son

PATERNA

The Autobiography of Cotton Mather

EDITED BY
RONALD A. BOSCO

SCHOLARS' FACSIMILES & REPRINTS
DELMAR, NEW YORK
1976

Published by
Scholars' Facsimiles & Reprints, Inc.
Delmar, New York 12054

First Printing 1976
Second Printing 1978

Library of Congress Cataloging in Publication Data

Mather, Cotton, 1663-1728.
Paterna: the autobiography of Cotton Mather.
Bibliography: p.
Includes index.
1. Mather, Cotton, 1663-1728. I. Title.
F67.M42145   973.2'092'4   B   76-10595
ISBN 0-8201-1273-9

PREFACE

The edition of _Paterna_ that follows is the first public offering of
the complete text of Cotton Mather's autobiography. However, for reasons
which I shall explain in the introduction, specificity concerning major
events during his life is not a prominent feature of either _Paterna_ or
Mather's other extensive autobiographical work, his _Diary_, which has been
published. I have attempted to compensate for Mather's unwillingness to
keep his reader informed of significant dates and events in his life in
both the chronological chart of Mather's life which appears below and the
detailed annotation which accompanies the text of _Paterna_. I would direct readers who desire more detailed information on Mather's life
first to Barrett Wendell's _Cotton Mather: Puritan Priest_ (New York:
Dodd, Mead, and Co., 1891), a yet unsurpassed biography which is the most
suitable companion to a reading of _Paterna_, or to Ralph and Louise Boas's
Cotton Mather: Keeper of the Puritan Conscience (1928; rpt. Hamden,
Connecticut: Archon Books, 1964), which is neither as detailed nor as
competently written as Wendell's Work. Kenneth Silverman's informative
introduction and commentary in his recently published _Selected Letters of
Cotton Mather_ (Baton Rouge: Louisiana State Univ. Press, 1971) provide a
competent and concise review of major events in Mather's life as does
Kenneth Murdock's "sketch" in the _Dictionary of American Biography_, Vol.
XII (1933). Perry Miller's comment on Mather in his _The New England
Mind: From Colony to Province_ (1953; rpt. Boston: Beacon Press, 1961)
and that of Robert Middlekauff in _The Mathers: Three Generations of
Puritan Intellectuals, 1596-1728_ (New York: Oxford Univ. Press, 1971)
are indispensable as informed estimates of Mather's position in New
England's intellectual history and as heir to the "Mather Dynasty."

iii

A Chronological Chart of Significant Dates and Events in the Life of
Cotton Mather

1662/3: Cotton Mather born, February 12, the eldest son of Increase and
Maria (Cotton) Mather, the grandson of two of the most promi-
nent ministers of Puritan New England, Richard Mather and John
Cotton.

1674-
1678: Enters Harvard College during his twelfth year, the youngest
student who had ever been admitted there; at Harvard is regarded as a prig by his peers and is severely "hazed" by them,
although quite popular among the masters and tutors at the
school; although personally convinced that he is predestined
for the ranks of the "heavenly priesthood," a stammer prevents
him from seriously entertaining thoughts of a life in the
ministry; demonstrates considerable interest and accomplishment in science; takes a bachelor's degree with distinction
and becomes a member of the Second Church of Boston, his
father's church, during his sixteenth year.

1679: Studies medicine and conquers speech impediment.

1680: Preaches his first sermon, at his grandfather Mather's old
church at Dorchester, August 22; by a unanimous vote of the
congregation, is invited to assist his father at the Second
Church.

1681: Takes the degree of M. A. at Harvard; refuses a call to a
church in New Haven; elected Pastor of the Second Church in
December.

1685: Ordained at the Second Church, where he serves as his father's
colleague until 1723 and holds office for the rest of his life;

becomes an Overseer at Harvard College; becomes greatly concerned with thoughts about his suitability for marriage;
begins to read and study the phenomena of witchcraft; visited
with the apparition of an angel.

1686: Publishes first work, a sermon preached to a criminal about
to be executed; marries Abigail Phillips, the daughter of a
prosperous Charlestown family, May 4.

1688: Assumes sole charge of the Second Church when Increase Mather
travels to England to petition for a new charter for the
colony; becomes a leader of the ministers and citizens who
opposed James II and his rule as expressed through Sir Edmund
Andros, the royal governor; takes a possessed young girl into
his house in order to study the manifestations of her possession and to purge her of Satan's influence through prayer
and fasting.

1689: Publishes the results of his observation of the possessed girl
in his Memorable Providences, Relating to Witchcraft and
Possession; sides with the insurgents when open rebellion
breaks out against Andros and publishes The Declaration of the
Gentlemen, Merchants, and Inhabitants of Boston, a seditious
tract against English rule in the colony; narrowly escapes
imprisonment by Andros.

1690: Baptizes Sir William Phips, who is later governor-general of
the colony; becomes Fellow at Harvard College.

1692: Increase Mather returns from England with a new charter and is
championed for his efforts by his son; Cotton and Increase begin to lose political power as critics of the new charter mount
attacks against their theocratic position; Salem witchcraft

trials begin; before the Salem court convenes, Cotton warns against the admission of "spectral evidence," usually unfavorable to the accused, and urges the judges to consider milder means of discipline than execution; although the Salem judges neglect to follow his advice, Cotton never publicly questions their decisions, many of which were at variance with his own view of the evidence.

1693:   At the request of the Salem judges, publishes Wonders of the Invisible World, a narrative of the Salem trials in which he argues for the justice of the verdicts in the trials he describes; plans Magnalia Christi Americana (published in 1702) and Biblia Americana (still in manuscript at the Massachusetts Historical Society); influences the political decisions of Sir William Phips, now governor-general as a result of Increase Mather's diplomacy in England.

1695:   Phips dies; Cotton Mather's political power quickly wanes.

1696:   Writes the Life of Phips; opposes lay Charter of Harvard College.

1697:   Finishes Magnalia; receives angelic assurances that his writing will continue to be a means of the advancement of the Kingdom of God in the world.

1698:   Brattle Street Church is organized by the Rev. John Leverett, President of Harvard College, and the Rev. William Brattle of Cambridge in order to provide a Congregational alternative to the Second Church's conservatism; Mather is incensed at the new church's rejection of a public relation as a necessary condition of admission to communion; publishes Eleutheria: Or an Idea of the Reformation in England; And a History of

Non-Conformity.

1699:   Petitions for a sectarian proviso in the Harvard College
Charter; son Increase born, July 9; begins Paterna, his autobiography, for the instruction of Increase in the paths of
righteousness.

1700:   With the encouragement of the leaders of the Brattle Street
Church, Robert Calef publishes his More Wonders of the Invi-
sible World, a work which accuses the Mathers of complicity in
the injustices carried out at Salem in 1692; Cotton Mather
attacks the Brattle Street Church in his "The Order of the
Gospel" and "Defence of Evangelical Churches;" sends his
Magnalia to London in search of a publisher; publishes his
Reasonable Religion.

1701:   Increase Mather deposed from presidency at Harvard; Cotton is
unsuccessful in his attempt to succeed his father as president
of Harvard; attacks Calef as a "vile tool" of Satan; becomes
interested in the formation of Yale College.

1702/3:   Joseph Dudley becomes governor at Cotton Mather's urging; much
to Cotton's dismay Dudley reveals himself to be of a politi-
cally independent mind once in office; Magnalia is published
in London, much to Mather's relief; wife, Abigail, dies
December 1; amorous young woman addresses Mather for his
affection with near scandalous consequences.

1703:   Appointed President of Harvard College by the House of Repre-
sentatives, but the action is overturned; courts and marries
Mrs. Elizabeth Clark Hubbard, a widow and neighbor; abdicates
his office in Harvard College.

1706:   Finishes Biblia Americana; actively engaged in the

Christianizing of Negroes and publishes _The Negro Christi-
anized_ on the subject; publicly denounces Governor Dudley in a
letter; all hopes for the presidency of Harvard are defeated;
son Samuel born, October 30.

1708: Publishes _Corderius Americanus . . . The Good Education of
Children_.

1710: Publishes _Bonifacius_; is made Doctor of Divinity by the University of Glasgow.

1713: Made Fellow of the Royal Society of London; favors Yale College
as the new hope for traditional Congregationalism; wife,
Elizabeth, dies November 9.

1715: Marries Lydia Lee George, July 5, but within a year begins to
believe that he has been deceived by her pretense of religi-
osity and maternal excellence.

1716: Lydia Mather begins to show first signs of mental disturbance.

1717: Son Increase charged in paternity suit; Cotton begins to look
upon son Samuel as new hope of the Mather line.

1718: Troubled by growing apostasy at Harvard; domestic difficulties
abound; begins to assume the financial responsibilities of his
widowed sisters, with near ruinous consequences for himself.

1721: Son Increase is charged in town riot; son Samuel begins at
Harvard; Second Church appears in danger of breaking up, Cotton
introduces inoculation as the small-pox spreads through Boston,
but is answered by a public panic against the practice; publishes his _Sentiments On the Small Pox Inoculated_.

1722: Publishes his _An Account . . . of Inoculating the Small Pox_.

1723: Father, Increase Mather, dies.

1724:   Writes and publishes <u>Parentator</u>, a biography of his father;
the death of Leverett revives Mather's hopes for Harvard presidency, but his hopes are disappointed; Lydia deserts him,
but later she returns; son Increase lost at sea; Cotton is
visited by young Benjamin Franklin.

1726:   Publishes <u>Manuductio</u> <u>ad</u> <u>Ministerium</u> and <u>Ratio</u> <u>Disciplinae</u>.

1727/8:   Dies, February 13.

CONTENTS

INTRODUCTION

I: The Dates of Composition and History of Cotton Mather's Paterna

When Increase or "Cresy" Mather was born on July 9, 1699, his father
allowed himself a considerable sigh of relief. While seven children were
born to Cotton Mather during his thirteen years of married life with Abigail Phillips, only three were alive in 1699 and these, all daughters,
were obviously unsuitable as heirs to the political and religious dynasty
so carefully established and preserved through three generations of
Mathers.[1] Cotton looked forward, therefore, to the birth of this child,
his eagerness and anticipation tempered through prayer and fasting and
the Puritan's reluctance to presume upon either the good will or the intentions of the Lord. Nevertheless, as the day of Cresy's birth ap-
proached, it was only with great difficulty that Mather was able to
moderate his rising emotions. His records of the events surrounding
Cresy's birth suggest the high pitch of the moment. Recalling that "A
Son had been foretold unto me, in an Extraordinary Way, some years before," Cotton spent July 8 in preparation for the child's arrival: "In
Praying and Fasting before the Lord, and Crying to Heaven," and in discoursing with his family, during the evening preceding Cresy's birth, on
John 16: 21, "A woman when she is in travail hath sorrow, because 'er
hour is come: but as soon as she is delivered of the child, she remem-
bereth no more the anguish, for joy that a man is born into the world."
Cotton then retired for a few fitful hours' sleep until a servant issued
forth with suitably prophetic tidings: "That a Son was born unto me."[2]

Mather viewed these events as a sign of the Lord's good will and
smiling providence toward both his household and the Mather line. He
writes that less than an hour after Cresy's birth, "I received a wonderful

Advice from Heaven, that this my Son, shall bee a Servant of my Lord
Jesus Christ throughout eternal Ages."[3] His communication with Heaven
continued through the next day when, after baptizing the "hearty, lusty
and comely Infant . . . in Honour to my Parent [Increase Mather (1639-
1723)]," it "was again assured mee from Heaven that this Child shall
glorify my Lord Jesus Christ, and bee with Him, to behold his Glory"
(<u>Diary</u>, I, 307-8). To assure the fulfillment of these promises Mather
immediately undertook to groom Cresy, "my only and lovely Son, a Son
given to mee in answer to many Prayers among the People of God, and a
Son of much Observation and Expectation" (<u>Diary</u>, I, 336), for the path
of righteousness. No effort or concern was spared on this "Son of Great
Hopes": Mather personally began to prepare him for his eternal and temporal inheritance, and the people of God employed "Thousands & Thousands
of <u>Prayers</u>" (p. 187) toward a fruitful outcome of the father's effort.
Nevertheless, it is well known among students of the Mathers that Increase
never lived up to the expectations of his father and the people of God.
From the middle years of his adolescence until his death at sea in 1724
Cresy proved to be a sorrow to his father and a disgrace to the Mather
name. Cotton expressed his disappointment at these unhappy facts with
poignant simplicity: "Yett after all, a Sovereign GOD would not Accept
of him" (p. 187).

Among the means chosen by Mather in 1699 to "show [Cresy] the Way
he should go" was his composition of an autobiographical document which
he thought appropriate to entitle <u>Paterna</u>. In the early pages of <u>Paterna</u>
Mather makes clear his reasons for writing this work. Acknowledging
first that "God, who hath given You to <u>me</u>, requires and Expects, my Endeavours, that on the most peculiar Accounts, You may be <u>His</u>," Mather

writes that he will select from his own Reserved Memorials, a favorite
term for his diaries, "a Number of those Experiences and Contrivances,
which I have had, in my own Poor Walk with God," for "[the] Instruction
of a Father, carries much of Authority and Efficacy with it" (pp. 1-2).
It is obvious from its first pages that Mather originally conceived of
Paterna as both an informational and an instructional document. To the
extent that Paterna would be informational, Mather promises Cresy that
he will eventually be told, "What have been my Prayers for you, both
before and after my Receiving of you from the Lord, and what Hopes I
have had concerning you" (p. 1). In reality Mather never bothers to reveal to Cresy "all my Prayers, and Hopes, and Faith about You." Rather,
from its early pages onward, Mather concentrates on the instructional
function which he builds into Paterna, as he writes "no more of my own
[life], than what may just Serve as a Direction to Yours" and limits his
"Experiences and Contrivances" to "Such of them, as may be your perpetual monitors" (p. 2). On the basis of these statements alone, there
can be no doubt that Mather placed great importance upon the composition
and intended effect of his Paterna. Interestingly, however, this document has never before been printed in its entirety and has been virtually ignored by scholars engaged in research on Mather for the past
two centuries. Those who have noticed the work have generally under-
estimated both its intrinsic value and the significance attached to it
by Mather. Too frequently, what scholars have written about Paterna
has been misleading and, in some instances, incorrect.[4]

Our first concerns must be the dates of the composition of Paterna
and the identification of its audience. The two most widely respected
Mather scholars to comment on Paterna, Barrett Wendell and Thomas James

Holmes, assume that it was written sometime during the 1720's for Samuel
Mather (1706-1785), Cotton's only son to survive his death in 1728.[5]
Since they place the time of composition during the latter years of
Mather's life, neither Wendell nor Holmes acknowledges the possibility
that the work was first meant for Increase. Their opinion on this matter
was corrected only ten years ago by William R. Manierre II, who is the
first to suggest that Paterna was written for Increase. Manierre moves
the date of the composition back from the 1720's to 1709-1710 and cites
Mather's references to Paterna in his Bonifacius, published in 1710, and
his previously missing diary for 1712 as proof for the change of dates.
Manierre further contradicts Wendell and Holmes when he states that
Mather finished Paterna sometime during 1721, with Increase still the object of his interest. He concludes that when Increase died in 1724,
Mather simply "reassigned 'Paterna' to . . . Samuel."[6] Importantly,
although they disagree over the intended audience of Paterna, both sides
agree that the work is a unified document initially written for one son.

My own work on Mather and the Paterna manuscript has led me to conclude that Wendell, Holmes, and Manierre, have all erred in their
findings. The fault for their error is not, however, entirely their own;
much of the blame for the problems they have had with Paterna must be
assigned to its author. A peculiarity of Paterna which Mather obviously
enjoyed and exploited but which has confused later scholars is both the
speaker's pose of anonymity and his refusal to identify his assumed audience. Although Mather provides a significant number of clues to his
identity in Paterna, he never acknowledges himself or his audience by
name. Equally confusing, he deliberately suppresses or obscures information which might help fix the date at which he is writing. I will discuss Mather's reasons for never revealing himself as the subject of

Paterna or Increase and, later, Samuel as its audience in a later section devoted to Mather's literary method in Paterna. I wish to argue now,
however, that there is sufficient evidence for us to define Paterna as in
fact a two part autobiography of which the first part, pages 1-193, was
written exclusively for Increase during the years 1699-1702 and later was
altered by Mather to appear as though it was written for Samuel, while
the second part, pages 193-355, was written exclusively for Samuel during
the ten year period from approximately 1717 to 1727. Much of the evidence
for my view in this matter has been gathered from passages found in the
first part of Paterna. Many of these passages were altered or deleted
by Mather during the twenty-eight years he was concerned with the work,
yet the passages can still be read and offer incontestable proof that the
first part of Paterna was intended initially for Increase, was begun and
completed by Mather during the two to three years immediately following
Increase's birth, and was viewed by Mather at the time he wrote "Lord,
Help me!" on page 193 as a complete and unified work.

The clearest proof in Paterna to confirm Increase as Mather's initial audience is found on pages 186-187. There Mather copies from his
Diary a significant portion of the entries dealing with Increase's birth.
In the passage as it now stands Mather appears to be impersonally addressing a third party, identified in the manuscript as his son, on the
events surrounding Increase's birth: "The Day before he was born, I
Spent in Praying and Fasting before the Lord, and Crying to Heaven, for
the Welfare of my Consort, and of her Expected off-spring. A Son had
been foretold unto me . . ." (P. 186). Nevertheless, Increase is clearly
the party to whom Mather first addressed these comments, for, according
to my reading of several deleted words in the manuscript, Mather originally wrote "You were" for "he was," "You" for "A Son," and "Your

Excellent Mother" for "my Consort." Most likely, Mather made these
changes between 1717, the year in which he appears to have returned to
Paterna with a new audience in mind, and 1724, the year in which Increase
died. In addition to this passage there also exist outside the work two
direct references by Mather to his Paterna and its audience. Mather's
first published reference to Paterna appears in Bonifacius,[7] popularly
known today as Mather's "Essays to Do Good." There, as Manierre notes,[8]
Mather introduces a lengthy passage on a minister's duty in "Pastoral
Visits" as follows: "But some have chosen the way of PASTORAL VISITS.
And from the memorials of one who long since did so, and then left his
PATERNA to his son upon it, I will transcribe the ensuing passages."[9]
The passages that follow this statement are taken nearly verbatim from
Paterna, pages 96-98. Although it is true that Samuel was alive at the
time Bonifacius was published, it is important to bear in mind that he
was barely out of his infancy; while Increase, as Mather writes in his
Diary on March 12, 1710/11, "is now of Age enough, to know the Meaning
of Consideration." In order to teach Increase "the Meaning of Consideration" Mather decides that he "would never lett him spend many Minutes
with me, without entring upon a Point of Conversation, that may instruct
him, and enrich him, so that he may be the wiser and the better for it"
(Diary, II, 49). It is in his second direct reference to the autobiography outside the work itself that Mather places to rest any question
concerning the identity of the son for whom he has written Paterna and
incidentally reveals his principal method for teaching Increase "the
Meaning of Consideration." Mather writes the following telling entry in
his recently discovered and published 1712 Diary: "[February 25, 1711/
12] My Son Increase, I will now have to sit by me, especially on the

Lords-day Evenings; and Read over to me, first the _Paterna_ I have written for him; and such other things as may be most Suitable to him; and
make them the Arguments of my most Winning Discourses with him."[10]

With the identity of Mather's initial audience for _Paterna_ established, a question still remains concerning the dates of composition for
that part of the manuscript directed to Increase and the extent to which
the _Paterna_ manuscript was complete when, by 1712, Increase was spending
his "Lords-day Evenings" reading it. On the basis of Mather's reference
to _Paterna_ in _Bonifacius_ and his entry in the _1712 Diary_ Manierre assumes
that _Paterna_ was begun in 1709, just prior to the publication of _Boni-_
facius, and that a considerable portion of the manuscript, the extent of
which he is not able to identify, was completed by 1712.[11] However, a
reading of several deleted passages in the first part of _Paterna_ clearly
indicates that Mather began to write _Paterna_ before 1702, seven years before he began to prepare _Bonifacius_ for publication. When these deleted
passages are read in conjunction with several passages not deleted in the
manuscript and some additional passages found in both _Bonifacius_ and
Mather's _Diary_, it becomes clear that the first part of _Paterna_ was begun
immediately after Increase's birth in 1699 and was in fact virtually complete by 1702.[12]

The first indications that the portion of _Paterna_ intended for
Increase was begun and completed several years earlier than generally
supposed are found in three deleted references to Abigail Phillips
Mather, Increase's "Excellent Mother," who died December 1, 1702. In an
early section of _Paterna_ which deals with _Dutifulness unto Parents_
Mather describes a number of heaven's _Retaliating Dispensations_ or
Remarkable Providences toward him as a consequence of his filial

obedience and generosity. Hoping that Increase will see how heaven sufficiently rewards good children for their sacrifices, Mather writes: "Many
more such things I might mention. But I give you these for a Taste; that
You, My Son, may be Encouraged in Your obedience to ye Fifth Commandment."
This is Mather's conclusion as it now stands. Yet in the manuscript two
additional lines were originally written and subsequently deleted which
prove that Abigail was alive and, presumably, in good health at the time
Mather was one-third of his way into the first part of Paterna. Originally, the above sentence continued as follows: "& Particularly, in your
Tenderness for Your Mother, (if she Survive,)[13] when I shall be gone to
a better World" (pp. 66-67). On another occasion, after he describes a
variety of "Methods to obtain ye Blessing of God, on [the] weighty Concern" of selecting a suitable wife, Mather reports that at the beginning
of his twenty-fourth year he "was by ye wonderful Favour of Heaven brought
unto an Acquaintance with a Lovely and Worthy Young Gentlewoman, whom God
made a Consort, & a Blessing to me." Once again, a reading of Mather's
deletions, with due notice taken of his shift in tense, indicates an
early date of composition for this section of Paterna. This sentence
originally ended, "whom God has made your Mother," which suggests that
Abigail was alive at the time Mather first wrote it (pp. 100-102).[14]
Finally, when it is read with the deletions inserted in the text, the
Paterna passage quoted earlier concerning the events surrounding Increase's
birth indicates that Abigail was alive at the time Mather was writing the
final pages of the part originally intended for Increase: "The Day before You were born, I spent in Praying and Fasting before the Lord, and
Crying to Heaven, for the Welfare of Your Excellent Mother . . . ".[15]

In addition to these deleted passages concerning Abigail Phillips,
Mather provides two additional clues in Paterna to its early date of

composition in comments which he retains in the manuscript on the age of his intended reader at the time he is writing. The first such comment appears on page 1 of Paterna. There Mather informs Increase that additional information on Mather's prayers and hopes for his son can be found in his diaries. He tells Increase, "perhaps you may Somewhat inform Yourself [of my Prayers and Hopes], if You should Live to Read, the Passages of My Life, Recorded from time to time, as they Occurr'd, in Reserved Memorials, which I Leave behind me." Mather's conditional phrasing of this passage--"if You should Live to Read"--is telling. Given our knowledge of Mather's extreme misfortune in the survival rate of his off-spring, it is apparent that Increase is yet an infant, unable to read what Mather is writing at this time, and about whose survival Mather has some reasonable doubt. The second such reference is toward the close of the part of Paterna written for Increase. After a brief summation of his purpose and method in composing Paterna Mather writes,

> But I was Willing to Lett no more Time roll away, before my doing of this work for you, My Son, Lest ye End of my Time, Coming upon me, in the Lustre that is now running, should Cause this work, wch I judged of Such Importance for you, to be never done at all. And it was the rather necessary for me now to do it, because I know not whether I may Live, to see you Capable of taking in my Verbal Discourses on such points as these, or, whether, you may be capable of Reading with Understanding, what I have Written for you, until I Shall be taken from all opportunities of any Verbal Discourses with you (pp. 185-6).

Interestingly, Mather here reverses his reservation as expressed on page 1. Rather than fear concerning the child's survival, Mather expresses a fear that his own death may prevent his personal instruction of Increase in the path of righteousness. So, he decides to leave behind this Paterna against such time as Increase will be capable of Reading with Understanding. It is apparent in this passage, as in that which appears on page 1, that the first part of Paterna is the product of Mather's intense effort during Increase's infancy, 1699-1702.

Finally, a close reading of Bonifacius reveals that Paterna is a source for more of what appears in that work than simply the passage on pastoral visits. Although Manierre neglects to note them, three passages found in Bonifacius are clearly derived from Paterna. While this does not offer conclusive evidence that Paterna was completed by 1702, it does suggest that the autobiography's first part was finished and revised and that its content was set in Mather's mind sometime before 1709. Two of the Bonifacius passages are expanded versions of Mather's experience and opinion first stated in Paterna; the third is taken nearly verbatim from Paterna. The first passage deals with societies of "YOUNG MEN ASSOCI-ATED," one of Mather's principal interests throughout his life. In Bonifacius Mather argues the usefulness of such societies for both the individuals involved and their neighborhood, and he outlines nine points of conduct to order the government of such groups (Bonifacius, pp. 66-68). These points of conduct as outlined in Bonifacius are, however, merely an expanded version of activities Mather first notes in Paterna, pages 8-9. Mather puts to similar use his outline of fourteen "Rules for Preaching" found in Paterna, pages 88-89. Although he does not re-produce them verbatim in Bonifacius, he does argue for the substance of these rules there (Bonifacius, pp. 71-72). In the third passage in question Mather reproduces nearly verbatim a paragraph from Paterna, pages 76-77, in which he describes a suitable method "to promote the Fear of God in [the] Hearts" of young pupils. Unlike the passage noted earlier on pastoral visits, Mather does not cite Paterna as the source for the material he quotes in Bonifacius. He writes only, "I have read this experiment of one who had pupils under his charge . . ." (Bonifacius, p. 85). Nevertheless, as in the case of the passage on

pastoral visits, Mather's introduction to this _Paterna_ material in _Boni-
facius_ suggests that the source for what follows is complete and authori-
tative and that the evidence offered by the anonymous author has been
tried and found true by Mather, sometime in the past, certainly before
1709.

Still to be answered is the question concerning the manuscript's
length at the time Mather viewed it as complete for Increase. Once again,
material which Mather at some time deleted from the manuscript proves
helpful. Throughout the first part of _Paterna_ Mather treats his life as
"Lustres," chronological blocks of years containing five years each. In
the _Paterna_ as it now stands Mather discontinues this practice in "The
SECOND Part," Mather's title for pages 185-355, which is "No Longer Distinguished into LUSTRES" (p. 185). Yet Mather originally twice wrote and
twice deleted "The Eighth Lustre" for "The SECOND Part." These deletions are significant, for the experience Mather would treat in his
"eighth lustre" is experience from his thirty-fifth through fortieth
years, 1697-1702, and would, therefore, include the experiences surrounding Increase's birth. In fact, as the breakdown between _Paterna_
passages and their _Diary_ sources in Appendix A indicates, Mather seems
to have decided to terminate _Paterna_ as it was written for Increase
shortly after relating the circumstances of his birth.

As we look to the opening paragraphs of what is now "The SECOND
Part" it is clear that Mather is preparing for the conclusion of his
Paterna in his eighth lustre. "Thus I have singled out," he writes,
"for Your more particular Consideration, _My Son_, certain Passages that
I Judged would be more Particularly Serviceable for your Instruction,
& Your Direction, in the _Paths of Righteousness_: Extracting them from

ye Larger Memorials which I have kept, of things that I have done or
Seen, in my poor pilgrimage, for Seven Lustres of it" (p. 185).
Following this statement is the paragraph quoted above in which Mather
explains that he has completed Paterna with all possible speed, lest his
death deprive Increase of the opportunity for instruction through verbal
discourse. After this paragraph, there follow in rapid succession the
passages in which Mather describes Increase's birth, a paragraph which
he added during or shortly after 1724 in which he notes Increase's death
"in the Atlantic Ocean," a paragraph which he added in 1717, the year in
which he returned to Paterna, in which he details a new method for the
autobiography, and four brief passages in which he summarizes the central themes of the first part of Paterna (pp. 185-193). Finally, on
page 193 Mather brings the first part of Paterna to a close. After he
observes that "the God of Heaven vouchsafes, Especially to Some of His
Faithful Servants, a more Singular Conduct of His Providence" (p. 192),
Mather pledges himself to "Observe what is Remarkable in the Divine
Dispensations toward me." He concludes, "And thus I would keep Waiting
on God in Christ perpetually, & Critically Eying of Him. Lord, Help me!"
(pp. 192-3). When they are read in context, these lines have a definite
ring of finality about them, and, interestingly, they closely parallel
Mather's ultimate conclusion to Paterna on page 355. These lines are,
according to my reading of the manuscript, the final lines of the first
part of Paterna as it was written for Increase between 1699 and 1702.
Except for occasional deletions and revisions the Paterna appears to have
remained in this state through approximately 1717.

While there is no evidence to prove conclusively that Paterna remained virtually untouched by Mather between 1702 and 1717, events

touching upon the relationship between Cotton and Increase and the effect of those events on Mather's initial purpose for Paterna strongly
suggest that in 1717 Mather returned to Paterna with a new audience and
a reconsidered purpose in mind. By 1717 there could be no question in
Mather's mind that his Paterna and the "Winning Discourses" derived
from it were not having their intended effect upon Increase. The biographical material concerning Increase's middle adolescent years (1712-
1717) is sketchy at best, but it is clear that during this time he began
to pursue the independent ways which eventually forced Mather to consider this son a "Castaway." Mather's Diary is the only substantial
record of Increase's decline in principles and promise during these
years. There we read that by April, 1717, Cotton concluded a search for,
and apparently found, a "suitable Companion" for Increase, "very much to
his Advantage." Mather must have felt the eventual effect of his find
to be questionable, however, for he concludes the April entry as follows:
"But, Oh! my unceasing Inculcations on the Child" (Diary, II, 447).
Mather's reservations proved correct. In September his paternal distress is obvious, but the cause is unspecified as he writes, "[September
10] O! My Son Increase, my Son, my Son!" (Diary, II, 474). The entry
for November 5, 1717, clarifies the source of Mather's distress: "The
Evil that I greatly feared, is come upon me. I am within these few
hours, astonished with an Information, that an Harlot big with a Bas-
tard, accuses my poor Son Cresy, and layes her Belly to him. Oh!
Dreadful Case! Oh, Sorrow beyond any that I have mett withal! what shall
I do now for the foolish Youth! what for my afflicted and abased Family?
My God, look mercifully upon me" (Diary, II, 484). Although Cotton immediately intensified his exercise of continual prayer with supplications

to the Lord, his effort appeared to him to be in vain. On November 10
he records, "My GOD humbles me exceedingly in the Circumstances of my
poor son Increase" (Diary, II, 486). On November 19 he concludes,
"Alas, I have this Day, an heartbreaking Intimation, that my God has not
heard me, in the main Point of my late Supplications . . . My poor Son,
has made a worse Exhibition of himself unto me . . . than I have ever
yett mett withal. O my God, what shall I do? what shall I do?"
(Diary, II, 489).

Mather was never able to direct Increase out of his path of waywardness.[16] Important for our interests is the fact that as Increase's fortunes decline in Mather's eyes during 1717 those of Samuel, Cotton's
younger and somewhat promising son, proportionally rise. Mather notes,
for instance, beside his September 10 entry concerning Increase that
"Sammy's writing." On September 17, while Increase is about the town
enjoying some physical diversions, Mather decides, "Diverse beautifying
Ornaments for his Mind, must I now recommend unto the Studies of my dear
Sammy" (Diary, II, 475). On October 8 Mather corrects himself for his
lax endeavor in this resolution: "I am very defective in the Degree of
exquisite and assiduous Cares, which I should use for the Education of
my desireable Samuel. Take it into the strongest Consideration" (Diary,
II, 478). When Samuel suddenly falls dangerously ill at the end of
October, Mather writes, "[October 29] Oh! what a Sacrifice am I now
call'd unto! But the Life of the hopeful Child, how must it be wrestled
for! And his future Improvement in all that is good, if he recover,
studied for!" (Diary, II, 482). Finally, Mather's entry for November 26
reveals that Samuel has replaced Increase as Mather's "Son of Great Hopes"
and that Cotton will spare no effort to see those hopes fulfilled: "The

sick State of my dear <u>Sammy</u>, must quicken my Resolutions, upon the more
exquisite Methods of prosecuting his Cultivation, first in Piety, and
then in all useful Accomplishments, if God will graciously spare him to
me" (<u>Diary</u>, II, 490-1).

God did spare the life of Samuel. It is my view that Mather thereupon returned to his <u>Paterna</u> as one of "the more exquisite Methods of
prosecuting [Samuel's] Cultivation." Since his references to Increase
in <u>Paterna</u> were relatively obscure and few in number, Mather could with
little difficulty revise the first part of the manuscript for Samuel's
use in such a way that would probably not arouse Samuel's suspicion that
the work was not originally intended for him. It is at this time too
that Mather deletes the title of the original concluding section on page
185 and decides on a slightly different method for what he now calls "The
SECOND Part." Instead of the systematic lustre approach which he uses
throughout the first part, Mather writes that he will proceed "without
any <u>Method</u> at all," for "the Less of <u>Method</u> there is in this Work, it
will be but ye more <u>Natural</u>, and <u>Beautiful</u>, and it may carry ye more of
a <u>Parental</u> <u>Authority</u> upon it" (p. 189). In fact, however, Mather proceeds with a method identical to that which he used in the first part.
While he refrains from using the lustre divisions, he continues to enter
into <u>Paterna</u> material from his <u>Reserved</u> <u>Memorials</u> largely in chronological order. The only noticeable difference in method between the part of
<u>Paterna</u> written for Increase and that written for Samuel is Mather's ex-
tensive use of material derived from sources other than his <u>Diary</u> and his
inclusion of passages which were most likely written specifically for
<u>Paterna</u>, since they do not appear to be derived from any other Mather
works. Complete records of Mather's use of material from his <u>Diary</u> and
other sources in <u>Paterna</u> are provided in Appendix A and Appendix B at

the end of the _Paterna_ text.

The only problem remaining to be resolved concerns the time at which
Mather completed the _Paterna_ manuscript as it now stands. Since pages
193-303 of _Paterna_ are taken exclusively from Mather's diaries for the
years 1702-1712 and from several of Mather's books which were in print
by 1714, it is reasonable to assume that Mather began this portion of the
manuscript shortly after he decided to return to the autobiography and
that he completed it with relative ease within a year or two (1718-
1719). These pages are important, for they represent Mather's last con-
centrated effort on his _Paterna_. His repeated references to his finally
arriving at "a _Finishing Stroke_" within them (pp. 270, 286, 296) indicate that Mather was preparing to conclude the manuscript at about page
303.

Nevertheless, _Paterna_ continues for another fifty-two pages. A
careful reading of the manuscript reveals some considerable differences
between these last pages and the three-hundred-three pages which precede
them and suggests a plausible defense for 1727 as the year in which
Mather considered the manuscript complete. It is important to observe
first that the sense of continuity which Mather consciously writes into
Paterna in order to satisfy the requirements of his genre--unity and the
appearance of completeness--is disrupted after page 303. In addition,
Mather's handwriting, which is generally clear and measured throughout
the first three hundred pages of the manuscript, appears rushed and occasionally erratic in this last section. Finally, two errors in pagi-
nation--Mather incorrectly numbers pages 344 and 345 as pages 244 and
245--and two premature conclusions on pages 336 and 350 indicate that
Mather was not giving his undivided interest and effort to _Paterna's_
final pages. On the surface these peculiarities lead to the suspicion

that Mather may have been concerned with Paterna only at irregular intervals after 1720. Reference to the sources of these last pages confirms this suspicion. After page 303 Mather uses his Diary as a source for only about fifteen pages of the manuscript, although he definitely had during this time relatively full diaries for six of the eleven years between 1712/13, the last year's diary from which Mather extensively quotes in Paterna, and 1724, the last year, apparently, for which Mather kept a diary. Since the sense of continuity in Paterna depends in large part upon Mather's chronological development of his life through his diary sources, unity and the appearance of completeness are disrupted in these pages. In the place of diary material Mather relies upon excerpts from his own works, some of which were printed during the 1720's, and upon meditative passages written specifically for Paterna and its audience (pp. 306-7, 316-7, 320-3, 337-9, 340-352) for matter to round out his life in Paterna.

It seems clear on the basis of his source material alone that Mather continued to work on and add to his Paterna at odd moments from 1720 until 1727. In these last pages he finally proceeds "without any Method at all," writing only when he comes upon matter which he judges "proper and useful" for Samuel and allowing time to be the ultimate arbiter of his autobiography's length. This view explains the work's loss of continuity as well as Mather's erratic handwriting and occasional errors in this section. This view also justifies Mather's anticipation of the language and form of his conclusion as it appears on page 355, for with time the legislator of Paterna's end Mather would with reason prepare his audience for the possible end of the manuscript as he concludes the two long sections which extend from page 329 to page 336 and from page 337 to page 350.

Sensing that his death was approaching, Mather probably returned to his _Paterna_ for one last review during 1727. At this time he evidently added the last five pages to the manuscript. Pages 351 to 354 provide a summary of the advice which Mather offers his son throughout the autobiography. In the "Supposed Cases" reviewed on these pages Mather brings together the major themes and concerns of _Paterna_ under the notion of "The Sentiments of a _Spirit Rejoicing_ in GOD my SAVIOUR," as he expresses it on page 351. These last pages are also noteworthy for the significant connection between the historical Cotton Mather during his last years, 1723-1727/28, and the individual whom Mather describes in his "Supposed Cases." There can be no question, for instance, that Mather is speaking of himself and the various tragedies he experienced as a father when he writes, "If it should be so, that in any Circumstances of my _Children,_ I should See Heart-breaking Spectacles; A Glorious CHRIST has brought me into an _Adoption,_ and into an _Inheritance,_ among the _Children_ of GOD: And while the SON of GOD makes me _His Own,_ what tho' I should not be _Happy in Sons & in Daughters?_" (p. 351). After he completed this summary passage, Mather quickly concluded the _Paterna_ with a brief exposition of the "TRINITY" as "a _Prelibation_ . . . of that _Final Blessedness_ wherein all the Gracious Designs of my SAVIOUR for me terminate!" (p. 355). By the end of 1727 there was really nothing left for him to say, as Mather himself implies in the last lines he wrote for _Paterna:_ "This is _the way that I take._ And in this way of _Living by Faith of the SON of_ God, I keep _Looking for His Mercy to me in Eternal Life._" Mather died on February 13, 1727/28.

There is no proof that Mather ever showed his _Paterna_ to Samuel before 1727. Yet, given Mather's purpose for the autobiography, it is reasonable to assume that Samuel was acquainted with the work as early

as 1717 and that he had a thorough knowledge of its contents long before
Mather's death. We do know for certain, however, the date when the manuscript was formally presented to Samuel, for on the title page of the
Paterna is written, in Samuel's hand, "Samuel Mather's" and below the inscription is written the date, "1727." Samuel made immediate use of the
manuscript for the biography of his father, The Life of the Very Reverend
and Learned Cotton Mather, D. D. & F. R. S., which he published in 1729.[17]
Although Samuel kept the manuscript in his possession during the remainder
of his life, it is not clear what use, if any, he made of the work after
1729. Upon Samuel's death in 1785 Paterna became the property of Hannah
Mather Crocker, his daughter, who presented the manuscript to the Reverend William Jenks of Boston in 1814. An inscription across the title page
of the manuscript provides us with the specific circumstances and date for
the change of ownership: "A Gift of Madam H. Crocker, June 1, 1814."
Shortly after Dr. Jenks' death in 1866 Judge Mark Skinner of Chicago purchased the manuscript during the sale of the Jenks library. Paterna remained in the Skinner family library until 1915. Then, as the following
inscription from the inside back cover of the manuscript indicates,
Paterna was presented to the Chicago Historical Society by Judge Skinner's
daughter: "This belongs to Elizabeth Skinner, formerly belonging to her
father--Mark Skinner--presented by her to the Chicago Historical Society,
of which he was one of the charter members--June 23rd, 1915." In 1951
the Chicago Historical Society sold Paterna to the Goodspeeds shop in
Boston from which it was purchased by the Tracy W. McGregor Library of
the University of Virginia in the summer of 1952. Paterna remains today
in the manuscript collections of the McGregor Library at Charlottesville.[18]

Written in black ink, the _Paterna_ manuscript is an octavo volume
with leaves 17.2 cm. long and 11.3 cm. wide. The leaves vary in length
between 17.15 and 17.3 cm., but the width remains almost constant. Its
make-up is as follows: a single leaf (unwatermarked); 2 conjugate leaves, with the binding thread evident in the fold; stubs of about 11 torn
out leaves; 12 8-leaf gatherings; a single leaf (unwatermarked); a
single leaf (unwatermarked); 9 8-leaf gatherings; an 8-leaf gathering
in which the bottom part of the seventh leaf has been torn out and the
eighth leaf is missing; stubs of about 33 torn-out leaves; a single
leaf showing part of a watermark. Thus, an appropriate collational
formula for the volume is: [unsigned: 1_1 2^2 $3\text{-}14^8$ 15_1 16_1 $17\text{-}25^8$
26^8 (-26_8) 27_1].

The manuscript contains 181 leaves, and the pages are numbered, in
Mather's hand, as follows: the first six pages and the last three are
unnumbered; the rest are numbered consecutively from 1 through 355 with
the following exceptions: pp. 7 and 60 lack numbers, the numbering skips
from 161 to 164, and Mather incorrectly wrote '244' for 344 and '245' for
345. Thus, an appropriate formula for the pagination is: pp. [6] 1-6
7 8-59 60 61-161 164-343 344-345 346-355 356-358 [= 356] .

The paper is laid watermarked paper all of one lot. The watermark
(a horn) is most similar to numbers 2724 and 2725 (and possibly 2738) in
Edward Heawood's _Watermarks_, plates 347 and 349; these watermarks occur
in books dated respectively 1671, 1668, and n.d. Precise identification
of the _Paterna_ watermark is rendered impossible, however, by the smallness of the octavo format. Furthermore, there is a barely discernible
countermark (some sort of flower) which differs from the countermarks of
Heawood 2724 and 2738.

The manuscript is bound in old calf, with gilt ornamentation around the edges of the front and back covers. On the spine there are eight sets of gilt double rules and the handwritten title (not in Mather's hand or the hand of his son Samuel) "C. MATHER'S / PATERNA', / MS.". The mark after "PATERNA'" may be a period; a slight smudge renders the reading of the mark imprecise. On the inside front cover a slip of nineteenth century (?) wove paper is pasted-in with the note "Cotton Mather's Life in his own handwriting written / for his son--."[18]

It is impossible to say with certainty what, if anything, Mather wrote on the approximately 11 missing leaves at the beginning of the manuscript and on the approximately 33 missing leaves at the end of the manuscript. It is highly likely that both sets of leaves were blank. Although I cannot prove my position, I am convinced that the 11 or so leaves at the beginning were reserved by Mather for additional quotations such as the ones with which he begins the manuscript as it now stands. Failing to fill in those pages by the time he passed the manuscript on to its first reader (Increase), Mather probably then tore them out. The case with the 33 or so leaves at the end is, I believe, much the same. As I indicated earlier, Mather continued to write his "Life" at odd moments during the 1720's. When, in 1727, it became clear to him that his "end" was drawing near, he wrote in the conclusion which appears on p. 355, and he probably then tore out the remaining pages of the manuscript, all of them blank, before he passed on the whole work to Samuel.

II: Mather's Motives in _Paterna_

According to the conventions then regulating the genre, there appear
to be three principal motives for autobiographical writing to which the
New England Puritan adhered during the seventeenth and early eighteenth
centuries.[19] First, he wished to convey to his children information concerning his pilgrimage through life, to document for them the course of
divine providence in his life, and to prepare them for their own life
of service to the Lord. Second, and not wholly distinct from the first
as a motive, he depended upon autobiographical writing as a means to convey to friends and neighbors, individuals with whom the writer had some
personal contact, his impression of the good and devout life and his
methods for pursuing it. Finally, the Puritan regarded autobiographical
writing in both the diary and the first person prose narrative forms as
a means of literary self-examination through which he could keep a
running account of his spiritual and worldly progress, as in the case of
the diary, and provide himself with a broad overview or review of his
life and experience, as in the case of the prose narrative, which was
often constructed out of diary material. In both his diary and his
narrative the writer could estimate the relative success or failure of
his life in terms of his spiritual and material accomplishments. In
actual practice, however, these three motives are not quite as distinct
as the terms I have used to describe them may make them appear. The impulse to write about oneself during this period, regardless of the audience which the Puritan author specifies in the work, stems from what
Alan Simpson has accurately defined as the essence of Puritanism in Old
and New England. "The essence of Puritanism," Simpson writes,

> . . . is an experience of conversion which separates the
> Puritan from the mass of mankind and endows him with the

> privileges and the duties of the elect. The root of the matter
> is always a new birth, which brings with it a conviction of sal-
> vation and a dedication to warfare against sin . . . The whole
> object of the Puritan's existence was to trace its course in
> himself and to produce it in others. He develops it in his ser-
> mons, systematizes it in his creeds, charts it in his diaries. 20

In fact, we should add, the Puritan's experience of his conversion and

his desire to convey as much of the specifics of his conversion experience

to others as he can is the central impulse in all Puritan autobiographical

endeavors. It is important for our purposes that during the several

phases of Paterna's composition Mather eventually comes to regard the

work from the perspective of each of these three motives and develops

the history of his life in order to fulfill the central impulse of all

Puritan autobiographical writing.

We have already noticed that Paterna was written principally for the

edification of Mather's sons. Throughout the autobiography Mather speaks

to his sons with all the authority of a parent, mindful, perhaps, of the

stern charge placed upon Puritan parents by his grandfather, Richard

Mather. In his 1657 "Farewel-Exhortation" to his congregation at Dor-

chester, Richard Mather states,

> Think it not enough to serve the Lord your selves alone in your
> own persons, but be sure to have special care that your Children
> & families may serve him also, and therefore remember to In-
> struct them and teach them the word and will of God.. . . The
> truth is you have but little love either to God, or to your
> children, or to your selves, if you make not conscience of this
> duty.. . . You know your selves must not live alwayes; there-
> fore it would be some Testimony of your love to his Majesty, if
> you be careful to train up a posterity for the Lord, and so to
> teach them in his wayes, that your seed may serve him when your
> selves shall be dead & gone. 21

In order to fulfill this charge placed universally upon Puritan parents,

Cotton Mather lays bare his spiritual life in Paterna in terms which

clearly indicate his purpose for doing so. Early in Paterna he tells

his son that his sole "Consideration" for his absolute honesty and attempt

at completeness in the work is that it "may be some Engagement upon You,
to hasten in ye Matters of Religion and Salvation" (p. 17). Mather frequently repeats the substance of this "Consideration" as he attempts to
make clear to his audience the consistency of his design or motive in the
autobiography. He reminds his son, for instance, that "my Design is to
Instruct You . . . [in your] Walk before ye Lord," that "my Poor Exemple"
in matters spiritual and practical ought to serve "[You] in ye Like
Employment," and that since the Lord has accepted "your poor Father . . .
in Services [to Him] . . . it is worth your while to Imitate his Desires
& Methods of becoming Serviceable" (pp. 53, 76, 158). Mather's fullest
statement on this aspect of his motive in Paterna appears in his conclusion to a passage in which he describes a period of significant distress
and disappointment. "My Son," he writes,

> I wish you may never have ye Occasions that I had for these
> humbling Wayes of proceeding in your Applications to Heaven.
> But if you have, Lett my Experience be your Direction and
> Encouragement. Had it not been for ye Hope of That, I would
> have Left this Part of my Experience as much unmentioned as
> I have done many others. I had some conflict in my own
> Spirit, whether I should have Related this or no; Lest there
> should be some Vanity in ye Relation. But, ye Hope of being
> Useful to you, has Carried it (p. 212).

Importantly, Mather does not limit his interest in Paterna to his
son's spiritual welfare alone. In the section initially written for
Increase as well as in "The SECOND Part," which was written for Samuel,
Mather expresses the hope that his son will be eventually admitted into
the ultimate service to the Lord, the ministry. Sensible, as he states,
that "To be a Christian, and a Minister too, Oh! tis no Easy Matter"
(p. 171), he includes in Paterna information designed to assist his son
in matters touching upon his practical and material welfare. Since the
proper ordering of one's ministry is the chief consideration among the
practical matters he addresses, Mather is careful to include in Paterna

extensive suggestions for and examples of the discharge of pastoral duties,
the correct preparation of sermons, the proper use of speech and language,
and the way to care for God's people through the continual, but silent,
doing of good (see, for Mather's most elaborate comments on these topics,
pp. 225-7, 272, 174, 235-6, respectively). In addition, Mather addresses
the civic and parental responsibilities which his son will eventually inherit as he describes at length the value and need of "reforming societies" and devotes several pages to "Some Special Points of Conduct . . .
in the Education of Children" (pp. 266-7, 227-232). Admittedly, Mather
is not so liberated from the standard of Puritanism as to conceive of
one's practical life as wholly distinct from one's spiritual life. However, to the extent that he addresses the practical and material aspects
of life and proposes methods conducive to his son's success in those
areas, Mather is consciously implementing his genre to the fullest degree
permissible by convention, and he is, accordingly, demonstrating the
breadth of Puritan motive for autobiography which is written for one's
children.

Beyond his view of Paterna as a guide for his son's spiritual and
practical welfare Mather does occasionally think of this autobiography
as a useful instrument for the instruction of friends, neighbors, and
other relatives. The impulse for Mather to regard Paterna as useful for
a wider audience than the one specified within the work probably derives
from his awareness of his responsibility, as a minister and a teacher,
to be a spiritual father to all the people of God within his reach.
Charles Chauncy, in his "Preface" to Richard Mather's "Farewel-Exhortation," addresses this aspect of ministerial responsibility and suggests
that an autobiographical statement, written or preached toward the close

or the anticipated close of a minister's life, is an effective way to
discharge this responsibility. Chauncy writes,

> It is warranted, and grounded upon the light of both nature
> and Scripture, 2 Cor. 12, 14. That Parents should lay up
> for their Children, and leave such an estate behind them,
> that their posterity after them may comfortably bee pro-
> vided for, which as it is requisite for the outward sub-
> sistence of Children in temporal regards: So it is most
> necessary for Spiritual Fathers . . . I mean for the faith-
> full Ministers of Christ, to leave a good stock . . . of
> Gods Testimonyes for his people committed to their charge,
> and their children in the faith: which care as it was
> always needful so especially it is in these times, where-
> in there is so much Apostacy & departing away from the
> faith & truth. In this regard we find it to have been the
> practice of the most precious servants of the Lord, that
> in their old age they have left . . . their swans songs
> (as they are called) which they sung not long before they
> departed this life. . . . 22

Importantly, throughout Paterna Mather does have a sense of the imminent
end of his time, so the autobiography is a "swans song" of sorts.
Equally important is the fact that although there is no evidence that he
ever acted on his intention, Mather does make several entries in his
Diary in which he determines to "lett out" his Paterna for the instruction of certain select individuals. Certainly, to judge by Mather's expression of it in both the Diary and his autobiography, there was enough
of "Apostacy & departing away from the faith & truth" in his time to
warrant such use of Paterna.

The first indication that Mather looks upon the audience of Paterna
as larger than that which he designates in the work appears in an entry
in his Diary for 1711. There he writes, "[May 1, 1711] What if I should
be so communicative, as to lodge my Paterna a while in the hands of my
Brother-in-Law, Mr. Walter; but with a due Care to preserve Modesty and
Concealment? It may sensibly assist him to discharge his Ministry, and
improve in experimental Christianity!" (Diary, II, 68). It is as a means

to improve the "experimental Christianity" of others that Mather twice
again considers passing on Paterna to relatives and friends. On March
22, 1712, he reminds himself to enter a section on "Christian Asceticks"
into Paterna. Although he does not enter this section, which begins in
Paterna on page 275, into Paterna at this time, he does within a week de-
cide to supply a kinsman with the section on "Christian Asceticks" along
with, presumably, the rest of Paterna, for use in his ministry: "[April
2, 1712] The Minister of Watertown-Farms, is my kinsman. I will give
him all the Assistances in his Studies that I can devise. I will Supply
his Reading, with the best things I can afford him. I will direct the
Discharge of his Ministry as well as I can. I will communicate of my
Christian Asceticks unto him, to render him a Man of God" (1712 Diary,
pp. 20, 23-4). And, nearly ten years later Mather again considers the
possibility of passing on Paterna to some "special Friends." Several
weeks after he writes, on February 26, 1720/21, that he has been "collecting into Paterna, several Methods of conversing with my Admirable
SAVIOUR," he proposes, on April 9, "also to communicate the same unto
some special Friends, that they may learn in the like Methods also to
glorify GOD" (Diary, II, 603, 611). Mather's stated intentions to make
such use of Paterna, regardless of his ultimate disposition of the work,
deserve our notice, for they clearly indicate his awareness of the conventional motives for autobiographical writing, at least in terms of
one's autobiography's social function, in Puritan America.

Finally, we should observe that Mather also regards Paterna as a
literary vehicle for self-examination, meditation, and self-evaluation.
Throughout the seventeenth and early eighteenth centuries Puritan ministers repeatedly exhorted their flocks to engage in methods of self-
examination. According to their theory, it was only through scrupulous

and continual self-searching that the individual Puritan could obtain
some indication that he was something more than a "refined hypocrite,"
that he was, indeed, a saint. The following statement on the subject by
Jonathan Edwards adequately represents the message that for over a century New England ministers delivered from their pulpits. In his Christian
Cautions; or, The Necessity of Self-Examination, Edwards writes,

> We ought to be much concerned to know whether we do not
> live in a state of sin. All unregenerate men live in sin.
> We are born under the power and dominion of sin, are sold
> under sin; every unconverted sinner is a devoted servant
> to sin and Satan. We should look upon it as of the great-
> est importance to us, to know in what state we are, whether
> we ever had any change made in our hearts from sin to holi-
> ness, or whether we be not still in the gall of bitterness
> and bond of iniquity; whether ever sin were truly mortified
> in us; whether we do not live in the sin of unbelief, and
> in the rejection of the Saviour. This is what the apostle
> insists upon with the Corinthians, 2 Cor. xiii. 5.
> Examine yourselves, whether ye be in the faith; prove your
> own selves; know ye not your own selves, how that Jesus
> Christ is in you, except ye be reprobates? Those who enter-
> tain the opinion and hope of themselves, that they are
> godly, should take great care to see that their foundation
> be right. Those that are in doubt should not give them-
> selves rest till the matter be resolved. 23

And, although Edwards neglects to take notice of it, meditation is the
only appropriate mood or atmosphere in which to engage in self-examination. The value derived from self-examination which is meditational
in mood is concisely stated by Thomas Hooker in his The Application of
Redemption. "Meditation," Hooker argues, "laies siege unto the soul,
and cuts off al carnal pretences that a wretched self-deceiving hypocrite would releeve himself by . . . Meditation meets and stops all the
evasions and sly pretences the half-hearted person shal counterfeit. If
a man should deny his fault, and himself guilty, Meditation will evidence
it beyond all gainsaying, by many testimonies which Meditation wil easily
cal to mind."[24] While the diary provided most Puritans with a literary
means of self-examination and meditation, many individuals employed the

first person prose narrative, the autobiography, toward the end of their
lives in order to arrive at a broad view of their life and its worth.
The popularity and significance of this literary form of late-in-life
self-examination is obvious from the many writers who use this form
during the period, among them John Winthrop, Anne Bradstreet, Thomas
Shepard, Roger Clap, and Increase and Cotton Mather.

In Paterna Mather frequently reminds his audience of the necessity
of self-examination and meditation and uses himself, as he engages in
self-examination in both his Diary and his Paterna, as his principal
example of how best to carry on these acts. We notice, for instance,
that among Mather's earliest concerns in Paterna is an explication of
"proposals of proceeding Methodically in that notable Duty of Christianity," meditation, which he defines as "[that] happy way of Preaching
to Myself" (p. 9). Later, in a section in which he addresses his methods
to achieve a proper degree of repentance (pp. 250-257), Mather notes that
the first movement in true repentance is self-examination and thereby reveals an important personal motive for Paterna. That Mather views his
autobiography as a vehicle for his own self-examination is made clear as
well in several of his references in his Diary to the personal value he
attaches to Paterna. Shortly after his statement in the 1712 Diary to
the effect that Paterna has been written for Increase's Lords-day evening
instruction and entertainment, Mather writes, "[March 22, 1712] I Perceive I must, in my Paterna, make a Recollection, of my Principal Projections and Intentions to carry on my Christian Asceticks, that so I
may frequently have Recourse unto it, and not Lose the Remembrance and
Influence, and Performance, of any of my Proposals and Resolutions"
(1712 Diary, p. 20). Again, in 1721, after he finished writing most of

"The SECOND Part" intended for Samuel, Mather notes in a diary entry, which underscores his personal motive for Paterna, that he has returned to the work: "[February 26, 1720/21] I am collecting into my Paterna, several Methods of conversing with my Admirable SAVIOUR, which of late Months I have been instructed in: that so having them together before me, for a frequent Perusal, I may keep in the lively Exercise of them, and may not lose them in my feeble and broken Conversation" (Diary, II, 603).

As we turn, in the following section, to consider the salient points of Mather's literary method in Paterna, it would be appropriate to bear in mind Mather's multiple motives for the work. There can be little question that much of what I would call the Paterna's "art" derives from Mather's awareness of the different audiences for the work and from the responsibility he feels to use language and images which best serve the needs of his audiences.

III: Mather's Literary Method in Paterna

In his recent study on the art of autobiographical writing, Design
and Truth in Autobiography, Roy Pascal observes that autobiographies
which are derived from diaries and previously published works are notoriously problematical in their method and style. On the one hand, Pascal
argues, the sense of continuity required of an autobiography in order
that it appear unified and complete is threatened when, in a chronological narrative, a writer borrows passages from other of his works in order
to tell about his life. On the other hand, he continues, since the method
one uses in writing a diary is at variance with the manner of unity and
completeness required of an autobiography, an autobiography which is
based solely upon one's other autobiographical writings for source material runs the risk of appearing not only disjointed or disunified but
also, frequently, incomplete.[25] While Pascal's interest is principally
with autobiographies written during the nineteenth and twentieth centuries, his theory may be used in considering the artistry of autobiographies written during the seventeenth and eighteenth centuries. Ironi-
cally, the recently published autobiography of Increase Mather,[26] which
dates from roughly the same time as his son's Paterna and which, like
Paterna, was written principally for the instruction of the author's
children, clearly reflects the dangers and limitations inherent in autobiography which is based upon information and passages borrowed from the
author's diary and other writings.

Although much of Paterna consists of passages borrowed from Cotton
Mather's Diary and other published works, its three hundred fifty-five
manuscript pages are remarkably uniform in method and style. While I do
not propose to exhaust all possible comment on Mather's method and style

in Paterna in the next few pages, I should like to indicate several of
the means through which Mather preserves a high degree of literary consistency throughout the work and to suggest that Mather is conscious of
the aesthetic requirements of his form as he pursues, for more than
twenty years, the history of his spiritual life. Among the methods
Mather uses to insure unity and to preserve the appearance of completeness in Paterna are his use of his conversion experience in order to represent his life as a continuous and dramatic unfolding of experience,
his use of the language and style of the Puritan sermon in order to sway
his audience to his point of view, his use of a "biographical parallel"
through which he measures the relative success or failure of his life
against that of an ideal, and his exploitation of his own and his audience's anonymity throughout the work.

By the time Mather was born in 1662, the process of conversion was
universally understood by Puritans as a formal, somewhat ritualized, experience, as William Perkins's outline of the process, which I have reproduced in Appendix D, indicates. Thus Mather could presuppose his
audience's familiarity with the theory of the process and he could,
therefore, exploit for his own artistic ends two prominent features of
the process: (1) the conversion experience is a life-long process which
concludes only with the ultimate judgment of God in the next world, and
(2) the conviction that one is converted and, therefore, saved, is never
to be regarded as absolute in this world. Mather introduces the conversion experience in the early pages of Paterna and continues to use it
throughout as the central experience of his life during each of the
phases he addresses in the work. Between pages 5 and 7 Mather acknowledges the first movements of his conversion in a form almost identical
to Perkins's outline of the process. Barely into a consideration of his

adolescent years, he writes on page 5, "I Apostatised from God, in diverse Miscarriages, which made me Suspect, that I have never yett Experienced any more than Some Common Works of His Holy Spirit, and that I was yet but a Refined Hypocrite." By page 6 he is experiencing the "Bodily Indisposition," including nightmares, fever, and delirium, which all good Puritan youth experienced and which "terribly Awakened" in the individual suspicions about his "Interior & Eternal State." As such suspicions continue to gather in intensity, Mather concludes that he is a "Castaway." By page 7, however, Mather's indisposition has passed, and he tells his reader that after an exhaustive effort at self-examination and meditation he received "Strange, and Strong, and Sweet Intimations, that I was Accepted of the Lord" and wonderful "assurances" that the promise of salvation "should be fulfilled upon me." In effect, young Mather achieves a conviction that he is welcome among the company of the saints. Yet as the reader of Mather's autobiography soon recognizes, this is only the beginning of Mather's conversion experience in Paterna. By page 16, for instance, the Lord is again "grinding [Mather] to peeces before Him" with doubts and anxieties concerning his fitness to be a minister of the Lord. No sooner are Mather's difficulties resolved than he is again, on page 17, so "much afflicted with the Ephialtes" that he has "great Expectation of Dying with it, or of its Turning to Apoplexy." Eventually, however, prayer and meditation provide relief and Mather's "Heart [is] . . . raised unto Extraordinary Hopes and Joyes" on the basis of the promises of "a faithful Creator and Redeemer." Lest his reader doubt either the accuracy or the sincerity of the conversion process as Mather presents it, he assures him that "the whole Work of Conversion [must be encountered] often over & over again" and he relates that he is prepared and

"Desirous to Begin the Work of _Conversion_ again, and anew go over all the
Sorrowful and Heart-breaking Hours [of it] . . . [in order to be] thereby
Strengthened in the _Warfare_, whereto I am Called" (pp. 22, 48).

The conversion experience is prominent throughout the first part of
Paterna and becomes accentuated in the second part as Mather begins to
measure the progress toward salvation of his "Interior & Eternal State"
against the model of spirituality represented by Christ. With each re-
newal of interest in his on-going conversion Mather relies upon the efficacy of the promises of the New Covenant to provide him with an assurance,
albeit temporary, that he is, indeed, saved. Through repeated reference
to the process of conversion in his own life Mather is able to indicate
to his audience the need carefully to chart the progress of its own spiritual condition through self-examination and meditation. Further, on the
basis of his own example, Mather is able to elaborate on the peculiarities of the conversion process, particularly the idea that conviction of
conversion is not absolute in this world, "for y^e _Spirit_ _worketh_ _how_ _He_
Liketh" (p. 200), and, therefore, to argue for individual commitment to
the requirements and promises of the New Covenant. Most important for
our consideration of Mather's literary technique, he is able to unify the
Paterna thematically around this continuous and pervasive aspect of his
life.

Also important to Mather's literary organization of _Paterna_ is his
use of the structure and language of the Puritan sermon. We have already
observed the personal value Mather attaches to his autobiography as a
means of self-examination and meditation and that his meditational procedure, which he incorporates into this autobiographical narrative, provides him with, as he says, a "happy way of _Preaching_ _to_ _Myself_." Interestingly, the structure of Mather's method for meditation, as he outlines

it early in Paterna (p. 9), is identical to the structure of the Puritan
sermon as the form was developed in New England during the seventeenth and
early eighteenth centuries.[27] In the passage that follows readers familiar
with either the Puritans' sermon techniques or Mather's own suggestions for
the proper preparation of sermons will recognize the striking similarity
between Mather's "Proposals of proceeding Methodically in that notable
Duty of Christianity," meditation, and the conventions regulating the sermon form in Puritan New England. After he describes briefly his efforts
at achieving a logical and regular method for meditation, Mather writes,

> . . . I finally Pitched upon this Method. My Meditation was
> to Consist of Two Parts. In the First Part, I proceeded more
> Doctrinally: To Instruct myself; Either with Answering of a
> Question, or with Explaining of a Scripture, or with Con-
> sidering (upon an Head) the Causes, the Effects, the Subjects,
> the Adjuncts; the Opposites, and the Resemblances of the Thing,
> which I made my Theme. In the Second Part, I proceeded more
> Practically; To Affect myself: In Three Several Steps: First,
> An Examination of myself: Next, An Expostulation wth myself:
> Lastly, A Resolution, in the Strength of the Grace of the New
> Covenant; All relating to what had gone before. (p. 9).

In Paterna Mather rarely departs from this method. He adheres closely
to the central "question" or "theme" of Paterna--"How to keep to and advance in the path of righteousness"--addresses this theme from a variety
of perspectives, all derived from his personal experience, and renders a
number of resolutions made "in the Strength of the Grace of the New
Covenant" for the edification of his audience.

Mather's method for meditation within Paterna is the principal indication that he is presenting the history of his life within the structural framework of a sermon. The fact that he incorporates into Paterna
passages from a number of his published works which were first preached
as sermons (see Appendix B at the end of the Paterna text) and that the
reader will not notice any break in the structure or continuity of the
autobiography as Mather introduces these passages into the text, suggests

that he viewed Paterna as a sermon and that he consciously worked at achieving structural consistency within Paterna through the use of sermonic devices. Thus we find that echoes of the Puritan minister's voice of pulpit authority ring throughout Paterna as Mather reminds his audience that to be taught of a natural and spiritual father is equivalent to being "Taught of God" (see, in particular, pp. 258, 295, 333). This voice is audible as Mather delineates, "without the Least Fiction in the World," those "Experiences and Contrivances" most conducive to a proper "Walk with God." Though Mather appears to say that his advice and personal example are limited to what may "just Serve as a Direction" for his audience, his qualification of that statement to the effect that these "may be your perpetual monitors" underscores his ministerial or preaching role in Paterna. Similarly, he employs a number of rhetorical devices that clearly serve the oratorical demands of his sermon in Paterna. Throughout the autobiography he uses capitals and italics to emphasize particular aspects of his theme and to suggest an oratorical pattern, should the work be read aloud. Although examples could be chosen from nearly every page of Paterna to illustrate both its sermon structure and its sermon oratory, the following selection from the concluding pages of the text sufficiently indicates Mather's technique as he applies it throughout the work. Notice the rhythm and mood which Mather creates as he writes,

> I think,
> If I were fastened unto a CROSS, and under all the Circumstances of a Crucifixion, What would be My Dispositions, What My Exercises? I should Look on my approaching Death, as Unavoidable; and the Approaches of it would not be Welcome to me, not having any Prospect of being any other way delivered from Numberless Uneasinesses.
> I should Look on all the Delights and Riches and Honours of the World from which I am departing, as things of no Use and no Worth unto me.
> I should have done Expecting of Satisfaction from any thing of This World; and no more propose a Portion in any thing that

is done under the Sun. . . .
   I should utter Words, that may be for the Instruction and
Advantage of People that are about me; and Lay hold on Oppor-
tunities to say what I Could for the Advancement of Piety
among them. . . .
   I should, with Continual Acts of Resignation, committ my
Spirit into the Hands of my FATHER, and my SAVIOUR; With
Assurances of my Speedy Reception into a Paradise, where I
shall be Comforted. . . .
   In these Things I should propound a Conformity to my
Crucified JESUS.
   Thus Dying, Behold, I Live!
   And finding myself brought into these Dispositions and
these Exercises, the Faith of what must most Certainly follow
hereupon fills me with Joy Unspeakable & full of Glory (pp.
352-4).

And, finally, there is Mather's extensive use of scripture to

verify all that he has to say in Paterna, regardless of the subject at

hand. I shall comment on the reasons for which Mather uses scriptural

evidence in both direct reference and allusion when I consider Mather's

style in Paterna; for the present, however, it is sufficient for us to

observe that the prominent use of the Bible in Paterna enables Mather to

assert a claim of eternal verity for all that he preaches in the work.

An important additional feature of Mather's literary technique in

Paterna is his use of an elaborate "biographical parallel" in order to

represent his life as a dramatic unfolding of experience and in order to

measure his own life against the ideal life of the historical figure with

whom he establishes the parallel. The device of the biographical paral-

lel, as it is used in Paterna, is borrowed directly from the pattern

around which Mather writes the biographies of godly men in his Magnalia

Christi Americana. In his "Biographical Technique in Cotton Mather's

Magnalia," Reginald Watters provides a concise outline of Mather's

pattern: introduction; names of parents, place and date of birth; edu-

cation; regeneration, if noteworthy; dedication to the ministry; call to

a church; persecution for non-conformity and flight to New England, if

the man was not born there; installation in a church there; quality of
his sermons; godliness of his life, with a series of virtues, illustrated with anecdote; opinions on church affairs; dying words and death;
epitaph.[28] At each stage of his development of the individual's adult
life Mather introduces an historical figure, usually from the Bible,
whose life is recreated in or paralleled by the life and achievements of
the individual under consideration. In effect, the historical figure is
a type who figures or foreshadows a corresponding reality or life of the
new dispensation (anti-type). While Mather does not assert an absolute
identity between the biblical figure and the individual under study, he
does use the parallel to define the character and to measure the achievement of the subject of his biography. Thus, William Bradford is the
"Moses" needed to lead God's people from the deprivations of Europe to
the edenic wilderness of America; Eaton and Davenport are the "Moses"
and "Aaron" respectively of New Haven; Governor Phips is "a Gideon, who
had more than once ventured his life to save his country from their
enemies."

While he can not, obviously, include information on his death and
epitaph, Mather does not significantly depart from his established
pattern for biography in his autobiography. We have already noticed
that his own conversion experience receives prominent treatment in
Paterna. The reader of Paterna will also notice Mather's "persecution"
for non-conformity during the reign of Andros, his godliness or virtue
and occasional failure in both, and his opinions on church matters and
the good life represented as well. And he will notice the biographical parallel which Mather includes in the work. In the first part of
Paterna the specific parallel is difficult to discern. Although Mather
argues that "A Christ is better to me" than any sinful delights, asserts

that Christ is "the Way," and tries to emulate the Way of Christ in his
pastoral duties and during times of personal trial (pp. 19, 42, 96, 153,
168), he does not appear to identify himself with Christ in any but conventional ways. Instead, the parallel that seems to emerge in the first
part is between Cotton Mather and, in general terms, an angel. Mather's
own interest in such a parallel is clear throughout the first one hundred
fifty pages of Paterna. Indeed, his comments on page 142 would lead us
to believe that this is the parallel through which he will describe and
judge his life, for there he writes, "I Considered, That as by the
Praises of God, I should become Like the Good Angels, thus it was a very
Reasonable Thing, that I should offer my Extraordinary Praises to Him,
for His Angels." Nevertheless, at the beginning of "The SECOND Part"
Mather's parallel becomes evident. Almost immediately after he begins
this part of the work he commences to judge his life and actions against
their degree of "conformity to my Lord JESUS CHRIST," and he describes
no significant event during his life from this point onward without
measuring himself against Christ, as represented by his attempt to be
Christ-like in his actions and experiences. Thus, for example, he describes his effort to bring "certain Wicked and Wretched people . . .
unto Saving Repentance, and Serious Religion" as an effort to emulate
"Some Image of JESUS CHRIST, in my Labours and Expensive Compassion for
those Miserables." While he asserts that this action has brought him
"unto the highest Pinacle of my Happiness," he admits that his "Conformity has been but Half carried through," for those to whom Christ
showed compassion "took Him, and Hang'd Him on a Tree, after all." However, he revealingly adds that among the "Libels" thrown at him for his
efforts toward these "miserables" was "ye Picture of a Man, hanging on
ye Gallowes . . . [with] my Name over it; and by the side of it [was

written], This is [Such an ones,] Desert" (pp. 216-7).

Mather continues to measure his personal worth and judge his life according to his degree of conformity to Christ throughout the remainder of Paterna. Incidents are drawn from his life which appear consciously to underscore the biographical parallel he has introduced. From page 218 on, for instance, Mather is steadfast in his pledge to love and to beg mercy for his enemies; and even as the Holy One did, Mather promises, "I should Pray for them, Father, Forgive them" (p. 353). He also enlarges on the meaning and instructional value of his Paterna, this sermon for his son, through the parallel, for the greater authority is conferred upon Mather's advice when he states that "a glorious CHRIST . . . has not only Instructed me by His Pattern, [a pun on the autobiography's title,] but Commanded me by His Precept also" (p. 244). Moreover, Mather uses the parallel to define himself, his motives as a man, and his view of the achievement of his ministry, for his son. Thus, for instance, while throughout the first three hundred pages of Paterna Christ is frequently described as the great sacrificer, the "high priest" of the "Heavenly Priesthood," Mather, on page 296, assumes the role of "A SACRIFICER" and a right to the "Heavenly Priesthood" for himself. He states, "My Poor Life has been full of Sacrifices; and by the Things I have Suffered, I have Learn'd the Obedience of, A SACRIFICER: By which my Title to the Heavenly Priesthood, is, I hope, a Little Cleared up." It is in such statements as this that Mather develops a definition of himself and evaluates his worth, while he also instructs his audience in the way or pattern of Christ, using himself as an example of one trying to lead a Christ-like life. Mather concludes the Paterna with a passage remarkable for both its emotional intensity and its elaborate use of the biographical parallel. In the meditative passage which begins, on page

352, "I think, If I were fastened unto a CROSS, and under all the Circumstances of a Crucifixion, What would be My Dispositions, What My Exercises", Mather summarizes the important experiences of the last years of
his life, indicates that the parallel between himself and Christ is consciously drawn, defines himself, in his Christ-like dispositions and
exercises, as a true Christian, and offers himself as a practical example
of "Living by Faith of the SON of GOD" for the edification of his reader.

Mather's use of the biographical parallel is his most significant
unifying device in Paterna. It allows him to represent his life not
only as a dramatic unfolding of experience but, through the crucifixion
passage at the end of the work, as a completed whole. In addition, the
history of a life modelled after the life of Christ provides sufficient
"Treats" and "Charms," to use Mather's language (p. 92), to persuade its
audience to follow the path of righteousness. While Mather can not be
too specific about the rewards to be gained through such a life, since
"'[the] Meditations [and Experiences] that are fullest of Devotion, Cannot be Remembred'" (p. 184), he promises the reader that the dispensations
or providences of God toward one who seeks to conform himself to Christ
are "marvellous," "wonderful," and "full of incredible satisfactions."

One final aspect of Mather's literary technique in Paterna deserves
our attention: the anonymity of author and audience throughout the work.
Manierre is at a loss to explain Mather's use of this device in Paterna,
observing that it is a "cause of 'Paterna's' relative worthlessness as a
source of historical fact" and a "perverse decision" on Mather's part.[29]
My own view is that Mather's anonymity in Paterna is of considerable
literary interest in that it anticipates the use of the persona in American autobiographical writing from Benjamin Franklin onward. Mather initially informs his son that "[Because] I know not what Hands, besides

Yours, this Work may fall into, I Will be careful to insert not One word, that shall discover unto any One man Living, who I am" (p. 2). In order to maintain this posture Mather pretends not to divulge any information in Paterna which would reveal his authorship of the work. He leaves unmentioned, therefore, facts such as, "When and Where (as well as, of Whom)" he was born, the name of the "Colledge" to which he was admitted, the age at which he became a minister, the titles, subject matter, and number of books he has written, and the various "Public Circumstances" of his first thirty years (pp. 3, 5, 15, 24, 46, 112, 115, 125, 129, 219). Yet there is more than sufficient information in Paterna for one to identify the author. In addition to a marginal note in which he identifies "The Title of a Book, which I had Published" on page 203, the speaker's various descriptions of himself, his occupations, and his possessions could refer to only one person alive between 1699 and 1727. He lets it be known, for instance, that he is a minister "in as Great a place, as any in these Parts of the World" and preaches "to greater Congregations, than most preachers of ye True Gospel in this world," that he has given away "many Hundreds, yea, . . . many Thousands, of Good Books," some of which were written by himself, that he is the "Pastor of a Church" and "Collegue . . . [of] . . . an Elderly and Eminent Person," that he has written to the churches of the civilized world in "More than Two or Three . . . Languages," indeed, he knows of no "Non-Conformist Minister now surviving in ye Nation [who] hath . . . written . . . so many books," and that his library, together with that of his father, is the largest in the colonies (pp. 20, 82, 45, 86, 265, 46). In addition, Mather frequently alludes to the titles of his published works and selects passages from them for inclusion in Paterna. Mather's inclusion of such facts and information indicates his wish to be not

wholly unidentifiable in Paterna and his use of anonymity as a literary
device. For Mather to be more specific about himself than he is in
Paterna would be, to some extent, unnecessary for his audience. Given
those for whom he intends the work--his sons, his select friends and
relatives, and himself--detailed information concerning his parentage,
education, and the like would be superfluous. Moreover, autobiography
does not require an endless catalogue of names, dates, and events, in
order to be authentic and to appear complete.

What end, then, is served by Mather's anonymity in Paterna? Anonymity, at least as Mather uses it, creates the illusion of objectivity
and truthfulness in his autobiography. What Mather writes in Paterna is
not to be read as the biassed view of a person writing his own life; it
is instead, presumably, the history of a person's life as any objective
biographer would write it. Such objectivity or honesty serves Mather in
several ways. It is, first of all, useful in reconstructing a righteous
life, a life of one conforming himself to Christ, as it helps to underscore the goodness and the humility of the individual. As such, anonymity
is of great value in an autobiography which is instructional, for the
audience can identify the devout and good life being taught in the work
with the life of the subject of the work without being distracted by personal idiosyncracies. Anonymity also enables Mather to be consistently
selective in the material he includes in Paterna without having to justify his selectivity. Since he is engaged in the composition of, principally, a spiritual autobiography, he does not have to worry about the
"Public Employments," among them the 1690's witchcraft episode, which he
would prefer not to treat. Finally, anonymity enables Mather to address
his several audiences without fear that because the work is designed for
a multiple audience it will, for any reason, offer insult or slight to

one or the other of them. With its specific audience and author left un-
named, Paterna allows Mather to address two sons, offer suggestions for
the ministry and for the spiritual welfare of several friends and relatives, and to catalogue his many promises and contrivances to serve the
Lord.

While Mather's method in Paterna enables him to write an autobiography which is unified and complete, it is his language which enables
him to be consistent in his method and to fulfill the primary purpose of
the work, instruction in the ways of righteousness. Since we have already noticed Mather's use of the structure of the Puritan sermon, it
would also be useful to consider his advice to ministers on the preparation of sermons. The fact that Mather looks upon Paterna as a "happy
way of preaching" has a considerable bearing on its style. In his
Manuductio ad Ministerium, a handbook for candidates for the ministry,
Mather writes the following passage, which will serve as a brief outline of his own stylistic approach in Paterna.

> In your Preaching that you may Save them that hear you,
> I wish you may with all possible Dexterity spread the Nets
> of Salvation for them. And therefore often exhibit the
> Terms of Salvation, and the Proposals of the Gospel, in
> such a Manner, and so importunately solliciting their Con-
> sent unto them, that by the hearty Speaking One Word, in
> the Echo's of Devotion thereupon, they may be brought into
> them. Exhibit unto them the Desires of PIETY, in such a
> Manner, that they must have their Hearts burn within them,
> & they must be Hearts of Stone indeed, if they take not
> Fire immediately. When you also describe the Graces of
> the New Creature, give the Description in the Language of
> PIETY, acting those Graces; wherein, if they come unto a
> Consort with you, their Souls are gained unto GOD, at the
> very Moment of your Instructing them. Oh! That you may
> be a Wise Winner of Souls! And while you are Preaching,
> may the Holy SPIRIT fall on them that hear the Word! ³⁰

Mather attempts to be a "Wise Winner of Souls" in Paterna by employing a style through which he can spread the "Nets of Salvation" over
his audience. The principal feature of his style is his use of

biblical references and allusions. Throughout the first and second parts
of the autobiography Mather relies upon evidence from the "Divine Oracles"
to underscore the urgency and applicability of his advice and to suggest
that there is an authority higher than his own for what he says. In
effect, Mather uses biblical evidence in order to "exhibit the Terms of
Salvation, and the Proposals of the Gospel" and to confer upon his advice
the prestige of gospel verity. Interestingly, he is more sparing in his
use of such evidence in the section of Paterna written for Increase than
he is in the section written for Samuel. It may be that he considered
his parental authority sufficient reason for Increase to act on his advice. If that is the case, then the failure of Paterna's intended effect upon Increase may account, to some extent, for Mather's extensive
use of biblical evidence to support his advice to Samuel. Most likely,
however, Mather's increased use of biblical evidence in "The SECOND
Part," in which the number of biblical allusions alone is nearly three
times that of the first part, derives from his intense development of the
biographical parallel in that section. As the examples which were used
earlier to demonstrate Mather's development of the parallel between himself and Christ indicate, Mather repeatedly supports his interpretation
of events touching upon his life and his definition of his "Way" with
references in which the "Way" of Christ foreshadows the "Way" of Cotton
Mather. Thus, his practice of the ministry is recounted in Paterna
according to its similarity to the pattern of the ministry of Christ and
his apostles as outlined in I Corinthians, chapter 4, and Hebrews,
chapter 8. Similarly, the spirit of resignation through which Mather
assents to the will of God in his many "Vehement Cries from ye Dust" re-
calls Christ's assent in Luke 23: 46 (see, for instance, pp. 321-2 of
Paterna). Since examples such as these are found on nearly every page

of Paterna, a complete index to all Mather's direct references and allusions to the Bible is provided in Appendix C at the end of the text.

Mather also uses a number of other stylistic devices to sway his audience to the "Desires of PIETY" and to make their "Hearts burn within them." Apparent throughout Paterna is Mather's fondness for punning. As indicated earlier, the title of the autobiography contains a double meaning. "Paterna" represents not only the advice of a father for his son's spiritual welfare but also a systematic statement concerning the way or pattern of righteousness as revealed in the pattern of "a Lovely SAVIOUR." In an equally serious vein Mather puns on Christ as the "SON of God" and the "Sun of Righteousness," using SON and Sun interchangeably to achieve the effect of a double reference as on pages 288 and 309. In a lighter vein Mather will use a pun to enliven Paterna for his sons, though he is always careful not to compromise the seriousness of his subject. Such is his aim, for instance, when after he describes his rejection of the "Wicked Words and Wayes" of his playmates, Mather writes of his first impulses toward the doing of good: "I Began Betimes, to aspire after Usefulness. I Could at first only play at Small Game" (pp. 4, 13).

Mather also effectively uses metaphor and simile in Paterna to enhance the instructional value of the work. Once again, the "pattern" element in Paterna is important to note, as it is the metaphor which controls the instruction of the entire autobiography. The use of simile, on the other hand, allows Mather to illustrate his teachings in terms his audience can understand and identify with. To this end Mather's similes vary from a tone of commonness or homeliness to a tone approaching poetic high seriousness. One of Mather's more elaborate homely similes appears on page 268, where he describes himself, in his effort to relieve the afflictions of his flock, as "the Wind [which though it] will

not fill the Hungry, yett it will turn ye Mill, that will grind the Corn,
that will fill the Hungry." Mather is able to underscore the importance
of a minister's close watch over his own conversion process through a
homely yet colorful simile when he writes, after a long description of
the "horrible Agonies and Amazements" which took hold of his soul one
day, "I was able afterwards, to make & preach Sermons, on the Duty of
Coming to ye Lord Jesus Christ, which (like the Silkworm) I had Spun out
of the Bowels of my own Experience" (p. 24). On the other hand, he occasionally uses more poetically elegant similes, one of which appears
early in the work. After he illustrates for his son the dangers of
melancholy as he has experienced it in his early years, he writes,

> But ye Troubles of Sin accompanied these my [melancholic]
> Confusions, which horribly overwhelmed me: Until once
> Crying to the Lord in prayer, and Casting my Burdens on
> ye Care of the Lord Jesus Christ, I sensibly felt an un-
> accountable Cloud and Load go off my Spirit, and from that
> Minute I was as much altered, by a New Light, and Life,
> and Ease arriving to me, as ye Sunrise does change the
> World, from the Condition of Midnight (P. 8).

Finally, there is Mather's use of vivid description in Paterna.
As it helps him call his audience's attention to the intensity of the
experience he recounts, his vivid description, which is frequently
hyperbolic metaphor or simile, complements his use of metaphor and
simile as stylistic devices. Mather's descriptions tend to be most
vivid when he considers the assaults of Satan upon his soul or when he
deplores his own sinfulness. Thus, he writes in the midst of spiritual
agony, "It may be, the Lord is fitting me, for some Service or Mercy,
and therefore is grinding me to peeces before Him" (p. 16). Frequently,
when the Lord is not grinding him to "peeces" with doubts, anxieties,
and fits of despair concerning his eternal estate, Mather finds himself
"wrestling with the Lord," as on page 209, for His influence in some

"Great Affayr" of this world. Again, he describes the world in which
those who survive him must remain as "a Land of Pitts & of Droughts, &
fiery flying Serpents" (p. 353). Finally, as suggested in these last
three examples, Mather's descriptions in Paterna reflect something of the
tendency of the puritan sermon to oratorical hyperbole. They often occur,
in fact, in Paterna's most sermonistic moments. We notice, for instance,
echoes of the Puritan ministers' rhythmical sermon voice as Mather describes the dangers of pride in Paterna:

> The Apprehension of the Cursed PRIDE, the Sin of Young
> Ministers, Lurking and Working in my Heart, fill'd me with
> inexpressible Bitterness, and Confusion, before the Lord . . .
> Yea, Lett me Remember, Pride Sooner than anything, will
> drive away the Good Spirit of God, from the Heart of a Poor
> Creature. And if that should be my Fate, Oh, Lord, have
> mercy! What a Monument should I be, of thy Ireful, & thy
> Direful Vengeance! (pp. 27, 29).

IV: Conclusion

Reluctant to overstep the limitations of an introduction to a work,
I have not set forth a detailed interpretation of Paterna here, although
I have attempted to suggest a number of reasons for our responding to
Paterna as an intrinsically valuable piece of hitherto ignored eighteenth century Puritan personal literature. Although Professor Manierre
argues persuasively to the contrary, Paterna deserves more detailed consideration than has been given it here or than scholars have given it in
the past, on the basis of its literary significance alone.[31] In addition,
Paterna provides us for the first time with a source of first hand information about Mather's first twenty years and offers important information on the progress of Mather's spiritual life during eight years for
which his diaries have not survived.[32] Ultimately, Paterna deserves the
attention of the literary critic, the theologian, and the student of autobiography. For the literary critic, Paterna represents an important
addition to the sources against which he must judge his theories concerning Puritan literary art. For both the literary critic and the theologian, the extensive use of biblical evidence in Paterna verifies recent
discoveries and discussion concerning the typological interest and exper-
tise of the Puritan writer and expands the field of reference beyond
texts of Puritan history and theology to include Puritan autobiography.
Finally, for the student of autobiography, the availability of Paterna,
the autobiography of one of the most significant figures of early America,
may help provide the impetus for much-needed study of the seventeenth and
eighteenth century American sources of the genre. An inevitable result of
such studies will be a better understanding of both the period and ourselves. After all, since the American character has evolved over three
centuries, the personal records left by Puritan settlers must serve us as
early sources through which to define that character.[33]

NOTE ON THE TEXT

AND STATEMENT OF EDITORIAL PRINCIPLES

The text of Paterna that follows is based upon the manuscript, in Mather's own hand, currently in the collections of the Tracy W. McGregor Library at the University of Virginia. The text is printed with the permission of the trustees of the McGregor Library.

Although the manuscript has been preserved in a reasonably good state, the smallness of the octavo format, the remarkable smallness of Mather's handwriting, and the occasional fragility of manuscript pages and their outside edges initially presented some predictable problems in the establishment of a correct text. Difficulties presented by the format and Mather's handwriting were able to be compensated for by the use of a xerox copy-flo of the manuscript which was enlarged to two and one-half times the original. Unfortunately, use of the copy-flo presented additional difficulties, principally in the copy-flo's distortion of capitals and its blurring of marginal entries. These difficulties were easily overcome, however, through reference to the original of the work with the aid of a magnifying glass. The absence of numerous blemishes and revisions in the manuscript (the latter are fully described in Appendix E) made the editorial process easier than it might otherwise have been and reduced the possibility of textual errors in the edition.

Since this is the first edition of Paterna beyond the manuscript, I have not "improved" its text. I have tried to reproduce the work as Mather left it to his son in 1727, believing that the principal audience for this edition (scholars and students whose interests are with the early period of American culture) will prefer a readable edition of the original as opposed to an improved, modernized text. My only personal intrusions into the manuscript have been to restore in it deleted phrases and passages as they occurred and were able to be read and to incorporate into it Mather's marginal notes and entries. In the case of both deletions and marginalia some personal judgments were called for. I have uniformly restored all readable deletions in the text unless (1) the deletion was occasioned by an error in spelling, sentence structure, and the like which Mather subsequently corrected in the text (in which case the deletion is noticed and described in Appendix E) or (2) the deletion was occasioned by Mather's discovery of his repetition of information contained elsewhere in the text (in which case notice of the deletion is taken in both Appendix E and the annotation). In no instance has my restoration of deletions violated Mather's desire to remain anonymous in the text and his concern for writing a coherent, instructive autobiography. In fact, whereas all of the unreadable deletions noticed in Appendix E were literally obliterated in the manuscript by Mather through both his excessive lining-through of words and lines and his smearing or smudging of lines and passages, most readable deletions were made by either a single wavy line or a single straight line through the middle of words and lines, suggesting, perhaps, that Mather had no objection to the readable deletions being read. All of Mather's deletions which have been restored in the text are setoff in this edition by the characters ⟨⟨ . . . ⟩⟩.

Marginal entries and notes presented little difficulty in determining either the propriety of the inclusion or the position of their inclusion in the text. In most cases, Mather's marginal entries consist of words, lines, or paragraphs intended as corrections of deleted material or used to incorporate inadvertently omitted material into the text. With few exceptions the proper position in the text of marginal material was indicated by a single, sometimes double or triple, caret. Generally, the proper position in the text of marginal entries which were not accompanied by a caret was easily determined by the content of the entry. In all instances in which the proper position of a marginal note or entry is open to question, a notice to that effect is taken in both Appendix E and the annotation. All of Mather's marginal notes and entries have been setoff in this edition by the characters ⟨ . . . ⟩.

Restored deletions, the characters I have used to set them off, and the characters I have used to setoff marginal notes and entries represent my principal intrusions into the text. In order to establish a consistent and permanent source of pagination for all future studies of Paterna I have included in the text too the page numbers of the manuscript, enclosing them in square brackets. This will be helpful, I believe, for those who may wish to consult the manuscript as well as this edition in their studies. Except for square brackets which enclose either manuscript page numbers within a line of text or a question mark within a deleted passage to indicate my doubtful reading of a word or line, all square brackets within the text are Mather's.

Readers of Paterna will notice many irregularities and peculiarities (by contemporary standards) in spelling, capitalization, paragraph indentation, and punctuation within the text. These are Mather's own, and consistent with my conviction that this first edition should not be improved, they have been preserved. In order to double-check against my inadvertent correction of the above, I have compared this edition against the manuscript on approximately twelve separate occasions during the past two years with an eye exclusively to preserving them. In fact, the irregularities and peculiarities of Mather's spelling, paragraph indentation, and

punctuation have been easy to preserve, as they are clearly represented
and readable in the manuscript. Admittedly, it was occasionally distressing to me (and it may be so to others) to observe exclamation marks
indiscriminately used for question marks, colons indiscriminately used
for semi-colons or periods. Yet to readers of colonial American manu-
scripts and material, Mather's inconsistencies should not prove an ob-
stacle to their reading of this work with understanding.

Mather's capitalization, however, did present some major problems
for me, as his system of capitalization can be described only as erratic.
While he often uses capitals along with italics either to emphasize a
point or to achieve an oratorical effect in those sections in which he
"preaches" to himself and others, he as often capitalizes adjectives,
adverbs, and, on occasion, prepositions seemingly without purpose. The
difficulty of making sense of such a system, although it is typical of
the systems used by most seventeenth and early eighteenth-century American
writers, is compounded in Mather's works by his carelessness in distinguishing between S and s, L and l, and W and w. I am confident that I have
correctly reproduced Mather's capitals in Paterna, as, once again, all
questions that I may have had at one time or other have been resolved
through reference to the original with the aid of a magnifier.

The relative ease of establishing a correct text has been offset
somewhat by the problem of annotation. Since in his effort to remain anonymous Mather left out of Paterna much information about himself, I found
myself confronted with two choices: annotate everything and write a running biography of Mather in footnotes or ignore annotation altogether.
My study of Mather has taught me the value of compromise, so I have pursued a "middle road" on the question of annotation. In addition to those
occasions for notes indicated above, I have provided notes only to clarify

Mather's obscure treatment of relatively important episodes during his life, to document Mather's biblical allusions the first time they appear (all additional allusions to the same text are noted in Appendix C), to indicate those passages in Paterna which are borrowed by Mather from sources other than his Diary or which are themselves sources for passages in other Mather works, and to provide translations for Mather's Latin and Greek passages in the text.

<u>Paterna</u>

Job. 9. 21.

Tho' I were perfect, --yett would I despise My Life.

Psal. 119. 74.

They that Fear thee will be glad when they See me;
because I have hoped in thy word!

Deinde plus me habiturum Autoritatis non dubitabem, ad
Excitandum Te, Si prius ipse Consurrexissen.[1]

Seneca ad Helviam

Quid utilius Filio? Quid jucundius Unico.[2]

Cic. de consol.

Vita hominis nihil aliud est, nisi Oratio, Gemitus,
Desiderium, Suspirium ad Misericordiam Dei.[3]

<u>Luther</u>.

A Father should bespeak his Children, as <u>Valerius Corvinus</u>
did his Souldiers; <u>Factu mea vos imitati vellem, nec
Disciplinam modo sed Exemplum</u>.[4]

1

A passage in <u>Jo. Halls</u> Essayes. P. 51. &c.

' The Description of Ones <u>own Life</u>, might be thought <u>Ambitious</u>; Were it
' not that it hath been done by Some Persons, either already <u>Satiated</u>
' with <u>Glory</u>, or not <u>Regarding</u> it; as among the Ancients, <u>Josephus</u>,
' <u>Nazianzen</u>, &c the Moderns, <u>Thuanus</u>, <u>Fr. Junius</u>, Etc. For <u>Fidelity</u>,
' they going out of the World, can have no great Desire to <u>Juggle</u>, and
' they have the most Liberty in Relation: For <u>Truth</u>, they are best able
' to be Accomptants of their own Actions; For <u>Authority</u>, they can best
' command Attention, Since their Past Life hath been the <u>Exordium</u> to
' what they Speak, and Every word is Raised from a Mass of <u>Experience</u>.
' So that it were to be Wished, that <u>Modesty</u> did not Withdraw many from
' this Task.

A Passage, in an Anonymous Book, Entitled, <u>An Account of the
Beginnings and Advances of a Spiritual Life</u>. P. 33.

' All such as are Renewed, have an Inward Principle of a <u>Divine Life</u> in
' them, which as it inclines them to all those things Comanded by God,
' Either by bringing them oft to their Remembrance, by driving the Con-
' trary Objects out of their Minds, by discovering the Excellence of the
' One, and the Baseness of the other, or by an inward Delectation, En-
' gaging to the One, & deterring from the other; All which with more of
' the Like nature, are Experienced by Pure Minds: So it also Setts them
' in the METHODS and Wayes that may Lead to an HIGH PITCH in those prac-
' tices. And tho' the General and Constant Methods be in Scripture,
' Yett there must be a Great <u>Variety</u> in these, Considering the Variety
' of Mens Tempers, Complexions, Educations, and Circumstances. Now for
' our Instruction in these, God gives a <u>Divine Light</u> unto all that ask

' it of Him, which Suggests means and METHODS to them for advancing

' This; and they feeling these prove Useful to them, may be well assured,

' they Came from God.

PATERNA.

To My SON.

Nullus Fidelior tibi ad Consulendum esse Potest, quait qui non tua Sed te diligit, quales profecto Sunt Parentes.[5] Gregor

---

God, who hath given You to me, requires and Expects, my Endeavours, that on the most peculiar Accounts, You may be His.

What have been my Prayers for you, both before and after my Receiving of you from the Lord, and what Hopes I have had concerning you, perhaps you may Somewhat inform Yourself, if You should Live to Read, the Passages of My Life, Recorded from time to time, as they Occurr'd, in Reserved Memorials,[6] which I Leave behind me.

From those Memorials, I am now going to Extract certain Passages, that may be Particularly Instructive to You; because to do so, I thought, would be one Reasonable Essay, That all my Prayers, and Hopes ((and Faith))[7] about You, may not be defeated.

The Instruction of a Father, carries much of Authority and Efficacy with it; It seems intimated in the Divine Oracles, That if the Servants of God WILL Command their Children, they SHALL keep the way of the Lord:[8] And some famous Orators going to Write Advice unto Young persons, have Ingeniously introduced, with a most Agreeable Fiction, the Dead Parents of those persons, as thus Advising of them. Tho' I shall quickly be Dead, Yett I am Still Alive; and because the Exemple of a Father added unto his [ms. p. 2] Instruction, may render it Singularly Efficacious, I have chosen to give you, without the Least Fiction in the World, a

Number of those <u>Experiences</u> and <u>Contrivances</u>, which I have had, in my own
Poor <u>Walk with God</u>.

I will not here mention, for my Vindication in this Action, the
Names of those Gentlemen, who Since <u>Josephus</u> have Written their own <u>Lives</u>;
or, have written Τῶν Ἐις ἑαυτὸν βιβλία.[9] For I am going to Write no more
of <u>my own</u>, than what may just Serve as a <u>Direction</u> to <u>Yours</u>. And, because I know not what Hands, besides <u>Yours</u>, this Work may fall into, I
will be careful to insert not One word, that shall discover unto any One
man Living, <u>who I am</u>; (as the Author of, <u>The Private Christians Witness</u>
<u>to Christianity</u>,[10] Lately Exemplified that Caution to me.) It may be,
the <u>Things</u>, which the Lord has helped me to <u>See</u>, and to <u>Do</u>, are Some of
those <u>Talents</u>; which I should Improve unto <u>His Glory</u>; And I know not,
how to make a better Improvement of them, than to Leave with You, <u>My</u>
<u>dear Son</u>, Such of them, as may be your perpetual <u>monitors</u>.[11] But tho' I
may Relate Such things, as May dispose You, to have a Good opinion of me,
(which 'tis not amiss for a <u>Son</u> to have of his <u>Father</u>, so far as it may
be had,) yett I Would not have you Conclude, that my Life has been free
from those <u>Failings</u> and <u>Follies</u>, which if they were all Related, would
Sufficiently Abase me: Nor shall I, where I may see it Useful for you,
forbear to touch upon them. [ms. p. 3]

THE FIRST PART

The First Three LUSTRES,

of a Fathers Life.

§ Being desirous to Discover myself unto None, but You, My SON, I must here Leave Unmentioned, When and Where (as well as, of Whom) I was born, Lest the mention thereof should afford some Light unto the Discovery, against which I would be Cautious.

Wherefore, I Begin with Observing to You, That I desire to bewayl unto the very End of my Life, the Early Ebullitions of Original Sin, which appeared at the Very Beginning of it. Indeed, Your Grandfather, tho' he were a Wise and a Strict Parent, would from ye Observation of some Dispositions in me, Comfort himself with an Opinion of my being Sanctified by ye Holy Spirit of God,[1] in my very Infancy. But he knew not how Vile I was; he Saw not the Instances of my going astray, even while I was yett an Infant.

§ However, there were Some Good things in my Childhood, in which I wish You, My Child, may do better than I. I began to Pray, even when I began to Speak. I Learn'd myself to Write, before my going to School for it. I used Secret Prayer, not Confining myself to Forms in it; And yett I Composed Forms of Prayer, for my School-mates, (I Suppose, when I was [ms. p. 4] about Seven or Eight years old) and Obliged them to Pray. Before I could Write Sermons, in y^e public Assemblies, I commonly Wrote what I Remembred, when I came home. (I Read the Scripture, with So much Ardour, that for one while nothing less than Fifteen Chapters a Day, Divided into three Exercises, for Morning and Noon, and

Night, would Suffice me.$\}^2$ I Rebuked my Play-mates, for their Wicked
Words and Wayes; and Sometimes I Suffered from them, the persecution of
not only Scoffs, but Blowes also, for my Rebukes: Which, when some-body
told Your Grandfather, I remember, he seem'd very Glad, Yea, almost
Proud, of my Affronts; and I then wondred at it, tho' afterwards, I better
understood his Heavenly Principle.

§ One Special Fault of my Childhood, (against which, I would have You,
My Son, be Caution'd,) was, Idleness. And One thing that occasion'd me
much Idle Time, was the Distance of my Fathers Habitation from the
School; which caused him, out of Compassion unto my Tender and Weakly
Constitution, to keep me at home in the Winter. However, I then much Employ'd myself in Church-History: And when Summer arrived, I so plied my
Business, that thro' ye Blessing of God upon my Endeavours, at the Age
of Little more than Eleven Years, I had composed many Latin Exercises,
both in Prose and Verse, and could Speak Latin so readily, that I could
Write Notes of Sermons after the English preacher, in it. I had Conversed with Cato, Corderius, Terence, Tully, Ovid, and Virgil. I had
[ms. p. 5] Made Epistles, and Themes; presenting my First Theme to my
Master,^{3} $_w$thout his requiring or Expecting as yett any Such thing of
me; whereupon he Complemented me, Laudabilis Diligentia tua!^{4} I had
gone thro' a Great Part of the New Testament in Greek: I had read considerably in Isocrates and Homer; and I had made some Entrance in my
Hebrew Grammar. (And I was upon a Strict Examination of ye President
& Fellowes, Admitted into a Colledge, the Name whereof need not here be
mentioned.) And, I think, before I came to Fourteen, I composed Hebrew
Exercises, and Ran thro' the other Sciences, that Academical Studies
ordinarily fall upon. I composed Systems both of Logick, and Physick,

in Catechisms of my own, which have since been used by many others. I
went over the Use of the Globes, and Proceeded in Arithmetic as far as
was Ordinary. I made Theses and Antitheses, and also disputed the main
Questions that lay before us. For my Declamations, I ordinarily took
some Article of Natural Philosophy, for my Subject, by which Contrivance
I did kill Two Birds with One Stone. Hundreds of Books I read over; & I
kept a Diary of my Studies.

My Son, I would not have mentioned these things, but that I may
provoke Your emulation.

§ Before I was quite arrived unto this Age, I Apostatised from God,
in diverse Miscarriages, which made me Suspect, that I had never yett
Experienced any More than Some Common Works of His Holy Spirit, and I was
yett but a [ms. p. 6] Refined Hypocrite. At length, upon occasion of
Bodily Indisposition, which I fear'd would End in Death, my Suspicion of
my Interior & Eternal State, was terribly Awakened. I Trembled, when I
thought, that after I had Hop'd Well of myself, & many Servants of God
had Spoke Well of me, I should be a Castaway after all; and I remember,
God Sett home that Consideration upon me, with a very particular Pungency, How Shall I be able to Look my own Father in the Face, at the Day
of Judgment? While I was under my Distresses, I heard Some Sermons, on
Luk. 7. 47. Her sins, which were many, are Forgiven; and on Rev. 22. 17.
Whosoever will, let him take of the water of Life freely. The Grace of
God in ye Lord Jesus Christ, and the Gracious Offer of the Lord Jesus
Christ, Wonderfully affected me; my Heart was Exceedingly Broken & Melted
at it; and it Embolden'd me to Come, and Lay Hold upon Him, who is able to
Save unto the uttermost all that come unto Him.[5] I had Frequent Returns
of Doubts and Fears; but I frequently Renewed my closures with ye Lord

Jesus Christ, as my only Releef against them. Once Labouring & Even
Languishing, under a Sense of my own horrible Vileness, and thinking, Will
the Lord Jesus Christ Accept of a Vile Wretch, that hath been & hath done,
as I have! I had some Discourse with Your Grandfather about it. He told
me, That as for that Matter, there was no Returning Sinner, but the [ms.
p. 7] Lord Jesus Christ would most freely Accept of him: For (Said he)
Observe it Even among men: There's a Vile Sinner, an Holy man Beholds
him and Abhors him: Yett if this Vile Sinner ever comes to be Converted,
the Same Holy Person, can & will, notwithstanding his former Loathsome
Vileness, Embrace him in his very Bosome; and This (he Said) is an Em-
blem & Effect of the Spirit of the Lord Jesus Christ. I shall never for-
get, how much these Words did Quicken me! In my Addresses to Heaven
under ye Exercises of my Mind, about my Reconciliation to God, I now
Sometimes received Strange, and Strong, and Sweet Intimations, That I was
Accepted of the Lord. Once Especially, having heard a Sermon, on Isa.
44. 3. I will Pour my Spirit on thy Seed, & my Blessing on thy off
Spring; I Pleaded that promise before ye Lord, and in my pleading of it,
ye Spirit of ye Lord, wonderfully dissolved my Heart, with Assurances,
That it should be fulfilled upon me.

§ I can't certainly Remember, (having by an unhappy Casualty Lost
some of my Records,)[6] when it was, that I began to keep Dayes of Prayer
with Fasting, alone by myself: but, I think, it was when I was about
Fourteen Years old: And I remember well, That I made Mr Scudders,
Christians Walk,[7] my Directory in those Duties.

§ Moreover, I may mention it unto You, That when I was about this Age,
I fell under the Power of Melancholy, to Such a Degree, that I Exceedingly [ms. p. 8] Wonder, ⟨ it had no worse Effects upon me.⟩ And

Studying Physick at this time, I was unhappily led away with Fancies, that I was myself Troubled, with almost every Distemper that I read of, in my studies: which Caused me sometimes, not only Needlessly, but also Hurtfully to use Medicines upon myself, that I might Cure my Imaginary Maladies. But ye Troubles of Sin accompanied these my Confusions, which horribly overwhelmed me: Until once Crying to the Lord in prayer, and Casting my Burdens on ye Care of the Lord Jesus Christ, I sensibly felt an unaccountable Cloud and Load go off my Spirit, and from that Minute I was as much altered, by a New Light, and Life, and Ease arriving to me, as ye Sunrise does change the World, from the Condition of Midnight.

§ I Will further inform you, My Son; That one Singular Advantage to me while I was thus a Lad, was my Acquaintance with, and Relation to, a Society of Young Men[8] in o^e Town, who mett Every Evening after ye Lordsday, for ye Services of Religion. There we constantly Pray'd, both before and after the Repetition of a Sermon; and Sang a Psalm; taking o^e Turns in Such Devotions. We then had a Devout Question, proposed a week before; whereto any one present gave what Answer he pleased; and I Still Concluded the Answer. As ye Lord made poor me, to be a little useful unto these (and other) meetings of young people, in my Youth, so He made these meetings very useful unto me. Their Loves to me, and their Prayers for me, and my Probationary Essayes [ms. p. 9] among them, had a more than ordinary Influence upon my After-Improvements.

§ I will bring you out of my Childhood at Last, by telling you, My Son, That while I was yett a Child, I was much affected with Reading Dr Halls Treatise of Meditation,[9] and with his proposals of proceeding Methodically in that notable Duty of Christianity. Hereupon I Read

Several other Books about that Subject; and I made many Essayes, at a
Logical and Regular Method, for daily MEDITATION. Yea, I went so far,
that I Wrote a Discourse on that Subject, which found some Consideration
among Several Ingenious persons. The Result of all, was, That I finally
Pitched upon this Method. My Meditation was to Consist of Two Parts. In
the First Part, I proceeded more Doctrinally: To Instruct myself; Either
with Answering of a Question, or with Explaining of a Scripture, or with
Considering (upon an Head) the Causes, the Effects, the Subjects, the Ad-
juncts; the Opposites, and the Resemblances of the Thing, which I made
my Theme. In the Second Part, I proceeded more Practically; To Affect
myself: In Three Several Steps: First, An Examination of myself: Next,
An Expostulation wth myself: Lastly, A Resolution, in the Strength of
the Grace of the New Covenant; All relating to what had gone before.
This happy way of Preaching to myself, the Lord began betimes to acquaint
me withal. But I mourn before ye Lord Exceedingly, for my not attending
it, with Such Constancy & Frequency, as I Should have done.

The Fourth Lustre

§   I find nothing in the <u>Sixteenth</u> year of my Life, that I think here
Proper to be mentioned.

§   Having Passed the First Sixteen years of my Age, I was by my
Friends, thought of Age Enough, to join Myself unto a <u>Particular Church</u>,
(of <u>Non-Conformists</u>, for I was, both by my Education, and upon Consci-
entious principles, One of Them:) which I did accordingly, and Renewed
my <u>Baptismal Covenant</u>.

§   My Approaches to the <u>Lords Table</u>, obliged me, to be very Particular
in <u>Self-Examination</u>. I once while yett Short of <u>Seventeen</u>, wrote ⟨⟨ the
following⟩⟩ unto this Purpose, on that Occasion.

'   Setting myself upon the work of <u>Self-Examination</u>, I find:

'   I. Concerning my <u>Faith</u>.

'   I am Convinced of the utter Insufficiency in my own <u>Righteousness</u>
' to procure my <u>Salvation</u>. I See the <u>Nothingness</u> of my own <u>Righteous-</u>
' <u>ness</u> in Point of Acceptance with God. I See indeed a woful <u>Hypocrisy</u>
' hath acted me, and <u>Sluggishness</u> and <u>Selfishness</u> hath attended me in
' the very best of all my Services.

'   I perceive now no other way for my <u>Salvation</u>, but only by ye Lord
' JESUS CHRIST; <u>Refuge</u> fails elsewhere on Every hand.[1]

'   I behold a <u>Fulness</u> and a <u>Bounty</u> in ye Lord JESUS CHRIST. He is
' worth Loving, worth Prizing, worth Following Hard after Him.

' [ms. p. 12]

'   Such is my Desire to obtain an Interest in Him, & make Him ye only
' <u>Support</u> and <u>Portion</u> of my Soul, that it is one of my greatest Griefs,
' to find my Heart so dull in its Out-goings after Him.

'   II.   Concerning my Repentance.

'   I Abhor Sin, because it is Abhorr'd by God & Contrary to Him.

'   Sin is my Heavy Burthen; Death itself would be welcome unto me, to
' free me from such a Burthen.

'   I am Heavily Troubled, for ye Sin in my Heart; and that Fountain of
' Corruption, the Plague of my Heart, afflicts me.

'   III. Concerning my Love.

'   I Long to See and Know ye Favour of God with mee; the Sight of That,
' would make all my Afflictions Light.

'   I desire to be as Active as may be, in promoting ye Honour of God;
' and I seldome Come into any Company without Contriving, whether I may
' not Act or Speak something for That in it, before I Leave it.

'   I am Sorry, that I Love God no more.

'   The Saints, that have ye Image of God, are those whom I Value most.

'   A mean person, with Grace, is more amiable to me, than another who
' is otherwise never so well-qualified, but Graceless.

I was also much Comforted about this time, with a passage, I found
in an Holy Book.

An upright man, is Like ye Needle touch'd with the Loadstone: tho'
he may, thro' boisterous Temptations, & Strong Allurements, oftentimes
Look [Ms. p. 13] towards the Pleasure, Garn, and Glory of this present
World, yett because he is truly touched with the Sanctifying Spirit of
God, he still inclineth God-ward, and hath no quiet, until he Standeth
Steady towards Heaven. And I found my Cares, to Speak Holily, Act Seri-
ously, and Live Usefully, did sensibly grow upon me.

§ Being about Seventeen Years of Age, ye Holy Spirit of God, Convinced
me more than formerly, of my Spiritual Sins, Especially, Pride, and

Sloth, and Envy; & fill'd me with unspeakeable Horror and Anger at them, & Caused me to Cry mightily unto Heaven for Help against them.

Sometimes also, I took up Devout Resolutions, which I recorded in my Reserv'd Papers.

One thing, which I Resolved as much as any One thing, (and Wrote it,) was,

' Tho' God never give me Sensible Demonstrations or Intimations of His
' Love, and any Shines of His Reconciled Face upon my Soul, yett I will
' follow hard after Him (in the Dark) as long as I have a Day to Live.

And I had much Peace in so Resolving.

§   But I will here observe One thing to You, My Son, which I desire you never to Forgett.

I Began Betimes, to aspire after Usefulness. I Could at first only play at Small Game. I first Sett myself to Contrive, what Good I might be able to do in my Fathers Family, by instructing my Brethren, & Sisters, and o^e Servants, & forwarding of all Piety there. [ms. p. 14] This I did, while a very Boy. I proceeded Then, to Impose it as a Rule upon My-self, That I would never come into any Company, where it should be proper for me to Discourse, but I would, if I could, so order my Discourse, as to be Serviceable unto ye Company. Afterwards, I was brought into ye Societies of Religious Young Men; and then my opportunities to Do Good among our Young Men grew upon my Hands. I Husbanded my Opportunities, tho' with much Folly and Frailty. And God, who of His Free Grace thus included the most miserable Sinner in the World, gave me to find from time to time, the Remarkable Fulfilment of that Promise, To him that have shall be given.[2] My Lord Jesus Christ hath gone on multiplying my Oppor-tunities, till I have Come to Serve whole Churches, Yea, whole Countreyes,

Yea, whole Nations. Poorly, I confess; And this is my own Fault: But I
must not Explain ye Demonstration, Lest I discover myself too far.

Now, My Son, I do from an happy Experience, advise you, To Study and
Contrive, as Early as you can, To Do Good. Love to Do Good; Count it a
Noble, and a pleasant Thing. While You, and your Opportunities, are but
Small, Invent as many wayes to Do Good, as you Can. Avoid Ostentation,
Avoid Immodesty, Avoid all Impertinency, in Your Essayes to Do Good.
But, Begin Betimes with your Little Talents: It may be, the Lord will
Do Great Things for you, and by you, before He hath done. [ms. p. 15]

§   I must ⟨⟨ now ⟩⟩ unavoidably acknowledge, That my Calling (Such has
been the Favour of Heaven to the cheef of Sinners,) is, To preach the un-
searcheable Riches of Christ. But at what Age I entred upon that Calling,
I will not mention, Lest it should Contribute any thing unto the Discovery, against wch I would use all ye Caution imaginable.

All that I shall here tell You, My Son, is, That I Wish You, if not
Later, Yett Better and Wiser, and Abler, than I was, at Entrance upon the
Solemnest Work in ye World, if you Should ever Enter at all upon it.

§   But it may not be amiss, for me, to treat you with One Observation.
For a Day or two before I preached my First (and Second) Sermon, (which
was to very great Congregations,) I had my Mind so horribly Buffeted and
Unhinged, that I verily Beleeve, There was an Immediate Energy of Some
Bivel, in ye Temptations that assaulted me. I could give no Reason for
my Disturbance; nor had I any Fear of Speaking to very Great Congregations: My Disorder was all over Unreasonable, but it was truly Unex-
pressible. I was very nigh Distracted, with an Intolerable Confusion
upon my Mind; and it was a Considerable while, before I was able to pray,
& mourn to Heaven for Deliverance. But upon Earnest cries unto ye Lord

Jesus Christ, who knowes how to Succour ye Tempted,[4] I was delivered;
and went Comfortably thro' ye Services that were before me.

In the midst of my Agony, I wrote [ms. p. 16] these, among the other
Thoughts, then working in my amazed Mind;
' It may be, the Lord is fitting me, for some Service or Mercy, and
' therefore is grinding me to peeces before Him.

At last, ye Clouds vanished, and I Concluded thus;
' Lord, what am I? A poor Firebrand of Hell, worthy to be Confounded
' forever! Thou mayst forever banish me from all Comfort, and sink me
' to the Lowest Hell of Desperation. But all thy Paths towarde me, are
' mercy & Truth.[5] And Shall I not now Love thee? Yea, O my Blessed Bene-
' factor: I will Love thee, as long as I Live: I will preach thy
' Praises, and perswade and invite the Children of men to Love thee.
' And when I Come to Heaven, Whither I am certainly assured, that I shall
' be brought, I will admire thee with Eternal Praises.

§ After I had been for Some weeks a publick preacher, Sitting one day
in my Study, my Heart was raised unto Raptures almost Insupportable, when
I was Expressing my Love to God, and Beleeving His Love to me, and Saying,
Lord, Thou wilt be with me,[6] and help me to do some Special Services for
my Lord Jesus Christ; Then shall I Lay down my Head in the grave, & my
Spirit shall go up to be with my Lord Jesus Christ. [ms. p. 17]

§ You must Expect, My Son, That there will be much Independancy, in y^e
rest of the Passages, which I may transcribe into these Memorials for You;
for I shall mostly take them out of my Records, in ye Order wherein I
find them; (only Sometimes make and add Remarks, as I see occasion;)
and often Specify ye Year of my Age, wherein they occurr'd; because That
very Consideration, may be some Engagement upon You, to hasten in y^e

Matters of Religion and Salvation.

§   While I was between Seventeen and Eighteen years of Age, I was much afflicted with the Ephialtes;[7] and it sometimes handled me so Severely, that I had great Expectation of Dying with it, or of its Turning to an Apoplexy. God Sanctified unto me, this Expectation, thereby awakening my Supplication to Him, and my Preparation for Death. And in my Prayers, on this Occasion, I had my Heart Sometimes raised unto Extraordinary Hopes, and Joyes. Once Particularly, I thus Expressed myself, and my Heart was Exceedingly broken & melted at ye Expressions.

'   Lord, my Soul is the most Precious thing I have in the World; yett
' I Leave That with thee, as with a faithful Creator and Redeemer. I
' have chosen ye Lord JESUS CHRIST, as my Lord-Redeemer: And now, thou
' wilt gloriously take the Care of my Soul, that has made Such a Choice.
' Thou wilt Sanctify it, & Glorify it, and Carry on the Works in it.
' When my Body shall be thrown down into the silent Grave, this my Soul,
' that has chosen ye Same God, that my Father, and my Grandfathers have
' chosen before me, shall be with them, in the Enjoyments of that God,
' whom in this world I have desired[8] above all things to Enjoy. Then
' will thy Grace have Eternal glory; Then will Hallelujahs be Sung unto
' thy Name Eternally. [ms. p. 18]

By the use of Paeony, and by Abstinence from all Flesh at Suppers, I obtained at Last, much Releef against my Malady.

§   One Special Design which about this time, & afterwards, I prosecuted, was, To Engage my Sisters, in the Service of my Lord Jesus Christ; Especially my Eldest, who was most Capable of minding my Discourses. Calling them aloud (successively) into my Study, I there in as pathetical Terms as I could, Laid before them the manifold & marvellous Obligations, which Lay upon them, to give themselves unto the Lord Jesus Christ; & then I

pray'd with them, in Floods of Tears for the mercies of the Lord. The
Lord Accepted and Rewarded these my poor Endeavours, & made them as Instru-
mental as perhaps any thing whatsoever, to bring those Children home unto
ye Lord.

My Son, Tis a Desireable thing, for a Brother, to be a Spiritual
Father unto his own Sisters. Indeed, One Effect of this my Conduct was,
That ye Children alwayes treated me, with more of Respect, than a Brother
use to have; they treated me rather as their Father, than their Brother.

§   On a Certain Lords-Day, I thus Renewed my Closure with the Lord
Jesus Christ.

I Considered, that God had offered Him unto me, Altho' I am a most
Sinful and Wretched Creature, Yea, Because I am so: and therefore it was
my Duty to Take Him. I then Examined, whether there were no Reserve,
that might herein prove Destructive to my Soul. I Sought unto the Lord,
That He would Search me, Try me, [ms. p. 19] See whether there were any
Way of Wickedness in me. I found the Things, whereof I had most reason
to be Jealous, were Worldly Honours, and Carnal Pleasures; and thereupon
I thus Renounced them.

'   Lord, I give my Name unto thee; If thou wilt have it Reproached, I
' am Content: Only give me thy Christ, and I shall be Satisfied. Yea,
' I will Seek the Honour of Thy Name, whether the Honour of My Own, be
' Advantaged, or Prejudiced, by my doing so.

'   Lord, If any of my Delights are Sinful, or as far as they are Sinful,
' I utterly Forego them; and I beseech thee, to make me Abhor them:

'   A Christ is better to me, than any of them, than all of them. If
' they are Lawful, yett will I Leave them, when Either the Comand, or
' the Glory of my Lord, calls me another way.

And I added; 'Now I beleeve, That the Lord is <u>Mine</u>, and I am <u>His</u>: and He

' will Carry on His Kingdome in my Soul, unto Perfection, in Spite of all

' Oppositions whatsoever. I Leave all the weighty Concernments of it,

' with Him, forever & Ever.

§   One Day, Your Grandfather (I thought) Encouraged me, to Accept an Invitation to a <u>Small</u> and <u>Mean Congregation</u>; & be willing to Leave all my Friends, for the Service of the Lord Jesus Christ. I had yett but <u>Little Grace</u>, and this was very <u>Trying Discourse</u>. The terrible Diffi- culties and Humiliations, of Leaving all my Friends, & Leading an obscure Life among ye poor Husbandmen, assaulted my Mind with sore Discourage- ments. At Last, I thus argued with myself;

' Alas, what an Heart have I, that can [ms. p. 20] Leave nothing for my

' Lord Jesus Christ. But hereupon, I thus gave up myself unto that

' Glorious Lord; <u>Lord</u>, Thou art Worthy of me; I am Willing to Spend, &

' be Spent for thee. Clearly call me, to any <u>Place</u> or <u>Task</u>; O my Dear

' Lord; I will then Leave all & follow Thee. I must Leave Every Temporal

' Comfort, within a Little Time, when <u>Death</u> Calls me away. But thy <u>Love</u>,

' thy <u>Favour</u>, thy <u>Mercy</u>, Lord, <u>That</u> is worth Enjoying; and I can Enjoy

' This in any place, where thou wilt Employ me in Service for thy Name.

Thus my Uneasy Soul was quieted. But it was not Long before ye Lord Called me to Serve Him, in as <u>Great</u> a Place, as any in these Parts of the world; and I know no <u>Non-conformist</u> that hath been so Enriched with opportunities of preaching to ye greatest Congregations.

Therefore, <u>My Son</u>, become <u>As a Weaned Child</u>.[10]

§   When I was come to be Eighteen years of Age my Mind was Exceedingly taken up, with the great Action, of, <u>A Closing with the Lord Jesus Christ</u>.

In the prosecution of this Action, I may Say, t'was y^e <u>Spirit</u> of God,
that was my <u>Teacher</u>; no <u>Man</u>, or <u>Book</u>, show'd me the Way of managing
this Action; but I was by y^e <u>Spirit</u> of God, Led on to a most Explicit[11]
procedure in it. One Day, I used Such words as these, among others, before my Lord-Redeemer.

' Oh, my dear Lord; Thy <u>Father</u> has Comitted my Soul into thy Hands:
' There is a [ms. p. 21] <u>Covenant of Redemption</u>, wherein I am Concerned:
' I know my <u>Election</u> by my <u>Vocation</u>, and my Concernment in that <u>Cove-</u>
' <u>nant</u>, by my being made Willing to Come under the Shadow of thy Wings
' in the <u>Covenant of Grace</u>. Now in that ancient <u>Covenant</u>, the <u>Father</u>
' Said unto the <u>Son</u>, <u>Such an Elect Soul there is</u>, <u>that I will bring into</u>
' <u>thy Fold, and thou shalt undertake for that Soul, as a Sufficient</u>
' <u>and an Eternal Saviour</u>. Wherefore I am now in thy Hands, O my Lord:
' Thy Father has Putt me there, and I have Putt myself there; O Save me,
' O Heal me, O Work for me, Work in me the good pleasure of thy Goodness.

    And afterwards, in the Same Day, I Said;
' <u>Lord</u>, I have been Leaving my Soul this day, with my Lord Jesus Christ,
' and thou hast bid me to <u>Beleeve</u>, that I shall be Saved by Him. <u>Lord</u>,
' I do <u>Beleeve</u>, that
there never Came a miserable Soul unto the Lord Jesus Christ in Vain;
and I do <u>Beleeve</u>, that I myself shall not find it in Vain. He will do
<u>Great Things</u> for me. He has already done Enough, to leave me without
any Cause of Repenting, that I have with So much <u>Agony</u> of Soul come unto
Him. Yea, But I <u>Beleeve</u>, That He hath <u>more</u> still to do for me. Having
been the <u>Author</u>, He will be the <u>Finisher</u> of my <u>Faith</u>.

    Two things I will observe unto you, <u>My Son</u>, concerning this matter.

    One thing is This; When I Renewed, (as I often did, and with great
Variety of Expression,) this Action of, <u>Coming to the Lord Jesus Christ</u>,

I frequently Sett apart Whole Dayes, for <u>Prayer</u> with <u>Fasting</u> in my Study; and in those Dayes, I Usually underwent, first of all, grievous Conflicts, and Sorrowes, and Horrors of Mind, and horrible Amazements about [ms. p. 22] the Condition of my Soul. These <u>Agonies</u> Came upon me, without my Calling for them; and they were accompanied with an inexpressible Bitterness, which made me dread the Repetition of them. When my want of a <u>Christ</u>, and the Worth of a <u>Christ</u>, was hereby Powerfully sett home upon me, I Still with unutterable Fervency Struggled, until I found myself assisted from on High, to Lay Hold on the Lord Jesus Christ, in all His <u>Offices</u>; and then a Sweet Satisfaction of Mind Succeeded. Thus I was (while an Ignorant Youth) Strangely Led on by y^e <u>Spirit</u> of ye Most High, to go the whole <u>Work of Conversion</u> often over & over again. And, tho' at ye Beginning of a Day Sett apart for Such Devotions, I Should even tremble in ye Thoughts of the <u>Travail</u> that I foresaw, I should pass thro', yett I Comforted myself, that my frequent <u>Renewing</u> of that Action, would be my <u>Assuring</u> of it.

Once particularly, I find in my Papers, that I have inserted this Record.

> Horrible Agonies and Amazements took hold of my Soul this day, when I was, as in the Beginning of such Dayes I ever use to be, Entertaining myself with the manifold Instances of my <u>Sinfulness</u> and <u>Wretchedness</u>. After the <u>Prayers</u> wherein these things were amplified, Sitting in my Chair, I had Such Thoughts as these.
> ' What intends my Lord for to do with my Soul? Why does He thus
> ' grind and break my Heart, and upon Every Turn Cast me into
> ' unutterable Anguishes? Most Certainly I am Entred at the <u>Strait</u>
> ' <u>Gate</u>, and walking in y^e <u>Narrow Way</u>!

After this, Essaying to go unto the Lord Jesus Christ, I found that
I <u>could not</u> Beleeve on Him. So, I cried Earnestly unto God, Even
as for my life, that He [ms. p. 23] would help me to Beleeve: And,
Oh! Blessed be His Name! He did help me: With a Moved, Melted,
Raised Soul, I <u>Laid Hold</u> on the Lord Jesus Christ; saying
' <u>Lord</u>, Tho' I am Lamentably full of Miseries, Yett, Blessed be thy
' Name, there is a <u>Christ</u>, in whom there is a <u>Fountain Sett Open</u>
' for me. And now, <u>Lord</u>, Thou hast bidden me to Go unto Him: It
' is thy <u>Commandment, that I should Beleeve</u>. My Lord Jesus Christ
' has also Encouraged me, with His gracious <u>Invitations</u>; & has
' told me, <u>He will in no wise Cast me out</u>. Oh! Blessed Words!
' What shall I now do, but <u>Come</u>? <u>Lord</u>, At thy Bidding, I <u>Come</u>.
' --And Now I will sitt down <u>Satisfied</u>. I know, That the Lord
' Jesus Christ, is both an <u>Able</u> and a <u>Faithful</u> Saviour, and by Him
' I shall be <u>Saved from my Sins</u>. <u>That</u>, <u>That</u> is the <u>one Thing which</u>
' <u>I have desired</u>, & <u>that I will seek after</u>: Even, that my <u>Iniqui-</u>
' <u>ties</u> may be <u>Subdued</u>, and that I may be <u>Sanctified</u> as well as
' <u>Pardoned</u>. And, Oh! what a glorious Word is This! <u>It belongs</u>
' <u>unto my Lord-Redeemer now</u>, to Destroy all my <u>Sins</u>. Why doth He
' call for my <u>Heart</u>? Is it not, that He might <u>work all His own</u>
' <u>works</u> in it! Why doth He <u>Knock at the Door of my Soul</u>? Is it
' not, that He may come in, to Sett up His <u>Kingdome</u> there! And is
' <u>That</u> it, O Lord! Oh! Lett that <u>Blessed Thing</u> be done. And now,
' I beleeve that I shall be <u>Saved</u>. Being a <u>Sheep</u>, in ye Hands of
' the Lord Jesus Christ, I never shall miscarry.

Go, <u>my</u> Son, Do Like wise.

But another thing is This. The Holy <u>Spirit</u> of the Lord, by this
<u>Experience</u>, was preparing me, to do Service for His glorious [ms. p. 24]

Name, which I Little thought of. I was able afterwards, to make & preach Sermons, on the Duty of <u>Coming to ye Lord Jesus Christ</u>, which (like the <u>Silkworm</u>,) I had Spun out of the Bowels of my own <u>Experience</u>. Yea, and Some of them, are Since printed; wherein ye Several Distinct Steps of a Distressed Soul, in <u>Coming to ye Lord Jesus Christ</u>, are so Punctually described, as I have not found them in any other Books. But ye Titles of my Books, I must not mention, because I would by no means discover ye Author.

§ About this Time, on a <u>Day of Prayer</u> kept in my Study, I made and wrote, the following,

· RESOLUTIONS, for my <u>Walk wth God</u>.

· Lord, Thou that Workest in me, to <u>Will</u>, help me to <u>Resolve</u>.

· I. As to my <u>Thoughts</u>.

· 1. To Endeavour, that I will keep <u>God</u>, and <u>Christ</u>, and <u>Heaven</u>,
· much in my <u>Thoughts</u>.

· 2. In a Special Manner, to Watch and pray, against <u>Lascivious</u>
· Thoughts, <u>Ambitious</u> Thoughts, and <u>Wandring</u> Thoughts in ye Times of
· Devotion.

· II. As to my <u>Words</u>.

· 1. To be, not of many <u>Words</u>; and when I do Speak to do it with
· <u>Deliberation</u>.

· 2. To Remember my Obligations, to use my <u>Tongue</u>, as the <u>Lords</u>, and
· not <u>my own</u>; and therefore to promote <u>Savoury Disco^ese</u>, if I can,
· wherever I Come.

· 3. Never to Answer any <u>Weighty Question</u>, without Lifting up my
· Heart unto God, in a Request, that He would help me to give a <u>Right</u>
· <u>Answer</u>.

'   4. To Speak Ill of no man; Except on a good Ground, and for a Good

' End. [ms. p. 25]

'   5. Seldome to make a Visit, without Contriving, What I may do for

' God in that Visit?

' III. As to my daily Course of Duties.

'   1. To Pray, at least Thrice, for the most part, Every day.

'   2. To Meditate once a day; in the Meditation proceeding after Such

' a Method as This: That there shall be Two Parts of the work, Doctri-

' nal and Applicatory; & the Applicatory to flow from the Doctrinal,

' into, Examination, Expostulation, Resolution.

'   3. To make a Custome of propounding to myself, these Three Ques-

' tions, at Night, before I Sleep.

'   What hath been the Mercy of God unto me, in the Day past?

'   What hath been my Carriage before God, in the Day past? And,

'   If I Dy this Night, is my Immortal Spirit Safe?

'   4. To Lead a Life of Heavenly Ejaculations.

'   5. To be Diligent in Observing and Recording of Illustrious

' Providences.

'   But in all, to be Continually going unto the Lord Jesus Christ, as

' only Physician and Redeemer, of my Soul.

'   Lord, Thou that workest in me to Do, help me to Perform.

The Lord knowes how miserably Defective, I have been, in Performing what

I have thus Resolved. But my Defects, have been ye matter of my Reflec-

tions and Abasements before Him. And these Flights of my Soul, in

Essayes to glorify God, have been [ms. p. 26] but the Lower, and Lesser

Flights of my Youth. You will E're Long, My Son, see more Comfortable

Effects, of Committing a Soul betimes, into the Hands of ye Lord JESUS

CHRIST.

§ About this Time, I had my Heart, much carried forth in Prayer, Yea, in Faith, also, That God would Lett me Live to Do, Yea, and in Time, to Write, Things that should be very Serviceable unto the Designs of Early Religion.[12] This hath been most Remarkably Accomplished: But how Remarkably, I must not say Particularly, Lest I be discovered.

§ Retiring one Day, to Walk solitarily in o^e Meeting-Place, I had a Strong Impression on my mind, there to Step into a Pew, belonging unto a Gentleman of Good Fashion,[13] who tho' he were a Non-Conformist, yett had made no great Progress in Religion; and fall on my knees, with a particular Prayer to Heaven, That the Lord would work Thoroughly & Savingly on ye Heart of that Gentlemen, to make him Seriously Religious. I had my Heart fill'd with a Strange Hope, that this Prayer was heard: And behold, About Eleven years afterward, ye prayer had a remarkable Answer.

§ On a Certain Evening, as I was in Meditation, Enquiring and Contriving, How I might Glorify God? I happened then to Look thro' the Window, upon the Heavens; and this Thought was after a most powerful and Refreshing Manner Cast into my Mind: Surely, If the Lord intended not forever to glorify me in [ms. p. 27] Heaven, He Would never have putt it into my Heart, that I should Seek to Glorify Him on Earth.

§ About this Time, I received One Special Effect of my having putt my Soul for Cure, into the Hands of my Lord JESUS CHRIST. My Son, I Charge you to take Notice of it.

The Apprehension of the Cursed PRIDE, the Sin of Young Ministers, Lurking and Working in my Heart, fill'd me with inexpressible Bitterness, and Confusion, before the Lord. In my Early Youth, ⟨ and even at an Age wherein I See Many Lads playing at their Marbles or Wickets, with one another in the Streets,⟩ I preached unto very Great Assemblies, and found Strange Respects amoung ye People of God. I fear'd, (and thanks be to my Lord Jesus Christ, that ever He struck me With Such a Fear!) Lest a Snare, and a Pitt, were by Satan prepar'd for Such a Novice. I Resolved therefore, that I would Sett apart a Day, to Humble myself before God, for the PRIDE of my own Heart, and Entreat that by His Grace, I may be delivered from that Sin, and from all the Dreadful Wrath, whereto I may be, by that Sin Exposed. I did so; And on this Day, I Examined myself by the Discoveries of Pride, which I found given in some Judicious Discourses on that Subject. But I found Especially Two Respects, wherein I was most Wofully Guilty before the Lord.

First, My Applauding of myself in my Thoughts when I have done any thing at all Significant; Pray'd or Preach'd with Enlargemts, Answered a Question Readily, Presently, Suitably, and the Like. Proud Thoughts, I Saw, fly-blow'd my best Performances. Next, my Ambitious Affectation of Prehemineucies, [ms. p. 28] far above what Could belong to my own Age, or worth, and above others that were far more Deserving than myself.

For My Humiliation, I then Wrote these Considerations.

'   I. What is my Pride, but the very Image of Satan on my Soul! The
' more any Man has of God and Christ in him, the more Humble will he
' be; & Low and Vile in his own Eyes, & Empty of himself. When the
' Lord Renewes His Image in us, He Pulls down, o^e Proud Thoughts. Tis
' True, My Pride is a most Natural Sin; but Grace would overcome That
' in a most Special manner & measure. And then, how Little Grace have
' I, to this very day? How unlike am I to Him, that Could say, I am
' Lowly? oh, Lett me for this Cause Abhor myself in Dust and Ashes![14]
'   II. Do I not, by my Pride, grievously Offend the Lord! It is a
' Breach of His Holy Command: And how often does He declare His

' Abhorrence of it? [see Psal. 138. 6. and Prov. 6. 17. and Hab.
' 2. 4.] His Holy Spirit is thereby Grieved: And how Vehemently does
' the Scripture Caution against all Tendencies thereunto? Shall I bear
' to think, of offending that God, who has been a Father to me, and
' whom I have Chosen, and Vow'd that I would Love and Serve Him, as my
' God and Father? Or, that Spirit, upon the Sweet Influences whereof,
' my Soul does Live, Sealed unto the Day of Redemption? Oh, the Inex-
' cusable Wickedness of my Heart!

' III. Is not my Pride, a most Unreasonable Folly and Madness? Have
' I any Just Occasion for Glorying in myself? Do I any thing Singular?
' Am I not [ms. p. 29] in most Attainments, Exceeded by most, of my
' Calling and Standing? But, Oh, Lett This be a Dagger to my Heart!
' Have I not a Cursed Nature in me? And hath not the Lord heretofore
' justly Left me unto some Abominable Iniquities, the Sense whereof
' should Cause me, to Walk Softly all my Dayes? Lord, I am Viler than
' a Beast before thee! Or, Why should I Seek Honour? (Tis not Seemly
' for such a Fool!) Am I fitt for Service? Or, am I not rather Un-
' savory Salt, fitt for nothing but the Dunghil? What am I better than
' the Least of Saints? If in any External Grandeurs I gett above any
' of them, I am thereby the more Obnoxious to Temptation, and Sin, and
' Wrath. Ly thou in the Dust before God, O my Soul.[15]

' IV. How Dangerous, how Destructive an Evil, is this Pride of Mine?
' I provoke the God of Heaven, to take away Every one of those Idols,
' which in my fond Pride, I dote upon; and if the Lord should now de-
' prive me of my Capacities, and Opportunities, where am I, but in an
' horrible Pitt of most Unpittyable Miseries? Yea, Lett me Remember,
' Pride Sooner than any thing, will drive away the Good Spirit of God,

' from the Heart of a Poor Creature. And if that should be my Fate,

' Oh, Lord, have mercy! What a Monument should I be, of thy Ireful,

' & thy Direful Vengeance!

' O that the Lord would sett home these Thoughts for my Humiliation!

' But what shall I do for the Cure of my Disease?

' I. In the first and cheef Place, I would Carry my Distempered

' Heart unto the [ms. p. 30] Lord JESUS CHRIST, and Putt it into the

' Hands of that Alsufficient Physician, for Him to Cure it.

' II. I would be daily Watchful against my Pride; and Continually

' keep an Eye upon my Heart, and Check the Least Beginnings and First

' Motions of this Corruption.

' III. I would Study much the Nature, the Working, and the Aggra-

' vations of this Evil, and the Excellency of the Grace that is Con-

' trary thereunto.

In One of my Supplications this Day, I thus Express'd myself.

' Lord, what shall I do for the Cure of this Disease, My PRIDE?

' Blessed be thy Name, that thou hast Show'd me a Way, and bid me

' Walk in it. Have I not heard thee Saying to my Stung, and Swol'n,

' and Sinful Soul, Oh, Look unto me, & be Saved! And therefore, by

' thy Grace I will do it. I have done it, and found, Yea, to this

' Day I find, the Benefit of it. Why is it, that I am not Insensibly,

' and Incureably forever Carried away Captive by the Lust, which I am

' now Warring withal? Tis because I had putt my Heart into the Hands

' of the Faithful Jesus; and Hee it is, that hath not Suffered me to

' go on unconcerned about ye Distemper of my Soul, but hath Awakened

' me to Seek Releef at His Hands, as I do this day.

' And, now, Lord, I come unto Him. He Sees, how I am Labouring and

' Heavy-laden, but He has bid me Come. Does not He Call for my Heart?

' But what kind of Heart? It is not Mention'd; but I am Sure, tis My

' Heart that is Called for.

' 　Hence, tho' My Heart be a Proud Heart, [ms. p. 31] Yett, as long as

' tis Mine, I am to bring it.

' 　Yea, O Lord, I bring it, Because it is Proud. And wherefore doth

' He call for it? Is it not, that He may sett up His Kingdome in it,

' and fill it with His Graces, & Manifest the Power of His Rich Goodness

' in it forever! Oh, then: Lett Him Take my Heart, and make it Humble!

' Tis Easy with Him to do it. Tho' I Can't overcome this Pride of mine

' Yett He Can do it. Oh, Lett Him do it; I Wait upon Him for it; Yea,

' I do Beleeve, I am Satisfied, and Assured, That He Will do it; I have

' not Sought thy Face in Vain!

While I was thus combating ye Vice, that I found my Heart so Tympanized

withal, the Lord gave me, in the Duties of this Day, glorious Assurances,

That He would never Leave the Works of His Grace, which He had begun up-

on my Soul; but fill me with His Holy Spirit, & Guide me by Counsil, and

Bring me to Glory: Yea, That He would Employ me to do Peculiar Services,

for His Blessed Name.

§ The Week after this Transaction, and while I was Yett in the Nineteenth

Year of my Age, I began a Practice, to which I never had Known of One,

or Heard of more than One, Accustomed. The Good Spirit of my Lord JESUS

CHRIST, having taken a Possession of my Sinful Heart, I became Inclined

and Instructed unto such Methods of Religion, as I had no Earthly Tutor

for. The Practice I now Particularly intend, was, that of KEEPing DAYES

OF THANKSGIVING, in Secret.

　On the first of the DAYES, which I thus kept, I Sett myself

I. To <u>Recollect</u> the <u>Merciful Dispensations</u> of God unto me.

[ms. p. 32]

II. To <u>Consider</u> the <u>Aggravations</u> of those <u>Mercies</u>; in the <u>Greatness</u>, and the <u>Freeness</u> of them.

III. To <u>Register</u> them in my <u>Memorials</u>.

IV. To <u>Acknowledge</u> them in my <u>Devotions</u>.

V. To <u>Contrive</u> what <u>Returns</u> I should make, by way of <u>Gratitude</u> unto ye Lord.

I Spent the Day in Such Exercises: and the Sweetness of the Exercises, with the Heavenly <u>Afflatus</u> which they brought upon my mind, made Me a rich Recompence for the Labour of them, tho' they were very Laborious.

In ye close of the Day, Coming to Ponder, <u>What shall I now Render to the Lord, for all His Benefits</u>? My Thoughts were thus written down.

' I. Shall I not <u>Love the Lord</u>, & be Fervent, Constant, Unwearied in
' the <u>Serving</u> of Him? Especially in the observation of the <u>Rules</u>, which
' I have written for my Conversation?

' II. Shall I not Endeavour to Shine by a <u>Good Example</u>? Yea, and
' <u>Orally</u> upon just occasions, as well as Practically alwayes bear a
' Testimony against the <u>Levity</u> of the <u>Young Generation</u>?

' III. Shall I not <u>Husband</u> and <u>Redeem</u> what I Can, the <u>Golden Hours</u>,
' which I enjoy in the Midst of So many <u>Smiling Providences</u>? And pre-
' pare for <u>Affliction</u> too, with all Speed and Care!

' IV. Shall I not <u>Every Day</u>, in Every Capacity, Relation, Company,
' be contriving, <u>what can I now & here do for God</u>? And Lay myself out
' accordingly!

' Oh! Oh! That God would help me thus to do!

And now Lett me bear this Testimony unto You, My Son; That Such
Dayes of Thanksgiving, which I have often [ms. p. 33] kept in Secret
Places before the Lord, have usually had a more than ordinary Influence
upon me, to Prepare me for the Special Mercies of the Lord.

§   One Morning, my Heart was exceedingly melted in Secret Prayer before
the Lord, using Such words as these.

'   Lord, I am in thy Hands; a poor, broken, Sorry, despicable Vessel.
' But it is with thee to make me a Vessel of Honour. Oh, Do so! This,
' Even This, is the greatest of my Desires. I am Worthy to be Nothing
' forever. But, oh, Lett thy Name have Glory by me. Thou art Worthy
' to be Glorified forever & Ever. Oh, Do these things in me, & for me,
' & by me, that upon my Account, it may be with Admiration, Said, O the
' Power, the Wisdome, the Grace, & the Truth of the Great Jehovah!

§   I lost abundance of Precious Time, thro' Tormenting Pains in my
Teeth and Jawes: which kind of Pains have indeed Produced me many a Sad
Hour, in my short Pilgrimage. In the Pains that were about this Time
upon me, I Sett Myself, as well as I could for my Pains, to Search and
Try my Wayes.

I considered,

Have I not Sinned with my Teeth? How? By Sinful, Graceless, Excessive Eating. And by Evil Speaches: (for there are Literae Dentales[16]
used in them!) The Lord thus Taught me, to Gett Good out of Every Thing.
May Hee Teach Thee also, My Son!

At last, by a Course of Washing behind my Ears, & on ye Top of my
Head, with Cold Water, I obtained a Deliverance from these Uneasinesses.
[ms. p. 34]

§ On a Certain Day, which I Spent in the Duties of a <u>Secret Fast</u>, I Earnestly Sought unto the Lord, That before the Day were done, He would manifest of His <u>Love</u> unto me. Immediately there upon, Sitting in my Chair, there was brought unto me, that Scripture, Joh. 14. 23. <u>Jesus Said, If a man Love me, He will Keep my Words, & my Father will Love him, & we will Come to him, & make o^e Abode with him.</u> My Heart was even Dissolved upon the Reading of these Words. I Said, <u>Oh, I feel! I feel! I feel! I Love the Lord Jesus Christ; I Love Him dearly, I Love Him greatly, Yea, I Love Him above all. And, What? Will God Love me? And will my Lord Come to dwell with me! Oh, Joy unspeakable & full of Glory! -----Oh, what Love, what Love, what Love is This! That I, who have been so Polluted and so Unworthy, should be Loved by the Great God! Now, oh, that I could Praise thy Name, and Love thee again!</u>

§ About this Time, I took up a Custome, which I found many wayes advantageous unto me.

My <u>Rising Thoughts</u> in ye Morning, I Chose to fix upon Some <u>Scripture</u>, (but sometimes upon Some <u>Question</u>,) which might be of some Special Consequence to my Everlasting Interests. I Judged, That my [ms. p. 35] <u>Morning Thoughts</u> being placed, on Some Divine and Holy Subject, I should be thereby the better disposed unto the <u>Fear of the Lord all the Day Long;</u>[17] And, that the passing of so many <u>Truths</u> as would thereby pass thro' my Mind, would have a Sanctifying efficacy upon me. The Text which I began Withal, was that in Zech. 13. 1. Whereon my <u>Thoughts</u> were under these Heads.

I. The <u>Blood</u> of the Lord Jesus Christ, is fitly Compared unto a <u>Fountain</u>.

II. Tis an <u>Open Fountain</u>.

III. The End of it is, the, Washing away of Sin.

IV. Sin is (therefore) to bee Look'd on as a Vile Uncleanness, ye Vilest of all Uncleanness.

I did for a while, Enter the Heads of my Morning-Thoughts, in certain Papers.

But at length I gave over doing so.

However, I went over many Portions and Chapters of the Bible, in these Morning Thoughts; and herein I also handled multitudes of Cases, referring to the most Important Points of Christianity.

My Son, Begin this Exercise as soon as you can. And make your Morning-Prayers out of your Morning-Thoughts. You'l never have any Cause to Repent of it. [ms. p. 36]

§ Keeping another Day of Thanksgiving, in Secret places before the Lord, (about Three or Four Months after the former,) I came in the close of the Day to Consider on that Question:

What shall I render to the Lord, for all His Benefits?

And now, besides the Resolutions formerly penned, I Resolved upon Two Things.

I. To have my Sett Times for Meditations on that Enquiry, What is there that I may do for the Interests of God?

II. To Act with as much Explicit Consideration as may be, for God, in Every Action.

And therefore,

Before I Study, or Preach, or Hear, a Sermon;

Before I make a Visit;

Before I Eat a Meal;

Before I Sett upon any Recreation;

Before I fall <u>Asleep</u> at Night;

I would still have Distinct Thoughts, <u>Lett me now do This</u>, [or, <u>I Will</u>
<u>do This</u>] <u>for God</u>!

The Lord having Taught me thus to fall into the way of <u>Living to Him</u>,
tis Incredible, what a <u>New Life</u> of Soul, I did thereby Experience. My
Soul was now Raised into an High, a Sweet, an Heavenly <u>Way of Living</u>. I
Something felt the meaning of <u>Dwelling in God</u>, tho' no Books or Men on
Earth, had Ever Instructed me how to do it. The Thoughts of <u>Being for</u>
<u>God</u> Continually, and of Expressly Interesting the Great GOD in all my
Motions, Exceedingly Ravished me.

Thus did ye Faithfulness of ye Lord Jesus Christ appear, in Carrying
on the <u>Sanctification</u>, for which I had Relied upon Him. And thus, while
I was yett a <u>Child</u>, [ms. p. 37] I fell into some Singular Methods of
doing those things, which, if Sad Slothfulness and Backsliding prevent
it not, might in time render One a <u>Man of God</u>.

§   Setting apart a Day, for the Duties of a <u>Secret Fast</u>, I Sett myself
to Write ye following,

'   <u>Arguments</u>, which Encourage me to Beleeve,

'   That tho' my <u>Sins</u> are <u>many</u> and

'   <u>mighty</u>, yett they are

'   all <u>Forgiven</u>.

' I. There are in the <u>Scripture</u>, Blessed Encouragements, unto the Vilest
' of Sinners, to Hope & Wait, & Seek, for <u>Pardoning Mercy</u>. Particularly,
' Psal. 130. 4. Exod. 34. 6,7. Neh. 9. 17. Isa. 55. 7. Mic. 7. 18.
' Isa. 1. 18.

' II. The Lord Jesus Christ is an Alsufficient Saviour, in and thro'

' Whom, the Worst of Sinners may Receive Atonement. Consider, Zech. 13.

' 1. Mat. 1. 21. Mat. 26. 28. Act. 5. 35.

'   Now, 1. I go to the Lord Jesus Christ for a Pardon. I now do it,

' and I have heretofore done it. So, Being Justified by Faith, I shall

' have Peace with God. Rom. 5. 1.

'   2. I attend those things, which are the Symptomes of a True Faith,

' & have the Promise of a Pardon thereunto annexed.

'   First. He that Confesseth and Forsaketh, shall find Mercy. Prov.

' 28. 13. Now I Confess my Sins; I do it on my knees. And, in my Af-

' fection I Forsake them all. Why Else do I Sett apart Such Dayes as

' these, to Combate and to Distress my Lusts, and obtain the Destruction

' of the most Beloved among them?

'   Again; He that Judgeth Himself, shall not be Judged of the Lord.

' 1. Cor. 11. 31. [ms. p. 38] I Judge myself, as the worst of Sinners;

' Hence, the Great God will, in & thro' His own Son, my Surety, Judge

' me Righteous. I Judge myself, as Worthy of Death forever; Hence the

' Great God, on the Account of Him that hath made Himself a Sacrifice

' for me, Will Judge me in Life Eternal.

Thus did I Try to Argue myself, into the Faith and Hope of my Justification. But I must Say, That I found Little Spirit, in all this
Rational way of Arguing: None of the Argument brought unto my Soul,
that Joyful Peace, wch I wanted. At Last, the Spirit of God powerfully
Came in upon my Heart, & Enabled me to Receive the Pardon of my Sin,
Offered freely unto me, with the Righteousness of the Lord Jesus Christ;
and this without any Distinct Considerations on my having these and
those Conditions wrought in me. Then Could I, and never till Then, Rejoice with the Joy unspeakable & full of Glory.[18] Afterwards, t'was

Comfortable for me, to see in myself the Conditions of a Pardoned Soul. Nor would I have Entertained ye Afflations & Assurances of ye perswasion, That I was Pardoned, if I could not at the same time, have Seen these Conditions.

§ About this Time, Taught of God, I grew into more Exactness, in the Methods of Employing my Mind (and Grace) at ye Table of the Lord.

I will here Transcribe for You, My Son, only the First of the many Instances, that I Recorded, of my more Methodical Procedures at ye Holy Table. [ms. p. 39]

'   Workings of Heart,

'   At the Administration of the Bread.

'   [The Prayer being Finished.]

' Do I Need the Lord JESUS CHRIST?

'   Yes; Infinitely. But cheefly on two Accounts.

' The Guilt of Sin on me, is Mountainous;

'   None but He Can Remove it.

' The Power of Sin in me, is Marvellous;

'   None but He Can Subdue it.

' But am I Willing to have ye Lord Jesus Christ?

'   Yes; Most Heartily. For

' There is a dreadful Necessity that the Miseries of my Soul should be

' Releeved.

'   Hee, and none but Hee, can Releeve them.

'   I cannot find any thing Unlovely in the Lord Jesus Christ; All His

' Offices, and all His Benefits are Desireable.

' And therefore, Lord, I am Willing.

' Art thou So? Thou take Him; Saies the Lord; I give Him to thee.

' And by this Time, the Sacramental Bread is brought unto me, to

' Seal this Gift: Which I Take [and Eat] accordingly.

' And Now, I Proceed: The Lord JESUS CHRIST is Mine; If I am ready

' to question it, I may now See it, I may Feel it, I may Taste it. And

' my Lord JESUS CHRIST, I may be Sure, will now Engage for my Good, and

' Perfect Every Part of my Salvation.

'   At the Administration of the Wine.

'   [The Prayer being Finished.]

' The First Covenant is broken: It Speaks nothing but Confusion to

' Fallen Man; The gracious God therefore Enters into a New Covenant,

' wch is of Grace. [ms. p. 40]

' In it is tendered all manner of Good, for Beleevers on the Lord Jesus

' Christ, the Mediator of that Covenant.

' Am I Willing to come under the Wings of this Covenant?

'   Yea, Lord; Thou hast made me Willing. Then, Saies the Lord, Here

' is the New Testament in my Blood.[19]

' By this Time, the Sacramental Wine Comes to me; and I Drink of it;

' and thereby I have all the Good of the Covenant Sealed unto me.

' And Now, I proceed, I shall have Repentance & Remission of Sins.[20]

' Yea, All my Changes in this World will be well-ordered for me. God

' Will Guide me by Counsil, & bring me to Glory. All the Very Great &

' Precious Promises of God, are my Heritage, and shall be ye Rejoicing

' of my Heart.[21]

This one Instance, may serve to teach You, <u>My Son</u>, how to manage
your <u>Sacramental Meditations</u>, with a certain charming <u>Elegancy</u>, and Sacred
<u>Curiosity</u>, when you shall come unto y^e <u>Supper</u> of the Lord. The <u>Sermons</u>,
which you hear preparatory to ye Communion, may be very Subservient unto
Your Meditations (as they were to <u>Mine</u>) in this way of <u>Regularly Mar-</u>
<u>shalling</u> of them on such Blessed Occasions. But the Lord be Your Teacher!
<u>My Son</u>, Go to Him, (as I did,) and He will be so. [ms. p. 41]

§   The Result of a <u>Self-Examination</u> preparatory to a Communion, I then
thus Recorded.

'   I Find,

' I. Not only my <u>Understanding</u> Sees, but my <u>Will</u> Chooses, the Great GOD,
' as my <u>Best Good</u>, and my <u>Last End</u>.

'   1. My <u>Interest</u> in Him, is my Greatest <u>Wish</u> and <u>Joy</u>. According to
' Psal. 73. 25. Psal. 16. 5,6. Lam. 3. 25. Isa. 26. 13.

'   Obj:

'   Then you would be more Careful and Earnest, for the Securing of it.

'   Ans:

'   1. I <u>Mourn</u> under, & Strive against, my own Coldness, & Endeavour
' to Stir up myself.

'   2. My <u>Zeal</u> to make Sure of any other Enjoyment, is not so Lively as
'   to make Sure of This.

'   2. I do heartily Embrace and Propose the glorifying of Him, as the
' main Design which I Would Be, and Live, and Work upon.

                         Quest.

                    How do you know That?

'   1. By my Frequent and Actual <u>Dedications</u> to His <u>Glory</u>.

'   2. By the Disposition of my Heart in <u>Prayer</u> for <u>any</u> Mercy; above

' all, for <u>That</u> Mercy.

'   3. By my Exceeding <u>Satisfaction</u>, when I see God acknowledged;

' Especially, when by <u>me</u>, or by <u>my</u> means.

' II. With much Detestation I Reject all that, which hath made a

' <u>Separation</u> between the Lord and my Soul.

' <u>Sin</u> is that <u>Accursed Thing</u>. Isa. 59. 2. Wherefore,

'   1. I Lament it.

'   2. I Abhor it.

'   3. I Labour to Avoid it.   [ms. p. 42]

' III. I assay to come unto the Lord JESUS CHRIST, the Ever-glorious

' <u>Mediator</u>, that I may be instated, in the full Enjoyment of God.

' According to Joh. 14. 6.

'   1. Thirsty after the <u>Fountain of Life</u> in God, I go to the Lord

' Jesus Christ, as the <u>Way</u>.

'   2. I would have <u>None but Him</u>, to be my Saviour.

'   3. I am free, that He should Execute <u>Every One</u> of all His <u>Offices</u>

' in ye Accomplishing of my Salvation.

' Blessed by ye Lord, who has not Left me destitute of His Eternal

' Mercies!

In Some <u>Self-Examinations</u> after this, wherein I Employ'd a Collection of <u>Marks</u>, which I had Lying by me, I proceeded Chiefly by <u>Direct</u>
Acts, rather than by <u>Reflex</u> ones; That is to say, Examining whether I
had Ever done, these & those <u>Good Things</u>, I putt it out of Doubt, by
now <u>doing them over again</u>.

Incredible <u>Satisfaction</u>, and, I hope, Some <u>Sanctification</u>, was y^e
Effect of these Blessed Exercises.   [ms. p. 43]

§ Soon after I had finished the Nineteenth year of my Age, I kept a Day of THANKSGIVING, in Secret before the Lord. On this Day, I deliberately Perused the Accounts, wch I had formerly Written, of the Lords Merciful Dispensations towards me; and then I distinctly Adored the Power, the Wisdome, the Goodness, and the Faithfulness of God, appearing in those His Dispensations. This took up the Forenoon. I proceeded in the Afternoon, to Consider my Present Enjoyments; And those I considered, as respecting, first my Particular Calling; both the Calling itself, and the Helps Afforded unto me, for my Comfortable management of the Calling: Secondly, My General Calling; my Recollections whereupon, I now made Subservient unto the Designs of a Self-Examination, which I was now Call'd unto.

Sunsett now being arrived, I sett myself to think on some Returns, agreeable to these Mercies of Heaven. Those were these.

' I. Lett me be more Active now, than ever in the Service of God.
' Wherefore,

'   1. Lett me more Watchfully Endeavour on all Occasions, Even before
'   Every more Observable Action, to have Distinct Thoughts unto this
'   Purpose, Lett me now do this for God! or, How shall I do this for
'   God!

'   2. Lett me more Carefully, take Some Sett Season, at Least once
'   Every Week, to Ponder on that Question,

'   What is there, that I may do for God?

' II. Lett me be more Exact, in Redeeming and Improving my Precious
' Time.²² And so,

'   1. On the Lords-Dayes, Lett my Holy Exercises be abundant. And
'   Lett me [ms. p. 44] Do nothing then in Committing my Sermons to
'   Memory, but just what may be a Working of them upon my Heart,

' rather than into my Head.

' 2. On the Week-Dayes, Lett me Rise Earlier; and be more Methodical

' in my Studies.

I must now observe to you, My Son, That I was very Defective, in Observing and Performing Some of these Purposes. However, I did Something, and it was an Help to me, that I had Purposed More.

Especially, in that matter of taking a Sett Season, for Contrivances on that Question, What is there that I may do for God? My Sett Season was for Some while on Mondayes; for some while on Thursdayes; for some while on Saturedayes, And tho' I did not Confine myself only to these Times, for my Thoughts on that Noble Question; tho' Likewise I had Thousands of Resolves upon it, which I never Entred in any of my Memorials: Yett I Wrote many Pages of Resolves at these Times: and at Length, I furnished myself with a Little Blank Book, wherein I Entred these My Contrivances by themselves, apart from other Memorials.[23]

At Last, I made it my Custome, upon Every Design for God, which I shaped in my Thoughts, to think upon Some Certain Promise or other, in ye Bible, which might Countenance & Encourage that Special Design.

But after Some Years, my Opportunities grew so many, and my Contrivances grew so frequent, and my Executions ran Parallel with [ms. p. 45] both; as that I Left off Writing my Purposes; Leaving them to be Written only in ye Lords Book of Remembrance.

I Suppose, My Son, that I shall in these Papers, now and then take some Notice of those my Purposes, where it may be Particularly Serviceable unto You, for me to do so.

§ I had, from my childhood, Employ'd at Least a Tenth, of what Money I gott, in Pious Uses; and now I had a Considerable Quantity of Money annually Coming in, I Employ'd much more than a Tenth on Such Uses. My Son, Do you alwayes Devote a Tenth of Your Gains, unto the Special Service of o^e Great Melchisedeck, ye Lord JESUS CHRIST, I Earnestly Exhort you, and Advise you: And you shall be no Loser by it, I Assure you.

But what I have here to note, is, That One of ye First Contrivances, for the Glorifying of the Lord, which I Recorded, was, To Spend much in Buying of Good BOOKS, to give away.

How many Hundreds, Yea, how many Thousands, of Good Books, I have thus given away, I Cannot reckon. I Suppose, I have given away near a Thousand, in One year.

But I will Observe Two Things unto You, My Son, upon it.

One observable is This. While I gave away Small Books unto others, [ms. p. 46] God gave Great Books unto me. I mean, That I had a Secret, & a Wondrous Blessing of God upon my Library. A Good Library was a thing, I much Desired & Valued; and by the Surprising Providence of God, it Came to pass, That my Library, without my Pillaging of your Grandfathers, did by cheap, and Strange Accessions, grow to have I know not how many more than Thirty Hundred Books in it;[24] and I Lived so near your Grand-fathers, that his, which was not much Less than Mine, was also in a manner Mine. This was much for a Non-Conformist Minister.

Another Observable is This. While I was giving away Good Books Written by other men, I had all along a Secret Perswasion, That a Time would Come, when I should have many Books written by myself Like-wise to give away. And I have Lived Since to see this Perswasion most Remarkably Accomplished. I shall too far Discover myself, if I should Particularly relate, how Remarkably. All I will Say, is, That no Non-Conformist Minister now Surviving in ye Nation hath had So many. [ms. p. 47]

§ It pleased my Gracious Lord-Redeemer while I was in the Twentieth Year
of my Age, to Cast into my Hands, a Little Book, of one Mr S. Shawes,
Entitled, The Voice of One Crying in a Wilderness:[25] Unto wch Book, I
must Record it, I owed more than unto most, that I had then Seen, in the
World. That Book, [My Son, Gett it, and Read it,] that Plain, Short,
Little Book, described so Livelily unto me, the right Skill of Conversing
with God, that, I shall never forgett the Words of it, for by them, O
Lord, thou hast quickened me! The Impressions which that Book left upon
me, are Eternal; and it Contributed, unto my having & using, the right
Spirit of Religion, more than most things, that I had yett mett Withal.
I found in it, a marvellous Agreeableness to the Designs, and the
Desires, with wch the Good Spirit of God, had already Touch'd My Soul;
and hereupon I Sensibly grew in my Essayes, to Consider God, as My All
in All.

But afterwards, I Came to Consider; That ye Considerations of the
Lord JESUS CHRIST, in o^e Conversing with God, were not so full, and so
clear, in this Book, as they should have been. I Endeavoured therefore
to amend this Defect, in my Meditations; and Remember, that there must
be a Most Explicit Respect and Homage unto my Lord JESUS CHRIST, in all
my Approaches unto God: I must Approach God IN HIM, With as much
Explicitness, as may be.   [ms. p. 48]

§ I will Record for You, My Son, the Result of another Self-Examination, which I Wrote, when I was betwixt Nineteen and Twenty Years of
Age.

' Asking the Help of Heaven in this Work, I professed, That if I were
' yett unsound, I was Desirous to Begin the work of Conversion again,
' and anew go over all the Sorrowful and Heart-breaking Hours, wch I

' had Seen in that Work: But that if I Saw my own Sincerity, my Hands
' would be thereby Strengthened in the Warfare, whereto I am Called.

'   I then found Such Things as these; Which made me Hope, that the Lord
' had begun a never-dying Work of His Grace upon me.

'   I. The Supreme Desire and Design of my Soul is, That GOD may be
' forever Glorious.

'   Inferiour Ends are become despicable in my Eyes; and I apprehend
' Those to be the Vilest-Fools, who Live only unto themselves.

'   The Voice of my Soul, is, Oh, Lett the Lord be magnified!²⁶ Hence
' I am Contriving Every Week, Yea, Every Day, & perhaps oftner than so,
' What can I do for the Name of God?

'   Hence my Thirst after an Enlargement in the Service of God, Yea,
' and after the Enjoyment of my own Salvation, does then after the most
' melting manner transport me, When I think, Hereby the Glory of the
' infinitely Amiable God, will be discovered!

'   Hence those things, whereby the Glory of GOD is obscured & Eclip-
' sed; Especially those Cursed Lusts of Mine, which have Robbed the Lord
' of that Glory, that I might have brought Him, do Vex & wound, & Cutt
' my very Soul within me. [ms. p. 49]

'   Finally; My Heart Rejoices, in any Revenues of Glory, brought any
' way unto the Lord. I feel my own Interest thereby gratified; and I
' See my Best Friend Honoured and Advanced.

'   II. My Heart is insatiably pressing after the High Attainments of
' Religion.

'   Oh! When I Consider, what it is, To Converse with God Continually,
' and not only to be Living alwayes With, and Upon, and Unto the Lord,
' but also to Love no Creature, Except in Him, and, for Him, & to have

' Him for my <u>All in All</u>, My Heart Springs at it: I Cry, I Strive, <u>Lord</u>,
' <u>Lett me thus Draw near unto thee</u>![27]

' And the Lord herein gives me some <u>Experience</u> that is Exceedingly
' Desireable.

' For, When I have been Mightily Carried forth in my Publick Dispen-
' sations, I have taken <u>Comfort</u>: In What? Not that any Gifts of <u>Mine</u>
' have been Seen; but that the <u>Power</u>, the <u>Wisdome</u>, the <u>Goodness</u>, & the
' <u>Truth</u>, of the glorious GOD, has glittered thro' me; as thro' a Sorry
' <u>Lanthorn</u>, is the View of many Hundreds at a Truth. This Even dis-
' solves my Heart, & Causes me to Love that God, who has Honoured Him-
' self by me.

' Hence also, my Spirit growes more Unconcerned, about Keeping or
' Losing any <u>Creature Comforts</u>; [Creaturulas Consolatiunculas;] for, I
' can <u>Encourage myself, in the Lord my God</u>.

' III. I drive a Continual Trade, of the most Exact, Express, <u>Ex-</u>
' <u>plicit Addresses</u>, unto the Lord JESUS CHRIST, the <u>God-Man</u>, who is the
' <u>Mediator</u> between God and Man; Solliciting Him to accomplish the <u>Great</u>
' <u>Work</u> of [ms. p. 50] Bringing my <u>God</u>, and my <u>Soul</u>, together; Yea, and
' Fulfill <u>all His Offices</u> in the doing of it.

' IV. My <u>Respect unto the Comandments</u> of God, is <u>Universal</u>. Be a
' precept never so Difficult, and never so Likely to be by <u>Flesh</u> and
' <u>Blood</u> recoyled at, if I See <u>Tis Gods</u>, my Soul Saies, <u>Tis Good</u>! Oh,
' <u>Lett me obey it, until I Dy</u>!

' V. Lett my <u>Own Iniquity</u> assault me with never so much Vehemence &
' Violence, I never Lett go the <u>Combate</u>. But if I am foiled, I <u>Mourn</u>,
' I am <u>Humbled</u>, I am <u>Grieved</u> Exceedingly; and With Extreme Ardor and
' Anguish, I keep <u>Crying</u> unto Heaven for Help; Resolving so to do while
' I have a Day to Live.

' Wherefore, <u>Bless ye Lord, O My Soul!</u> [28]

§ One Day, I was Thinking; When <u>Creatures</u> take themselves Wings, and Afflictions and Vexations roll in upon me, t'wil be my Happiness, to Converse with God as <u>Alsufficient</u>, and to take Satisfaction in God, as that Object, wch will make up the Want of all things Whatsoever.

But here I raised a <u>Question</u>; How Can I take my <u>Comfort</u> in the <u>Alsufficient God</u>, when my <u>Interest</u> in Him is uncertain? Will not the Lord frown upon my Presumption, and Say, <u>I have rejected thy Confidences?</u>

I answered, <u>No</u>. I Laid this down for a certain Truth; An <u>Heart</u> inclined unto a Converse with GOD, as the object whose <u>Alsufficiency</u> makes up the want of all creatures, is a most undoubtful [ms. p. 51] <u>Sign</u> of an Interest in Him. He that <u>Can</u> Do such a Thing, <u>May</u> do it, without any objection, and against Every Discouragement.

§ Reading a Little Book of Mr <u>Boyles</u>, Entitled, <u>Seraphick Loves</u>, [29] I mett with some charming Passages in it, about a Mans Resigning up <u>Himself</u>, and Especially <u>His Will</u>, unto the God of Heaven. I then Resolved, That I would Sett apart a DAY, on Purpose to give up <u>Myself</u>, and <u>My Will</u>, unto the Lord; and so Seek a <u>Preparation</u> for an actual & Entire <u>Submission</u> unto Him, in every One of my Concernments.

Accordingly, after previous Meditations, I addressed myself unto the Lord, much after Such a manner as This.

' Most Glorious Lord God! Thou hast offered <u>Thyself</u> unto thy Crea-
' tures, and many a time Called upon them, to Take <u>Thee</u> for <u>Their God</u>.
' This, This is that which I am Willing, I am Desirous, I am Resolved
' this Day to do. Oh! Thou <u>El-Shaddai</u>, [30] I Take <u>Thee</u>, to be <u>my God</u>;
' and hence I take <u>thy Glory</u>, for the <u>End</u>, which I will <u>Bee</u> and <u>Live</u>
' unto; I take the <u>Enjoyment</u> of <u>Thee</u>, for my Great and Sole <u>Happiness</u>.

' And, which, is the peculiar Thing, that I am now aiming at, I take <u>Thy</u>
' <u>Will</u>, to be <u>My Will</u>. As for my <u>Own Will</u>, Dear Lord, I find it a <u>Blind</u>
' <u>Will</u>, a foolish, Wicked, Hurtful <u>Will</u>, and therefore I Renounce it, I
' Reject it, I Resign it and I Say again, & again, <u>Lord</u>, Lett <u>thy Will</u> be
' <u>My Will</u>. I have Great <u>Concernments</u>; Concernments as to this World;
' Concernments as to the World to come; They are Weighty and Many. But,
' O God, Thou art the <u>only Wise</u> God; There is [ms. p. 52] <u>Perfect Know-</u>
' <u>ledge</u> with Thee; Thou art of <u>Great Power</u>; Thy <u>Understanding</u> is <u>infi-</u>
' <u>nite</u>. Yea, and in the Lord JESUS CHRIST, that Sweet Reconciler of God
' and Man; Thou art wonderfully <u>Gracious</u> and <u>Merciful</u>, unto them who
' draw near unto thee, as I do this Day. Unto thy <u>Wisdome</u> and thy Good-
' <u>ness</u>, I Committ my Concernments, One and All. <u>I Cast all my Cares</u>
' <u>upon my God</u>.[31] Oh! Thou most <u>Wise</u> and most <u>Good</u> God, I Resign All
' unto Thee. Is it not thy pleasure, That I Should so do? <u>Yea, It is</u>.
' And hast thou not pleasure in Seeing of me do so? <u>Yea, Thou hast</u>. I
' then profess it in thy presence; All my <u>Concernments</u> are putt into Thy
' Hands, and Left unto thy <u>Managements</u> forever. And, now, I am Happy;
' The Lord, Yea, the Lord God Almighty, will <u>Perform all things for me</u>;[32]
' and all Things now shall be <u>well-performed</u>. Whatever now befalls me,
' Will be an Effect of the Great <u>Jehovahs</u> infinite <u>Wisdome</u> and <u>Goodness</u>.
' Yea, tho' it be never so really Cross to my <u>Humour</u>, and Seemingly Cross
' to my <u>Welfare</u>, I will take a Contentment in it; because I will now Look
' upon it, as the <u>Will</u> of Him that is infinitely <u>Wise</u> and <u>Good</u>; the <u>Will</u>
' of Him that is my <u>Friend</u>, my <u>Father</u>, my <u>God</u>; the <u>Will</u> of Him that hath
' undertaken ye Conduct of all my Assayes forever. And, Oh, my <u>Will</u>;
' Oh, my <u>Soul</u>; Remember thou, after This, never to be disturbed about
' <u>Future Events</u>, and alwayes to Approve the <u>Present Dealings</u> of the Lord.
' [ms. p. 53]

§ 'Ere[33] the Twentieth Year of my Life Expires, I will Remark to You, My Son, Two or Three more Signal Favours, which I received from the Lord, before I was Twenty Years old.

One Great Thing done for me, by the Spirit of my Blessed Saviour was This. Hee taught me, not only after the Hearing of a Sermon, to Consider, What Improvement shall I make of these things! but also to Write Still in my Papers, the Special Resolutions, which I entertained, in the Strength of Heaven, upon thus Considering. Many Sheets would not Contain the Resolutions, which I thus Entred in my Memorials, & which I carried unto the Lord, for His Help to be vouchsafed me, in my performing of them. Only because in my Gathering together these broken Remembrances of my Life, my Design is to Instruct You, My Son, with Some Experiences of a Poor Walk before ye Lord, I will Single out One Instance of the Practice, about which I am now giving you my Instructions.[34]

I had heard a Sermon upon, Delighting in God: [from Psal. 37. 4.] The Preacher of the Sermon, had managed ye matter, not Extraordinarily. But when I Retired (according to my Custome,) to Ruminate on what I had heard, I then Wrote the following Purposes.

'   My Improvement.
' At the Invitation of Davids Counsil,[35] My Awakened Soul, in a Sweet
' [ms. p. 54] Retirement this Afternoon, doth Resolve after this manner,
' to Delight in God.
'   I. I will ever Mourn over the Distempers of my Heart, which incline
' me, to take an Unchast Sort of Delight, in Creatures, in Idols, in
' Vanities.
'   II. I will Bless God, for those Dispensations, be they never so
' Afflictive, whereby He is Curing those Disorders in me.

'   III. I will alwayes Count myself <u>Happy</u> in the <u>Favour of God</u>; tho'
' I should have no Earthly thing to give me any Satisfaction.

'   IV. I will reckon any <u>Opportunities</u> for my being brought into a
' <u>Converse with God,</u> as <u>Treasures</u> to be preferr'd above all Riches.

'   V. I will never be any other, than in a raging <u>Disquiet</u> of Soul,
' until I find all my <u>Ends,</u> to be swallowed up in y^e <u>Glory of God</u>.

'   VI. I will relish <u>all</u> my <u>Enjoyments,</u> Even to my very <u>Meat</u> and
' <u>Drink,</u> Mainly, and, if I can, <u>Meerly,</u> under ye Notion of my being
' thereby assisted in the <u>Knowledge</u> or the <u>Service</u> of God.

'   VII. I will Endeavour to be Continually abounding in the <u>Thoughts</u>
' of God; Nor would I be ordinarily One Waking <u>Quarter of an Hour</u> with-
' out them.

'   VIII. It shall be my <u>Pleasure,</u> to be Waiting upon God, in all the
' wayes of His <u>Worship,</u> wherein I may have Communion with Him; Especi-
' ally in frequent <u>Prayer</u> unto Him.

'   <u>Lord,</u> Assist me, & Accept me; Yea, <u>Delight</u> in me. [ms. p. 55]

Another Great Thing done for me, by y^e <u>Spirit</u> of my Redeemer, was
This. <u>Hee</u> powerfully disposed My Heart unto the daily Making of OCCA-
SIONAL REFLECTIONS: Insomuch that, whereas Mr <u>Boyl</u>, Dr <u>Spurstow</u>, Sr
<u>William Waller</u>,[36] and others, have written Little Books of Divine & De-
vout <u>Thoughts,</u> Raised from the Commonnest Occurrences of Humane Life, I
have Scarce had a <u>Day</u> without Such kind of Thoughts, from the Time I
first Litt upon this <u>Way of Thinking,</u> until <u>Now</u>; and sometimes I have
had very many of them in a <u>Day</u>. I have Seen, that Every man, has his
Little <u>Intervals</u> of Business every day, and this very often; wherein his
Mind Either is but <u>Ill-Employ'd</u>, or Else Lies <u>Not-Employ'd</u> at all. I
have been desirous to Redeem those Little <u>Intervals,</u> for <u>Occasional Re-
flections</u>; and I have reason to Bless the Lord Exceedingly, for His

Inclining of me, to this _Method of Piety_. Hereby tis, that besides my
Opportunities to Sharpen, and Quicken my Dull _Witts_, I have made all sorts
of _Objects_ very Serviceable unto my Everlasting Interests. The _Meannest_
Objects in the House, or in ye Street, have afforded me Thousands of
Lessons, which I have immediately Sent up to Heaven, formed into _Ejacula-_
tory Prayers. I have Successively made, almost Every thing that I Could
See in my _Study_ preach me a _Sermon_; that One thing, the _Fire_ on my Hearth,
yeelded me a Large _Book_ full of _Meditations_, (for I Wrote Such an one for
an Experiment;) and when I [ms. p. 56] have been Travelling on the _Road_,
I have, perhaps Hundreds of times, in this Charming way, preached unto
myself; and Sometimes Communicated the Instructions thus Extracted from
Accidents in ye Journey, unto my _Fellow-Travellers_. Thus I was help'd
from Heaven, to fall upon a _Custome of Thinking_, wherein, together with
the pleasing of my Fancy, I have had many Thousands of _Thoughts_ & _Prayers_,
which have more Enriched me, than if many _Thousands_ of Silver & Gold, had
been bestow'd upon me.

A Third Favour of the Lord unto me, was His Causing me, to _Consider_,
to _Determine_, and to _Exemplify_, the Particular Seasons for _Ejaculatory_
Prayers, wherewith I am continually furnished. As now;

For _Ejaculatory Hosannah's_, or Petitions,

Before I Sett on any Signal _Act_ of _Worship_, an _Ejaculation_ may ask
for Help in that Act.

While I am joining with another, in _Social Praying_, I may fix my
wandring Heart, by annexing Such a Pertinent _Ejaculation_, unto Every Sentence that is uttered, as, _Lord, I own it_, or, _Lord, I Ask it!_

In Hearing of a _Sermon_, I may tack a Serious _Ejaculation_ upon Every
thing that shall be offered; at Least upon Every _Head_, & upon Every _Text_,

that shall be proposed in it. [ms. p. 57]

Before my Preaching of a Sermon, I may Revolve it, in a Meditation, that Shall turn Every Part of it, into some Ejaculation.

A Course of daily Meditation is to be Carried on; but agreeable Ejaculation is to be intermixed in the whole Exercise.

Numberless Ejaculations, are at the Lords-Table, highly Seasonable.

In Singing of a Psalm, and in Reading of a Chapter, I may Try, Whether I cannot form some Ejaculation, out of Every Verse, as I go along.

Fetching Lectures and Lessons from ye Creatures of God, at my Liesure-Minutes; Why should I dismiss any of them, till I have putt them into agreeable Ejaculations?

When any new Comfort is Conferred on me, here is room, for an Ejaculation, Lord, Help me to Employ this Talent for thy Glory! When any new Trouble is Inflicted on me, here is room for an Ejaculation, Lord, Help me to Bear and Hear thy Rod!

Every New Matter of Care, brings with it a New Matter of Prayer. What shall I do, but, at Least by a short Ejaculation Carry it unto the Lord? Thus the Smile of that God, who Performs all things for me, may be asked upon all that I have to do.

Especially, If any Weighty Question, be propounded unto me, Lett me not Answer it, until I have by some Ejaculation address'd Heaven for a Right Answer!

Such Ejaculations for ye Whole Church of God, as, Lord, Save thy People! are often Called for. [ms. p. 58]

It was a Good Rule of One, When I think of my Friend, Lett it be with a Praying Thought.

When I am informed of any Neighbour in Affliction, my Charitable Ejaculations are bespoke upon it.

Yea, While I Walk in the Street, or Sitt in a Room, with my Mind otherwise unemploy'd, its Pitty this Time should wholly be Lost. Is it not possible, for me to use my Witt, as well as my Grace, (both Little Enough!) in Contriving of some Suitable Blessing, for such & Such Persons, as are there before me, & then form it into Some Ejaculation for them, which I will discover to none, but that God, who knowes my Thoughts afar off.[37]

For Ejaculatory Hallelujahs, or Thanksgivings.

All the Occasions which may occur for my Prayers, will sollicit Sometimes for my Praises too.

Every Dispensation of God, May afford me, matter for some Ejaculation to Him.

Especially, when any Conspicuous Mercy is bestow'd upon me, then I may Express my Gratitude, by some Grateful Ejaculation upon it, Saying, Lord, Thou art Good, & thou dost Good.[38]

Yea, whenever any Perfection of God, is by any Effects, manifested unto me, I may, by some adapted Ejaculation Celebrate that perfection; & Say, Lord, How Great is thy power, thy Wisdome, thy Justice, thy Sovereignty, thy Bounty!

And this is one Remarkable Expedient, whereby whether I Eat, or [ms. p. 59] Drink, or whatever I Do, I may Do all to the Glory of God. I may String almost Every more Extended Action of my Life, upon a Thread of Religion, by such an Ejaculation over it, as, Lord, May this be done for thy Glory.

Such as these were the Essayes and Salleyes of my Soul, My Son, before I was Twenty Years of Age. I must bewayl it, I have Exceeding often, fallen short in these my Essayes, to Walk with God. However, while I thus kept _Aiming_ at these things, I found it my unspeakable Advantage, that I had _Prescribed_ them. Tho' in my _Practising_, I fell short of what I had _Prescribed_, Yett I _Practised_ very very much what I had _Prescribed_; and my _Prescribing_ it, was a Vast help & Step to my _Practising_.

And so there is my _Fourth Lustre_ finished. ⟨⟨ I am now Twenty years Old! ⟩⟩ [ms. p. 61[39]]

The Fifth Lustre

§   My Son, I Lately mentioned unto you, a Contrivance, to Carry on
Ejaculatory Prayers, while I walk'd in the Street, or Satt in a Room
(with my mind otherwise unemploy'd;) by Contriving of some Suitable
Blessing for such Persons, as I should have before me, & then Directing
it in the form of an Ejaculation unto Heaven for them, Unobserved by any
but Heaven, in the doing of it. In the Twenty first Year of my Age, I
carried on this Exercise of Religion and Charity, to more of Exactness,
and it hath ever Since been with me, a frequent Exercise, and as Pleasant
as it has been frequent.

The Lord only knowes, how many Thousands of Ejaculatory Prayers, I
have thus made for my Neighbours. But that you, My Son, may be Assisted
in your Imitation, I will only Recite a few Such Ejaculatory Prayers,
from whence You may Conjecture, how I did, and You may, use to Shape Such
Devotions.

At a Table, where I being the Youngest of the Company, it was not
Proper for me, to Discourse at all, & the Discourses of others were
too trivial to be Worthy of my Attention.

Looking On the Gentlewoman that [ms. p. 62] Carved for us, (Ejaculations.)

Lord, Carve of thy Grace and Comforts, a rich Portion to that Person.

A Gentlewoman stricken in years.

Lord, Adorn that Person with the Vertues, wch thou prescribest unto Aged
Women, and Prepare her for her Dissolution.

A Gentlewoman Lately Married.

Lord, Espouse & Marry the Soul of that Person to thyself, in a Covenant
never to be forgotten.

A Gentlewoman very Beautiful.

Lord, <u>Give that Person an Humble Mind, and Lett her Mind be most Con-</u>
<u>cern'd for those Ornaments, that are of great Price in thy Sight</u>.

One of o^e Magistrates.

Lord, <u>Inspire that Person, with Wisdome, Courage, & Goodness, to Seek</u>
<u>the Welfare of thy people</u>.

One of o^e Ministers.

Lord, <u>Incline & Assist that Person to be a faithful Steward in thy House</u>.

One unhappy in his Children.

Lord, <u>Convert the Children of that Person, and Lett him have the Joy to</u>
<u>see them walking in thy Truth</u>.

One Crazy and Sickly.

Lord, <u>Lett the Sun of Righteousness arise unto that Person, with Healing</u>
<u>in His Wings</u>.

A Physician.

Lord, <u>Lett that person be Successful in his Practice, & Lett him Success-</u>
<u>fully Carry the Distempers of his own Soul, unto the Lord, his</u>
<u>Healer</u>. [ms. p. 63]

One that had mett, with great Losses.

Lord, <u>Give to that Person, the good Part, which Cannot be taken away</u>.

A Servant giving Attendance.

Lord, <u>Make that Person a Servant of Jesus Christ, & One of thy Children</u>.
In Like manner, when I have been Sitting in a Room full of People, at a
<u>Funeral</u>, where they take not much Liberty for <u>Talk</u>, and where much Time
is most unreasonably Lost, I have usually sett my poor Witts a Work, to
Contrive <u>Agreeable Benedictions</u>, for Each Person in the Company.

And thus, in Passing along the <u>Street</u>, I have Sett myself to <u>Bless</u>
Thousands of Persons, who never knew that I did it; With <u>Secret Wishes</u>

after this manner Sent unto Heaven for them.

〈Ejaculations.〉

  Upon the Sight of a Tall man.

Lord, <u>Give that Man High Attainments in Christianity: Lett him fear God</u>
  <u>Above Many</u>.

  A Lame Man.

Lord, <u>Help that Man, upon Moral Accounts, to Walk uprightly</u>.

  A Negro.

Lord, <u>Wash that Poor Soul; Make him white by ye Washing of thy Holy</u>
  <u>Spirit</u>.

  Children Standing together.

Lord, <u>Lett the Blessing Hands of my Lord Jesus Christ, be Putt upon</u>
  <u>those Children</u>.

  Children at Play.

Lord, <u>Lett not these Children alwayes forgett the Work, which they Came</u>
  <u>into the World upon</u>.

  A Merchant.

Lord, <u>Make that man a Wise Merchant</u>. [ms. p. 64]

  A Very Little Man.

Lord, <u>Bestow great Blessings upon that Man, and above all, thy Christ,</u>
  <u>the Greatest of all Blessings</u>.

  A Man Carrying a Burden.

Lord, <u>Help this Man to Carry a Burdened Soul, unto his Lord-Redeemer</u>.

  A Man on Horse-back.

Lord, <u>Thy Creatures do Serve that Man; help him to Serve his Creator</u>.

  Young People.

Lord, <u>Help these Persons, to Remember their Creator, in the Dayes of</u>
  <u>their Youth</u>.

Young Gentlewomen.

Lord, <u>Make 'em Wise Virgins, & as the Polished Stones of thy Temple</u>.

A Shop-keeper, Busy in the Shop.

Lord, <u>Lett not this World Cause that Person to neglect ye One thing that is Needful</u>.

A Man, who going by me, took no notice of me.

Lord, <u>Help that Man, to take a due Notice of the Lord Jesus Christ, I Pray thee</u>.

One in Mourning.

Lord, <u>Give that person the Comforts, wch thou hast Promised for ye Blessed Mourners</u>.

A Very Old Man.

Lord, <u>Make this an Old Disciple</u>.

One Leaning on a Staff.

Lord, <u>Teach this person to Lean on a Christ</u>.

One, who (as I had heard) had Spoken very Injuriously & Reproachfully of me.

Lord, <u>Bless, & Spare, & Save that Person, Even as my own Soul: May that Person Share with me, in all the Salvations of the Lord</u>.

[ms. p. 65]

One that was reckon'd, a Very Wicked Man.

Lord, <u>Rescue that poor man, from Satan, who (tis to be fear'd) Leads him Captive</u>.

But, <u>My Son</u>, it were <u>Endless</u>, and it is now <u>Needless</u>, to Exemplify a thousandth Part of those <u>Ejaculations</u>, which I found, a Person may, without any <u>Loss</u> of his <u>Time</u>, or any Prejudice and Obstruction to any of his Affayrs, thus dispatch unto the Heavens. And I had this Comfortable Thought, for my Encouragement, That if I did not Obtain for my <u>Neighbours</u>,

the Blessings which I thus asked for them, I should obtain them for Myself: the Prayers would not be Lost.

However, while a Man is in the Exercise of Grace, he is gloriously
answering his End: and it is a glorious Consolation, to be alwayes thus
Exercising the Grace of Love.

§ In pursuance of that Intention, (the Exercise of Love,) about this Time,
I resolved upon Two Things.

The First was; To take ye Bills, that are putt up for Prayer and
Praise in o^e Congregation, and afterwards present the Particular Cases,
there Exhibited, before the Lord, in my Study; where I may more Particularly Implore the Grace of God for Each of them, than I did or could
in the Publick. The Second was; To ask myself, before my Evening-Prayers
in Secret, Who hath in the foregoing Day show'd me any Kindness? And
particularly Supplicate the God of Heaven, that He would bestow Spiritual & Eternal Favours, on Each of them that have so obliged me.
[ms. p. 66]

§   It may not be amiss for me, My Son, if now & then, I mention a
Remarkable Providence, and intersperse these Memorials, with some Remarks, on what I have Seen, in ye Retaliating Dispensations of Heaven
towards me. One thing, that I will observe at this time, is what I mett
Withal, in the Twenty first Year of my Life. I Can tell you, My Son,
That ye Lord has in many Instances, most notably and Charmingly Retali-
ated, my Dutifulness unto my Father. Some of the Instances whereof I
have taken some Notice, may Seem, Trivial; but yett ye Retaliation that
I Saw in them, gave them a Relish.

As now: I was owner of a Watch, whereof I was very fond, for the

Variety of _Motions_ in it. I Saw, my Father took a Fancy to this _Watch_,

and I made a Present of it unto him, with some Thoughts that as it was

but a peece of due gratitude unto such a Parent, so I should not go with-

out a Recompence. Quickly after This, there came to me, a Gentlewoman,

from whom I had no Reason to Expect So much as a _Visit_: But in her

Visit, she, to my Surprise, Pray'd me to Accept, as a Present from her,

a _Watch_; which was indeed preferrible unto That wch I had before parted

withal. I Resolved hereupon, to Stirr up, _Dutifulness unto Parents_, in

myself & others more than Ever.

At another time; I bought a _Spanish Indian_ Servant, & bestow'd him

upon my Father. Some years after this, a Knight whom I had Laid under

many Obligations, bestow'd a _Spanish Indian_ Servant upon me.[1]

Many more such things I might mention. But I give you these for

[ms. p. 67] a Taste; that You, _My Son_, may be Encouraged in Your obedi-

ence to y^e _Fifth Commandment_, ⟨⟨& Particularly, in your Tenderness for

Your _Mother_, (if she Survive,) when I shall be gone to a better World.⟩⟩

§ I will touch upon a Mystery of _Practical Christianity_, which in the

Experiences of this year occurr'd unto me.

One Day, at the _Lords-Table_, I Resolved, That I would _Crucify_ the

Lusts of my _Flesh_; inasmuch as Either they had Killed the Lord Jesus

Christ, or Else My Soul would be Killed by them.

I now Sett about this Work, by doing unto my _Lusts_, as the _Jewes_

did unto the Lord Jesus Christ.

They Enquired, _Who_ and _Where_ He was? And I Said, _Lord, Make me to

know my Transgression & my Sin._[2]

They brought _Him_ then before the _Rulers_. And I presented my

Corruptions before _God_.

They sollicited, That He might be Slain, as Worthy of Death. And I professed unto the Lord, That for Innumerable Reasons, I thought my Iniquities Worthy to Dy: And I besought the Lord, now to Destroy those Enemies in my Heart that would not have Him to Reign over me!

And I purposed, That I Would hereafter be as Active in the Extinction of those Evil Inclinations, as ye Jewes were in the Crucifixion of my dearest Remeeder.

§   I Commend unto You, My Son, a Little Book, Entitled, Self-Employment; wch about this Time, gave me Some Good Employment. It was Written by Pious Mr Corbett,[3] and Contains his Experiences; With Some Notes at the End, which I Sett an high value upon, as Expressing many Points of Piety, which my own Heart, was much sett upon. [ms. p. 68]

I Singled out Several of his Notes, to charge myself unto the observation of them. I shall not here Transcribe any of these Notes; only mention one wch I added of my own.

'   I may do Something for God, in my Visits. And therefore, as an
' Effect of my Constant & Earnest Cares, to Carry on Holy Designs, in my
' Occasional Diversions, I now think of One Rule, which I have not for-
' merly so much observed: That I should, for my Ordinary Farewel to my
' Christian Friends, at ye Conclusion of a Visit, Contrive, as hand-
' somely as I can, to Commend unto them, some suitable Text of Scripture,
' whereof they may think, when I am gone from them.

§ Lett this passage, be Excused, if it Seem Impertinent. Perhaps, it will not be Unprofitable.

Using of Sacred Meditations (with mixed Supplications) at my Waking Minutes, Every Morning in my Bed, and in this Course going over many portions of the Scriptures, a Verse at a Time; the Thought of Isaac, having his happy Consort brought unto him, <u>When</u> and <u>Where</u> he was Engaged in Holy Meditations,[4] Came into my Mind; And I had a Strange Perswasion, That there would a Time Come, when I should have my <u>Bed</u> blessed with such a Consort given unto me, as <u>Isaac</u> ye Servant of the Lord was favoured Withal.

I Confess, This Thought comes a Little <u>too Soon</u>; Yett I thought it not amiss to Write it, where it comes, in my Reserved papers. [ms. p. 69]

§ Setting apart a Day (as I did many a Day) this year, for Prayer, with Fasting, in my Study; I Judged myself before the Lord, for my horrible Transgressions of all Sorts; and in the Distresses of my Soul, beholding my Miseries, by my unavoidable <u>Exposedness</u> to the Wrath of God, and my insuperable <u>Estrangedness</u> from the Fountain of all Good; but Beleeving that the Lord Jesus Christ, ye Only Mediator, was yett Willing to have Mercy on me, after all the Indignities that I had Putt upon Him, if I <u>Now</u> Look'd unto Him; I Earnestly besought Him, that He would graciously take the Care of all that Concerned my Salvation, <u>and</u> rescue me from all the Confusions which I had brought upon myself, by my Leaving of God, & be my <u>Priest,</u> and <u>Prophet,</u> and <u>King</u> forever. And I professed unto Him, That I Left my Immortal Spirit in His Blessed Hands, and that I would Expect Every Part of my Welfare, as the fruit of His Blessed <u>Satisfaction</u> and <u>Intercession</u>; and that I would Submitt unto His glorious <u>Dominion</u> and <u>Power</u> and <u>Wisdome,</u> So as never Wittingly & Willingly to Withdraw from the Regulations thereof; but I would fly unto the precious <u>Blood,</u> for a <u>Pardon,</u>[5] whenever I Perceive in myself any Deviation. And I concluded, with a Triumphant Faith, That He would now Delight in me to do me Good; and that God would have no Controversy with me; and that I should after a desireable Manner Know Him, Love Him, Honour Him; And that I should find my neverdying Soul, to be under a Peculiar Care of a Loving

& Faithful Redeemer, in ye times of the greatest Extremity, that shall Ever Come upon me. [ms. p. 70]

§ But in the Close of this Day, I formed Certain Contrivances about my Walk with God, which, I confess, are Liable to c nsure; and I am Contented, that they should be censured.

I was desirous, not only to Entertain Purposes of glorifying my Glorious Lord Jesus Christ, but also to Honour Him with my Substance,[6] Particularly thro' my being thereby quickened unto Stedfastness in those Purposes; and yett more Particularly, Aweing myself into Faithfulness unto Them, with Forfeits upon That.

Such Penalties I also Saw, would Lay me under a Necessity to Do Good, Still one way or other.

Herein I was very far from any Vile Imagination, That I could Buy off the Guilt of any Omission, whatsoever. I knew, and I own'd, That only the precious Blood of the Lamb, (and Son,) of God,[7] Signified any thing for the doing[8] of That. But I imagined, That for me to make my Omissions more Painful and Costly unto my Flesh, would be to furnish myself with Effectual Monitors of my Duty.

Wherefore I now Purposed, That if I did any Day, (for Some while) Omitt Such or Such Exercises of Religion, which I had prescribed unto myself, I would Forfeit a certain peece of Money (besides & beyond my Tenths,) to be given unto the Poor.

These usages I Continued for Some While; until I found my Dispositions unto Such Methods of Conversing with God, so Strengthened, that I had not so much Need of using these Incitements any Longer. [ms. p. 71]

Thus, I have sometimes Laid a Penalty for Some while upon myself, That if in Joining with the Prayers of another, I did Lett more than One

Entire Sentence pass me, at any time, without annexing some Ejaculation Pertinent thereunto, I would forfeit a Peece of Money, to be given unto the Poor. And I found this Effect of it, that in a Week or two, I had Little Occasion to lay my Penalty: for I found my Distractions in these Duties (a Sore Plague upon my Soul!) wonderfully Cured.

Thus also, I have sometimes Laid a Penalty upon myself, on a Lords-Day, that if thro' ye whole Day, I Spoke One Word, which I could not Judge proper to be Spoken on Such a Day, I would in Like manner forfeit. And I found myself marvellously Strengthened by this Caution, in keeping the Lords-Day, at Such a rate, as was unto me, a Little prelibation of the Rest remaining for the People of God.[9]

I was a Youth, when I first Practised a thing of this Nature; and it was a proposal of pious Mr Thomas White, in his Book about, The Power of Godliness,[10] which first Led me into it. But upon further Consideration I find ye Practice Liable to Some objection, For which cause, My Son, I would not have you Look upon it, as recommended unto you any further (than if it had been Left unmentioned.)

§ Moreover, Because at this Time, I kept a Diary of my Daily Actions, I now purposed, that I would note no Action in my Diary, Except it had been Prefaced or Attended, with some such motion of Soul as This: O Lord, This is that thou mayst be glorified! or, Thy Service[11] is in this aimed at, O my God!

That I may but just Exemplify to you, My Son, the Watch, which the Lord in those dayes helped me to keep over my Walk, I will here Transcribe only the Actions of One Day then occurring, which I entred (as the rest) in characters. [ms. p. 72]

28.^d 6.^m Legi, Exod. 34, 35, 36. ‖ Oravi. ‖ Examinavi Adolescentes. ‖ Legi Cartesium. ‖ Legi Commentatores in Joh. 6. 37. ‖ Jentacul: ‖ Paravi concionem. ‖ Orationi interfui Domest: ‖ Andivi Pupillos recitantes. ‖ Legi Salmon pharmac. ‖ Pransus Sum. ‖ Visitavi quosdam amicos. ‖ Legi Varia. ‖ Paravi concion. ‖ Audivi pupillos recit: ‖ Meditat ‖ ⟨⟨ On the Exceeding Willingness of the Lord Jesus Christ to do Good unto those that Come to Him. And, I RESOLVE, As to be Encouraged in my Addresses unto the Lord for His Mercy fro ye Thoughts of His Mercifulness, thus also to Endeavour that I may be Like unto Him, in Humble & Ready Helpfulness, unto others.⟩⟩ Oravi. ‖ Caenavi. ‖ Paravi Concion: ‖ Orat. Domest. interfui. ‖ [12]

Thus my Diary Sometimes Entred, it may be, Twenty Actions in a Day wch had been all of them explicitly Dedicated unto God. And I continued thus noting my Actions in my Diary, till my sinful & slothful Heart grew Weary of it. Besides, at Length I Saw, this Recording of Every thing, took up too much time, however Specious to be attempted, it was neither Easy, nor very useful.

I was also Willing to Forgett what was behind;[13] & I threw my papers into ye Fire. [ms. p. 73]

§ If you Look back, My Son, You will find, That I had required of myself, an Answer to be given unto Three Questions, at my going to Rest, every Night.[14]

Now, that I might Make a more Convenient Pause, on Each of these Questions, I Composed the following Hymn, to be sung sometimes in my Evening-Walk, with due Deliberation.

Psal. 68. 19.

I. Blest be the Great JEHOVAH, who

Doth me with <u>Daily Blessings</u> Load.

Thou, with a <u>Saviour</u>, dost bestow

<u>Salvations</u> on me, O my God!

Psal. 139. 2, 3, 4.

II. To Thee my <u>Wayes</u> have all been known;

Known all my <u>Words</u> have been to Thee:

Thou know'st my <u>Thoughts</u>: My <u>Faults</u>, I own:

May All, thro' CHRIST, now <u>Pardon'd</u> bee.

Phil. 1. 21.

III. Thy CHRIST is now my <u>Life</u>; I fly

To CHRIST with an Enliven'd <u>Faith</u>.

And <u>Now</u> t'wil be my <u>Gain</u> to <u>Dy</u>,

To CHRIST fetch'd by a <u>Stingless Death</u>.

§ And then, that I might celebrate[15] the Favours of God, <u>every Morning</u>, I
Composed another <u>Hymn</u>, to be Sung <u>Every Morning</u>, at my first Coming into
my Study. It was This.

<u>Lord</u>, Bought by thy All-worthy <u>Blood</u>,

<u>Life</u> Worthless I receive:

Nourish'd with Health, & Peace, & Food,

Free from Just plagues I <u>Live</u>. [ms. p. 74]

By Thy great Friendship I enjoy

<u>Friends</u> that my <u>Jewels</u> are;

Mee in thy <u>Work</u>, thou dost Employ:

And Still accept my <u>Prayer</u>.[16]

CHRIST, with His Promises, is Mine,

His <u>Angels</u> are my Guard;

Now I will my <u>Long Praises</u> join

With thy <u>Good Angels</u>, LORD.

§   When I was in the <u>Twenty first</u> year of my Age, I was vexed &
humbled with hateful Temptations. ⟨⟨17⟩⟩ ⟨ I found my Mind haunted with
<u>Ideas</u>, on the occasion whereof,⟩ I Sett apart so many Dayes for <u>Prayer</u>
with <u>Fasting</u>, in my Study; (rarely Letting <u>One Week</u> pass me, without
Such a <u>Day</u>, for many months together; and Sometimes keeping more than <u>one</u>
Such Day in a <u>Week</u>;) that I broke y^e <u>Sixth</u> Comandment, for ye Exact
keeping of ye Rest.

Herein, I was Like to have proved a Sad Instance, of one betrayed
by the <u>Devices of Satan</u>: which I mention, <u>My Son</u>, for Your Caution; That
you may beware, Lest When you <u>fight</u> against Satan in One Point, you do
not, before you are aware, <u>fall</u> by him in another.

I <u>Bear down my Body</u>, in these Exercises of Piety, Lest I Should
Prove a <u>Castaway</u>. But I brought <u>Splenetic Maladies</u> upon my <u>Body</u>, and I
was in hazard of having my <u>Duties</u> turned into <u>Murders</u>. [ms. p. 75]

§   Among ye Contrivances, about this Time Entred in my Memorials, One
was This.

In all places, (not Excepting the very <u>Kitchen</u> of the Family where
I Live,) wherever I Come, I would be Studious, not only to <u>Discourse</u>
<u>Profitably</u>, but also I would be careful, that my <u>Last Speech</u>, may still
be of a peculiar <u>Weight</u> and <u>Use</u>. For, <u>That</u> will be most Remembred; and
for ought I know, it may truly prove, <u>My Last</u>.

§   Another was This. Out of Reverence unto the <u>Word</u> of God, which I
See profaned Sometimes, even by Religious people: and out of Respect

unto the Souls of men, which I observe, Cannot Read at any Time afterwards, a Text in the Bible, whereon they have heard any unlucky Jest made, without a Vain Reminding of that Jest, I Resolved, That I would not Laugh at, Much Less would I Relate and Recite a Jest, wherein a Text of Scripture has been Ludicrously introduced.

§   This place will do, as well as another, to tell you, My Son, That Ever Since my being Seventeen years old, I had, for Seven years together, the Charge of Scholars: Yea, Some have been under my Tuition, that were older than myself. These my Pupils I carried thro' all the Parts of Academic Learning, as far as I was able; & by Instructing them, I Confirmed myself in many Points of Literature. The Methods, how I taught them the Hebrew [ms. p. 76] Language; How I heard their daily Recitations, from the Originals of both Testaments; How I Composed Catechisms of the Several Arts for them; How I directed their Declamations and their Disputations; I might have mentioned, it may be, with some Advantage to You, for Somewhat of Curiositie therein occurring. But I will mention only This to you, that so You may be a Little taught, by my Poor Exemple, if ever you should Come to do any thing, in ye Like Employment of a Tutor. The Lord helped me, to have many Contrivances, how I might Save the Souls of the Young Men, who have been Committed unto my Charge. I therefore, besides my Cares to check all Ebullitions of Sin in any of their Conversations, did Successively use to Send for them, One by One, into my Study, and there, in ye Solemnest & Liveliest manner I could imagine, Seldome Dismissing any of them without Floods of Tears, I have Discoursed with them, about their own Everlasting Interests; and I have then bestowed Good Books upon them, to further the Work of God and of Grace upon their Spirits. Moreover, I made it my Custome, That in every <u>Recitation</u>, I would, from Something or other occurring in it, make an Occasion to Lett fall some <u>Sentence</u>, which might have a Tendency to promote the <u>Fear of God</u> in their Hearts: Which thing Sometimes did indeed, putt [ms. p. 77] me upon a Little Strain of my Witts, but, I hope, it Left Good Effects upon my Pupils.[18]

And God at Length gave me to see, some Harvest of these my Labours; for Several of these Young Men, have proved Able and Holy Preachers, and among the Hopefullest of the Rising Generation. Yea, I must here sincerely insert, a very Abasing Acknowledgment. I would give all I am Worth in this World, for those Measures of <u>Grace</u> and <u>Sense</u>, which I now See, in some that were once my <u>Pupils</u>.

§ Of a Certain Day, Sett apart for Secret <u>Prayer</u> with <u>Fasting</u> (in the Twenty Second Year of my Age,) I made this Record; w^{ch}, for your Sake, <u>My Son</u>, I will here Transcribe.

' This Day, having Humbled & Judged myself before the Lord, for my many
' Provocations, and <u>Watered my Couch w</u>th <u>my Tears</u>, in the Apprehension
' of my own Exceeding Vileness, at Length, whole Floods of Tears gushed
' from me, in my Laying Hold on the pardoning Mercy of God in ye Lord
' Jesus Christ. The <u>Spirit</u> of the most High God, brought me to a <u>mar-</u>
' <u>vellous Temper</u>, which was to me, Like the very Suburbs of Heaven;
' Wherein Hee assured me, That my <u>Sins were all Forgiven</u>;[19] and that His
' Anger, in the sense whereof my Soul trembled, Should no more Burn
' against me. [ms. p. 78] Hereupon I called unto mind, the <u>Names</u> of as
' many Persons, as I could any wayes Learn, had Reproached me, or In-
' jured me; and I most heartily begg'd the God of Heaven, on the behalf
' of them, One after One, That they might be <u>Blessed with all the</u>
' <u>Blessings of Goodness</u>,[20] and Such Blessings especially as were Most
' Suitable for them.

'   I also herewith besought the Lord, That I might never Sin against
' Him, with Will, or Design, or Delight any more; I professed unto Him,
' That I should Rejoice to Dy this very Day, if I might thereby be Ever-
' lastingly Delivered from Sinning against Him; I declared before Him,
' That I was very Sure, I should E're Long be with the Lord Jesus Christ,
' & Joyfully behold His Face with Sinless Glory.

And on this Occasion, I will observe to You, My Son, That about
this Time, there was Like to be, thro' some Fine-Spun Devices of Satan,
Some Opposition from Certain Ill-disposed persons, unto my Settlement in
the Place, where I was now a Preacher. To Conquer this Opposition, I do
not know, that I Consulted or Addressed so much as One Man in the World:
but I knew, that Prayer with Fasting, was a Sovereign way to Cure En-
chantments; and I was Resolved, That I would be Concerned with none but
ye Lord Jesus Christ, about my Settlement in Opportunities of Service
for Him. Accordingly, I kept close to Prayer with Fasting, and with
a Broken Spirit, I Earnestly protested unto ye Lord, That I would be any
thing; do [ms. p. 79] any thing, and go any where, that He would have me.
The Effect was, That by a meer Work of Heaven, on the minds of all Concerned, the Difficulties all blew over, & my Settlement mett with no
Contestation. My Son, This Experience of your Father, may at some time
or other, do you a kindness.

§   On another Such Day, about this Time, I find in my papers:[21] That
I did with Plenty of Tears, Lament my own wretchedness; And herein I was
Carried forth, to Declare, unto the Lord, That having Dishonoured His
precious and Glorious Name, if there were no other way, for the Honour
thereof to be Recovered, Except in My Ruine, I Laid myself down at His
Holy Feet, by Him forever to be Disposed of, as Hee should please. But

I therewithal Said, That His Name was, A God that Will abundantly Pardon;[22] and that He had provided a Way for the Glory of it; and that whosoever Will Accept of Salvation in & thro' the Lord Jesus Christ, Should upon His Word, be sure to have it; And so I Concluded, with a Full Assurance, That the Lord Jesus Christ was now Interceding for me, and that because He had Lived and Dyed, I should not Dy but Live.[23] And these Motions of Soul in me, were accompanied with very Rapturous Hallelujahs, Yea, with Transports of Love and Praise; Telling the Lord, That Now I would be His forever, and I Longed now to be with my Redeemer, in the mansions that are above, where I shall certainly [ms. p. 80] be, Within a very Little While, but that for One Reason I desired Still to Live, a few Dayes more upon Earth; Even that I might Labour for Him, and Suffer for Him, and Serve Him, where I had Sinned against Him: And This, even to Serve Him, (I Said) should be my only Work, all the Day Long, while I had a Day to Live.

§   One Day, about this Time, Thinking, How to glorify God in ye Family, where I Sojourned, I thus Designed.

I would Sett before ye Family, a Good & Grave Exemple, in all things; and Scarce Ever Come among them in the Room of Resort, without Letting fall some Savoury Expression, before I Leave them; And, besides this, I would on one Lords-day in a Month (at Least) which I shall find fittest for it, Single out Some One of the Children or Servants in ye Family (for there were many of them) till All who shall be fitt so to be treated, shall be so treated, & bring them into my Study; where I would Endeavour by Serious Discourses, to Obtain the Consent of their Souls unto the New Covenant; and E're I dismiss them, I would Pray with them, to Confirm that Consent, & their Everlasting Welfare.

My Son; If you come to Board, at a fitt Age do so too. And God give
to You as good Success, as He gave to mee! [ms. p. 81]

§   Entring upon the Twenty Third Year of my Age, I Resolved upon a
Method of Spending the whole Afternoon of Every Saturday, in peculiar
Transactions between the most High God, and my own Soul. And I continued
acting according to my Resolution, until the Encumbrances of my Publick
Ministry, made it necessary for me to abate it. The Method was This.

I. Making Three Prayers.

The first (as I began other Afternoons,) Consisting of Praises unto
God, for His Mercies unto me, and my Requests on the behalf of Others.

The Second, Consisting of more Signal Converse with God, in Renewals
of Covenants and Closures with the Lord Jesus Christ, and the Like..

The Third, Consisting of Petitions, relating to the Ministerial
Capacity wherein I Stand; & Particularly, the Services of the Day ensuing.

II. Thinking on that Question, What is there, that I am further to
do for the Name of God?

III. Meditating on the Truths of God; & Especially such as I am to
deliver on the Morrow.

IV. Reading of Books, and Singing of Hymns; Wherein Graces may be
Exercised.
I kept some Records of these Blessed Sature-day Afternoons. But, I shall
Transcribe only the First of them, that You, My Son, may be Somewhat
Assisted, in your own Walk with God.

'   After, and amidst the usual Devotions of this Time, I considered
' with myself, [ms. p. 82] Why do I Beleeve the Scriptures to be the Word
' of God? And having Settled the Conviction thereof upon my Mind, I took

' into my Hands the BIBLE, whereof I Ordinarily make use, in my Publick
' Ministrations; and presenting myself with it, on my knees before the
' Lord, I professed unto Him, <u>That I did Embrace the Precious Book, as</u>
' <u>His Word; Resolving Ever therefore to Credit all the Revelations of it;</u>
' <u>That I would Love it, Prize it, Converse With it, as His; That I would</u>
' <u>be so Awed by the Promises & Threatenings & Histories of it, as to</u>
' <u>Study a Conformity to the precepts of it, while I have any Being.</u>[24]
' So, I Blessed Him, for His vouchsafing His Invaluable Word unto me.

§   Altho' I have had, for the most part, ye conveniency of preaching
to Greater Congregations, than most preachers of ye True Gospel in the
World; Yett One Day my Auditory was Thinner & Smaller than Ordinary. I
began thereupon to Entertain some foolish Discouragements. But I presently Encountred them, & Vanquished them, with writing the following
Meditation.

'   Consider, O my Soul, How unworthy my Sins have rendred me, of the
' Least Acceptance among the people of God; [ms. p. 83] and that, if
' there were nothing Else, besides the <u>Meanness</u> which attends my Minis-
' trations, <u>This</u> were Enough to Cause in my Auditors, a Withdraw there-
' from, unto the Assemblies, where they may easily Mend themselves.

'   Consider Likewise, how many Hundreds were my Auditors this day;
' doubtless more than to make a <u>Thousand</u>: and that many far more Ex-
' cellent Persons than myself, would Count themselves Happy, if they
' might preach quietly to Assemblies One Quarter so big as mine.

'   Consider also, Tis possible, the Hearers that went from me, found
' their <u>Edification</u> to be promoted Elsewhere; And it is not Impossible,
' Some of that Number that Staid with <u>Mee</u>, did also Reap some Little
' Benefit. And then, Be glad, that the Church of God is Built, <u>per</u>

' <u>Alios</u>, when that, <u>Nos non Sumus Digni</u>.[25] But in the mean time, Triumph

' in it, as a most undeserved Favour of the Most High, that I may be Cap-

' able of Helping forward the Salvation, of so much as <u>One</u> Immortal Soul.

' And Since I have heretofore had the <u>Temptation of being Flock'd after</u>,

' Lett me now Suspect, that I need a Rod, for some Irregularities of

' Spirit under it. But if a Wise Redeemer, will now Try me another way,

' Lett me now humbly act the <u>Graces</u>, that shall be Suitable thereunto;

' And Especially, be Careful to apprehend, that an affectation of dis-

' playing ones <u>Gifts</u> before <u>Throngs</u>, is too often an abominably Proud

' Fishing for Popular Applause. But my Work in the pulpitt, must be,

' rather to acquitt myself well in the Discharge of the <u>Duties</u> incumbent

' on me there, before y^e <u>All-seeing Eye</u> of that Majesty, who to me,

' shall be <u>Theatre</u> Enough.

'   <u>Satis mihi Pauci Auditores, Satis Unus, Satis Nullus</u>.[26] [ms. p. 84]

§   About this Time, One Day walking in my Retirement, my Soul was after

an unusual manner, transported in this Thought.

'   I desire above all things to <u>Glorify God</u>, & show forth His vertues

' & His praises forever. And I shall now be Sure, never to have this

' Happiness Denyed unto me: And therefore now nothing shall ever make

' me miserable.

     Another Time, soon after this, my Heart was much melted in Thinking

Thus.

'   If On the one side, there should be profered unto me, all that can

' be Desired of <u>this worlds Good</u>, attended with the <u>Degrading Misery</u> of

' Living only to <u>Myself</u> in the midst of all: If On the other Side, there

' should be profered unto me, the Happiness of bringing very much <u>Glory</u>

' unto my Lord Jesus Christ, Even in a Life of many and bitter

' Afflictions; I should with an unspeakably Strong Bent of Soul Choose
' the Latter. And so, I assuredly infer, That I shall not miss of so
' great Salvation.

§ Being Somewhat Sensible of the Vast Importance, of Abstaining frō y^e
Sins of ye Time and Place, wherein I Live, I now Resolved, That I would
now and then Single out a Season, [On a Lords-day Noon,] wherein to
Consider,

What are the Special Sins of this Time and Place?
And how to bear my Testimonies against them. [ms. p. 85]

§   On a certain Day of Prayer, which I kept this Year, (the Day for
the Meeting of a Parliament, the Event whereof was a matter of great
Concern to me, & caused me to be much in prayer before ye Lord;)[27]
The Lord having Assured me, That all Controversy between Him & Me, was
done away, I Solemnly thus Renewed, and Subscribed His Covenant, and
gave up myself unto Him.

The COVENANT.

' I Renounce all the Vanities, and Cursed Idols, and Evil Courses, of
' this World.
' I Engage,
'   That I Will Ever have the Great GOD, my best Good, my last End, &
'   my only Lord.
'   That I Will Ever be rendring of Acknowledgments unto the Lord
'   JESUS CHRIST, in all the Relations which He bears unto me.
'   That I Will ever by Studying, What is my Duty in these Things, and
'   wherein I find myself to fall short, I will ever make it my Grief,
'   & my Shame, and for Pardon betake myself unto the Blood of the
'   Everlasting Covenant.[28]

' Now Humbly Imploring the <u>Grace</u> of the <u>Mediator</u> to be <u>Sufficient for me</u>,

' I do,

'   as a further Solemnity hereunto, Subscribe my <u>Name</u>, with both <u>Hand</u>

'   and <u>Heart</u>.

I Commend Such a Transaction to You, <u>My Son</u>; But be sure, you be very

Serious in it. [ms. p. 86]

§   I need not Conceal from You, That tho' I was Long Since chosen a

<u>Pastor</u> of a church, Yett, being a <u>Collegue</u> with another, an Elderly and

Eminent Person, & being in some other Circumstances inviting me to Con-

tinue so, I chose all this while, to Decline the <u>Pastoral Office</u>, and

continued only as a Candidate of the <u>Ministry</u>, and without <u>Ordination</u>.[29]

But when I was Twenty Two years Old, the Necessity of my Receiving

<u>Ordination</u>, was become Irresistible. And it was performed in a very

publick, and Solemn, and Aweful Manner.[30]

In Order to it, I kept many Dayes of <u>Prayer</u> with <u>Fasting</u>, in my

Study. And in One of those Dayes, having declared unto ye Lord, That

not Expecting any <u>External Advantage</u>, but rather <u>Sorrow</u>, and <u>Sickness</u>,

and <u>Obloquy</u>, & many <u>Persecutions</u>, I would out of <u>Love</u> to Him, undertake

ye Work now before me, and <u>Feed</u> a Precious & a Numerous Flock of HIS:[31]

I then Promised unto Him:

I. That I would ever Endeavour to be a <u>Faithful Pastor</u> unto those,

over whom He should sett me.

II. That I would Endeavour to be very <u>Humble</u>, under whatever <u>En-</u>

<u>largements</u> He should Vouchsafe unto me.

III. That if He would give me to Build up His church, with an <u>un-</u>

<u>blemished Reputation</u>, I would $Endeavo^e$ to be Contented with whatsoever

Estate He shall order for me, in the World, tho' never so poor, & many

other wayes Afflicted. [ms. p. 87]

§   While I was preparing for my Ordination, I had my Spirit Strangely
Buffeted, & mortified & macerated with Strong Temptations, & broken to
peeces, until I was Content Even to be any thing in the World, if so be
the Lord might have Glory from me. But when the Day arrived, as I was
in ye Morning of the Day, on my knees in my Study before the Lord, an
astonishing Irradiation from Heaven came upon me, which Dissolved me into
a Flood of Tears, and Assured me, That I should Enjoy a mighty Presence
of ye Lord Jesus Christ with me, in ye Ministry, whereto He was now more
than ever calling me.

But after ye Day was Over, I considered, That my Lord Jesus Christ,
Entring on His publick Ministry, mett with very Sore Temptations: and
it may be, my Ordination to ye Ministry, might likewise be followed with
Temptations. I Resolved therefore,

I. That I would immediately go Read a Profitable Book or two, Concerning Temptations.

II. That I would now and then Sett apart a Time, to think; What is
the Temptation, wherewith I am now most of all Endangered? [ms. p. 88]

§   My Son, Because This is upon some Accounts a proper place for it, I
will here Introduce diverse

Rules of Preaching, [32]

Which I drew up for myself, Long before You were Born. And if God should
Accept and Employ You (which I beseech Him to do,) as a Preacher of the
Gospel, You may do well to Consider them.

I. When I am at a Loss for a Text, I would make a Prayer unto the Holy
Spirit of the Lord Jesus Christ, for His Direction, and Assistence, as
well to Handle my Text, as to Find and Fitt One for me.

II. Before I undertake to Go over any Larger Portion or Doctrine of the

Bible, which may require many Sermons, I Would, with more Solemn Supplications Address Heaven, for ye necessary Succours⟨⟨ of Alsufficient
Grace⟩⟩.

III. I would Weigh well the Original Tongues, as well as the usual and
needful Commentaries, for a Scripture, before I preach upon it.

IV. In pitching upon Subjects to be discoursed in my publick Ministry,
Especially more Occasional Ones (for which I would Reserve myself a
Liberty, whatever Course I may be in,) I would Still have some Design of
Suiting and Serving ye Edification of my Hearers; --Ever, Preach upon
Design.

V. I would not use to Stand Long upon any One Text ordinarily; but
Study an Acceptable Variety. Nor use One way of Treating upon Every
Text; but be Various in my method.

VI. I would be Scriptural in all my Exercises; and ordinarily Dismiss
no Head, without some Scripture well adjusted unto it. [ms. p. 89]

VII. I would alwayes Endeavour to Fill my Hour Well, and Croud every
Sermon, as full of Matter, as I may, without obscuring.

VIII. In uttering my Sermons, I would not Begin, either Too Fast, or,
Too Loud.

IX. I would not make my Sentences too Extended, for the Writers to take
them readily or for the Hearers to have Easily the Sense of them.

X. Before I preach any Sermon, I would in a Devout Meditation, work
every Head of it upon my Heart, Even until I turn it into a proper
Supplication.

XI. I would Have Notes, and Use Notes, in my Preaching; but Yett I would
not so Read my Notes, as to take off in the Least, the Vivacitie of my
Eye, my Voice, my whole Action.

XII. I would in all my Ministry, have much of CHRIST, who is <u>All</u>: As
Knowing, That the <u>Holy Spirit</u> of God, Loves to glorify CHRIST, and I
shall have much of that <u>Holy Spirit</u> with me, in my Ministry, if I sett
myself to do so too.

XIII. And I would have a great Care, Lest in my Ministry, I do at all
Confound, the <u>Methods of GRACE</u>; Upon a due <u>Stating</u> and <u>Owning</u> whereof,
the <u>Success</u> of my Ministry does exceedingly Depend.

XIV. To Conclude a Sermon ordinarily, with Some Agreeable Text of Scripture, Pungently & Livelily Left with ye Consideration of the Hearers,
will be a practice very edifying. [ms. p. 90]

§ About this Time, I Entertained Several further Methods of Walking with
God.

    I. I thought it would be a Thing many wayes Agreeable and Pro-
fitable, if on ye close of Every <u>Satureday</u>, I may be found by the
approaching <u>Lords-day</u>, Engaged in some Fixed Meditation on the Lord
JESUS CHRIST.

    II. When I pray with any <u>Sick-person</u>, I would use what Ingenuity
& Application I can, to Do Good upon the Souls of them that attend in
the Room where I give the Visit, as well as ye Sick person Visited.

    III. I would on <u>Lords-Day</u> Mornings, not Seldome have my Rising
Thoughts Employ'd on this Question: <u>What Service may I do for the Lord
Jesus Christ, as I am a Pastor, to a Flock of His</u>?

    IV. While I am Dressing myself in a Morning, Oh, Lett it be my
frequent Thought, <u>What Special Service may I do for the Lord Jesus
Christ, in the Day Ensuing</u>?

    V. When I have heard a <u>Sermon</u> preached, I would, as I go out of
ye Assembly, still send up an <u>Ejaculation</u> to Heaven, <u>That ye Truths</u>

newly delivered, may have an happy & lasting Effect upon me. [ms. p. 91]

§   About the Middle of this Year, I began One of the Most Holy and Useful Practices, of all that ever the Good Spirit of the Lord, has taught me, in the Whole Course of my Life.

This was, A Course of Reading the Scriptures, with such a Devout Attention, as to fetch at Least One Observation, and One Supplication, (a Note With a Wish) out of every Verse in all the Bible.

I had a prospect of more than a Little Truth and Grace, to pass thro' my Soul, in thus Waiting upon God; and my prospect has not failed me.

This Reading of the Scriptures, with Such an Attention, has proved unto me, a most glorious Opportunity of Conversing with God.

And, I give more Thanks unto the Lord, for Teaching mee, this Way of Living, than if He had bestowed the greatest Earthly Revenues upon me.

My Dear Son; As Soon as ever you are able to do it, Begin (and having Begun it, Hold On,) this Method of Reading the Scriptures; Read a Portion of ye Bible, after this manner, for the most part Every Day. If you do not find it One of the most Profitable, and Comfortable Exercises, that ever you were advised unto, I dare be Content that my Advice may Signify nothing with you.

The Method which I thus used in Reading I also took up for Singing; and, I hoped, this way to make Melody in my Heart, Singing unto the Lord.[33]

Yea, and for Hearing of Sermons also, I took up this Laborious Method; That not One Head, nor one Text, brought by the preacher should pass me, without some [ms. p. 92] agreeable Ejaculation. And I often, (tho' not alwayes) Practised it; but alwayes unto my incredible Advantage.

§   Another thing, I find recorded in my Papers this Year; which I will

mention to you, My Son, for your Imitation.

I had in my Conversation with a Young Gentleman, used many Endeav-

ours for his Everlasting Happiness. At Last I prevailed with him, to

Spend a whole Day with me, in my Study, at the Devotions of Prayer with

Fasting. Towards ye close of the Day, having drawn up in Writing, a

Solemn Covenant, I Left him not, until his Conquered Heart and Hand, most

affectionately Subscribed it; and so he forever bound himself unto the

Service of the Lord.

This Day, thus painfully Laid out, for the Gaining of a Soul unto

the Lord Jesus Christ, had a Blessed Success. The Young Gentleman after-

wards joined unto my Church, & Lived & Died a Serious Christian.[34]

Since that, I have done more of ye Like Nature, for ye Engaging of

Young Gentlemen, of great Gifts & Hopes, unto my Lord Jesus Christ.

After many Preliminary Treats, in my Conversation with them, and as

agreeable Charms as I could think of, I have had them with me, in my

Study, when I have been there Praying and Fasting before the Lord: and

there I have With Floods of Tears Carried them unto the Lord, and Ex-

pressed [ms. p. 93] for them their Consent unto the Covenant of Grace;

and the Lord hath Rewarded me, with Good & great Effects of these Actions.

§   I did this year also form Several other Designs of Christianity.

I.   The Apostles Advice to a Young Minister was, Exercise thyself

unto Godliness.[35] I Resolved, I would now Read over Mr Swinnocks[36] fine

Discourses on that Subject; & Employ my Particular Ejaculations upon

Every Article, as I go along.

II.   I had Mett with an Observation, That ye Want of Mortification

in a Minister, procures a Sad unsuccessfulness to his Ministry.[37] That

I might not be a deplorable Instance of it, I Resolved, I would immediately Read over Dr Owens Treatise of Mortification,[38] & Endeavour to follow & apply the Directions in it.

    III. I took a Catalogue of all the Communicants belonging to my
Church; and in my Secret Prayers, I resolved that I would go over the
Catalogue, by Parcels at a Time, upon my knees; praying for the most
Suitable Blessings, I could think of, to be bestow'd on Each person, by
Name distinctly mentioned.

    IV. In perusing my Sermons before I preached them, I Resolved,
That I would make Even That, an Exercise of Devotion, by Endeavouring to
fetch an agreeable Ejaculation, out of Every Head, and Every Text produced in them.

    V. I had one Design more, which I expressed in these Terms:

'   It will cost me very bitter Toyle and Pains; Yett perhaps I may be
' very Serviceable in it: If I procure to myself an Exact Account of
' those Evil Humours, which [ms. p. 94] the place where I Live, is at
' any time, under the Observable Dominion of; and whereas, those Divels
' may be Cast out, by Fasting and Prayer, Sett apart Still a Day of Sec-
' ret Prayer with Fasting, on the occasion of Each of them; to Deprecate
' my own Guiltiness therein, and Supplicate for such Effusions of the
' Spirit from on High, as may Redress, Remove, and Banish Such Distempers
' from the Place.[39]

§   This Year, I kept Several Dayes of Thanksgiving, alone in my Study.
I will give you, My Son, the Method of no more than One of them.

The Forenoon I Spent;

I. In Acknowledging of my own Vileness before God; whereby I have become, after an aggravated Manner, Unworthy of all that Goodness & Mercy,

which has followed me all my Dayes.[40]

II. In Acknowledging of those Glories, which belong unto the Great God,
as Hee is infinitely Excellent in Himself; and as He is the Creator and
Governour of all the World; and unto the Lord Jesus Christ, as He is One
Altogether Lovely.

In these Exercises, my Heart was rapt into those Heavenly Frames,
that would have turned a Dungeon into a Paradise.

In the Afternoon, I went over the Former Kindnesses of God unto myself, in my Thoughts, my Psalms, my Praises.

But I more Emphatically Singled out Three Things, wherein I have
Seen the Favour of God.

1. Answers to Petitions. [ms. p. 95]

2. Rescues from Temptations.

3. Those Afflictions, by means whereof, I have Enjoy'd Both.

I assay'd then, to Bless the Lord, for those Favours, wherewith I
am at present, on Every Side Surrounded.

1. My Life and Health.

2. My Accomplishments in any Points of Learning.

3. My Exceedingly-well-furnished Library.

4. My Improvement in the Ministry of the Gospel.

5. My peaceable Settlement in a place of great Opportunities.

6. My Success in my public & private Labours.

8.[41] My Acceptance and Interest among the people of God.

9. My Enjoyment of my Father, unto this Day.

10. The Notable Growth and Peace of the Flock, whereof I am the
Pastor.

Having Employ'd my Admirations and Adorations, upon the Grace, from
whence these things do come unto me; I then came to Consider the Free-

Grace of God unto me, in,

    1. The gift of the Lord Jesus Christ unto the World.

    2. The Offer of the Lord Jesus Christ unto myself in particular.

    3. The Sense of the Need of the Lord Jesus Christ, which God has given me.

    4. The Union with the Lord Jesus Christ, which ye Holy Spirit has brought me into.

    5. All the further Operations of the Holy Spirit upon my Soul, whereby He is Continually making me more Meet for the Inheritance of the Saints in Light.[42] I concluded the Day with Considering; What shall I render to the Lord? [ms. p. 96] I then gave My Self, my Whole Self, all my Powers, Members, Interests, and Capacities, (which I own'd, was the Least that I owed) unto the Lord.

    In Particular, I added,

That Since I owed all my Good Things unto the Compassion of God,

    I would alwayes be contriving, How to Honour Him; and I would

    immediately procure Some Testimony, against Some Common Evils

    in ye Land, which are doubtless very offensive unto Him.

And Since it was ye Mediation of the Lord Jesus Christ, unto which I owed the Procurement of all,

    I would quickly preach a Sermon unto a very great Auditory, the

    Scope whereof should be, to magnify the Lord JESUS CHRIST, &

    invite the minds of People unto an assiduous Contemplation of

    His glories.[43]

§   This Year I Sett upon Visiting all the Families belonging to my church; taking Sometimes One, Sometimes Two Afternoons in a Week, for that purpose.[44]

I Still Sent before hand unto the Families, that I intended at Such a Time to Visit them. And when I came unto them, I assay'd with as Handsome and as Pungent Addresses, as I was able, to treat Every person particularly, about their Everlasting Interests.

First, I discoursed with the Elder people, upon Such Points as I thought most proper for them.

And Especially, I charged them, to maintain Family-Prayer; and obtain'd their promises for it, if they had yett neglected it. ⟨ Yea, I pray'd with them, that I might show them How to Pray[45] as well as to obtain their Purposes for it.⟩ [ms. p. 97]

I likewise pressed upon them, the Care of Instructing their Children and Servants in the Holy Religion of the Lord Jesus Christ, and bringing them up for Him.

If any that I should have Spoke withal, were Absent, I frequently Left a Solemn Text or Two, of the Sacred Scripture, which I thought most agreeable for them; desiring Somebody present, That they would Remember me Kindly to them, & from me Recomend unto them that Oracle of God.

I then Called for the Children and Servants. And Putting unto them Such Questions of ye Catechism, as I thought fitt, I would from the Answers, make as Lively Applications unto them, as I could, for the Engaging of them unto the Fear of God.

I frequently gott Promises from them, relating to Secret Prayer, and Reading of ye Scriptures, and Obedience to their Parents and Masters.

And I frequently Sett before them ye Proposals of the New Covenant, after I had first Laboured for their Conviction and Awakening. So with Floods of Tears, they have Expressly declared their Consenting to, & Accepting of, the Proposals of ye Covenant of Grace, which I distinctly Sett before them.

Some of the Lesser Folks, I would order to bring their Bibles unto me, and Read unto me from thence, two or three verses whereto I turned them. I then Charm'd them, to think on Such things, as I thence observed for their Admonition, and never Forgett those Faithful Sayings of God.

I would sometimes Leave Some Awful Questions with them, which I told them, they should not Answer to Me, but Answer to Themselves; As, What have [ms. p. 98] I been doing ever Since I came into the World, about the great Errand, upon which God Sent me into the World? And, If God Should now Call me out of the World, what would become of me, throughout Eternal Ages? And, Have I ever yett by Faith Carried a Perishing Soul unto the Lord Jesus Christ, for both Righteousness & Salvation?

Many Other Such Methods, I took for the Winning of Souls in this Discharge of my Ministry, before I had seen Twenty Three Years in the World. And I Enjoy'd a most Wonderful Presence of God with me, in this Undertaking; & Seldome Left a Family, without many Tears of Devotion, dropt by all sorts of Persons in it.

I Could Seldome Dispatch more than Four or Five[46] Families in an Afternoon; and the Work was as Laborious as any in all my Ministry; I rarely Came home, without uneasy Bones, from ye Excessive Labours of it.

My Son; If ye Lord should Accept you, So far as to make you a Minister of His Glorious Gospel, I advise You, to Sett a Special Value, upon that Part of your Ministry, which is to be Discharged in Pastoral Visits. You will not only Do, but also Gett, more than a Little Good, by your Conversation with all Sorts of Persons, in thus Visiting of them, from House to House. And You will never more Walk in the Spirit,[47] than when you thus Walk about your Flock, to Do what Good you can among them. [ms. p. 99]

§ There was this Year also, another Design, Which I prosecuted, for
the Good of myself and others.[48] I Singled out a Number of <u>Students</u>,
who had passed thro' their <u>Cursus</u> in Philosophical and Academical Studies, & were just Entring into the World. These Young Gentlemen mett
once a Week at my Study; where we carried on a Course of <u>Disputation</u>
upon the Body of <u>Divinity</u>. In the Several Common-place Heads of <u>Divi-
nity</u>, where any notable <u>controversie</u> had been managed in the Church of
God, We had a Solemn <u>Disputation</u> on the <u>Controverted Question</u>. In this
<u>Disputation</u>, I was alwayes the <u>Moderator</u>, and Still Concluded with a
Discourse, which by Argument Established y^e <u>Truth</u>, Defended by the <u>Re-
spondent</u>. But, because upon Every Head of <u>Divinitie</u>, there were Multitudes of <u>Questions</u>, not so Worthy of a Solemn <u>Disputation</u>, These I
Laboriously gathered up; and giving them to the Society, at Some of o^e
Meetings, We Came all prepared, with <u>Brief</u>, but <u>Strong</u> and <u>Prov'd</u>
Answers to them; which we accordingly delivered in our Order. And it is
incredible, how much We advantaged o^e selves, by these Exercises.
[ms. p. 100]

§ Many of my Neighbours were now often proposing to me, a <u>Married
State of Life</u>. But I thought it necessary to Address Heaven with more
than Ordinary <u>Prayer</u>, and <u>Fasting</u>, before I took a Step in an Affayr of
Such Importance. I kept many <u>Dayes</u> on this Occasion, in Such Devotions.
    On One of those Dayes, I find this Record of my Proceedings.
' I acknowledge unto the Lord, my own Unworthiness of any Good Thing;
' Especially of That <u>Good Thing</u>, which is found by them that <u>obtain
' Favour of ye Lord</u>.[49] I professed, That I would Study to do nothing
' hereabout, that should be Displeasing unto Him. I Declared, That I

' desired nothing in this World, which might prejudice my glorifying of
' Himself. I Said, That if He Saw any thing would Hinder me from Hon-
' ouring of Him, I should be glad if He would Hinder me from Having of
' That, whatever my Misguided Appetites, might plead unto the Contrary.
' I Said, That if He would have me to Embrace a Celibacy, I would Ever-
' more take a Contentment in it, as that which would Capacitate me to
' Serve my Parents, & His people, to whom I owe my All. Nevertheless,
' to This Subjoined, That Since my Inclinations and Invitations did now
' Seem to Recommend a married Estate unto me, I begg'd of ye Lord, That
' He would Lead me in the Way wherein I should Go.[50] And I made a VOW,
' That if the Lord would prevent all Obstructions of my Desireable
' Settlement, in a Marriage with one, who should be a Blessing to me, in
' Evangelical Services,. I Will Twice at Least, Every Year, join with her,
' in keeping a Day of Thanksgiving, [ms. p. 101] privately unto Himself;
' --Except His Providence at any time, give a Sufficient Cause for the
' Omission of it.

On another of these Dayes, I thus Recorded, what occurred.

' This Day, with Anguish of Soul, in the Sense of my own Sinfulness
' and Filthiness, I cast myself prostrate on my Study-floor, with my
' Mouth in the Dust. Here I Lamented unto the Lord, my Follies, w^{ch}
' might have an Influence to deprive me of ye Blessings which I was now
' pursuing. I Judged, I Loathed, I Hated Myself, because of those
' Accursed Things, & besought the Forgiveness thereof, thro' ye Blood of
' the Covenant. I then Begg'd of the most High, That He would, notwith-
' standing all my miscarriages, bestow upon me, A Companion for my Life,
' by whose Prudence, Vertue, Good Nature, I might, while I am alive in
' this world, be Assisted in the Service of my Master, and Who might
' accompany me to[51] the Heaven of the Blessed forever. I pleaded, That

' Marriage was His Ordinance; and that He had Promised, No Good Thing

' shall be witheld from me. I Said unto Him, That I Cast the whole

' Burden of the Care about this Affayr, upon Him:[52] Expecting, That He

' would mercifully divert my Inclinations from this Matter, if it would

' prove Displeasing to Him, or Disadvantageous to my Opportunities of

' Serving Him: Entreating, That if it may be best for me to proceed, He

' would please to Direct my Choice, & Order my Way, & Over-rule the

' Hearts of my Friends, and of Her unto whom I may make [ms. p. 102] my

' Addresses, to favour what I prosecute: And in His due Time, so Settle

' me, as to give me Rich Demonstrations of His Loving-kindness: Engaging

' herewithal, That I would more than Ever glorify Him, and Spend my Time,

' in making of Blessed Matches, between the Son of God, and the Souls of

' Men.

Having taken these Methods to obtain ye Blessing of God, on this

weighty Concern, I may now tell You, My Son, I was wonderfully Blessed

in it. When I was Entring the Twenty Fourth Year of my Age, I was by y^e

wonderful Favour of Heaven brought into an Acquaintance with a Lovely and

Worthy Young Gentlewoman, whom God made a Consort, & a Blessing to me.[53]

In Managing my Acquaintance with her, it will not be amiss for me

to tell You, That I propounded unto myself, the Methods, the Divine and

Sacred Methods, wherein the glorious Lord Jesus Christ, Engages ye Hearts

of His Elect unto Himself; and I Studied, with Distinct Meditations

thereupon, how to make my Addresses unto that amiable Young Gentlewoman,

analogous unto those. But, alas, I am Foolish & Sinful in all my under-

takings.

And I will add, for Your Instruction, if you Live to have ye Like

affayr before you; That for a whole Quarter of a year, during my Court-

ship, I think, I did Lett Scarce one week pass me, without a whole Day of Prayer unto the Lord, for the Good Success of the affayr, wherein I was Engaged, and Lest any Unholiness might gain upon my Distempered Heart. And I beleeve, never any body Saw [ms. p. 103] more Sensible Answers of Prayer, in a Marriage, than your poor Father did in his.

My Wedding was attended (with unusual circumstances of Respect and Honour,) when I was Three Months above Twenty Three, and my Consort[54] was One month under Sixteen years of Age.

In ye morning of my Wedding-Day, the Lord filled my Soul, while Secretly at Prayer before Him, with Celestial and unutterable Satisfactions, flowing from the Sealed Assurances of His Love unto me. And my Heart was Particularly melted into Tears, upon my further Assurances, that in my Married State, He had Reserves of Rich and Great Blessings for me. ⟨⟨55⟩⟩

After this, going to the House of my Bride, and of o^e Splendid Entertainments, & having Some Liesure, before the Arrival of those Persons of Quality, which were Expected, I carried my Bible with me, into the Garden; where I Singled out the Story of the Wedding in the Second Chapter of John,[56] & fetched for myself One observation and one Supplication, out of Every Verse in that Story. In the doing of This, I received further Assurances, from the Spirit of my Heavenly Lord, That I was Blessed; & should be Blessed by Him forever.[57] [ms. p. 104]

§ About this Time, I drew up for myself a Proposal, of this Importance.

' Lett it be a Part of my Business Every Day, To be Applying of the
' PROMISES. There are certain Promises, that are of Continual Use, in
' ye Christians Daily Walk; & I wish I might Every Day have Some De-
' lightful Reflections upon Several of them.[58]

' Every Day, I shall have occasion for a Promise, of a Supply for all
' my wants in the Day. Such an one is That, in Phil. 4. 19. God will
' Supply all your Needs.

' Every Day, I shall have occasion for a Promise, of Grace to manage
' the Day for the Glory of God. Such an one is That, in Zech. 10. 12.
' I will Strengthen them in the Lord, they shall walk up & down in His
' Name, Saith the Lord.

' Every Day, I shall have occasion for a Promise, of a growing Victory
' over Sin. Such an one is That, in Mic. 7. 19. He will Subdue o^e
' Iniquities.

' Every Day, I should have a Promise, of Success in my undertakings.
' There is One in Psal. 1. 3. Whatsoever he doth, shall prosper.

' Every Day, I should have a Promise, of Protection from Dangers.
' There is one, in Psal. 91. 10. No Evil shall befal thee.

' Every Day, I should have a Promise, of Counsil in my Difficulties.
' There is one, in Psal. 32. 8. I will Instruct thee, and I will Teach
' thee in the way, which thou shouldest go.

' Every Day, it were Good, I should have a Promise, of not being the
' Worse, by whatever happens to me. Tis to be found, in [ms. p. 105]
' Rom. 8. 28. All things shall Work together for Good.

' Every Day, I can't be without a Promise, of Eternal Happiness at my
' Dying Day. Here it is; Luk. 12. 32. It is Your Fathers Good Pleasure,
' to give you the Kingdome.

' Oh! That I might often Every Day, be glancing at such Promises as
' these! It would be Heaven upon Earth, to be doing so; & it would have
' a charming Efficacy upon me, for the Perfecting of Holiness in y^e
' Fear of God.

§ This year, I kept Several Dayes of THANKSGIVING. The Exercises peculiar to these Dayes, (besides ye Ennumeration of Special Blessings, wherewith God had favoured me,) Were Especially these.

I Laid out Large portions of Time, in Meditations, upon Some Collections of Texts, which represent, the glory of <u>God</u>, in His <u>Nature</u>, <u>Trinity</u>, and <u>Attributes</u>, and wonderful Works of <u>Creation</u> and <u>Providence</u>; and the <u>Glory</u> of the Lord Jesus Christ, in His <u>Natures</u>, <u>Person</u>, <u>Offices</u>, <u>Life</u>, <u>Death</u>, <u>Resurrection</u>, and <u>Exaltation</u>. I dwelt upon the <u>Scriptures</u> which exhibited these things unto me, with Innumerable <u>Ejaculations</u>, and multiplied <u>Hosannahs</u> and <u>Hallelujahs</u>, magnifying the Most High, until failure of Strength obliged me to break off.

Again, I went from Room to Room in my <u>House</u>, now newly, but richly, furnished; Deliberately looking upon the Several Possessions, whereof I was become the <u>Steward</u>; And with a Ravished Soul, I gave Every thing back to ye Lord; variously <u>Contriving</u>, and so, <u>Declaring</u>, <u>How all that I have, should be made Serviceable unto His Glory</u>. [ms. p. 106]

§ Being Settled, in my <u>Family</u>, I took up this Course for <u>Family-worship</u>.

Before my <u>Morning-Prayers</u>, I Still Read a <u>chapter</u>, or part of a <u>chapter</u>, and then Composed my <u>Prayers</u> out of it.

Before my <u>Evening-Prayers</u>, I Singled out Some <u>Text</u> of Scripture, or some <u>Head</u> or <u>Case</u> of Divinity, and made a short <u>meditation</u> upon it: Then digesting it into ye Prayers. Thus I went thro' the Body of Divinity, and a Considerable Portion of the <u>Bible</u>.

§ Partly from ye provision which I had already made, of <u>Methods</u> to <u>Serve God</u>, & to <u>Do Good</u>; and Partly from ye Variety of <u>Publick Employments</u>, whereinto I was now fallen, after these <u>Methods</u> had Somewhat fitted me; but Partly, and, I doubt Cheefly, from y^e <u>Sinfulness</u> and <u>Slothfulness</u>

of my own Heart, I find very Little Recorded, in ye Twenty fifth year
of my pilgrimage.[59]

What I will fetch from that year, for You, My Son, is; That ye Lord
having bestowed upon me a Daughter,[60] (and perhaps One of the Comeliest
Infants that have been seen in ye world,) I underwent a particular Trial
thereupon. I had been Invited often to Look upon its Lovely Features
and Actions, but I commonly replied, No, Tis Mortal, and I will not En-
tangle my Affections with it![61] God gave me now to reap the Benefit of
this Disingagedness. The Child, being about Five months old, Suddenly
Dyed of Convulsions, on ye Lords-Day, in ye Forenoon, as I was [ms. p.
107] Returning from my public Labours. In ye Afternoon, I Preached on
the words of Bereaved Jacob, Me have Yee bereaved of my children;[62]
and, I hope, I glorified the Lord, who mightily still bore in that
Thought upon me, God will never hurt me! My God will never do me any
Harm![63]

I took my dear Consort with me, to make a Consort, in ye Confessions, and Petitions, of Prayer with Fasting on this occasion; and y^e
Lord helped me to lay hold on His Free Grace in Jesus Christ, & with
a Joyful Reliance thereon, to Beleeve, That all my Sins are forgiven
me forever.[64]

§ I remember, that Gregory Nazianzen, speaking of the Prayers, which
his Father poured out, at the Celebration of the Eucharist, Saies,
They were dictated πᾶσα τῷ ἑνὶ πνεύματο,[65] by the Holy Spirit of
God. While I was Yett but a Young Person, and a Younger Pastor, and
had but Little of the Holy Spirit of God, & had horribly Grieved Him,
& Vexed Him, & Resisted Him, Yett I rarely administered before the Lord,
on the Eucharistical occasions, but His Holy Spirit, (I hope, it was)

Irradiated my mind, with some very Enlarging Influences. My Employments
were so many, that I could not keep <u>Written Memorials</u> of those Passages;
However, I did preserve a few of those Heaven-ward <u>Expansions</u>, which I
found in ye Administration of the <u>Eucharist</u>, at the Beginning of my Ministry. But instead of here Inserting any of them, I shall only advise
you, <u>My Son</u>, to be more Careful than I was, in Recording Such passages,
if Ever you should Enjoy them; You will find ye Remembring & Recording
of such things, to be of more than ordinary Advantage. [ms. p. 108]

§   Once this year, I made a Short Collection of Instances, wherein I
had Seen the <u>Faithfulness</u> of God, unto His <u>Promises</u>.

It was to This purpose.

'   According to that <u>Promise</u>,

'   Psal. 91. 15.

'   <u>He shall call upon me, & I will answer him.</u>

' I have many & many a time found, That my God hath not bid me <u>Seek His</u>
' <u>Face in Vain</u>; I have gott more by <u>Prayer</u>, than by any other <u>Endeavour</u>
' or <u>Contrivance</u> in ye world.

'   According to that <u>Promise</u>,

'   Psal. 37. 5.

'   <u>Committ thy way unto the Lord, & Hee shall</u>

'   <u>bring it to pass.</u>

' I never found my Affairs to Prosper better, than when I have, with a
' Quiet Heart, <u>Resigned</u> those Affayrs, unto ye management of my Almighty
' Father, who <u>Performeth all things for me.</u>

'   <u>According to that Promise,</u>

'   Prov. 16. 7.

'   <u>When a Mans Wayes please the Lord,</u>

' <u>He maketh even his Enemies to be</u>

' <u>at peace with him</u>.

' I find, that when I have Engaged the <u>Friendship</u> of God, I never Want

' a <u>Friend</u>; Engaging y^e <u>Friendship</u> of <u>God</u>, is the best way of Encount-

' ring y^e <u>Malice</u> of <u>Man</u>.

' According to that <u>Promise</u>,

' Prov. 15. 33.

' <u>Before Honour is Humility</u>.

' I do continually find, That my Laying myself in the Dust, is the <u>best</u>

' <u>mean</u> to prevent my being Laid there, by the Abasing Dispensations of

' Heaven: While I maintain a <u>Low Opinion</u> of myself, I grow in favour

' with God and Man.

' According to that <u>Promise</u>,

' Prov. 19. 17.

' <u>He that hath Pitty on the Poor, Lends</u>

' <u>to the Lord, & that which he hath given,</u>

' <u>will He pay him again</u>. [ms. p. 109]

' When a <u>Wrong End</u>, hath not, Like a <u>Dead Fly</u>, Spoiled the Ointment of

' my <u>charity</u>, I find no part of my Estate, putt out unto so good Inter-

' est, as that which I have employ'd upon <u>Pious Uses</u>.

' According to that <u>Promise</u>,

' Mal. 3. 10.

' <u>Lett there be meat in my House, and prove me</u>

' <u>now, Saith the Lord, if I do not poure you out</u>

' <u>a Blessing</u>.

' While I have been, with a Publick Spirit, Serving the <u>House</u> of my Lord

' Jesus Christ, I have been thereby Building <u>my own House</u>, & Providing

' for the welfare of it.

§ Besides my <u>Evening Sacrifices</u> with my Family, in the Beginning of the
Evening, I have taken a Custome, to Sing with my Family, ye Last thing
we do, before we go to Rest, a Verse or two of a Psalm; to wch I alwayes
annex ye Last verse of the IV Psalm.

<u>In Peace with God Ly down I Will</u>;

<u>My quiet Sleep I'l take</u>:

<u>In glad Assurance me to dwell</u>,

<u>Thou, glorious Lord, wilt make</u>

Or,

<u>In Peace with God Ly down I will</u>;

<u>My Quiet Sleep I'l Thankful take</u>.

<u>In glad Assurance me to dwell</u>,

<u>My Great Redeemer, Thou wilt make</u>.

Sometimes I thus varied it.

<u>In Peace with God, & far from Fear</u>,

<u>I'l now Ly down to Rest</u>;

<u>My God, In thy kind Love and Care</u>,

<u>Safe & forever Blest</u>.

[ms. p. 111][66]

The Sixth Lustre

§ My Son; For Some following years,[1] my ((Private)) Memorials were not so filled with Varieties of Contrivances for my Private Walk. My Public Work was indeed so very much, that I could not be so Various in my Private Walk, as heretofore. And it may be an useful Hint unto you, if I tell you; That God, who intended me for very much Public Work, did Strangely prepare me for it; by putting me upon ye Excogitating of such methods for my Private Walk, in ye dayes of my Youth, while I had more Liesure for them.

§   I was no sooner Entred the Twenty Sixth Year of my Age, but a Storm of Persecution from ye Church of England fell upon me. Some Neighbouring Justices fell upon me, for my Breach of the, Act of Uniformity; and they were tearing me to peeces, with their horrible Talons. I was desirous to glorify the Lord JESUS CHRIST on this occasion, and represent how the Spirit of Glory does rest upon those that are Confessors, and Sufferers for Him. I preached therefore, in the very midst of my Troubles, to an Assembly of near two thousand people, gathered from all parts; on Rom. 8. 31. If God be for us, who can be against us? And I Expressed a glorious Triumph, over Enemies & Sufferings. But by ye Strange providence of God, it came to pass, That a Wonderful Change of things upon the Nation, delivered me from ye Storm that was gathering; it all came to Nothing![2] [ms. p. 112]

One thing that makes me mention This but very briefly, and will make me wholly Omitt very many other things full of Remarkables, ((Changes,)) is the Law which I imposed upon myself, at the Beginning of this Collection, To Say nothing, that shall discover, who I am.

And therefore I must very particularly Avoid Saying, What <u>Books</u> I
Wrote from Time to Time, (tho' Some of my most Exquisite <u>Contrivances</u> to
glorify ye Lord, were Still managed in those <u>Books</u>;) Because it will be
impossible to do it, without some Discovery.

§   This year, I found once ye Liesure, to Record, the Result of a SELF-
EXAMINATION, proceeding upon these Articles.

'   Proofs of my REPENTANCE.

' I. I have never been at more Pains for any thing in this world than

' for y^e <u>Mortification</u> of Every Lust.

' II. <u>Afflictions</u>   themselves are Welcome to me, when I See my <u>Sins</u>

' thereby Subdued & Embittered.

'   Of my FAITH.

' I. My Soul is Exceedingly affected with the blessed <u>Fulness</u> and <u>Glory</u>,

' that is the Lord JESUS CHRIST.

' II. My Heart most affectionately closes with the <u>Gospel-way of Salva-</u>

' <u>tion</u> by Jesus Christ, so that I can cheerfully Venture thereupon.

'   Of my LOVE.

' I. Any thing that has a Tendency to promote the Honour of God, is

' readily Embraced by me, and preferred before all the Riches in ye world.

' II. I count no Service too much to be done, for the <u>People of the</u>

' <u>Saints of the Most High</u>. [ms. p. 113]

§ In the Twenty Seventh year of my Life, Once,[3] I dreamt that the Lord
Jesus Christ was coming to <u>Judge</u> the world; at which, with some Raptures
of <u>Joy</u>, and yett Mixtures of <u>Fear</u>, I went forth to meet Him. When I came
into His awful presence, I dream't He Spake to me, after this manner;
<u>Child, Is it Your Sincere Desire to Serve the God of Heaven?</u> and I re-
plied, with Tears, to this purpose, <u>Lord, Thou knowest all things, Thou</u>

knowest that I desire this above all things! Upon which He Said unto me,
Well then; I will not yett have You taken out of ye world; You shall yett
go back, and Live, and Serve the great God! Soon after this Dream, I
fell into a Feavour, which threatned my Life: but yett I Lay Ill no more
than a Little while: In two or three dayes, the Feavour was Conquered.
When I was Recovered So far as to walk into my Study, I found my Heart
wonderfully Expanding, in Desires to be a more Holy and a more Useful man,
than I had been heretofore. But with many Distresses of mind, I Saw,
that I was utterly unable to Be or Do any thing that is Good; that I cannot Resolve, much less Perform, any thing whereby my Redeemer may be glorified. Wherefore, I lay before the Lord, with Humble Groans and Cries
unto Him, to work all in me, & for me: I begg'd of Him, to take full
possession of me, by His own most Blessed Spirit; Unto wch Possession I
did now most affectionately Resign myself: Beleeving, That I should now
be a Temple of that Sacred Spirit, and that He will Dispose me, & Strengthen me, by His Grace, to glorify the Name of my Glorious Lord.
[ms. p. 114]

§   Some Time after this, the Lord brought me to Look upon Dying, with
certain Motions of Soul, which I had not hitherto been ordinarily used
unto. I had been used unto Some Terrors and Recoyles, in ye Thoughts of
Death; unless at the Times of my more near Approaches unto my Redeemer,
in Comunion with Him. Whereas Now, in whatever Company I came, the
Thoughts of Death (accompanied with Hopes, that when my Death shall come,
it will be Natural, and Sudden, and Easy,) had a Strange Kind of pleasure
in them. I Look'd upon Death, with a very Sensible perswasion, of the
Admission, which I shall thereby receive, into Enjoyments to be Impati-
ently Longed for. Tho' I Live Surrounded with Comforts, and few in the

world have so much Content in their Exteriour Concerns as I, yett the Day
of my Death, methinks, will prove, the Best Day that ever I Saw.

As I was Thinking at this rate, with some Company, at the House of
a Knight of my Acquaintance, I Lett them Talk of other things, While I
silently Thought on these. And as I walked in the Room, I took up a Book
in the Window, where I found a Leaf turned down, unto these words:

'   To Think of the Day, in which the Lord will deliver us from the hand
' of all o^e Enemies, & from ye Hand of SIN; Oh! it should fill o^e Hearts
' with Raptures of Joy, & Cause our Hearts to Leap and Spring within us.
' It is an allowable thing, to be almost angry with Time, and Call upon
' Slow Time, Fly apace, Fly away, O Time; Come, O Eternity, come, & fetch
' me into ye presence of ye Lord. '

I Laid this matter up in my Heart. [ms. p. 115]

§ About this Time, I Learn'd the French Tongue; which I would not have mention'd, but that I may tell you, My Son, the Good Providence of God, hath
made it many wayes very advantageous to me. It proved a Key unto Rich
Treasures, in French Authors, wch ye Lord putt into my Hands; & gave me
opportunity also to Write & Print Some things for ye French churches, in
their own Language, which they had occasion for.[4]

I afterwards mastered another Living Tongue of a Nation considerable both in Europe and America, so far that I composed and published a
Book in it, for ye prosecution of some great Evangelical Designs. But
what it was, I will not mention, Lest I be discovered.[5]

§ One of ye Fancies, which I find Collected in my papers about this Time,
I will mention to you, My Son: because you may do well to follow it,
how Fanciful soever it may appear unto you.

I rarely, if Ever, See a Torn Leaf of the Bible, Cast about the Street, Without Stooping, to take it up, and lay it by, with some Respect. But at the Same Time also, I Look into it, as not knowing, but that there may be Some Special Text, by which the Lord would at this Time, send unto me some Heavenly Admonition. I have often found This to be, a profitable practice! [ms. p. 116]

§ In my Public Ministry, in the Twenty Eighth year of my Age, I largely handled ye Doctrine of Temptations; & preached upon ye Temptations of our Lord. Now I had a Special Remark, to make upon it; That no part of my own Life, had been so filled with Buffeting Temptations, as that which ran, while I was thus discoursing on that subject.

My Son; You may Live, to See some use of this Remark: which indeed I have seen since Confirmed in further Instances, that were very Remarkable.

§ I made it a Special Errand of my Praying with Fasting before the Lord, often in this Lustre of my Life; That He would prosper my Studies upon the Apocalyptical Affairs, and accept me in some Service of proclaiming unto the World ye Approaches of the Glorious Things, that are Spoken about the City of God. I conceived, That our Lord Jesus Christ was now hastning apace, towards the Revealing & Erecting of His glorious Kingdome in the World; and I understood by Books, that the Desolations of the Church by Antichrist, were very near accomplished. I therefore Sett myself to Seek of God, That He would Illuminate me, with a right Knowledge of the Mysteries that concern His Kingdome; that He would help me to Discern the Signs of ye Times;[6] & that He would give me such a Sense thereof, as to know what His Israel ought to do.[7]

I had Some Signal and Wondrous Answers to these my poor Supplications; but I must not mention them. [ms. p. 117]

§ My Son, I will here declare to You, an Experiment, that may be a perpetual Encouragement, of your Faithfulness to ye Lord Jesus Christ.

Several very Considerable Gentlemen, in my Church, successively, and unhappily fell into some Scandals. Tho' I were but a Young Man, (& Even before I Entred this Lustre,) I would not permitt the Quality or Interest of those Gentlemen, to intimidate me. I faithfully stuck to ye Rules of ye Lord Jesus Christ, & of His Holy Discipline in His House. I Extended the Discipline of ye Lord unto those Gentlemen, & Compelled them to Submitt unto it. They were Angry: It was not Easy for them to Forgive my Impartiality. But, behold, ye Providence of God! These very Gentlemen afterwards proved, some of the Best Friends I had in the world; no men in ye world, more Loved me, & Served me, & honoured me; Yea, I was hundreds of Pounds the better for some of them. With This Favour, did ye Lord reward my faithful Rebukes of my Friends, for Sinning against Him!

§ I have told you, My Son, That my Publick Work, in this Lustre of my Life, did exceedingly take me up. I very much Lived upon ye Methods formerly Contrived, for my Private Walk. Indeed, I mett with an huge Heap of Experiences in this Time; & my Contrivances to glorify ye Lord Jesus Christ, were more than ever in any part of my Time. Nevertheless, they were so Interwoven into my publick Circumstances, and had Such Dependence on them, & Relation to them, that I [ms. p. 118] cannot here Conveniently Entertain you with them, without hazard of Laying myself open unto further Discovery, if this Book should fall into any Hands but Yours. You will find many of them therefore confined unto Some Other Papers, that are kept under more of Reservation.

I pray God, Bless unto you, the Communications of those other papers,
for your Assistance in being Serviceable in Your Generation. [ms. p. 119]

§   However, this Lustre shall not be passed over, without observing to
You, My Son, One of the most observable Things, that have occurred unto
me in my Pilgrimage.

Good Men that Labour and Abound in Prayer to the great GOD, Sometimes arrive to the Assurance of a PARTICULAR FAITH, for the Good Success of their Prayer.[8] As there is a certain Satisfaction of Soul, in
which all the Faithful are to Encourage themselves, that all their Supplications in general are Heard, by the gracious Lord unto Whom they
Supplicated; and a Praying in Faith, which is a Duty in Every Prayer;[9]
So Sometimes, while the Faithful do Supplicate unto God, they do by a
Special Operation of His Holy Spirit, arise to a Particular Faith, for
the Success of their Supplications, in the most peculiar Instances. The
children of God, in the most of their Supplications, for this or that
Particular Mercy, Sometimes find their Hearts very Comfortably, but unaccountably, Carried forth, to a Strange perswasion, That they shall certainly Receive this Particular Mercy from the Lord: And this perswasion
is not a meer Notion, & Fancy, but a Special Impression from Heaven,
upon the Minds of the Saints, that are made partakers of it. This Particular Faith for a Peculiar Mercy, is not the Attainment of Every Christian: It is only here and there, a Christian, whom the Sovereign Grace
of Heaven does favour with ye Consolations of a Particular Faith; And a
Christian that Enjoyes that Favour, has nothing therein to be boasted of;
inasmuch as there may be persons more eminent for Self-Denial, & for
patience, & for many other vertues, that go without it. And this

Particular Faith for a Peculiar Mercy, is not so much ye Duty of a Chris-

tian, as his Comfort, his Honour, and his Priviledge; A Particular Faith

in prayer, for the Bestowal of Such Blessings, as God bestowes not on

all His Chosen ones; This is not Incumbent on a Christian: tis not Re-

quired of him. There is no Command of the [ms. p. 120] Lord Jesus Christ

broken in it, if we remain in the Dark, about these and those Particular

Events, wch we Spread in o^e prayer before ye Lord. This Particular Faith

is a thing very near akin to ye ancient Faith of Miracles; [Quare,

whether This be not compatible to Reprobates, as well as That?] Highly

Preferr'd, and Advanc'd, and even Lifted up to Heaven, were those persons,

who So tasted of the Powers of the world to Come: Nevertheless it was

not the Sin of Men, to remain destitute of those Powers, until the Lord

should please to Confer them from on High. Now, tis ye Holy Spirit of

the Lord Jesus Christ, that with a Special Operation, does produce in a

Christian this Particular Faith. We read (Jam. 5. 16.) of a, δενϐ/ς

Ενεsγrωεvν.[10] An Energumen is a Possessed person. There is a Posses-

sion of the Holy Spirit, as well as of the Wicked Spirit. Lett a man

Seriously & frequently Resign himself unto the Influences of Heaven, &

by a circumspect Walk watchfully Conform himself unto those Influences:

Thus he will come to be Possessed by the Holy Spirit. When this Pos-

session has proceeded unto some Degrees of Elevated Christianity, y^e

Holy Spirit after a most Wonderful manner, Directs, & Quickens, & En-

flames ye Prayers of the Christian; and there is indeed Something Pro-

phetical in the prayers thus produced. Nor does the Principal Effici-

ency of the Holy Spirit, in these Illapses, Exclude and Hinder y^e

Instrumentality of ye Holy Angels in them. The Holy Angels of the Lord

Jesus Christ, are ye usual Instruments of the Holy Spirit, in those

Operations of His, that we count Extraordinary. We know [ms. p. 121]

ye Message, whereupon _Angels_ Came to _Daniel_, and _Cornelius_;[11] and now, tho' the Visible Appearance of _Angels_ be not now to be Look'd for, yett the _Angels_ of the Lord Jesus Christ, may be They that more Invisibly bring such a Message and Advice from Heaven unto us, & by an Inexpressible Impulse bear it in upon o^e Souls.

My Son; I am now to tell you, that Your Sinful Father, (one of the most Sinful and Shallow Men upon Earth,) has often & often in his Life received this Gift from Heaven, _A Particular Faith in Prayer for Special Mercies_. And tho' I was no Stranger to this _Faith_, before my Coming into _this Lustre_ of my Life, yett I have chosen to defer ye mention of it, until _Now_, because _Now_, I had one of ye Signallest Instances of it, that ever I had in my Life.

While I was _Praying_ and _Fasting_ before ye Lord, for a _Special Mercy_ of great Consequence unto me, & unto many others, and whereof indeed we were in Some Expectation, my mind was marvellously Irradiated from Heaven, with an _Assurance_, That I should receive that _Special Mercy_: And I made a Record of this my Assurance. But, behold, Within a few Hours after my _Particular Faith_, Tidings came to us, That o^e Expectation was all Disappointed; & that things were so unhappily Circumstanced as to leave me very Little Prospect, of my Ever Enjoying the _Special Mercy_, whereof I had been so Assured. Well, I waited with some Astonishment, under the _Sentence of Death_, which I Saw Written upon my _Particular Faith_. But, behold! Almost Three years after, ye Thing was wonderfully accomplished, with all the Advantages imaginable.[12] [ms. p. 122]

As Easy were it for me, to give a Blind Man an _Idea_ of _Light_, as for me to _Describe_ in Words, unto ye understanding of another Man, how one _Enjoies_, and how one _Discerns_ ye Heavenly Favours of a _Particular Faith_. However, I will _Transcribe_ out of my Papers, a Little of what I have Recorded there, from One Instance, instead of many.

'   After I had finished all the other Duties of the Day, I did in my

' Distress, Cast myself <u>Prostrate on my Study-floor</u> before the Lord:

' [Which has been a very frequent <u>Posture</u> of <u>Praying</u>, with me.] There I

' acknowledged my own manifold and horrible <u>Sinfulness</u>, and my worthiness

' by reason of that <u>Sinfulness</u>, to be putt off with <u>Delusions</u>, and have

' a <u>Serpent</u> given to me, when I ask'd and Look'd for y^e <u>Holy Spirit</u>.

' Nevertheless, I that am <u>Dust</u> and <u>Ashes</u>, and worthy to be made so, by

' <u>Fire</u> from Heaven,[13] Crav'd leave to plead with Heaven, Concerning the

' Matter of the <u>Particular Faith</u>, wch had been wrought in my Mind, as I

' thought, by the Lords own Holy Operation. I pleaded, That my Lord

' Jesus Christ, had Invested me with His own glorious <u>Righteousness</u>, and

' was now making <u>Intercession</u> for me in y^e <u>Holy of Holies</u>; and because

' of <u>His</u> Interest there, I might approach the most High God, with Humble

' <u>Boldness</u>, as to a Prayer-Hearing Lord. Having told the Lord, That I

' had alwayes taken a <u>Particular Faith</u>, to be a Work of Heaven on the

' Minds of the Faithful; but if it should prove a <u>Deceit</u>,[14] in that Re-

' markable Instance, which was now ye Cause of my <u>Agony</u>, I should be cast

' into a most wonderful confusion. I then begg'd of the Lord, That if

' my <u>Particular Faith</u> about the matter [ms. p. 123] now Exercising of me,

' were not a Delusion, He would please to <u>Renew</u> it upon me. All this

' while, my Heart had the Coldness of a Stone upon it, and the Strait-

' ness that is to be Expected from the bare Exercise of <u>Reason</u>. But now,

' <u>all on the Sudden</u>, I felt an Inexpressible Force to fall on my Mind;

' an <u>Afflation</u> that Cannot be described in Words; <u>None knowes it, but he</u>

' <u>that has it</u>: If an <u>Angel</u> from Heaven had Spoken it Articulately to me,

' the Comunication would not have been more powerful & perceptible. It

' was told me, That the Lord Jesus Christ Loved me, and that He had not

' permitted me to be Deceived, in my <u>Particular Faith</u>; but that I should

' Live to See ye Accomplishment of it; and that a <u>Sentence of Death</u> shall

' be written on the Effect and Success of my <u>Particular Faith</u>; but y^e

' Lord Jesus Christ, who <u>Raises the Dead</u>,[15] and is the <u>Resurrection &</u>

' <u>the Life</u>,[16] shall give a New Life unto it; He will do it! <u>He will do</u>

' <u>it!</u>

'   And so, having left a Flood of Tears, fetch'd from me, by these

' Rayes from the Invisible world, on my Study-floor, I Rose and Went

' unto my chair.

Thus, <u>My Son</u>, many & many a time, when I have been asking to be Employed

or Assisted in Such & Such Eminent <u>Services</u>, or for y^e <u>Recovery</u> of my

Sick Friends, Especially my children Lying at the point of Death, Yea,

and for some Remarkable changes in the world, I have, in ye Dust before

the Lord, received inexpressible Irradiations upon my Mind, from the

<u>Invisible World</u>, which have Dissolved me into[17] a Flood of Tears, and

Assured me [ms. p. 124] That the Things which I have Desired, would be

performed of the Lord. For my Part, I cannot <u>Beleeve</u>, What and Where I

will; but y^e [18]<u>Particular Faith</u> Produced in me hath still been an Im-

pression from Some <u>Superiour Cause</u>. And I must bear this <u>Testimony</u> for

the Lord, That, tho' oftentimes my <u>Faith</u> has been Try'd unto ye utmost,

by y^e <u>Long Delay</u> of ye Mercy, wch I have Expected, and by its being

thrown into Circumstances, that have Look'd altogether <u>Hopeless</u>, ⟨⟨yea⟩⟩

(and there be three or four very Remarkable Things, that yett remain,

but not <u>Hopeless</u>, to be accomplished,) Yett I cannot Remember, any one

Instance, wherein it has miscarried: but I have known many & many an

one, wherein it has had a⟨⟨n astonishing⟩⟩ Fulfilment unto Amazement.

     I will not go to Illustrate & Embellish, the Story of my own poor

<u>Experiences</u> in this matter, With Parallel <u>Exemples</u> of Others. Tho' I

can Scarce tell how to Leave altogether unmentioned One passage, which
you may find, if you Live, concerning that Blessed Martyr of the Lord,
Mr Holland.

' After Sentence was read against him, he Said, --And now I tell you,
' That God hath heard the Prayer of His Servants, wch hath been poured
' forth with Tears, for His afflicted Saints, which you daily persecute.
' This I dare be bold in God, to Speak; and I am by His Spirit moved to
' Say it; That God will shorten your Hand of Cruelty; For after this Day,
' in this Place, there shall be no more putt unto ye Trial of Fire &
' Faggott. Which accordingly came to pass; He was the Last that was
' burnt in Smithfield. [ms. p. 125]

All that I will here Say further upon it, is This; My Son, Be sure to
maintain, a Prayerful, a Watchful, a Trembling walk with God, and have
an Heart sett up on doing all the Good that Ever you can. It may be,
the Spirit of the Lord JESUS CHRIST, (and this also, not without Surprising Operations of His Holy Angels,) may do Wonderful Things for you.
But if you are favoured with any Special Comunications from Heaven, be
sure to make a Very Humble, & Modest use of them; & Think meanly of yourself, & be not ready to Speak, much Less, to Boast of your Singular
Entertainments;[19] Lest you Grieve the Holy Spirit of God.[20]

§   Thus I have brought you to the Thirtieth Year of my poor, vain,
barren Life. And I will break off, with the Memorable Words in Chanutes
Memoirs. Cum Natalis Dies Februarii admonuisset AEtatis Numerande, Et
TRICESIMO reperissem, invasit me Subita Mæstitia, Et Perculsit admir-
antem, quomodo Sine Sensu Vitae, ad Ejus Culmen Pervenissem, a quo Lux
quælibet fit obscurior, Et Dies nostri ad occasium inclinare incipiunt.
Visu est mihi rerum facies Momento mutata; Et tunc primum me Hominem
agnovi.[21]

❴ But after Several years,[22] I must in ye Margin Enter a Caution
about this Difficult and Marvellous matter. I have had, what I thought
a <u>Particular Faith</u> so baffled in one or two Considerable Things, after a
Strange Course of Experiences, in wch it never fail'd, that I am at a
<u>Perfect Loss, what to make of it</u>. I must not Reproach ye Work, or say,
That it is not <u>often a Gracious Work of Heaven</u>. Yett I must Caution you,
<u>My Son</u>, against Laying too much <u>Stress</u> upon it; Lest it Plunge you into
a <u>Distress</u> that Shall be Wonderful.

A <u>Particular Faith</u> may be a <u>Jewel</u> of God. But y^e <u>Counterfeits</u> of
this <u>Jewel</u> are So very fine, that it will require a Judgment almost <u>more</u>
<u>than Humane</u>, to <u>discern</u> them.[23] I would have you afraid of <u>Enthusiasms</u>;
afraid of <u>Delusions</u>; Content with y^e <u>ordinary Satisfactions</u> of <u>Praying</u>
and <u>Waiting</u>, for ye mercies of God.

It may be, ye Glorious Lord has humbled me, with Some <u>Disappoint-</u>
<u>ments</u>, and <u>Confusions</u>, on purpose that I may be Serviceable unto you
and others, against Certain <u>Errors</u>, into which you might have run, if my
Experiences had alwayes remained Such as they were, when I wrote the
<u>Pages</u> of this Book, & if I had never mett with an Occasion to Lodge in
ye Margins, Such a Caution as I now Sett before you.❵ [ms. p. 127][24]

The Seventh Lustre.

§ My Son, My Employments are still so Publick, and Many, that I rather Live

upon my Old Methods of peculiar Christianitie, than think upon any New

Ones. And tho' I am Still Contriving Innum rable wayes to glorify the

Lord JESUS CHRIST, yett these also are attended with such Public Cir-

cumstances, that I cannot mention them, without being too far discovered.

However, I may find Something or other, in my Reserved Papers, that may

do you Service. ⟨⟨ My Birth-day, at my Finishing the Thirtieth Year of

my Age, falling on a Lords-day, I preached, as Agreeable Things as one

of my Small Capacity Could, on Psal. 102. 24. I Said, O my God, Take me

not away in the midst of my Dayes. At another Time in my Life, my Birth-

day So falling on the Lords-day, I preached on Job. 14. 1. Man that is

born of a Woman, is of few Dayes. At another Time, I did, as blessed Mr

Crook on ye Like occasion alwayes did; Even preach on that, in Luk. 18.

13. God be merciful to me a Sinner. I found Each the Thoughts, whereto

Such Texts Led me at these Times, highly Serviceable to me; and it may

be, they were so to others.⟩⟩   [ms. p. 128]

§   On a certain Day of Prayer with Fasting, which I kept in the Thirty-

first year of my Age, my Special Errand unto the Lord was, This: That

whereas His Good Angels did by His Order, many Good Offices for His

people, He would please to grant unto me, the Enjoyment of those Angeli-

cal Kindnesses and Benefits, which use to be done by His Order, for His

Chosen Servants. I Requested only those Kindnesses, which ye Written

Word of God mentioned, as belonging to the Heirs of Salvation;[1] but I

Requested, that I might Receive those Benefits, in a Manner and Measure,

more Transcendent, than what the great Corruptions in the generality of

Good Men, permitted them to be made partakers of.

Now, that I might be <u>Qualified</u> for this Favour, I first Entreated,
that I <u>May</u> not, and Engaged that I <u>Will</u> not, on the score of any <u>Angeli-</u>
<u>cal Communications</u>, forsake ye Conduct of the Lords <u>Written Word</u>, but
apply myself more than ever, to the assiduous and reverent Contemplation
of that <u>Word</u>.

I proceeded then, to Consider, What things would render me Singularly Agreeable to ye Holy <u>Angels</u> of God; and for my Assistence in those
things, I humbly Implored the Grace of the Lord.

It was now my purpose,

To be Entirely <u>Devoted</u> unto God, in all the wayes of <u>Dedicating</u>
<u>Holiness</u>.

To be Continually <u>Contriving</u>, how to glorify God, in being Eminently
<u>Serviceable</u>.

To be much in Studies upon the <u>Person</u> and upon the <u>Kingdome</u>, of the
Lord JESUS CHRIST; which things the <u>Angels desire to Look into</u>.[2]
[ms. p. 129]

To be more Useful than ever unto my Neighbours in their <u>Afflictions</u>;
that by my Hand there may be done, Things that the <u>Angels</u> Love to do.

Finally, To <u>Conceal</u> with all <u>Prudent Secrecy</u>, the <u>Extraordinary</u>
<u>Things</u>, which I may perceive done for me, by the <u>Angels</u>, who love <u>Secrecy</u>
in their Administrations.

In the close of these proceedings, I wrote these words;

<u>I do now Beleeve, That Some Great Things are to be done for me, by</u>
<u>the ANGELS of God</u>.

And now, <u>My Son</u>, It is <u>not Lawful for me to utter</u>,[3] the marvellous
and amazing Favours, which I have Since received from ye Blessed ANGELS.
I have Seen, and felt, most wonderful Effects of their <u>Ministry</u>,

Directing my Studies, Assisting my Labours, Preventing of Wrong Steps which
I have been just ready to take; Supplying my Wants, and Comforting me under
& against my Temptations. Yea, their Ministry hath proceeded So far, that
I must here bear this Testimony, against the Sadducism of this Generation,
That I have as infallible Demonstration of the Existence and Agency of
those Heavenly Spirits,[4] as I have to prove any matter of Sense in the world.
It is possible I may Leave to you, My Son, a particular History by itself,
of Angelical Operations, and of Matters of Fact, relating to things done
by Good and Bad Angels, whereof I have been myself an Attentive Witness:
Tho' I must not Forgett my promise of Concealing Such Things as are not
proper to be Exposed. [ms. p. 130]

I will therefore dismiss this matter for the present; With only mentioning Two Remarkable Passages.

One is This. Very Soon after the Day of Prayer, which I have Specified, a Squadron arrived from the West-Indies, on board of which, there
was a Considerable Army, return'd from a Fruitless Expedition there. I
was desired, by many of the Officers, to give them a Sermon, on a certain
Lords-day, upon an Island, where they putt ashore, to Air themselves. I
rashly undertook it; but while I was in his Excellencies Barge, I was
taken So very Sick, that my Friends would needs carry me back again. I
was well as Soon as I came home; and the Admiral afterwards told me, It
was well for me, that I went no farther. For ye Army, had newly Suffered
a fearful Desolation, by a Sickness more Infectious & more Destructive
than ye Plague itself; And had I gone, and Conversed among So Infectious
a Company, it would probably have Cost me my Life, as it proved Mortal
unto very many others of my Neighbours, who were so hardy as to go down
among them. I have cause to think, It was a Good Angel, wch then struck
me Sick, & so Sav'd my Life.

Another is This; There fell out in my Neighbourhood, not many months
after the Day of Prayer above Said, an astonishing Thing, which I am well
Satisfied, is true; It were unreasonable for me, to desire a greater Satisfaction, than I had for ye Truth of it.   I will insert it, as I chose then
for some Reasons, to insert it, in ye Language, wch I thought most proper
for it.

Res Mirabilis, et Memorabilis.   Post fusas, Maximis Cum Ardoribus
Jejunijsqu preces, apparuit Angelus, [ms. p. 131] qui Vultum habuit Solis
instar Meridiani Micantem, Caetera Humanum, at prorsus Imberbem; Caput
Magnifica Tiara obvolutum; In Humeris, Alas: Vestes deinceps Candidas et
Splendidas: Togam nempe Talarem, et Zonam circa Lumbos, Orientalium
Cingulis non absimilem.

Dixitqum hic Angelus, a Domino JESU Se missum, ut Responsa Cujusdam
Juvenis Precibus articulatim afferat.

Quamplurima retulit hic Angelus, quae hic Scribere non fas est.
Verum inter alia Memorata digna, futurum hujusce Juvenis Fatum, optime
Posse Exprimi asseruit, in illis Vatis Ezekielis Verbis.[5]

EZEK. 31. 3, 4, 5, 7, 8, 9.

Behold, He was a Cedar in Lebanon, with fair Branches, and with a
Shadowing Shroud, & of an High Stature, and his Top was among the Thick
Boughs.

The Waters made him Great, the Deep Sett him up on high, with her
Rivers running about his plants.

His Heighth was Exalted above all the Trees of the Field, and his
Boughs were multiplied, and his Branches became Long, because of the
multitude of Waters, when they shott forth.

Thus was he fair in his Greatness, in the Length of his Branches,
for his Root was by the great Waters.

Nor was any Tree in the Garden of God, Like unto him, in his Beauty.

I have made him fair by the multitude of his Branches; so that all the Trees of Eden, that were in the Garden of God, Envied him.

Atqu Particulariter clausulas, de Ramis Ejus Extendendis, Exposuit hic Angelus, de Libris ab hoc Juvene Componendis, Et Publicandis. Addiditqu peculiares quasdam praedictiones, [ms. p. 132] de Operibus Insignibus, quae pro Ecclesia Christi, in Revolutionibus jam appropinquantibus, hic Juvenis olim facturus Est.

Domine JESU! Quid sibi vult haec res tam Extraordinaria? A Diabolicis Illusionibus, Obsecro te, Servum tuum Indignissimum, ut Liberes ac defendas.[6]

At another Time, and in another place, tis possible, My Son, I may tell you more. All that I will here Say, is; Be Sure to Beleeve, That there are Holy Angels, and Behave yourself So Holily that ye Good Angels may take pleasure to do you Good; But keep close to the Written Word of God, in your whole Conduct, and affect not Extraordinary Dispensations, Lest you run into Delusions and Confusions, of ye worst Consequence imaginable. Your Sinful Father, has more than Ordinary Cause, to Bless ye Lord, for his own preservation from them. [ms. p. 133]

§ This year, I buried, both a Son and a Daughter. But I must here bear this Testimony for the Lord; That while one of ye Children was Lying Sick, I had my Heart wonderfully Melted in Prayer with it; Not for ye Life of it, but with Rapturous Assurances, of ye Divine Love unto me and Mine; wherein so great was my Unspeakable Joy, that I wrote upon it, It would have made Amends for the Death of more children, if God had Called for them.

Indeed, I have buried Five children, Two Sons, and Three Daughters;[7]

But the Lord has alwayes assisted me to glorify Him, with some Degree of

Patience and Cheerfulness, under my Bereavements; and Exemplify unto my

Flock, ye Way of <u>Living by Faith</u>,[8] under Such a <u>Death</u> of Dear Enjoyments.

And it may not be amiss, here to mention, that, as Expressions of

my poor <u>Faith</u>, I ordered y^e <u>Epitaphs</u>, on ye Gravestones of ye children.

On, ye First;

<u>Of Such is the Kingdome of Heaven</u>.

On ye Second;

<u>Reserv'd for a glorious Resurrection</u>.

On ye Third;

<u>Gone, but not Lost</u>.

On ye Fourth;

<u>Your Bones shall flourish as an Herb</u>.

On ye Fifth;

<u>Not as they that have no Hope</u>.

They are Since, all of them Lodg'd in one <u>Tomb</u>, together. [ms. p. 134]

§This year, my Little and only Bird, ((who is now, <u>My Son</u>, Your Eldest

Sister,)) was taken so dangerously Sick, that Small Hope of her <u>Life</u>, was

Left unto us.[9] In my Distress, when I saw ye Lord thus <u>Quenching the Coal</u>

<u>that was Left</u>[10] unto me, and rending out of my Bosom, One that had Lived

so long with me, as to Steal a <u>Room</u> there, and a <u>Lamb</u> that was indeed unto

me <u>as a Daughter</u>, I cast myself at the Feet of His Holy Sovereignty.

When I was going to Resign the Dying Child, in a <u>Prayer</u> for that purpose

over it, I took the <u>Bible</u> into my Hand, Resolving to Seek and Read first,

some agreeable Portion of the <u>Scripture</u>. The <u>First</u> place, that accident-

ally fell under my view, was, the story of o^e Lords Raising the <u>Little</u>

Daughter of the <u>Ruler of the Synagogue</u>, in the Eighth Chapter of <u>Luke</u>.[11]
Amazed at the pertinency of the place, I readd it with <u>Tears</u>; and then,
with more <u>Tears</u> I turned it into a <u>Prayer</u>; wherein I freely gave up this
child unto ye Lord; Assured, That it should be a <u>Vessel</u> of His <u>glory</u> forever. But I also begg'd for ye Life of the Child in this World; promising to the Lord, with His Help, That I would bring her up for <u>Him</u>,
and that I would Likewise assay to do Some Special Service quickly for
ye Young people of my Neighbourhood. Immediately, the child fell into a
Critical and plentiful <u>Bleeding</u>, and Recovered from that Hour, unto the
Admiration of us all. However, <u>This Day</u> to prepare my own Heart for all
Events, and Express what should be in ye Heart of others, I preached a
Sermon on those words, <u>The Lord is able to give thee much more than
this</u>.[12] [ms. p. 135]

§   I'l transcribe one short passage, wch I find in the Beginning of my
Thirty Second year, occurring on a Day of Secret Supplications.
'   God helped me this Day, Solemnly to Accept of Him, as my <u>Father</u>, in
' the <u>New Covenant</u>, and solemnly to Devote myself unto the Work of
' <u>Glorifying</u> His Name, in my Generation. Whereupon I concluded, That
' without any anxious <u>Carefulness</u>, I might Safely Leave all my Concerns
' unto His All-wise Disposals forever. <u>He Careth for me</u>.[13] Upon this I
' queried; Is not here the <u>Spirit of Adoption</u>, crying, <u>Abba, Father</u>.[14]

My Son, I must not Stay with you. Behold, I instruct you, how to
make sure of a <u>Father</u>, that will <u>never Leave You, nor Forsake You</u>.[15]

§ Much of ye Spirit of my Devotions, in my <u>Prayers</u> with <u>Fastings</u>, (whereof
I kept many whole Dayes, and for a Long while usually at Least one Every
week,) this year, was a <u>Resignation</u> of myself unto ye Lord <u>Jesus Christ</u>,
and a <u>Supplication</u> for His <u>Holy Spirit</u>, that I might be Employ'd in

Considerable Services for Him. Now inasmuch as there have been some Re-
markable Effects of these my Addresses unto ye Lord; and I am very much
Concerned, That you, My Son, may do more Considerable Services, for y^e
Lord Jesus Christ, than ever your poor, Shallow, Slothful, & Sinful
Father did, I will transcribe a few of the passages, which I have Record-
ed, of these my Addresses unto Heaven. [ms. p. 136]

At one Time,

' The Agonies of my Soul this Day, Caused me to cast myself prostrate on
' my Study-floor, where in the Dust, I Several times Poured out my Soul
' before the Lord.

'   There I received wonderful, and Heart-melting Assurances, That the
' God of Heaven had Pardoned all my Sins, for the Sake of the Lord Jesus
' Christ.

'   But this is not all. I cried unto God, with Floods of Tears, That
' His Holy Spirit may take possession of me, and Gloriously Fill me, and
' Act me, and make me an Instrument of doing very Great Services for His
' glorious Name. While I was doing thus, my Soul was in a manner Ex-
' tasied, with Powerful perswasions, That it would be so.

At another Time.

' While Fasting and Praying in my Study before the Lord this Day, pros-
' trate on my Study-floor, I received a Fresh & Strong Assurance, That
' the Lord Jesus Christ, unto the Glorifying of whom, I have Consecrated
' all my Interests, would Accept me, & Employ me, even Mee the vilest of
' men, to Do Some Great Services, for the glory of His Blessed Name.

At another Time.

' I Received & uttered a Strange Assurance, That God would make use of
' me, to Glorify ye Name of my dear Lord Jesus Christ; and that after-
' wards, when I came to Dy, I should not only have a Happy, but also an

' <u>Easy, Pleasant, Joyful Death</u>, and go away Triumphing wth Joy into y^e

' Paradise¹⁶ of God. [ms. p. 137]

At another Time.

' I essayed, with a Wrestling Soul, to give myself up, unto the Service

' of <u>Glorifying</u> the Name of my <u>Everglorious Lord Jesus Christ</u>; and unto

' y^e <u>Special Possession</u> of His <u>Holy Spirit</u>, that so I might be Prepared

' & Employed for His Glory. Tho' this be a thing, which I have been

' doing for so many thousands of times, for many years together, yett I

' now did it with a <u>Singular Effort</u> of Soul. And in doing of it, I Con-

' fessed my own Worthiness to be Rejected from this Happiness; But I

' Beleeved, That the <u>Disposal of all Opportunities</u> to Glorify the Lord,

' were Entirely in His own Hands, for which Cause, I Resigned myself unto

' Him, with a Sweet Acquiescence of Soul, about all my <u>Future Improve-</u>

' <u>ments</u>. I Beleeved, That He had <u>Himself inclined</u> me now to Cry unto

' Him, that He would make use of me, because He had a <u>Secret Purpose</u> in

' His own Heart so to do. I Beleeved, finally, That He had some <u>Signal</u>

' <u>Services</u> for me to do unto His Interests.

Yea, t'was after an unaccountable manner bore in upon my mind, what

the <u>Services</u> were. And unto my Astonishment, I have Since beheld the

Things almost unaccountably accomplished.

At another Time.

' The Lord helped me this Day, in a more Particular manner, to bewayl the

' Sin of <u>Selfishness</u>, Wofully cleaving to my Soul. I am Exceedingly prone

' to Consider my <u>Self</u>, as my <u>End</u>, and from <u>Self</u>, to take the measures

' both of my Comforts, & of my Troubles; not Subordinating distinctly all

' things unto the Great <u>GOD</u>, nor Swallowing up all <u>my</u> Interests in <u>His</u>.

' God gave me to See the [ms. p. 138] Wickedness of my own <u>Selfishness</u>,

' and Condemn and Abhor my <u>Self</u>, on ye Score of it. Now, begging my
' <u>Pardon</u>, thro' the Lord JESUS CHRIST, who <u>Pleased not Himself</u>,[17] I
' humbly Dedicated <u>myself</u>, and all that I <u>Have</u>, and all that I <u>Do</u>, unto
' the Lord. Yea, in the Lively Salleyes of my Soul, to Converse with
' GOD, as my <u>All in All</u>, I proceeded so far, as to Consent unto Him,
' <u>That if I have any One Enjoyment, which it was not for His glory, that</u>
' <u>I should Still possess, He should, at His Pleasure deprive me of it</u>.
' And this Day, the Lord Renewed my Assurances, That He would Accept me,
' & Employ me, in some Eminent Services, for ye Name of my precious Lord-
' Redeemer.

At another Time.
' This Day I did again, as in the Last Week, draw near unto the Lord,
' <u>Fasting</u> and <u>Prayer</u>. I had a peculiar presence of the Lord with me, in
' the Duties of the Day; Especially, when Crying to God, That <u>I might</u>
' <u>glorify my precious Lord Jesus Christ</u>. I pleaded with the Lord, That
' He often gratified the children of Men, when they asked <u>other Great</u>
' <u>Things</u> for themselves, with a more <u>Selfish</u> Disposition of Mind; Yea,
' He often did <u>Great Things</u> for them that never asked Him. Whereas, I
' did not ask for <u>Long Life</u>, nor for the <u>Riches</u> and <u>Honours</u> of this Life.
' Instead thereof, His own <u>Holy Spirit</u> had Inclined me, to ask nothing
' but <u>This</u>. Lett me be <u>Little</u>, and have <u>Little</u> in the matters of this
' world; but, <u>Oh, Lett me do Great Things</u> [ms. p. 139] <u>for the Name of</u>
' <u>my Glorious Lord Jesus Christ</u>. Oh, Lett me glorify that matchless Lord
' Exceedingly! I know, The Eternal God infinitely desires the <u>glory</u> of
' the Lord JESUS CHRIST, in whom His <u>Delight</u> is infinite. And I now
' made my Humble offer unto Him, that I might be accepted & Employed by
' Him, in the doing of Some Eminent things for the <u>glory</u> of that peerless
' LORD. He knowes, That this <u>is all my Salvation, & all my Desire!</u>[18]

' Glorious now was the Satisfaction of my Soul, in a Powerful & a Raptur-
' ous <u>Assurance</u>, That my Lord JESUS CHRIST, would, with the Directions
' and Assistences of His Holy Spirit, employ me, in the Doing of Services
' for the <u>Glory</u> of His Name.

  In another part of this Day, I cried Earnestly to God, That He would
' make me very <u>Like</u> unto His <u>Holy Angels</u>; and having obtained an <u>Assur-</u>
' <u>ance</u> of my being a <u>Fellow-Servant</u> with those Blessed Spirits, I pro-
' ceeded then to Implore this of the Lord: That His <u>Holy Angels</u> might
' marvellously take <u>Possession</u> of me, Lead me, Act me, Incline me, Assist
' me, Defend me, & <u>Apply</u> me to such Blessed Purposes, as may be Continu-
' ally for the Service of that Great LORD, Who is <u>Theirs</u> and <u>Mine</u>. And
' my Assurance hereof Carried me into ⟨⟨19⟩⟩ an uncommon Satisfaction.

  At another Time.

' This Day, Sitting in my Chair, I burst into an unusual Flood of Tears,
' which ran down my Face, in the Consideration of my being a Wretched,
' Filthy, Loathsome Creature, and one fearfully Empty of what might Rec-
' ommend me to God or Man. But my Heart was then Raised with Admiration
' at the [ms. p. 140] <u>Free-Grace</u> of God, which will Employ Such a Crea-
' ture to be an Instrument of His Glory. The <u>Unutterable Communion</u> with
' God in Christ by the Spirit, which I was hereupon admitted unto, no
' pen may, or can Relate.

  At another Time.

' When I was uttering some of my <u>Unutterable Groans</u>[20] before the Lord,
' That I might be Improved, in ye doing of some <u>Great Things for the Lord</u>
' <u>JESUS CHRIST</u>, my Importunate Soul, received an Answer equivalent unto
' a Voice from Heaven, <u>That it shall be so!</u>

  At another Time,

' I Sett myself to cry unto the Lord this Day, <u>That He would Employ me</u>

' in great Service for the glory of my Lord Jesus Christ. And when I
' was, prostrate on my Study-floor, with a Confession of my own infinite
' unworthiness, to be thus employ'd, & of the wonderful & Illustrious
' Grace which must be display'd in it, if ever I, the Silliest, Yea, the
' Sinfullest of my Generation, should come to be thus Employ'd; Pleading
' yett, That the Lord had Eminently Employ'd Many, that never had Asked
' this Favour, with so much Importunity, as the Lord, by His own Spirit,
' had Caused poor me, to Ask it; for Hee knew, how frequently & fervently
' I asked it, & indeed Chose it for my Greatest Happiness, undervaluing
' all things in Comparison of it: A Flood of Tears now gushed from me;
' My Tears ran down upon my Study-floor; in a Strange Assurance, That
' the Lord had heard my Supplications.[21] But because I am very Unfit,
' for the service [ms. p. 141] of the Lord Jesus Christ, I Lifted up my
' Cries from the Dust, unto the Lord, That His own Holy Spirit might See
' me, and find me, Sieze me, & fill me, there: and make me a Discreet,
' Reserv'd, Holy, Humble, Prayerful and Watchful Man; and give me
' Another Spirit.

My Son; It is not fit for Me to mention at any Time, (and Especi-
ally in these Papers, where I am to Study all possible Concealment,)
what Marvellous and Amazing Answers, ye Strange Providence of Heaven,
hath given to these Prayers of a Vile Sinner before the Lord.[22] It is
Enough, if I tell you, the Answers have been Enough, to Encourage You,
My Son, unto ye Imitation of Your poor Father, in Such Intentions and
Petitions, as I have thus taught you, to become[23]Serviceable in Your
Generation. [ms. p. 142]

§   This Year, I kept one Day of THANKSGIVING, in Secret before the
Lord, whereof I will give you, My Son, a more Particular Account, than

of ye rest, because of Something more Singular and Instructive, in it.

I Considered, That as by the Praises of God, I should become Like the Good Angels, thus it was a very Reasonable Thing, that I should offer my Extraordinary Praises to Him, for His Angels.

I Saw, That the Scriptures mentioned the Ministry of the Good Angels, about the Heirs of Salvation, with a very glorious Frequency: and I Saw, That my Life had been wondrously Signalized, by the Sensible Ministry of those Angels. Wherefore, Lothe to be Guilty of Such an ungrateful and unthoughtful Neglect of the Angels, as the Generality of the Faithful, who Enjoy the Assistences of these Heavenly Guardians, are, I Devoted this Day, To glorify the God & Father of my Lord JESUS CHRIST, for the Ministry of ANGELS, which has notably befriended me, unto this very Day. And I expected, in this way, not only to render myself more agreeable to those Excellent Spirits, but also to obtain from Their and My Lord, a more Notable Share of their Influence, than had ever yett been granted me.

In the Evening before this Day, I was Amaz'd when I beheld, but Happy that I Plainly beheld, the happening of Several things, that Seemed, as it were, Contrived on purpose, to Indispose me for the Duties now before me; But I Comfortably gott over all those Indispositions. [ms. p. 143]

How many Hymns, referring to the Angels, I Sang this Day, t'wil be needless for me to Relate.

In the morning, I wrote an Illustration upon a Text, about the Angels. And I made my Family-Offering Suitable to the Designs before me.

And one Law, which I Laid upon myself this Day, was, That in all the Intervals of more Stated Thinking, as I passed from one object unto another, I would make Ejaculatory Thanksgivings unto the Lord, upon all the Occasions which offered themselves unto me. But how many Scores of Ejaculations thus Occasionally acknowledging the Greatness and Goodness of God, passed from me this Day, I can make no Computation.

My Chief Exercise in the Forenoon, was, To Consider Exactly, and with as much of Scripture and Learning, as I could, the Existence, the Properties, and the Relations of the Good Angels; and the Honour, tho' not Worship, due to those Benign Spirits: And then, to Run over the Marvellous References to their Ministry, which I found Scattered here and there in the Oracles of God; Whether towards Particular Saints, or towards the Church in general. These Considerations, with a Vast Varietie, took in the chief of the Story of the Bible, together with the Apocalyptical prophecies, Especially in the Trumpetts, and Vials, wherein Angels are concerned. But my Considerations were still directed unto the Lord, with my Desires, That He should be forever Magnified and Glorified, for all the Things, in which He had thus Commissioned His Angels, to be His Messengers & His Instruments. [ms. p. 144]

Tis impossible for me, to Express fully, the Elevation of Soul, wherewith I went thro' these noble Exercises; Which Exercises, at Last, I Concluded, with Assurances, That I should one Day Come to Praise Him that Sitts upon the Throne, and ye Lamb, in the Company[24] of His Holy Angels forever.

In the Afternoon, I look'd over Some Catalogues of Mercies received from the God of Heaven, which I had heretofore Entred in my Diaries; and by Comparing of what I Read in y^e ⟨⟨ Sacred⟩⟩ Book of Heaven, about the Agency of Angels, I Examined, where I might make an Allowance, for their Subordinate Agency, in my own Affairs.

The main Heads of _Kindnesses_ done for me, which the Word of God permitted me to count _Angelical_, were these.

I. I have Reason to think, That the _Parental Government_, which in my Childhood, was a Thousand wayes a Blessing to me, had a _Biass_ very often given to it, by the _Angels_ of God.

I considered, Judg. 13. 12, 13. and Mat. 2. 13.

II. I have been _Preserved_ from and in many _Dangers_, while I was yett a child; by the _Angels_ Looking after me.

I considered, Matth. 18. 10.

III. In my _Education_ I was wonderfully Circumstanced, by Helps and Means of _Learning_, and a Capacity to Learn, and a Kind Conduct of _Tutors_: which doubtless the _Angels_ influenced.

I considered, Gen. 21. 17, 18, 19.

IV. When Epidemical _Sicknesses_ have carried off many of my Neighbours, [ms. p. 145] and I have been in the midst of them, I have been kept unto this Day; by an Hedge of _Angels_ about me.

I considered, Psal. 91. 3, 4.

V. I have made many _Journeyes_; but never yett Came to any Harm in any of them: Why? The _Angels_ were my Keepers.

I considered, Psal. 91. 11, 12.

VI. I was Blessed with an Early _Conversion_ to God; and the Eternal Spirit of God, hath been Ever Since, marvellously at work upon my Soul, to fitt me for ye Society of _Angels_ in a better world. Here was a _Joy_, and as to many Circumstances of it, a _Work_, of _Angels_.

I considered, Luk. 15. 10.

VII. My Call to the _Ministry_ of the Gospel, and the Hearts of People being so disposed, that I have had my Call in so remarkable a place, as where my Lott is Cast, has been a Thing full of _Wonders_, and I don't fear to Say, full of Angels.

I considered, Act. 16. 9, 10.

VIII. The Door of Utterance opened for me, hath Some Surprizing things in it, wch I am Certain have proceeded from the Angels of God.

I considered, Luk. 1. 20. and, Isa. 6. 6, 7.

IX. My Strange Opportunities to Serve the Church of God, both by Speaking and Writing, and the astonishing Impulse oftentimes on my Mind thereabout, I have been amazed thereat! But there hath been the Energy of Angels in it all along.

I considered, Act. 10. 30, 32. and Act. 8. 29.

X. My Marriage was under a Direction of Angels; and the Condition of my Family Ensuing thereupon.

I considered, Gen. 24. 7.   [ms. p. 146]

XI. The Provision of a Food Convenient for me, hath been so Stupendously Nick'd many times, that I were Blinder than a Stone, if I should not see Angels my Providers.

I considered, Psal. 78. 25.

XII. Unreasonable Men that had no Faith, have zelously Sought my Ruine, for my Faithfulness to ye Interests of the Lord; but I have had an Host of Angels for my Guard.

I considered, Gen. 33. 4. and, Dan. 6. 22.

XIII. My Lost Health has been Restored & Prolonged; Have not the Angels been my Physicians?

I considered, Joh. 5. 4.

XIV. Many a time, have I been Ready to do those things, which would have been very Contrary to Gods glory, very pernicious to my own welfare; but I have been very Strangely Hindred: By Whom? Truly, by ye Angels of the Lord.

I considered, Num. 22. 32.

Such Things as these, I did, prostrate on my Study-floor, acknowledge unto the Lord, with multiplied Hallelujahs. And in the midst of
ye Rapturous Hallelujahs, I could not forbear Saying, Bless the Lord, O
my Soul, & forgett not all His Benefits! Yea, if any Good Angels of the
Lord are now nigh unto me, do you also Bless the Lord, Yee Heavenly
Ministers; And, Oh, Adore that Free-grace of His, which Employes You,
to be Serviceable unto so poor, So mean, so Vile a Wretch, as is here
Lying in the Dust before Him. [ms. p. 147] From hence I went on, unto
Supplications, That the Great GOD would now go on more than ever, to
Employ His Good Angels for my Good; Which I then also Particularized in
many Articles: And that He would also preserve me from ye Illusions and
Injuries of Evil ones.

I then Considered, What Returns I should make unto the Lord, for the
Benefits, which I have Received by His Angels. And here, I Thought on
the Message, which an Angel brought from Heaven, unto One of his Fellow-
Servants, towards the Close of a Day Spent in Extraordinary Devotions;
Thou art a Desireable man. [Dan. 9. 23.] So I Spent an Hour or two,
in Considering, What would render me Such a man.

One Special Thing, Wherein I proposed unto myself, a way to become
Desireable, was, to become Angelical.

Accordingly, I Considered;

How the Angels were Continually Engaged in Beholding and Admiring
the Glories of the Great GOD. [Matth. 18. 10.]

How the Angels were Continually Studying the Mysteries of Redemption
by the Lord JESUS CHRIST, and the characters & Approaches of His Kingdome. [1 Pet. 1. 12.]

How the Angels were Continually upon the Wing, to go upon whatever Errands, the King of Heavens shall Employ them in. [Psal. 103. 20, 21.]

How the Angels were Continually Doing of Good, among the people and the Churches of the Lord. [Heb. 1. 14.]

How the Angels took particular Satisfaction in the Conversion of Miserable Sinners. [Luk. 15. 10.]

How the Angels, in fine, were Holy Angels. [ms. p. 148]

These Things I Considered, for my own Imitation.

But, for the Close of all; Because I thought, it would be a Little Angelical, as well as otherwise Agreeable, I took a List of many poor people in my Flock, with some Care to have their Necessities Releeved against the approaching Winter.

And so the Day Ended.

§ In ye following Year I kept Several (more than one or two) Dayes of THANKSGIVING, in my Retirements. And one of them also, I will single out, here to give you, My Son, Some Account of it, because there may be for you something Instructive in it. I find it Recorded in Such Terms as these.

' Having Spent one day this week in Secret Humiliations and Supplications
' before the Lord, I thought it was not amiss to Spend another in Secret
' THANKSGIVINGS; and I sett apart this Day accordingly.

'   I did this Day Endeavour, to fetch out of all sorts of Objects,
' that occasionally occurr'd unto me, occasions for Ejaculatory Thanks
' givings: And perhaps many Scores of Hallelujahs were thus formed in
' the Intercalar, and Intervening Thoughts of the Day; [ms. p. 149] by
' which I was kept in better Tune, for the more Solemn Exercises, that
' were before me.

'   I began the Day, with singing some Hymns, which I had Composed from
'   certain passages of the New Testament, in Honour of my Glorious Lord
'   JESUS CHRIST; and afterwards I intermixed Such Hymns, with the other
'   Duties of the Day.

'   Indeed I designed, that the Special character, by which this Day of
'   Thanksgiving should be distinguished, with me, should be, The payment
'   of Acknowledgments unto my Lord JESUS CHRIST.

'   I Read over the Records of many former Thanksgivings, Entred in my
'   papers, with Pauses and Praises upon the Several Articles thereof.

'   With my Family, I Readd the Hundred & Third Psalm, and Largely
'   paraphrased in Prayer upon it.

'   Part of the Day, I had my Consort with me, in my Study; and We to-
'   gether Praised the Lord, for the Mercies & Effects of o^e Conjugal
'   Relation.

'   My Present Good Circumstances, I did in my Study, on my knees, Con-
'   fess unto the Lord; ennumerating them under those Two Heads; My Life,
'   and the Comforts of That; My Work, and the Supports of That.

'   But intending a Special Consideration of my Lord JESUS CHRIST, in
'   this my Thanksgiving, I shall here preserve to myself, the memory of
'   Especially Two Transactions, which I now had, relating thereunto.

'   One was in the Forenoon; When I did Particularly Recapitulate in my
'   Devotions, the glories of my Lord JESUS CHRIST; therewithal [ms. p.
'   150] Declaring, That He is infinitely Worthy that I should make the
'   Glorifying of Him, to be my Chief End, and Aim, and Happiness. Where-
'   upon I did, with Tears, Give up myself unto Him, Entreating, That
'   under the Influences of His Holy Spirit, I might Serve Him forever.

'   T'other was, in the Evening; When, Recounting the Comfortable Things,

' wch I do Enjoy, I did Particularly Enquire and Ponder, How my Lord

' JESUS CHRIST in His Humiliation, did Suffer Afflictions just Contrary

' to my Enjoyments; and unto these bitter Sufferings of His, did I as-

' cribe the Purchase and the Reason, of all those good Things which are

' bestow'd upon me.

'   In the Close of all, I gave Thanks unto my Lord JESUS CHRIST, for

' Spiritual and Eternal Mercies, & the Benefits of the other World, where-

' to He had Entitled me, & was preparing me; the Inchoating Marks where-

' of, I did, upon a Self-Examination, Thankfully mention before Him:

' And then, for the Ministry of His Holy Angels, who, being Sent by Him,

' had often & often done me very wonderful Kindnesses, and I beleeved,

' would still do so.

'   By way of Gratitude for these things, I Renewed my Dedication of my-

' self, unto my Lord JESUS CHRIST; and I Resolved, That it should be more

' than ever, my main Business Every where, to Render and Procure Acknow-

' ledgments of His Glories: And, I Said, That with His Help, I would

' Endeavour particularly to Vindicate the Name of Christianitie, by

' preaching publickly on a Case of that Importance, What is a Christian?

' or, What it is to be a Christian! [25] [ms. p. 151]

'   But apprehending myself, now fallen into a more than ordinary Speed-

' ing Time, for whatever Concern I would Spread before the Lord, I took

' this Time, to say before Him, That I now knew, He would, for the Sake

' of my Lord JESUS CHRIST, be ready to grant me any thing, that I should

' Wisely ask of Him. If there were any thing for the Glory of my Lord

' JESUS CHRIST, which I would Now Petition for, in ye Conclusion of a Day

' Spent in the Praises of my most precious Lord, I was very Sure, it

' should not be denyed unto me. Accordingly, One of my Supplications now

' was, That my Lord JESUS CHRIST, may have England, Scotland and Ireland

' given unto Him; That He may quickly take glorious Possession of those

' Kingdomes; & bring about Mighty & happy Changes there, & make ye Cor-

' rupt Church-State ⟨⟨there⟩⟩ for to Vanish before ye morning Light of

' a Wonderful Reformation. And my Soul could not but think, That ⟨⟨26⟩⟩

' Something should anon be this way Endeavoured & accomplished; Tho' no

' Great Matter will be done before ye Coming of ye Lord.

My Son, I have proposed, in Transcribing these things, to teach you some Varieties for Your Thanksgivings. Oh, Lett your Life be as full of them as you can; They will make you a Lively Christian. [ms. p. 152]

§   One Lords-day in this year, Preaching on Luk. 2. 8. The Shepherds keeping a Watch over their Flock; & Propounding This, among other observations upon it, They that have any Flocks belonging to them, should faithfully, Carefully, Watchfully Look after their Flocks: I Lett fall certain Passages in ye Application thereof, which I am Willing to Transcribe in this place, as carrying in them some Instruction, for which, I hope, You, My Son, may Live to make some Improvement.

' Lett me Entreat of My own Flock, this Kindness, this Justice. Oh, help

' Mee, by Your Compassionate Prayers, That I may neglect nothing of the

' Duty, which I owe unto my Flock. If you say, That I owe you my All,

' All my Love, All my Strength, All my Time, I Confess the Debt. But

' then You owe Something too; Even Your Prayer unto o^e Common Lord for

' me, That I may well & truly discharge this Debt. My Soul desires to

' walk humbly under the Awe of that Word, Heb. 13. 17. They Watch for

' your Souls, as those that must give an Account. In the Day of Judg-

' ment, when I shall give up my Account unto ye Judge of all, I would

' fain be able to Say,

'   I Watched, that I might see what Special Truths from time to time

' were most Proper to be inculcated on my Flock, and I thoroughly

' preached those Truths. I would fain be able to Say,

'   I Watched, that I might See, what Sort of Temptations did most

' threaten my Flock, and I Sett myself to Strengthen them against those

' Temptations. [ms. p. 153]

' I would fain be able to say,

'   I Watched, that I might See, what Sort of Afflictions, did most

' assault my Flock: and I sett myself to Comfort them under those

' Afflictions.

' I would fain be able to say,

'   I did Watch, to Learn, what sort of Duties, were most Seasonably to

' be recomended unto my Flock, and I vigorously recommended them in the

' season thereof.

' I would fain be able to say,

'   I did Watch, to see what Souls of my Flock, did call for my more

' Particular Addresses, and I still, for the most part, Every Week,

' Addressed Some or other of them.

'   Now, that I may not fail of this Good Account, I come unto You, with

' the Language, that has been used, by such as had far Less occasion to

' use it; Brethren, Pray for me!

§   One Special Character upon my Experiences in this year of my Life,

was a greater & clearer Application than ever I had yett made, unto the

Righteousness of ye Lord JESUS CHRIST, for my Justification before the

Holy God.

    My Son, I cannot possibly Entertain you with an Article of more

Importance!

    I will therefore Transcribe a few Select Passages from the memorials, which I Recorded and Reserved for this year; And I charge you to Consider them, with a more than ordinary Attention.

At one Time, I have Written thus.

' In the former part of this Day [a Fast,] I humbled myself before the
' Lord, with Inexpressible Agony of Soul, for all the Filthiness of my
' Heart and Life: And [ms. p. 154] Especially a Fear, Lest under my
' Extraordinary Trials from the Invisible World, I have at any time
' gratified the Hidden Desires of Evil Angels, or Entertained any Dis-
' position to see broken ye Good, Wise, Right Order, wherein Humane
' Affairs are fixed by the Lord. I did, with Tears, Bewayl my own Sin-
' fulness; and Submitting myself unto the Divine Soveraignty, wch might
' uncontroleably make me a Vessel of Dishonour, and an Instance of Con-
' fusion, I further acknowledged, that ye Divine Righteousness added
' unto Sovereignty, had further advantages to proceed against me, &
' make me a dreadful Monument of the Divine Displeasure.

'   While I was in the midst of my disconsolate Reflections, the Spirit
' of the Lord Caused me, to behold, the Obedience, and the Sacrifice,
' and the Suretiship of my precious Lord Jesus Christ, as provided by
' God the Father, for the Releef of my Distresses. And that good Spirit
' Caused me to Rely hereupon; so that, with a Flood of Tears, I Said
' before the Lord; Now I know, that my Debts are all paid; My God will
' now make no Demand of me, but that I Love Him, and Praise Him, and
' Glorify my glorious Redeemer forever. I know it! I know it! I know
' it! And now I will do so forever! I can do no other.

     At another Time.

' I Experienced an unspeakable Satisfaction of Soul this Day, when taking
' part with the Lord against myself, I approved all His Lawes, and I
' abhorred myself on the Score of my Contrariety to them, (and my

' Violation of Sin;} and I Justified all the [ms. p. 155] Chastisements
' that had therefore befallen me: And when, with a Ravished Soul, I
' felt the Lord assuring of me, That His Free-grace would Impute unto me
' the Righteousness of the Lord JESUS CHRIST, and at the same time Im-
' print upon me, an Holy Disposition to Conform unto that Righteousness
' in my own Heart and Life.

    At another Time.

' This Day, my Spirit was Exceedingly Distressed at the View of my own
' manifold, former and present Vilenesses, which I bitterly bewayled be-
' fore the Lord. But my Humiliations, I thus Concluded:
'' And yett after all this, I do Beleeve, Lord, Help my Unbeleef![27] I
'' Beleeve, That my precious Lord JESUS CHRIST, o^e Immanuel, hath fully
'' Obeyed and Suffered thy Will, as a Surety in ye room of Elect Sin-
'' ners. I Beleeve, That the Righteousness of this o^e Surety, is offer-
'' ed unto my Acceptance, that for the Sake thereof, I may become Accept-
'' ed with God. I Beleeve, That whenever thou dost Enable me to Rely
'' upon this Righteousness, thou dost immediately Absolve me from all my
'' Guiltiness, and Pronounce me a Dear Son, a Pleasant Child, whom thou
'' wilt Surely have mercy upon. Yea, I Beleeve, That the horrible, Enor-
'' mous, Prodigious Greatness of my Sins, does nothing to render me un-
'' capable of this Free and Rich Grace of Heaven. Oh! My God; In this
'' Beleef, I Cast myself at the Feet of the Lord JESUS CHRIST. There
'' will I now Ly, Waiting, Looking, Yea, Assured, there to Receive thy
'' Favours. [ms. p. 156]

§   This Year, as well as the Last, I find frequent Mention in my
Memorials, of Wonderful, Tearful, Joyful Assurances, granted me from the
Good Spirit of God, as I Lay prostrate in ye Dust before Him on my

Study-floor; That the Holy Spirit of God would fill me, and Apply me to, & Employ me in, Special Services for the Name of my Lord JESUS CHRIST.

I will Transcribe a few Passages, that they may be Assistences & Encouragements unto you, My Son, in your devoting yourself unto the LORD.

One was This.

' When I went on to Petition, That I might not only be Defended from the
' Evil Spirit, but also be Possessed by the Holy Spirit, I fell into a
' Flood of Tears, which gushed out on my Study-floor, where I now lay
' prostrate before the Lord. My Joyful Assurance grew almost into a
' real Extasy. I felt the Lord of Glory, after an inexpressible manner
' perswading of me, That ye Spirit of the Lord JESUS CHRIST, should
' Sieze me, and Fill me, and Irradiate me, and Sanctify me throughout,
' & Cause Heaven to come into me, & fetch me away to Heaven at ye Last.
' But the Rapture of my Soul grew yett more Unutterable, and almost Un-
' tolerable, when I came to Say, That I was desirous to Deny and Re-
' nounce all things, in Comparison of this Blessedness, To glorify my
' precious Lord JESUS CHRIST, who indeed is not known, Lov'd, Serv'd,
' and Priz'd, by this Miserable World; and that I was now Sure, the
' Spirit of the Lord JESUS CHRIST, would make me an Instrument of His
' glory, and Employ [ms. p. 157] me in some Eminent Services for His
' Blessed Name. Hereupon I magnified the Free-grace of the Lord, in that
' He would make this Use of me, who am One of the most Sinful, Silly,
' Shallow, & Filthy Wretches upon Earth.

Another was This.

' This Day, after I had Confessed and Admired the Free-grace of Heaven,
' which would appear in it, if Such a Lothsome, Filthy, Wretched Sinner
' as I am, should Ever be made a Vessel of Honour for the Lord, I gave

' up myself unto the Lord JESUS CHRIST; and I Earnestly professed, That

' I desired nothing in this world so much, as to glorify that precious

' Lord; I Earnestly Entreated, That He would Accept me, & Employ me, to

' glorify Him. And whereas, I am a Poor, Ignorant, Impotent Creature,

' I gave myself up unto the Spirit of the Lord JESUS CHRIST, whose Of-

' fice, and whose Delight it is, to Glorify Him; And as I could not but

' hope, That it was the Spirit of the Lord JESUS CHRIST, who had made my

' Importunitie to glorify Him, Vehement Like ye Coals of a Vehement

' Flame,[28] so I now Cried unto Him, That He would Sieze me, Fill me, Act

' me, & make me a Servant of ye Lord.

Another was This.

' This Day, prostrate on my Study-floor I Poured out a Prayer unto my

' glorious & Precious Lord JESUS CHRIST; Wherein I gave myself unto the

' Lord, under the Sense of my manifold Obligations, to be His, forever.

' In the doing of This, a Flood of Tears issued from me; and my Rap-

' tured Soul received from the Lord, a Strange Assurance of Two Things.

'   First, That nothing should ever befal me in any of my Interests,

' but what should [ms. p. 158] be Serviceable unto His. And, Next; That

' He would yett make use of me, to Do Some Eminent Services for His

' Blessed Name.

Another was This.

' Tis not possible for me, fully to describe ye Agony of Soul, wherewith

' I did, in a whole prayer for that purpose, Devote myself unto ye Ser-

' vice of the Lord JESUS CHRIST. My Soul was Grieved, when I thought,

' how Little that precious Lord is known in the world; and I Cryed fer-

' vently unto Him, that by My Means, many may come to Know Him, and

' Prize Him, and Love Him, and Serve Him. I wondred, when I Considered

' the Free-Grace of the Lord JESUS CHRIST, in Accepting Such a Poor,

' Vile, Filthy Wretch as I am, to be a Companion of Bright Angels, in
' Glorifying of Himself: but I Beleeved, That it would be so. I Re-
' nounced all the Delights of this Life, not asking for Them at all; but
' unspeakably above and beyond all of them, asking for This as my chief
' Happiness, That I may bring much Honour to the Name of my Lord-Re-
' deemer. I Apprehended & Acknowledged, all Opportunities, to be in the
' Hands of the Lord JESUS CHRIST, who hath All Power in Heaven & Earth[29]
' belonging unto Him; And, Oh! I Cried unto Him with Unutterable Groans,
' That He would give me great Opportunities, to Glorify Him Exceedingly.

My Son, I would not have Transcribed these Passages, if I had not
propounded a more than Ordinary Advantage to You, by my Transcribing of
them. All I will add upon them is, That tho' your poor Father be one
deservedly of Little Account in ye World, yett ye Lord has Accepted him
in Such Services, as to render it worth your while to Imitate his Desires
& Methods of becoming Serviceable. [ms. p. 159]

§ One Action of a Special Importance, I find recorded in my poor papers
this year, which I will describe to You, My Son, from thence, for your
Instruction.

'   Being to morrow, to preach about the ANGELS, I thought it, upon many
' accounts, Convenient for me, to Day, to Pray with Fasting before the
' Lord: which I did, in my Study, with Devotions very Singularly Cir-
' cumstanced: They all bore some Aspect upon ye ANGELS of my Lord Jesus
' Christ.

'   I Endeavoured this Day, to Confess and Bewayl unto the Lord, my many
' Sins against Him; Especially under this Aggravation, The Grief which I
' had thereby given to His Holy Angels. And the Sins, which I thought
' had been more particularly grievous to the Angels, I did particularly

' enumerate with an Abased Soul. This I did, after I had first Expressed
' my Adoration of the Divine Power, Wisdome, and Goodness, appearing in
' the Creation, and Condition of those Blessed Spirits. And, in my
' Family-Duties, I Lamented the Disorders in my Family, which had been
' offensive unto the Good Angels, by whom so many Kindnesses had been
' done for my Family. Having both Privately and Secretly, Obtained from
' the Lord, that He would, Imputing to me the Obedience of the Lord JESUS
' CHRIST, Pronounce me, even before His Holy Angels, A Pardoned Man; I
' then gave up myself unto the Lord JESUS CHRIST, professing, that I had
' no Satisfaction, Like that of, Being Employ'd in Service, for this my
' most precious Lord. So, I besought the Lord, that His Holy Spirit
' might now take a Glorious Possession of me, and make [ms. p. 160] me
' very Like unto the Lord JESUS CHRIST, and Fitt for Great Services unto
' His glorious Name. With a Joyful Assurance, that I was heard in this
' Petition, my Tears gushed out on my Study-floor, where I now Lay Pro-
' strate before ye Lord; and I wondred at it, that Such a Filthy Crea-
' ture as I had been, should Ever be made use of, to glorify the Lord
' JESUS CHRIST. But then I pleaded, That the Good Angels of my Lord
' Jesus Christ, might be very Assistent unto me, in that Service, where-
' in I had Them to be indeed my Fellow-Servants. I pleaded, that I might
' be made an Angelical Man, and then that the Angels might notably be-
' friend me, with such a Ministry, as the more Serviceable Heirs of Sal-
' vation use to be favoured withal. I declared, That their Visible Ap-
' pearance to me, was a thing which I was far from desiring; but I
' desired, that from their Invisible & Effectual Operations, I might
' be Comfortably Carried thro' the Services of the Lord Jesus Christ,
' which I had before me; and that my Life, my Health, my Subsis-
' tence, my Studies, & my whole Ministry, might receive more than a

' Little Advantage, from their <u>Wondrous Agency</u>. I Enlarged on these
' Matters, and had my Heart melted with Assurances of Great Things to be
' done for me by the Hands of <u>Angels</u>.

On the Day following, I Entred this among my Experiences.
' I have often observed, That when I preach a <u>Sermon</u>, wherein the Minis-
' try of the <u>Good Angels</u> is much insisted on, I find a very Singular
' [ms. p. 161] Assistence, Enlargement, and Energy, attending of my Dis-
' pensations.

§   A Little Daughter, wherewith God had Enriched me, was on a certain
<u>Lords-day</u> in this year, taken with Sore Convulsion-Fitts, that so fol-
lowed it, as that its Life was despaired of. The Lord helped me, not
only to go on cheerfully with my other work, but also to Resign ye Child
unto Him: Yea, to make and Sing, over ye Dying child, ye following <u>Hymn</u>,
in the midst of my Distresses.

> Heb. 11. 17. with Gen. 22. 12.
>
> The dearest Lord of <u>Heaven</u> gave
>
> <u>Himself</u> an <u>Off'ring</u> once for me:
>
> The dearest Thing on <u>Earth</u> I have,
>
> Now, Lord, I'l offer unto Thee.
>
> I <u>See</u>, my best Enjoyments here
>
> Are <u>Loans</u>, and <u>Flow'rs</u>, and <u>Vanities</u>;
>
> E're well-Enjoy'd they disappear:
>
> Vain <u>Smoke</u>, they pierce and Leave o^e <u>Eyes</u>.
>
> But I <u>Beleeve</u>, O Glorious Lord,
>
> That when I Seem to <u>Lose</u> these <u>Toyes</u>,
>
> What's <u>Lost</u>, will fully be Restor'd,
>
> In <u>Glory</u>, with Eternal <u>Joyes</u>.

I do <u>Beleeve</u>, That I and <u>Mine</u>,

Shall Come to <u>Everlasting Rest</u>;

Because, <u>Blest JESUS</u>, We are Thine,

And with thy <u>Promises</u> are <u>Blest</u>.

I do <u>Beleeve</u>, That Every <u>Bird</u>

Of Mine, which to the ground shall fall,

Does fall at thy Kind <u>Will</u> and Word;

Nor <u>I</u>, nor <u>It</u>, is hurt at all.

Now my <u>Beleeving Soul</u> does Hear

This among the Glad <u>Angels</u> told:

<u>I know, Thou dost thy Maker Fear</u>,

<u>From whom thou nothing dost withold</u>.

Now, to o^e Admiration, ye child Recovered. [ms. p. 164][30]

⟨⟨§ In this Year, I oftentimes had my Mind Strangely Irradiated in my
Supplications, with Assurances, of Mighty and Happy Changes, to come
Shortly upon Great <u>Britain</u>.

I will Reserve those matters, as not proper to be inserted in these
papers. Only One Passage I will here Transcribe.

' <u>Lords-Day</u>. In the Evening of the Day, after my public Work, I Cast my-
' self on my Study-floor, drowned in Tears of Agony, for this mercy from
' the Lord JESUS CHRIST, That I might See more of His infinite <u>Glory</u>, &
' be Fitted with, and Helped by His Holy Spirit, unto the doing of Great
' Things, for His <u>Glory</u> in the world.

'   I hereupon, Cried unto the Lord JESUS CHRIST, That He would please
' to make Himself <u>Glorified</u> on the Island of Great <u>Britain</u>, and glori-
' ously take Possession of the Island for Himself. In the doing of This,
' my melted Heart received a wonderful Assurance from the Lord, That He

' would Shake and Change the Affayrs of Great <u>Britain</u>, & mightily over-
' turn [?] the Throngs that opposed His Interests, & Sieze that Land
' for a place where He would [?] His Kingdome gloriously. Yea, and
' all of [?].

§ But ye Mention of this, gives me an Agreeable Occasion, to introduce the
mention of Something that I find Recorded among my Memorials, for the
next year of my life.⟩⟩

  §   On one of the <u>Fasts</u>, which I kept, ⟨⟨ that year, ⟩⟩ I wrote these
things, among others that I think not so agreeable to be now Transcribed. [ms. p. 165]

'   Having first Confessed and Bewayled my manifold <u>Sinfulness</u> before
' the Lord, & obtained the Hope of Pardon, thro' the Lord Jesus Christ;
' I Sett myself to Consider, That altho' in my Devotions, I had Still
' Remembred the <u>Churches</u> and <u>Int'rests</u> of my Lord JESUS CHRIST, abroad
' in the world, Yett I had not arrived unto a due <u>Enlargement of Soul</u>
' in my doing so.

'   Wherefore, I now Lamented before the Lord, the <u>Privateness</u> and
' <u>Selfishness</u> of Spirit, which in my former Devotions had attended me;
' and I Resolved, that I, as Poor, and as Vile as I am, would now be-
' come a <u>Remembrancer</u> unto the Lord, for no less than whole <u>Peoples</u>,
' Nations, and Kingdomes.[31] I apprehended, That if I should thus Lay
' to Heart the Concerns of ye Lord JESUS CHRIST, and the State of Whole
' <u>Peoples</u>, and Contrive with extraordinary Supplications, Crying to
' Heaven, for Mercy to them, I should be more <u>Angelically</u> Disposed and
' Employed, than I have been heretofore; and I should prepare myself
' also, for very <u>Extensive Services</u> to be done by me; and I should Enjoy
' unutterable <u>Communications</u> from the <u>Holy Spirit</u> then Delighting in me,

' yea, and perhaps <u>Manifestations</u> of what the Lord is <u>going to do in y</u>^{e}

' <u>Earth</u>.

'   This Day, from the Dust, I Lifted up my Cries unto ye Lord,--

'   [<u>For things not here to be mention'd.</u>] ^{32}

' In my Cries to Heaven about these matters, my Spirit was Rewarded and

' Comforted, with some Inexpressible Irradiations; and in some things I

' arrived unto Joyful Assurances, That the Lord had heard my Supplications.

'   This Day, an honest man of another Town,^{33} gave me a Visit, at the

' very Time, when the Lord was Entertaining of Me, [ms. p. 166] with some

' of my chief Employments and Enjoyments in the Day. When I came out of

' my Study to him, he oddly gott me into his Arms, and Pray'd me, to Lett

' him Serve me; but he fell to Discoursing, How Prone we all are to <u>Spir-</u>

' <u>itual</u> Pride, and what Need we all have to Watch against it; & what

' poor, sorry, silly, <u>Earthen Vessels</u>^{34} ye both of us are, after the <u>best</u>

' that God has done for us, or we for Him. Now, he not knowing in y^e

' Least, how I had been Engaged this Day, I could not but <u>Wonder</u> at these

' Discourses, & <u>Ponder</u> with myself, whether the <u>Good Angels</u> of my Lord

' Jesus Christ, might not have a Particular Design in them.

Now, <u>My Son</u>, I hope, you will not need any Annotations, on ye passages

wch I thus Transcribe one after another, out of my <u>Reserved Memorials</u>, to

make you understand y^e <u>Directions</u> which I intend for you, in singling out

these Passages, from very many others, which I do not in this place and

way Expose unto your Notice. If you <u>Consider</u>, you will easily <u>understand</u>,

as you go along, what those <u>Points of Piety</u> are, which I would have you

from hence Directed unto.

    My dear Son; <u>The Lord give thee understanding in all things!</u>^{35}

[ms. p. 167]

§   Upon occasion of Certain Passages, which I find Recorded in my Papers
about this Time, I will in this Place mention to You, My Son, an Observation, which if it Seem to be too Fanciful, yett it may be worth my
Mentioning.

My Heart being Somewhat Sett upon the glorifying of my Lord JESUS
CHRIST, I was willing to Consider that Glorious LORD, On as many occasions,
& for as Many Purposes, as I could. I thought, it would render a Particular Glory unto my Lord JESUS CHRIST, for me to Consider Him, as not only
Dispensing, but also Purchasing, all my Temporal Benefits; and Carry on
ye Contemplation with so much Particularity, as to behold ye Sufferings
of my Lord JESUS CHRIST, in the Points of His Humiliation, which were
directly Contrary unto those Benefits, as having some Influence thereupon.
I will now Illustrate this matter unto You, My Son, by singling out Three
or Four of my many Experiences, thereupon.

I.. Bitter Pains in my Jaw, not only hindred me from other Devotions,
but had Like to have hindred my Ministrations at the Table of the Lord.
Nevertheless the Lord gave me such a Release, that I could Wait upon Him,
in His Public Ordinances; and that Release came so Suddenly, upon a Meditation particularly Circumstanced, that I thought it not amiss to Write
the Summ of the Meditation.

'   My Blessed Lord JESUS CHRIST, whom the Iniquity of us all, was Laid
' upon Him,^{36} Suffered Bitter Pains in His Holy Jawes. He did so, when
' His Bloody Persecutors did there Smite Him, with the Fist of Wickedness.
' Now, by that Suffering of my Lord, all the Sins of my own Jawes, [ms.
' p. 168] as well as my many other Sins, had an Atonement made for them.
' And if God will now mercifully take away the Pains, that so grievously
' afflict me there, I will humbly Receive it, and Reckon it, as a Mercy,

' Purchased by that Particular Suffering of my Lord.

I found my pain, so immediately Retire, upon this Meditation, without Returning as before, (altho' I was using of no new means for it,) that it a little Surprized me.

II. I had been, for about a Fortnight, vexed with an Extraordinary Heart-burn; and none of all the Common Medicines would Remove it, tho' for the present some of them would a Little Releeve it. At Last, it grew So much upon me, that I was almost ready to faint under it; but under my fainting pain, this Reflection came into my Mind. There was this among the Sufferings and the Complaints of my Lord JESUS CHRIST, My Heart, Like wax, is melted in the midst of my Bowels.[37] Hereupon I begg'd of the Lord, that for the Sake of the horrible Heart-burn undergone by my Saviour, I might be delivered from the Other and Lesser Heart-burn, wherewith I was now incommoded.. Immediately, it was darted into my Mind, That I had St Philip Paris's plaister in my House, which was good for Inflammations; and Laying this Plaister on, I was Cured of my malady. Upon its Return, I fell into a Course of taking Conserve { of Roses in Milk, which totally & forever delivered me.}

III. When I undertake Journeyes for the Service of my Lord JESUS CHRIST, I am generally accomodated with Incomparable Horses, wch is indeed a very sensible Accomodation: { or perhaps with Chariots or with Coaches.} But that wch usually prepares me for it, is, A Serious Meditation, [ms. p. 169] that when the Lord JESUS CHRIST, was to Ride a Little Journey, He had none but such a sorry Creature as an Ass to Ride upon: and ye prophecy thereof,[38] I find by the pagan Kings of Persia Exprobrated unto ye Jewes, as a matter of Derision upon their Messiah. O^e Lord Submitting to Mean Circumstances in the Journey, Procures Good-Ones (think

I) for me, in mine; and why may not This be one of them?

《 IV. My Cloak being Somewhat so Old, that it was Time to Seek a New One, and I being just at that Instant, [?] a Little imcomoded in my Capacitie to furnish myself, I Sett myself to affect my own Heart, with the Humiliation of my Lord JESUS CHRIST; when they Stript Him, and Robbed Him of His Garments.³⁹ I assured myself, that for yᵉ Sake of that Humiliation, I should never want Such Garments as would be proper for me.⁴⁰ Immediately after these Thoughts, a Lady belonging to my church, Surprised me, with a present of an Handsome & a Costly Cloak, which could not but Raise in my mind some Reflections. 》

But these few Instances will Serve as a Taste, which is all I intend, for the Instruction of my dear Son, in the Methods of glorifying the Lord JESUS CHRIST. My Son, very Small Enjoyments will become very Great Ones, if you can therein come to Enjoy Something of the Lord JESUS CHRIST, and this way of acknowledging His Humiliation, as purchasing Every contrary Blessing wherein you may be Advanced, is one way of doing so. [ms. p. 170]

§ One morning, in the Thirty fourth year of my Life, praying in my Study for Each of my children by Name, I Left yᵉ Name of One unmentioned. I Wondred at this Omission, when my prayer was over; & blam'd and chid myself, that when I had but Three Children I should forgett one of them. Immediately there came in a messenger, that gave me to understand, That yᵉ Child had been Dead, by a Sudden Expiration in its Nurses Arms, about an Hour before, about a Quarter of a Mile off my House.⁴¹ I hope, the Spirit of the Lord Jesus Christ helped me, to a Patient & Cheerful Submission, under this Calamity.

On this occasion I made and Sang, this Hymn, (from Job. 1. 21.)

I Stript of <u>Earthly</u> Comforts am;

    <u>Stript</u>, Lett me duely mourn:

<u>Naked</u> from <u>Earth</u> at first I came,

    And <u>Naked</u> I Return.

What, but <u>Gifts</u> from above were They?

    GOD <u>gave</u> them unto me.

And now they <u>Take</u> their Flight away,

    <u>Taken</u> by GOD they be.

The Name of my Great GOD, I will

    Forever then Adore;

Hee's <u>Wise</u>, and <u>Just</u>, and <u>Sovereign</u> Still,

    And <u>Good</u> forevermore.   [ms. p. 171]

§ How often I Sett apart whole Dayes for <u>Prayer</u>, with <u>Fasting</u>, in my Study, this year I shall not Mention, any more than in the years that are already rolled away.

Only I think it not amiss, to instruct you, <u>My Son</u>, with one or two Passages Concerning them.

On a Certain Day, I find this Intimation recorded in my papers.

'   I was again Engaged in the Exercises of a <u>Secret Fast</u> before the
' Lord, on the very same occasions, that I was this Day Se'nnight so
' Engaged. I thought, that I could not obtain and Enjoy the Assistences
' of y^e <u>Holy Spirit</u>, necessary to the Discharge of my Ministry, &
' necessary for the Several Conditions and Relations, whereinto the Lord
' may bring me; Except I be much in <u>Prayer</u> wth <u>Fasting</u>, before the Lord.
' I soon Lose that Serious, that gracious, that generous, & that watch-
' ful & useful Disposition of Mind, that I begin to gain by these
' Devotions, if I do for many Dayes Intermitt them. To be a <u>Christian</u>,

' and a <u>Minister</u> too, Oh! tis no Easy Matter!

Moreover, There were sore Degrees of the <u>Terrible Famine</u>,[42] at this time, advanced upon ye Towns all round about us. And I Considered hereupon, That it was my Duty to be much in <u>Fasting</u> before the Lord, that so I might procure Food for my distressed Neighbours. There were <u>Three</u>, Renowned in ye Scripture, for <u>Fasting</u>; and the Lord made use of all those <u>Three</u>, to be miraculous <u>Feeders</u> of other men. And wonderful was the Experience, wch I had in this Time, of Seasonable Supplies by ye good Providence of God Sent in, as unto my own Family, so unto more than the whole County; in ye procuring of Supplies whereunto my Influences were otherwise not inconsiderable. [ms. p. 172]

§ Being Invited unto a more than ordinary Action of Publick Service, for the Lord, and for His people, I thought myself Concerned in a more than ordinary manner, to Abase myself before the Lord. And that I might keep myself under a Lasting Abasement, I not only kept many <u>Dayes of Humiliation</u>, but I also Composed a Writing of Several pages, Entitled, <u>The true picture of</u>--myself.[43] Herein I did, with Black, but yett with too True, characters, describe my own Vileness at such a rate, that it cannot be Look'd upon, without Horrour of Soul; but I Resolved, often to Look upon it.

§ On one of my Dayes this year, I have inserted this passage. <u>My Son</u>, You may make it useful to you.

' This Day, as I was Crying unto my Lord JESUS CHRIST, and Lying be-
' fore Him, with Agonies of Desire, That whereas there were Quickly, very
' <u>Great Things</u> to be done for His Name and Church in the world, He would
' please to Accept of such a Loathsome Wretch as I am, and Employ <u>me</u>, to

' Do <u>Some of those Things</u>: And pleading, That it was doubtless a Law-
' ful Thing, for me to Desire this Favour; For indeed, I had chosen it
' as my chief Happiness, <u>To Glorify my Lord</u> JESUS CHRIST, and I would
' Relinquish Every thing, Overlook Every thing, for ye Sake of <u>This One</u>
' thing: I was melted into a Flood of Tears, wch ran down my Face; and
' the <u>Spirit</u> of my Lord JESUS CHRIST assured me, That He would grant me,
' <u>that</u> which I thus desired of Him. [ms. p. 173]

§   Now, <u>My Son</u>, that you may not only come to be inspired & inflamed
with such Desires, but also be directed, how to gett the Desires accomplished, I will transcribe unto you another passage, wch I find about
this Time Entred in ye Stores, from whence I fetch these Collections
for you.

'   The Lord Exceedingly Irradiated my Soul, by His Good <u>Spirit</u>; Espe-
' cially, when Praying for that <u>Spirit</u>, and Saying:

''   <u>Lord</u>, we know, Wee that are <u>Parents</u> feel it so, that if One of o^e
'' <u>children</u>, should come and Say unto us, <u>Father, There is One thing,</u>
'' <u>that would make us perfectly & forever Happy, and it is a thing that</u>
'' <u>you can do for us, by Speaking of One Word, if you please to Speak it</u>:
'' We could sooner Dy, than Deny that Thing unto them. Now the Hearts
'' of the Kindest <u>Fathers</u> on Earth, are <u>Stones</u> and <u>Flints</u>, in Comparison
'' of thy more <u>Fatherly</u> Compassions. Wherefore we now Come, and Say unto
'' thee, <u>Father. There is one thing that would make us wonderfully Happy</u>:
'' <u>One Word of thine can do this thing for us: Yea, and we are Sure, tis</u>
'' <u>infinitely pleasing unto thee, that we should ask for this Thing</u>:
'' Tis, that thou wouldest please to bestow thy <u>Holy Spirit</u> upon us.
'' [ms. p. 174]

§   I thought it needful to Renew and Revive the Cares of my mind, about the Government of my SPEECH. I wrote therefore the following <u>Rules</u>, which I had heretofore in part observed, that I might after this observe them, yett more Watchfully & Exactly before the Lord. And I therewithal, gave up all my <u>Speaking</u> powers and organs unto the <u>Holy Spirit</u> of my Lord Jesus Christ, that being possessed by Him, I may be by Him assisted unto the observation of the <u>Rules</u> thus imposed.

I.   May I not affect <u>Loquacitie</u> in my Discourses; but Contrary thereunto, affect much <u>Deliberation</u>. The <u>Gravitie</u> and the <u>Discretion</u>, accompanying Such a Caution, will be of more Consequence to me, in all Companies, than the Reputation of <u>Witt</u>, which by a greater <u>Volubility</u> of Tongue, might Easily be acquired: And, <u>in many words there wants not Sin</u>.

II.   May I Studiously decline to utter any thing, that I foresee may be <u>Useless</u>, and much more, Every thing that may be <u>Hurtful</u> and <u>Sinful</u> to be uttered. It must be my Ambition Every where to Speak <u>Usefully</u>, and only those things that some one may be the <u>Better</u> or the <u>Wiser</u> for.

III.   May I, with all ye Contrivances imaginable, improve Opportunities to Say Something or other, that may Particularly Sett off some <u>Glory</u> of my Lord JESUS CHRIST. I would Every where Contrive, if it be possible, to Lett fall Some <u>Sentence</u> or other, whereby Some <u>High Thoughts</u> of the Lord JESUS CHRIST, may be produced in them that hear me. [ms. p. 175]

§   I began the <u>Thirty-fifth</u> year of my Age, with a Day of THANKSGIVING to God in my Retirements; from a Sense of the great obligations, unto Thankfulness, wch my Life had now for <u>Thirty four</u> years together been filled withal.

From ye Records of this Time, I will here Transcribe a Word or two, My Son, for your more Instructive Entertainment.

' Unto Each of my Acknowledgements of the Divine Favours this Day, I
' annexed a Threefold Amplification.

' First, I Confessed, That I had observed many in the world, Lesser
' Sinners than myself, Labouring under ye Contrary Miseries.

' Secondly, I Ascribed still unto Some such Sufferings of my Lord
' JESUS CHRIST, the Purchase of my Deliverance from Sufferings, in my
' Several Enjoyments.

' Thirdly, I owned, from Such Parallels as the Scriptures of Truth
' afforded me, the Agency of the Good Angels, employ'd by the Lord of
' Heaven, to Convey unto me, the Enjoyments wherein I am Rejoicing.

' Then I Sang Suitable Things.

' But in the Evening, tho' I were so Spent with the foregoing Exer-
' cises, that I thought, I had not Strength to proceed any further, I
' Laid myself prostrate, on my Study-floor before the Lord.

' And there did the Spirit of the Lord Jesus Christ, after a wonder-
' ful Manner, Irradiate my Mind, and Quicken me, and Comfort me, with
' wondrous Assurances, that He would Possess me, & Employ me, & grant
' me to glorify my Lord JESUS CHRIST Exceedingly. Yea, [ms. p. 176] the
' Good Angels of that Holy Spirit, were So near unto me, in my raptur-
' ous praises of my Lord-Redeemer, that the Prelibations of Heaven,
' which I Enjoy'd in this matter, are not fitt here to be uttered.

' But perceiving, that it was now a Time with me, wherein I might
' obtain Even what I would, of the Lord, I took this Time to Cry unto
' Him, That the Spirit of Reformation may mightily come down upon y^e
' Nations of Europe; and that a mighty Revolution, ⟨⟨ upon France, and

' upon Great Britain >> particularly, may accompany it. << It will be

' so! This poor man Cried, & the Lord heard his Cry, [44] for this

' glorious Matter. >>

§ I have also Recorded, That on a certain Lords-Day in that Month; At the Lords-Table, it was a perswasion powerfully produced in my mind, That I Should E're Long be with the Innumerable Company of Holy Angels, [45] and that when they came to call for me, I should go away Easily, and Joyfully; and that my Off-Spring which I Leave in this Evil World, shall be the Servants of the Lord JESUS CHRIST, who will, as a most Merciful Father, take such Care of them, that they shall want for no Good Thing. [46]

My Son, This Faith of your poor Father, is here Left with you, because I desire, it may have a very great Influence upon you, to make you, both Trust in the Lord, [47] and also Do Good. [ms. p. 177]

§ From the Memorials of that Month, I will, for Some Reason, Transcribe one passage more.

' I Sett apart this Day, as I did this Day Se'nnight, for the Exercises

' of a Secret Fast before the Lord.

' My Heart Expanded, in a fervent Importunity, for the Cure of those

' Distempers in my Soul, (Pride, Sloth, Envy, Selfishness, Sensuality,

' Earthly-Mindedness,) which rendred me unfit for the Kingdome of God,

' or for any Eminent Service to that Kingdome. I pleaded, That nothing

' but the Almighty and Infinite Spirit of the Lord JESUS CHRIST, could

' cure the Lusts which disordered my Soul. Nevertheless, the Blood of

' the Lord Jesus Christ hath purchased the Favours of His Good Spirit

' for me, whereon I now placed my Dependence for ye Comunication there-

' of.

'   In the close of the Day, when I Lay prostrate on my Floor, in the
' Dust before the Lord, I obtained Fresh and Sweet Assurances from Him,
' That altho' I had been the most Loathsome Creature in the world, yett
' His Holy Spirit would, with Sovereign and Glorious Grace, take posses-
' sion of me, and Accept me, and Employ me, to glorify His Name Exceed-
' ingly. ((And I Successfully Renewed my Cries unto the Lord, That He
' would Visit France, and Great Britain Speedily, with a mighty Revolu-
' tion.))

§   About this Time, having my Thoughts more than ordinarily Exercised,
about ye Approaches of the Great Sabbatism,[48] I thought, it was my Duty
to prepare for it, especially by being very Careful and Watchful, in the
Sanctification of [ms. p. 178] the christian Sabbath, which recurs Every
week unto us.

I did now therefore Exceedingly Revive my Zeal to Sanctify the
Lords-Day; Particularly Resolving upon these Instances.

First, I would not Speak any One Word all the Day Long, but what
shall be Holy, or Useful, or Proper for the Day.

Secondly, I would abound in Religious Exercises throughout the
whole Day; Especially in Reading & Thinking of CHRIST.

Thirdly, I would at Noon Still Address Heaven, with a prayer in my
Study, on Purpose, to Implore ye Favours of Heaven for ye Distressed, or
Depraved Churches of the Lord upon   Earth, & for the Hastning of the
Great Sabbatism.

§   Among other things which I Entred this year, in my Memorials, I
will here Extract one for you, My Son, which may do you no Little
Service.

'   I Seldome am to be much Improved & Assisted, in the Service of my

' Lord JESUS CHRIST, but I am just before it, Buffeted with Very sore

' Temptations, and my Mind is One way or other, Strangely Vexed and

' Broken, and made Uneasy. Tis after a very Long Experience, that I now

' insert this observation; and tho' by having so Long & oft Experienced

' it, I can, when the Disturbances of these Temptations arrive, by my

' Reason, see the Satanical Original of them, yea, and Even Foresee the

' Arrival thereof [ms. p. 179] before they come; Yett such is the Energy

' of them, that I cannot by any Force of Reason overcome them.

§   I know not whether it will signify any thing, but only to Confirm

You, in some thing that I have already mention'd, if I transcribe another

passage, akin to a former, wch this year afforded me.. It is This.

'   Setting apart this Day, as I did this Day Se'nnight, for the Devo-

' tions of Secret Prayer with Fasting, (especially on the behalf of Some

' churches among us, miserably out of Order,)⁴⁹ I received in the close

' of the Day, when I Lay Prostrate before the Lord, a Sufficient Reward,

' and a Wonderful Answer, unto all the Labours of the Day.

'   For, being dissolved in Tears, it was from Heaven told unto me,

' That altho' I am as miserable a Sinner as any upon Earth, yett the

' Spirit of the Lord Jesus Christ shall fill me, & use me, to glorify

' Him. And, whereas He had inclined me, to make choice of this

' Happiness, My glorifying of my Lord JESUS CHRIST, as Heaven itself,

' even as the Brightest and Sweetest Heaven that I aspire unto, I shall

' be Wonderfully gratified in this One thing which I desire, and I

' shall be Employ'd in eminent Services.

((' It was then told unto me, That my Lord JESUS CHRIST, shall Quickly

' be Glorified in England, Scotland, and Ireland, and Glorified in

' France, and glorified throughout Europe, and Glorified over the whole
' world with very marvellous Dispensations. ⟩⟩

'   And inasmuch as my Lord JESUS CHRIST hath granted me, my Good ANGEL,
' I have this Evening attained unto a [ms. p. 180] Particular Satisfaction,
' That We, who Love and Prize, and unspeakably Long to Serve the Same Lord,
' shall do so; and that I shall Enjoy wonderful and Familiar Assistences
' from Him, in doing so. But I mourned Exceedingly, That by my unholi-
' ness I had rendred myself so Disagreeable unto the ANGEL of the Lord.
⟨⟨§And now my Hand is in, You shall have one more, After which I will

    Suppress ye rest.

'   Lords-Day. This Day, at Noon, before my publick Services, I took a
' Time, as I sometimes do, on the Lords-Day, to pour out my Soul, before
' the Lord, with Supplications, for ye Hastening of the Great Sabbatism,
' and the great Revolution and Reformation, that is to bring in the King-
' dome of God. Now, To Day, I pleaded with the Lord, That there were in
' the world, Some Huge Trees, of a very Malignant Influence, concerning
' which the Watchers and the Holy Ones, [50] doubtless made their humble
' Demands, for the Casting of them down. And I would now, tho' I were a
' Vile, & Sinful, & Lothsome Wretch, (yett thro' the Righteousness of
' Christ Accepted with God, and They themselves had not a more glorious
' Righteousness!) Humbly [?] for ye Casting down of those terrible
' Trees. One of ye Trees which I now Specified, was, The French Tyranny,
' and with the Fall thereof, I proposed Such a Shake to be given unto
' France, that the Persecutors of o^e Holy Religion should find, That they
' had Laboured in the very Fire, & wearied themselves for very Vanity. [51]
' Another of the Trees which I now Specified, was, ---------- a thing
' whereby the Knowledge & Service of Christ, was [ms. p. 181] much kept
' in the English Nation.

'   While I was pleading with the Lord, for the <u>Casting down</u> of these

' <u>Trees</u>, I received a wonderful Assurance from Heaven, That it should be

' done <u>Quickly</u> and that the <u>Mighty Angels</u> of the Lord, should <u>Quickly</u>

' have <u>Orders</u>, to do those things, that should be the Astonishment of

' the World. ⸙⸙

§ In my Records, concerning a Day of Secret THANKSGIVING, which I kept in

this year, I find This, among other passages.

' In the former part of the Day, when I was on my knees, Confessing the

' <u>Glories</u> of GOD in my Lord JESUS CHRIST, after I had Requested and Ob-

' tained ye Irradiations of His Holy Spirit for that Service; I received

' an Heart-melting Assurance from the Lord, That inasmuch as my Heart

' was become Desirous to <u>Praise</u> Him, He would never Send me down to that

' miserable World, where they do not <u>Praise</u>, but <u>Hate</u> Him, and <u>Curse</u> Him,

' and <u>Blaspheme</u> Him forever: No, but He would grant me a State of <u>Eter-

' nal Blessedness</u>, wherein I shall carry on that Blessed work of <u>Praising</u>

' Him, which I was now Beginning to do.

'   But the more Special matter of <u>Thankfulness</u>, for which I intended

' this Day, was, The USE, which the infinite <u>Grace</u> of Heaven, has made

' of MEE, the most Filthy Sinner out of Hell, <u>To Glorify</u> my Lord JESUS

' CHRIST.

'   In the Prosecution of my Design, to glorify the Sovereign <u>Grace</u> of

' God, in this matter, I first Confessed & Bewayl'd [ms. p. 182] my own

' horrible Sinfulness, by which I have Deserved, forever to be Rejected

' from the Service of the Lord. I then Solemnly Declared, unto the Lord,

' That I made <u>choice</u> of <u>This</u>, as my <u>Chief Happiness</u>, To be a Servant of

' my Lord JESUS CHRIST, and an Instrument of His <u>Glory</u>. Therewith, I

' magnified the <u>Favour</u> of the Lord unto me, in those Operations of His

' Holy Spirit, upon me, by which He has brought me to such a choice.

' And so I proceeded unto Particular Articles, of that Use, which ye Lord

' had made of me; --[Not here to be mentioned, Lest I be thereby dis-

' covered.] 52

§ My Son, Do you Learn something from this passage.

One Day, discoursing with a worthy Minister, who Lay dangerously

sick, I Said unto him;

'   To Praise Christ in the midst of Myriads of Angels in Heaven, may

' in some Respects be as good, as to Preach Christ, in ye midst of Hun-

' dreds of Mortals on Earth.

He replied; Its True.

I added, (for o^e Discourse was managed with a certain Serious &

Sacred Hilaritie,)

' But, Syr, have you prepared a Song? Have you thought, what to Say,

' when you arrive among the Blessed Angels?

He replied, Why, Pray, what do you intend to say?

I answered;

' I'l Say, Behold, O Yee Holy Spirits, ye most Wretched & Lothsome Sin-

' ner that Ever arrived among you; but it is a glorious Christ that has

' brought me hither! I'l Say, Syrs, [ms. p. 183] Here is one Come among

' you, that was the most abominable Sinner, that ever was in the World,

' and yett I have as good a Righteousness as any of you! I'l Say, Oh!

' Yee Illustrious Angels of the Lord, if you don't wonderfully glorify

' the Grace of the Lord JESUS CHRIST, in fetching so vile a Sinner into

' these mansions, You'l never do it!

This Excellent Man, soon after went unto the Angels, and Poor I am

Left yett in a Sinful & Woful world.

§ In ye close of a Day Sett apart for Secret <u>Prayer with Fasting</u> before the Lord this year, Prostrate in the Dust on my Study-floor, I received a New, a Strong, a Wonderful <u>Assurance</u> from Heaven, (melting me into Tears of Joy,) That my <u>Sins</u> are all Pardoned thro' ye Blood of Christ,[53] and that notwithstanding my horrid Sinfulness, I shall be Employ'd in great Services for His Name. Whereupon I Resolved, That inasmuch as the GRACE of Heaven, was never more magnified, than in Pardoning & Employing so Vile a Wretch as I am, I would sett myself to glorify <u>Free-Grace</u>, by Preaching, and Writing y^e <u>Doctrines</u>, y^e <u>Riches</u>, and the <u>Glories</u> of it, with all Possible Application.[54]

In ye close of another such Day, <u>this Thought</u> was with Inexpressible Joy, Sett home upon my Mind;

' That since my Heart was Exceedingly sett upon Promoting and Advancing
' the <u>Glory</u> of the Lord <u>JESUS CHRIST</u> in this world, God will Certainly
' grant me the <u>Siglet</u> of that <u>Glory</u>, in another and better world; I
' shall Certainly be <u>with Him, where</u> [ms. p. 184] <u>Hee is, to Behold His</u>
' <u>Glory</u>:[55] And there I shall be Happy throughout Eternal Ages.

§ <u>My Son</u>, I Conclude my first <u>Seven Lustres</u>, with telling you, I should have been able to have given you a much Richer Entertainment, than any that I have yett sett before you, if I had not all my Days found ye Truth of an observation, which ye pious Mr <u>Thomas White</u> has Express'd in such Terms as these.

' Many times, the <u>Secrets</u> of o^e Communion with GOD, are of that Nature,
' that it is <u>not</u> Possible to utter y^m; Because the <u>Affections</u> are so in-
' tensely employ'd, <u>Invention, Memory</u>, and <u>Intellectual Actings</u> of y^e
' Soul, during ye Time, do almost cease. An Experienced Christian, his
' <u>Inward Thoughts</u> of Love, Joy, Grief, and Admirings of GOD, are above

156

' all that his Tongue doth or can utter; so that ye Secret Expressions

' which he uses between God & his own Soul, when his Thoughts are full

' of Heaven, & of GOD, are much beyond what he can Invent, or by Study

' Express. The Meditations that are fullest of Devotion, Cannot be

' Remembred. The Prayer, the Devout Soul, when it hath Ended, forgetts;

' So that if one might gain a World, when ye Heart is overwhelmed wth

' Grief, or inflamed with Love, or ravished with Joy, one Could not

' Remember ye Pourings out of ye Soul. [ms. p. 185]

The SECOND Part.
No Longer Distinguished into
LUSTRES.[1]

§   Thus have I Singled out, for Your more particular Consideration,
My Son, certa'n Passages that I Judged would be more Particularly Serviceable for your Instruction, & Your Direction, in the Paths of Righteousness:[2] Extracting them from ye Larger Memorials which I have kept,
of things that I have done or Seen, in my Poor Pilgrimage, for Seven
Lustres of it. {{3}}

I Exceedingly mourne before Him, for ye many Sins, and the horrible
Foolishness, and Filthiness, and Unfruitfulness, with which these years
have been attended. And I fly, with Hope, to His pardoning Mercy, in
the Blood of ye Lord Jesus Christ, which cleanses from all Sin.

But I was Willing to Lett no more Time roll away, before my doing
of this Work for you, My Son, Lest ye End of my Time, Coming[4] upon me,
in the Lustre that is now running,[5] should Cause this work, wch I judged
of Such Importance for you, to be never{{6}}done at all. And it was the
rather necessary for me now to do it, because I know not whether I may
Live, to see you Capable of taking in my Verbal Discourses on such points
as these, or, whether you may be capable of Reading with Understanding,
what I have Written for you, until I Shall be taken from all opportunities [ms. p. 186] of any Verbal Discourses with you.

For, My Son, it was not until after Seven Lustres of my Life were
Expired, that God bestow'd upon me, a Son that Lived unto an Age to Read
what I write.[7]

The Day before he was born, I Spent in Praying and Fasting before
the Lord, and Crying to Heaven, for the Welfare of my Consort, and of
her Expected off-spring. A Son had been foretold unto me, in an

Extraordinary Way, some years before; and, in the Evening of the Day, which I had now kept, I Entertained my Family, before o^e Evening-Prayers, with a Meditation on Joh. 16. 21.[8] A Woman, when Shee is in Travail, hath Sorrow because her Hour is come; but as Soon as she is delivered, of the Child, she remembreth no more the Anguish, for Joy that a Man is born into the world.

After I had Commended my Consort unto ye Lord, I Laid me down to Sleep (after midnight,) that I might be fitt for ye Services of ye Day Ensuing, wch was ye Lords-Day; and in a Chamber by myself, because of her Expecting at this Time her Travail. But after One a clock in the Morning, I Awoke, with a great Concern upon my Spirit, which obliged me to Arise, and Retire into my Study. There I Cast myself on my knees before the Lord, Confessing my Sins that rendred me unworthy of His Mercy, but imploring His Mercy to my Consort, in the Distress now upon her.

While my Faith was pleading, that the Saviour, who was Born of a Woman, would send His Good Angel to Releeve my Consort, the people ran to my Study-Door, with ye Acceptable Tidings, That a Son was born unto me! ⟨⟨9⟩⟩ [ms. p. 187]

In ye Forenoon following, I preached unto o^e Great Congregation, on that Scripture, Psal. 90. 16. Lett thy Work appear unto thy Servants, and thy Glory unto their Children; managing this Doctrine; That the Enjoyment of the Precious Christ, who is the Glorious Work, of God, is the Great Blessedness desired by Good Men, both for Themselves and for their Children.

⟨⟨ It may not be amiss for You to Remember That. ⟩⟩

But tho' this were a Son of Great Hopes, and One Son who Thousands & Thousands of Prayers, were Employ'd for him; Yett after all, a Sovereign GOD would not Accept of him. He was Buried in the Atlantic Ocean.

And You, my only Son, Surviving, are the Person for whom these Memorials
are intended & reserved. And now, because I may upon my Looking back,
meet with Several Passages yett Unmentioned, that may be as Instructive
to you, as those whereof I have already made mention; and others are
occurring, in that part[10] of your Fathers Life, which is now running; ⟨⟨11⟩⟩
I shall proceed without any Method at all, to Sett before you what I may
think proper & useful for you. And it may be, the Less of Method there
is in this Work, it will[12] be but ye more Natural, and Beautiful, and it
may carry ye more of a Parental Authority upon it. [ms. p. 188]

§   On a certain Lords-Day, after my Public Labours, Retiring into my
Study, at the Evening, I there Cast myself prostrate in the Dust, on my
Floor before the Lord. And there, a wonderful Thought with an Heavenly
Force came into my mind, That God Loved my Lord JESUS CHRIST infinitely,
and had given Worlds unto Him, and made Him the Lord of all;[13] And that
I had, thro' the Efficacy of His Grace upon me, My Heart Exceedingly
sett upon the Glorifying of my Lord JESUS CHRIST, and was Entirely de-
voted unto Him. Hereupon an Unutterable Joy filled my Mind, from an
Assurance, That God, for the Sake of my Lord JESUS CHRIST, had great
Things to do for me; That He would even Delight in me, and Delight in
Using me, & Use me in eminent Services for Him, who is dearer to me than
all things.

§   In a SELF-EXAMINATION, my Soul Sallied forth unto those Three Acts
of Elevated Christianity.

   I. LORD, I am so Satisfied in the Infinite Glory and Greatness
of my Lord JESUS CHRIST, & of thy Infinite Regard unto Him, that I
wholly give up myself unto that Illustrious Lord, and I Pitch upon it,
as my Cheef Happiness, To Serve Him forever.

II. LORD, I am in such Ill Terms with my <u>Sin</u>, that I most heartily <u>give Thanks</u> unto thee, for all the most <u>Bitter</u> and <u>Humbling</u> Dispensations, of thy <u>Providence</u> towards me, that have had any Tendency to <u>Mortify</u> it.

III. <u>Lord</u>, I will be alwayes at <u>Work</u> for Thee, and for thy People, and be so [ms. p. 189] far from thinking much of any <u>Work</u>, wch I may do for them, that whatever <u>Sufferings</u> do befall me for the sake of that <u>Work</u>, I will Rejoice in the <u>Sufferings</u> Exceedingly.

§ Now and then One or other of my Church, have unhappily fallen into <u>Scandal</u>; and I have been obliged thereby to Pass the <u>Censure</u> of ye Lord & of His Church on the Scandalous Offendors. In so very Numerous a Flock as mine, it Cannot Easily be otherwise. But on these Lamentable Occasions, I have Still thought it necessary for me, Exceedingly to Humble myself with Prayer and Fasting before the Lord, in Secret, Lest the Anger of the Lord should burn & break forth against <u>me</u>, for ye Sins found in any of my Flock, and that the Divine Anger may be diverted from y^e <u>Flock</u> as well as from myself, on ye account of y^e <u>Great Sacrifice</u>, wch I Pleaded on o^e behalf. The Effect of these <u>Humiliations</u> hath been, That I have Still Enjoy'd a more than ordinary presence of the Lord with me, in managing of His Holy Discipline, and it hath been Carried on wth Such a Majesty, Authority & Efficacy, & made Such a <u>Futuri Judicii Prae-judicium</u>,[14] as to Leave a Lasting Impression upon ye many Hundreds more than a Thousand Spectators of it.

What I have here Especially to Commend unto you, <u>My Son</u>, is, That a Minister must from y^e <u>Sins</u> in his <u>Flock</u>, be Led Seriously to Think on his <u>Own Sins</u>, yea, and Think how far <u>these</u> also may be <u>his own</u>. [ms. p. 190]

§ One Day, when I was Pouring out my Prayers unto the Lord, I mentioned the <u>Prolongation of my Life</u>, to Enjoy and Improve more opportunities of Glorifying Him. In my prayers, I humbly Represented unto the Lord, That there were Two Objections against my Dying, wch my Flesh would be ready to make; but thro' His Grace I had Conquered them.

First, My Flesh pleaded, That the Comforts of Earth were too agreeable Things to be Easily forsaken. But my Faith is Perswaded & Satisfied, That the Delights of Heaven are Sweeter than the Comforts of Earth; and I can freely Leave all the Entertainments of this Evil World, that I may be with Christ, where to be, is by far ye best of all.

Secondly, My Flesh Pleaded, What will become of my Poor offspring, when I am gone? But my Faith is Perswaded & Satisfied, That God will be a Father to my Fatherless Offspring; and my Lord Jesus Christ, whom I have Served, without Seeking, as many others would have done, to Enrich myself with a Portion for my Children, will marvellously become such a Guardian to my Orphans, that they shall never want any Good thing.

My Mind being on these Two Accounts, thus Easy, and Ready to Dy, I then besought of the Lord nevertheless, that He would yett Spare my Life, to Work for Him a Little more, among His people. [ms. p. 191]

§   Finding, that whenever I go abroad into other Towns, the Curiosity and Vanity of the People discovers itself, in their Great Flocking to hear me, with I know not what Expectations: This hath still Caused me aforehand Exceedingly to Humble myself before ye Lord, (even with Fasting and Prayer oftentimes) that the fond Expectations of the People, may not be chastised upon myself, in His Leaving of me to any Inconvenience. By this Method, I not only am in a Comfortable measure kept from ye foolish Taste of Popular Applause in my own Heart, but also from the Humbling Dispensations of Heaven, whereto ye Fondness of the people might otherwise Expose me.

My Son, You may Live to make some Use of this Hint.

§   Keeping a Day of Secret THANKSGIVING, my Soul was raised unto more than ordinary Delights and Raptures. The Holy Lord Even dealt Familiarly with me; I went into the very Suburbs of Heaven; the Spirit of my Lord Carried Me thither, and made known unto me Glorious Things; Yea, Heaven Came near unto me, & fill'd me with Joy unspeakable and full of Glory. I Cannot, I may not, Utter ye Comunications of Heaven, whereto I was this Day admitted. All that I shall observe to you, My Son, is, That within a few Hours, I was Buffeted wth some things in my Neighbourhood, that had a more than ordinary measure of Temptation, & Vexation in them. And Lett my Experience Confirm unto you this observation, That immediately after Extraordinary Communion with Heaven, you shall ordinarily meet with some Accident on Earth, wch will mortify you with some Special Affliction and Abasement. [ms. p. 192]

§ I have seen Cause to Enter this Memorandum among my other Memorials.

I Beleeve, That the God of Heaven vouchsafes, Especially to Some of His Faithful Servants, a more Singular Conduct of His Providence, with the Management and Ministry of His Holy Angels. And, not altogether in-sensible of the Sweetness attending such a Life, I desire to have all the Affayrs and Motions of my Life, more than Ever, under that Singular Con-duct of Heaven.

It is therefore necessary, That besides the Gravity, and Sanctity, and Fruitfulness of a Conversation in Heaven, there be these two things Endeavoured.

First, I would, with more Explicitness than ever, Continually Spread before ye Lord, the Concerns, wherein from Time to Time I may want His Direction and Assistence. Now, for this Purpose, I find it has been a wrong unto me, that I have so much Confined these Representations of my Concerns, unto my more Stated Prayers, at the Hours constantly recurring for them. Wherefore I would, for the Time to Come, Use at any Hour of the Day, when a Case or Care offers itself unto my Thoughts, to make a brief Supplication to Heaven distinctly upon it. Thus I shall be going to Heaven continually; and have Opportunity not only to Converse with the Commandments and Promises of God, and Sacrifice and Righteousness of Christ, more fully on all occasions; but also to have an High Respect Ennobling all my Concerns.

What an Excellent way of Living would This be!

But, Secondly, I would more Exactly and Curiously than Ever, Observe what is Remarkable, in the Divine Dispensations [ms. p. 193] towards me. I would Observe most of all, What Answers of Prayer I receive; and I would Observe ye Efforts and Effects of a Particular Faith. And thus I would keep Waiting on God in Christ perpetually, & Critically keep Eying of Him.

Lord, Help me![15]

§   When my Birth-day has recurr'd on a Lords-day, I have diverse times found it Profitable for me, to insist on Some Agreeable Text, in my pub-lic Sermons, (tho' not alwayes thought it Necessary to tell my Hearers ye reason of my taking such a Text.)

Once on my Birth-day, my Text was, Job. 14. 1. Man born of a Woman, is of few Dayes. Another Time I Remembred my Nativity wth a Sermon, on Luk. 13. 8. Lord, Lett it alone this Year also.

Another time, on my Birth-day, my Text was, Psal. 102. 24. I Said, O my God, Take me not away in the Midst of my Dayes. I was then just Thirty Years old.

⟨ Another time, I had on my Birthday opportunity to preach on this Text;
Act. 26. 22. Having obtained Help from God, I continue to this Day.⟩

Another Time, on my Birth-day, my Text was, Luk. 18. 13. God be
Merciful to me a Sinner. And tho' I durst not alienate this Day, from
ye Celebration of my Lord-Redeemers New-Birth, for which He Sanctified
it; Yett I improved the Sense of my Circumstances this Day, to quicken
my Apprehensions of the Need which I have of such a Lord-Redeemer.
Wherefore, in the Ensuing Evening, I Sett myself to Call over ye Special Dispensations of the Divine Providence towards me, & Write, Mercy
to a Sinner, upon them all; and therewithal to Consider, What Conditions
I had pass'd thro', what Relations I had Sustained, what Employments I
had Managed, and Cry, God be Merciful to me a Sinner, upon ye view of my
Miscarriages in all of them. ⟨ Once I made my Birth-day an opportunity
for preaching, on Psal. 90. 9. We Spend o^e Years as a Story; And of
pressing as a Proper Exercise for such a Day, A Recollection of our own
Story, wth Endeavour, that it may not prove an unhappy Story.⟩
[ms. p. 194]

§   On a Certain Lords-day, being to preach on Renouncing our own Right-
eousness, & Repairing to and Relying on, ye Righteousness of a Glorious
Christ; as I was on my knees in my Study, before my going forth to
Preach, Imploring (as alwayes) ye Help of Heaven, I had that Scripture
darted into my Mind, Psal. 71. 16. I will go in the Strength of the Lord
God; I will make mention of thy Righteousness, even of thine only. Here-
upon I thought, That Ministers, when they go to preach on that great
Point of the Gospel, A Sinners being Justified by ye Righteousness of the
Lord Jesus Christ, Even by That Only, they might Expect for to go in the
Strength of the Lord God, and Enjoy Singular Assistences from on High.

I was verily perswaded, that I should find it so; and I did this Day find it so; and I have at Several other Times, (in Vast Congregations) found it so.

§ I have had ye Repetitions of another Experiment, When I have been to preach on the Temptations, or Devices of Satan, I have been after an Extraordinary Manner myself buffeted with his Temptations. No part of my Life, has been So Signalized with horrible Temptations assaulting me, both from Within, & from Without, as that wherein I have been to discourse on Temptations in my public ministry: As, to handle ye beginning of ye fourth Chapter of Matthew,[16] or other such portions of Scripture. When therefore I have been going to handle Such portions of Scripture, I have thought it necessary for me, to Cry unto God, with Fasting and Prayer, That He would not Suffer me to be Tempted above what I am able.[17] [ms. p. 195]

§ Considering, that for Men, & even Good Men, to Speak Evil of one another, was the Special Vice of the Place (and more Especially of ye Time) wherein I Lived, I Sett myself to bear my Testimony against the Vice. But that I might be qualified the better to bear my Testimony, I took up these,

RESOLUTIONS,

in the Strength of the Lord Jesus Christ, &

His Good Spirit of Grace.

First, That I will never Speak Falsely of any Man.

And, Next, That if I must Speak what is Evil of any man, it shall be under these

Limitations and Regulations.

I. I will keep a Charity for the Person of whom I Speak, Wishing most
heartily, that all Good might be Spoken of him; And I will Speak from
charity for those to whom I Speak, alwayes thinking when I Speak, Is
what I Speak, for the Good of the Hearers?

II. If I Speak what is Evil of any Person, I will carefully Watch over
my Heart, that I do not Speak it with Delight. I will ever manage it,
with Brevity and Aversion, as a very ungrateful Subject.

III. When I must Speak what is Evil of any man, if I know any Good, that
can be Spoken of him, I will be sure to Ballance the Evil, with y^e
mention of the Good.

IV. Before I Speak Evil of a Man, I will Consider, whether I should not
first Speak to him; and be it how it will, I will ordinarily Speak nothing but what I could be Content he were present at my Speaking of it.

V. I will Aggravate Nothing, and when I Speak of an Evil, I will not go
to make it Worse than it is. [ms. p. 196]

I Resigned my Speech unto the Possession & Management of the Holy
Spirit of the Lord JESUS CHRIST, that I might keep these RULES forever.

And, My Son, I Cannot Express the Satisfaction and Serenity of Soul,
wch I find, when I do most Religiously keep these Wholesome Rules.

§ My Heart has been Strangely Transported, with a Meditation of this
Importance!

I not only desire to make the Imitation of the Lord JESUS CHRIST,
the very character of my Life; but there is a further Article of Resemblance to Him, whereto I desire to aspire Exceedingly. The Place where
I Live, hath in it, many People, that are full of Enmity to the Interests of the Lord JESUS CHRIST; and if He were on Earth again, as once
He was, He would be Persecuted with Wonderful Malignity, by Vast Numbers

of People, that now go by the Name of <u>Christians</u>. By my <u>Faithfulness</u>
unto the Interests of the Lord JESUS CHRIST, and of <u>Holiness</u>, I Cannot
but Expose myself unto a Deal of raging and railing Malignity. Well, If
I now find myself <u>Hated</u>, by them that <u>Hate</u> the Lord JESUS CHRIST, or that
<u>Hate</u> what is <u>Loved</u> by the Lord JESUS CHRIST, and if the <u>Reproaches of</u>
<u>them that would Reproach Him, fall upon me</u>,[18] I will Triumph in all such
<u>Conformity</u> to Him, as being indeed <u>Good</u> for me, and in these my <u>Suffer-</u>
<u>ings</u>, as being really my <u>Honours</u>; and <u>my Spirit will gloriously Rejoice</u>
<u>in God my Saviour</u>.[19] [ms. p. 197] When I was thus thinking, it was
Powerfully sett Home upon my Heart, that I have in this Disposition, an
<u>Infallible Symptom</u>, That my Lord JESUS CHRIST will E're Long fetch me
away to <u>Heavenly Glory</u>; and that He will <u>glorify</u> me with Himself, World
without End.

§ <u>My Son</u>, I will mention to You another Matter of <u>Experience</u>, which I advise you to Improve; but so that you do not make it a Matter of <u>Super-</u>
<u>stition</u>.

I Considered, That ye Primitive Christians, in Obedience to that
Commandment of <u>Watching unto prayer</u>,[20] sometimes had their VIGILS, which
were of great use unto them in their Christianity. To Spend a good Part
of a <u>Night</u> sometimes in <u>Prayer</u>, and so take the Advantage of a <u>Nocturnal</u>
<u>Solitude</u>, and abridge themselves of their usual Rest, for the sake of a
Devout Conversation, with Heaven; They found God often Rewarding y^e
Devotions of such <u>Vigils</u>, with a more than ordinary Degree of Heavenly
Consolation. And so hath your Poor <u>Father</u> done! I have sometimes made
an Essay towards a VIGIL. I have ⟨⟨21⟩⟩ withdrawn from a Lodging agreeable
Enough unto me; and in the Dead of ye Night I have Retired unto my Study:
and there I have Cast myself on my Study-floor, prostrate in ye Dust

before the Lord, and Wrestled with Him, for a long while together.   In
doing thus, I have been Rewarded with Comunications from Heaven, which
Cannot be uttered. [ms. p. 198]

§   Among the Remarkables, which I am willing that You, My SON, should
know, of my Life, perhaps this may go for One.

I have Several Times observed, That God hath Strangely Stirred up
my Heart Sometimes to Visit persons, that were Strangers to me, & Employ
very Particular Methods to Excite and Assist, their giving Themselves up
to Him, in His Covenant; and they have presently after Dyed, with great
Symptomes of Regeneration upon them.

Once (among ye rest of the Instances) On a Satureday-night, I was
very Strongly accosted in my Sleep, with a Dream of this importance. A
Certain old man, to whom I was almost a total Stranger, (only I had Seen
him, & heard his Name,) was brought into my Sight; and it was (I know
not how) said unto me, Take notice of this Old man, Speak to him, Do for
him. On the Day following, I Saw the Old man, in my Congregation,
(where, I Suppose, he had not usually attended,) very attentive to my
Sermon. On the Day after this, I mett the old man in ye Street, and I
Lett fall some such words as these unto him; How d'yee do, old Man! I
am glad for to see you Still in this world; I pray God, prepare You for
another! I suppose, it won't be Long before You are Called away: Can I
do you any Service? And so I turned from him. On the Day after That,
ye old man Came to me at my House: And I then instructed him, how to
prepare for Death; and I gave him a Little Book farther to Assist him in
it: Adding a Peece of Money, to Encourage him. Afterwards he came to
me Several Times: but in about Seven Weeks [ms. p. 199] after o^e first
Interview, he Died Suddenly. On ye Day of his Funeral, I was told, by

some who did not understand, how much I had been Concerned for him; and afterwards I had it more fully Reported unto me, from ye people of ye House, where the old man had Lived: That he had been a Poor, Carnal, Sorry Old man, till about Seven Weeks before he died; but in his Last Six or Seven Weeks, they had observed a Wonderful Change upon him: he Spent his whole Time in Praying and Reading; and a Certain Little Book, (ye Same that I had given him,) they said, was his Continual Companion Day and Night. They never Saw a man so Altered; and they were verily Perswaded, he died a Regenerate Man.

§ My Son, I am very Particularly Sollicitous, That you may not only Entertain Right Thoughts about, The SEALING WORK,[22] of ye Holy Spirit on the Souls of ye Faithful, but also have ye Experience of that work in your own.[23]

I take it for to be a Solid and Joyful, a Grounded and Powerful Assurance, produced in the Soul of a Beleever, by the Holy Spirit of God, Comfortably Perswading him of his Interest in the Benefits of the Lord Jesus Christ, and the Promises of His Covenant. The Holy Spirit of God, in this Work, brings Home unto us, the Electing, ye Redeeming, ye Pardoning Love of God, with an astonishing Efficacy, wch no man knowes but he that has it, and no Tongue is able to utter. In Sealing of us, the Holy Spirit, with a mighty Light breaking in upon o^e Minds, Raises in us a Triumphant perswasion, That we are the children of God, and that o^e Father [ms. p. 200] has Good and Great Things to do for us. O^e Souls are mightily Irradiated, and marvellously moved & melted & overpowered, so that being dissolved into Tears of Wonderment at ye Riches of Grace, We cry out, God is my Father, Christ is my Saviour, Heaven is my Inheritance![24] Inexpressible Peace and Joy, and Heavenly Rapture, accompanies

this work of the Holy Spirit; a transporting Satisfaction of Soul, that
antedates Heaven upon Earth. But then, to distinguish the Seal from a
Counterfeit, it alwayes Leaves a Stamp of more Holiness upon the Soul.
It is often in a way of Self-Examination, and upon the Sight, which in
that Exercise, the Holy Spirit gives us of His Vertues and Praises and
the Marks of a Regenerate Soul wrought in us, that He Comes to Seal us.
Tho' Sometimes tis done in a more Absolute Manner, and the Marks of Regeneration are not under any Actual View of o$^{\textrm{r}}$ Minds, when y^e Holy Spirit
Comes to Assure us of His having Sett us apart for Everlasting Blessedness. But Lett it be done One way or t'other, (for y^e Spirit worketh
how He Liketh!) the Sealing Work of y^e Holy Spirit, is alwayes attended
with y^e Symptomes of a Sanctifying Work. There is with it, an Image
wrought and Left by the Holy Spirit on ye Soul of the Saint: And whose?
But the Image of o^e GOD and SAVIOUR! [25]

I will no Longer discourse to you the Theory of the matter; I will
choose rather to give You, what I take to be ye True Stroke of it, in
One Instance, which I find Recorded in my Reserved Papers.

Having preached on that glorious Priviledge of being Sealed with the
Holy Spirit of God; [26] and being arrived unto my Last Prayer at the fol-
lowing Administration of that Sealing Ordinance, the [ms. p. 201]
Eucharist, I felt an inexpressible Irradiation from Heaven upon my Mind,
which Caused me with Weeping Supplications thus to Express myself, and
Exemplify unto my Flock, that Favour of the Lord.

'   And now, Surely, Thou are o^e Father; Else thou wouldest never have
' inclined us, to Repair unto thee as unto o^e Father, with Prayer & with
' Pleasure, on all occasions; and to desire nothing in this World so
' much, as to Glorify o^e Heavenly Father. Surely, Thy Christ is o^{es}; or
' Else thou wouldest never have Caused us to Accept of Him in all His

' Offices, and Value and Admire all His Benefits. Surely, Thy christ

' has Loved us, & Washed away o^e Sins in His own Blood;[27] or Else thou

' wouldest never have made o^e Sins to become so Bitter and Loathsome

' unto us, and made us Wish for nothing so much as Deliverance from o^e

' Sins. Surely, We Stand before thee in ye Righteousness of thy Christ;

' or Else thou wouldest never have made us to Renounce and Abhor all o^e

' own Righteousness, & fly to His Righteousness as o^e only Refuge, and

' make mention of That, even of That only. Surely, Thy Christ has o^e

' Names written on His Breast, & appears as o^e Advocate in the Heavens;

' or Else thou wouldest not have made us Carry His Name so much on o^e

' Hearts, & be so much Concerned above all things to advance His Name,

' & be so willing to appear on Earth as Advocates for His Labouring

' Interests. Surely, Thy Holy Spirit has taken a Saving Possession of

' us, or Else we should never have undergone such a change upon us: We

' should never have been Reconciled unto the most Mortifying and Self-

' denying Points of Christianity; We should never have Chosen rather to

' be Afflicted, than to be abandoned unto Sin against thee; We should

' never [ms. p. 202] have Relished it as the chief Delight under Heaven,

' yea, a Very Heaven itself, To be alwayes doing of Good. Surely, These

' are the Seals of God upon us; and they Seal us for the Heavenly Inheri-

' tance. God uses not Such Seals as these upon Reprobates: God would

' not Seal us for Damnation with such things as these upon us; These are

' not the Marks of those that must go down unto ye Congregation of the

' Damned. No, o^e God has now Sealed us for glory; Sett us apart for

' glorious & Eternal Happiness.

' Oh! O^e God, O^e God! We find a mighty Light broke in upon o^e Minds;

' a Joyful Perswasion and Assurance, That thou hast Loved us with an

' Everlasting Love;[28] and that o^e Sins are all Pardoned in the SON of thy

' Love; and that we shall be <u>kept by thy mighty Power thro' Faith unto</u>

' <u>Salvation</u>.[29] We are <u>Sure</u>, This perswasion, must Either be from <u>Satan</u>,

' and from a Deceived & Deluded <u>Heart</u>, or Else it must be from y^e <u>Holy</u>

' <u>Spirit</u> of God. But we are Sure, the perswasion is not from <u>Satan</u>, &

' from o^e own Sinful <u>Heart</u>; because we no sooner Entertain it, but it

' fills us with <u>Love</u> to God, and <u>Care</u> to Please Him & Serve Him; it makes

' all <u>Sin</u> most Hateful unto us; it Leaves an <u>Heavenly Impression</u> upon us;

' it causes us to <u>abound in the Work of the Lord</u>;[30] it inspires us with

' a <u>Zeal</u> for thee; it Constrains us to a Watchful, Useful, Fruitful and

' Humble Walk before Thee. We are <u>Sure</u> then, that the perswasion is from

' y^e <u>Holy Spirit</u> of God. And now, <u>Behold, What manner of Love is This!</u>[31]

My Design to Teach You, <u>My Son</u>, in a way of <u>Exemplifying</u> Every

thing, & of <u>Parental Exemplification</u> too, hath caused me to transcribe

this [ms. p. 203] Passage. And as I here give You the right meaning,

and Purpose and Process of that Illustrious Thing, <u>The Seal of the Spirit</u>,

so I importunately urge You to be most Restlessly Importunate, until you

Can Rejoice in your own Happy Experience of it.

§ How often have I declared it with Tears unto ye Lord; That I Chose and

Begg'd This, as ye very <u>Heaven</u> of my Soul; To be made an <u>Instrument of</u>

<u>Exhibiting</u> y^e <u>Glory of</u> y^e <u>Lord Jesus Christ</u>, unto His People, & Inviting

and Inducing Others to Glorify Him!

I received once a Letter, a short Letter, from an Holy Servant of

that glorious LORD, which had this (and Little more than This,) Passage

in it.

' You'l Pardon my Troubling You, with a Line or two, to Thank you for

' Your <u>Maschil</u>, ⟨[The Title of a Book, which I had published.]⟩[32] Which

' I think may be called <u>Mictam</u> as well as <u>Maschil</u>.[33] You help me to this

' Thought; How full of Excellency is the Glorified Man, the Lord JESUS
' CHRIST; if by His Holy Spirit, He so fills One of His Admirers, that
' he is Enabled to fill a Book with such Excellent Things!

My Son, Tis impossible for me to Express the Satisfaction of Soul,
which the Sight of this passage raised in me. [ms. p. 204] That Holy
Ones, whose Hearts are Sett upon the glorifying of the Lord JESUS CHRIST,
should by any thing of Him in me, be Led unto ye Contemplation of His
glories! This, This I Look'd upon, as the Highest Pitch of my Felicity.
I thought, I aspired unto nothing Higher than this, throughout Eternal
Ages. It ravished me, when I saw my Good God beginning to Grant this
Felicity. I despised the Diadems of Emperours in Comparison of it. I
cried out, I am Happy! I am Happy! Lord, I am Swallowed up with the
Extasies of thy Love!

§   A Young Minister (and One doubtless of much more Grace than myself)
came to me, desiring my Advice about his Distressed Case: For, he told
me, he was fully Convinced of his being to this Day an unconverted and
unregenerate Creature.

Lord, (thought I,) What Cause have I, to Examine Seriously &
thoroughly my own State, if one so much better than I, hath such Thoughts
of his?

But, Setting myself to Comfort him, I found a Wonderful Comfort
convey'd unto my own Soul, with a Dialogue of this Importance.

I Pray, Syr, What is it that Stands upon ye Mantle-tree before you?

A Repeating clock, & a very Curious One.

What Use do you think I will putt it to?   [ms. p. 205]

Syr, You'l assign it a convenient and an Honourable place in Your
Study, & putt it unto ye Noble Use of Measuring your Time.

How do you know, that I shall not make it a Stool to Sitt upon, a Block to tread upon, a Backlog to be thrown into my Fire?

Syr. The workmanship of it, makes it appear to be intended for no such miserable use.

Well then; Have not You upon your Soul, a Divine Workmanship, far more Excellent, than the most curious clock-Work in the World? A Soul is a most noble thing; but I will venture to say, A Work of Grace upon ye Soul, is more noble than the Soul itself. A Work of Grace, is a Work of God; Even of Him, who does nothing in Vain. You find in Yourself a Disposition, a Strong Disposition and Inclination, to Glorify God, & Serve ye Interests of the Lord JESUS CHRIST, and hate, & slay, & shun all Sin, as most Contrary to that Holy Lord. This is a Work of Grace. You know no Delight Comparable to that of Serving the Lord Jesus Christ. God has Wrought this in you: and herein He has Wrought you for that Self-Same thing, of being to the Praise of His glory forever. What Use can you think, He will now putt you to, but that of Serving the Lord JESUS CHRIST in His Heavenly World? Such a peece of Workmanship (Created unto Good Works) as what is wrought in you, was never intended for to be thrown into ye Fire of Hell. No, There is No Use of it there. God intends you for an Heavenly Use undoubtedly!

This Thought gave to me, an inexpressible Consolation; whatever it might give to him, to whom I directed it. [ms. p. 207] [34]

§ My Son, Having drawn up the Glorious COVENANT of Grace, in a Poem, which I have often Recited, (with New Expressions of my Consent unto it) with Tears before the Lord, I will here Transcribe it, and Tendar it, unto you, for you to do so too. [35]

AND now to Life Rais'd by the Heavenly Call,[36]

Henceforth, Vain Idols,[37] I Renounce you all.

   Vile Flesh, Thy raging Lust, & Sordid Ease,[38]

My Winged Soul now shall not Serve & Please.

   False World, Thy Lawes shall be no longer Mine,

Nor to thy Wayes my Newborn Soul incline.

   Satan, Thou wilt, I know, my Tempter be,

But thy Temptation shall not govern me.

   Foolish I've been; O Lord, I blush, I grieve;

And Gladly would my Woful Folly Leave.

Fain would I Turn to God, but can't alone:

Help, Sovereign Grace, Or it will ne'er be done

To the Great GOD of Heaven I repair,

And Help'd by Heaven thus to Him declare.

   Great GOD, Since to be Mine thou Willing art,

Oh! Be thou mine! Replies my Conquered Heart.

To Glorify Thee, Glorious Lord, I Take

For That alone which can me Happy make.

   O FATHER, of all Things Creator Great,

Wilt Thou all Happiness for me Create?

   Eternal SON of God, Wilt thou me Save,

That I the Hopes may of Gods Children have?

   Eternal SPIRIT of God, Poor me Wilt thou

With Spiritual Blessings of all sorts Endow?

   Lord, Ravish'd at thy wondrous Grace, I do

These gracious offers now Conform unto. [ms. p. 208]

   O Alsufficient ONE, Wilt thou Supply

My Wants from Stores of Rich Immensity?

Shall boundless <u>Wisdome</u> for my Good Contrive?

And boundless <u>Power</u> ye Fruits of <u>Goodness</u> give?

Shall Spotless <u>Holiness</u> on me imprint

An <u>Holy Temper</u>, with thine Image in't?

   <u>Lord</u>, Thy <u>Perfections</u> all I do adore;

And to a <u>Perfect Love</u> my Mind would soar.

   A State of BLISS, according to thy Word,

Thou Wilt unto thy Chosen ones afford.

   A State of Blissful <u>Rest</u> and <u>Joy</u>, wherein

Rais'd from the <u>Dead</u>, they shall be freed from <u>Sin</u>.

There, bath'd in Rivers of Eternal <u>Joy</u>,

No <u>Sorrowes</u> more shall them at all annoy.

GOD shall be <u>All in All</u>; Brought nigh to God,

In <u>Him</u>, they shall forever make Abode.

They shall <u>See God</u>; The <u>Beatific Sight</u>!

And <u>their own God</u> shall take in them Delight.

   <u>My Soul</u>, Make now thy Choice. O Say: Is This

What thou doest Choose for thy chief Blessedness?

Things of this <u>Present Time</u> I now Refuse;

My Blessed GOD, Thee, <u>Thee</u>, and <u>This</u>, I chuse.

May the Sweet JESUS me to <u>Glory</u> bring,

And be my Glorious <u>Prophet</u>, <u>Priest</u>, & <u>King</u>.

   Does the Almighty CHRIST of God, to those

That <u>Will</u>, an <u>Union</u> with Himself propose?

<u>My Lord, I Will</u>! The <u>Will</u> thou didst bestow;

To Thee, Oh, Lett me be <u>United</u> so.

   The full <u>Obedience</u> which my <u>Surety</u> paid

To God, may <u>That</u> my <u>Righteousness</u> be made.

A Wretched Sinner would appear in That,

Righteous before ye dreadful Judgment-Seat.

   Show me thy Way, O Lord, Lest that I shou'd

Fall by those Mockers that will me delude.

To thy Pure Scriptures-Way I will adhere,

And find the Rule of my Whole Conduct there.

   All the Rebellion of my Heart Subdue;

And for thy Work, O Lord, my Strength Renew.

From thy Vast Fulness Lett my Faith derive

Strength to do all things, & to Thee to Live. [ms. p. 209]

   May thy Good SPIRIT me Possess, & Fill

With Light and Zeal, to Learn and Do thy Will.

With His Kind Flames may He upon me Sieze,

And keep me alwayes on my Bended knees.

May all I am and have, be us'd for Him

Whose is my All, for He did me Redeem.

To Thee, Good SPIRIT, I Lift up my Cries,

That thou Wilt fall upon ye Sacrifice.

   May the Bright ANGELS be my Guardians then;

For Thee they'l Guard and Guide ye Sons of Men.

   By Thee assisted, LORD, thus I Consent

Unto thy Everlasting COVENANT.

§ My Spirit had been for a Considerable while distressed, & full of Supplication and Resignation to ye Lord, about a Matter of great Consequence
to me, Doing, or, Undone, in another Countrey, at a Considerable Distance from me.[39]

   In One of my Vigils, When I Sang the Hundred & thirty first Psalm,

that passage Exceedingly affected me; My Soul is even as a Weaned Child;
Lett Israel hope in the Lord FROM HENCEFORTH. I had been wrestling with
the Lord, for the Good Success of my Great Affayr. In the Midst of this
my Wrestling, I found myself become as a Weaned Child. I Submitted the
whole Concern unto the ordering of the Lord; I Resolved, that I would be
Satisfied, with whatsoever He shall order. But it was [ms. p. 210] now
Powerfully Sett home upon my Mind, That I might now Hope in the Lord
from Henceforth, to see a good Issue of it. And before the Year was out,
it Came to pass accordingly.

§ There was a Time, and a Thing, wherein I was full of Distress.[40] My
Temptations, my Difficulties were Extraordinary. I was Called into more
than ordinary Humiliations, and Supplications, and Resignations. The
occasions were full of Agony. In this Time, I rarely Lett a Week pass
me, without Setting apart a Day for Prayer with Fasting, for many Months
together; and I every now & then had my Vigils, for a Conversation with
Heaven; and Every Day for the most part I had one Secret Prayer more than
I use to have, & Lay prostrate in the Dust, with Tears before the Lord.
Yett I thought it necessary to do something more than all of this.

I had often in my Life, kept no Less than Two Dayes of Prayer with
Fasting, in One Week. But I now took up a Resolution to Spend THREE
DAYES TOGETHER, in Prayer with Fasting in my Study; and Beseech the Lord
Thrice, Knocking at the Door of Heaven,[41] for Three Dayes together. And
the Lord Carried me thro' that undertaking, even before what One of my
Feeble Constitution could have Look'd for.

I was desirous, that Each Day should have its peculiar Character;
tho' there were many General Strokes of Devotion, which were Common to
all the Dayes.[42]

The <u>Singular Character</u> of y^e <u>First Day</u>, was <u>Confession</u> of, and <u>Con-</u>
<u>trition</u> for, the <u>Sins</u> which Exposed me to the Displeasure of Heaven;
(wherein I [ms. p. 211] used a <u>Catalogue</u> of Things <u>Forbidden</u> and <u>Required</u>
in ye Commandments, as well as the Ingredients of <u>Original Sin:</u>) and
<u>Petition</u> for the Pardon of all, thro' ye Blood of the Lord JESUS CHRIST.

The <u>Singular Character</u> of the <u>Second Day</u>, was, <u>Resignation</u> to the
<u>Will of God</u>, in whatever Sorrowes had already befallen me, and in all the
sorrowful things, which I could imagine hereafter to be inflicted on me,
by the Sovereign Will and Pleasure of Heaven.

Astonishing Entertainments from Heaven, were granted me in and from
this Action. God Opened Heaven to me, after a Manner, that I may not,
and indeed Cannot, Express in any Writing. The Thought of <u>Dying</u>, (and
going to the Heavenly World,) was become ye most Easy & pleasant thing
in the World unto me. I was now advised from Heaven, That God is Mine,
and I am His, and He had wonderful Things to do for me.

The <u>Singular Character</u> of the <u>Third Day</u>, was, <u>Request</u>, first, for
Help under and against, all the Assaults of <u>Temptations</u> upon me; and
then, for the <u>Angelical Ministry</u> to be Employ'd on my behalf, & for my
Help in those Cases, wherein the <u>Heirs of Salvation</u> use to be befriended,
by y^e <u>Ministers, who do the Pleasure of the Lord</u>.[43]

Astonishing Things were now again done for me, that cannot be related. I will only say, The <u>Angels</u> of Heaven are at Work for me. And I
have <u>my own Angel</u>, who is a better Friend unto me, than any I have upon
Earth.

My <u>Three Dayes</u> Left me in a very Desireable Frame; Very Fearful of
[ms. p. 212] Sinning against God; Very Raised in my Thoughts of Christ &
Heaven; Very Watchful to Do Good, & bring forth Fruit unto the Lord.

But because an Admission to Extraordinarily Intimate Communion with

Heaven, uses in my Experience, to be followed with sore Buffetings from Satan, Either by Internal Impressions, or by External Occurrences, I had a Trembling Expectation of what might follow upon that Intercourse with Heaven, whereto I had newly been Admitted.

The Evil that I feared, came upon me. But yett, I received a Glorious and a marvellous Harvest of these Three Dayes. The Design of them, was obtained unto Admiration!

My Son; I wish you may never have ye Occasions that I had for these humbling Wayes of proceeding in your Applications to Heaven. But if you have, Lett my Experience be your Direction and Encouragement. Had it not been for ye Hope of That, I would have Left this Part of my Experience as much unmentioned as I have done many others. I had some conflict in my own Spirit, whether I should have Related this or no; Lest there should be some Vanity in ye Relation. But, ye Hope of being Useful to you, has Carried it.

§ On a Day of Prayer with Fasting, wch I kept, under Sore Temptations, I find I have Entred this Record.

' It was a Day full of astonishing Enjoyments; a Day filled with Resig-
' nations and Satisfactions, and Heavenly Astonishments. Heaven has been
' opened unto me this Day. Never [ms. p. 213] did I so long to Dy, and fly
' away into Heaven! I have seen and felt unutterable Things. I have Tasted
' that the Lord is Gracious.^{44} I can by no means Relate, the Communications
' with Heaven, whereto I have been this Day admitted. I am now sure, That
' the Great GOD is my God; that I stand before God in the Righteousness of
' my Lord JESUS CHRIST; that no Good Thing shall be Witheld from me; that
' God will make an amazing use of me, to Glorify Him; and that I shall be
' an object, for the Everlasting Triumphs of Sovereign & Infinite Grace.
' I was not able to bear the Extasies of Divine Love, into which I was

' Raptured: They Exhausted my Spirits; they made me Faint, & Sick; they
' were Insupportable; I was forced, even to Withdraw from them, Lest I
' should have Swoon'd away under the Raptures.

But, I can tell you, My Son: there soon followed a Storm of Great
Reproaches & Confusions upon me. Gett Good by what I tell you!

§   After many Prayers, and Tears, and Fasts, on a great Occasion, I
found my Temptations, and Confusions, Continued and Multiplied. These
Rebukes of Heaven, were improved by Satan, very much unto my Discouragement. But my weeping Soul, kept humbly professing before the Lord;
'Lord, I will not give over Seeking thee,
' tho' it appears as if I Sought thee in Vain: I will alwayes Love thee
' and Serve thee, though thou dost Seem as if thou wouldest Lay me by
' from Serving thee: Tho' thou shouldest not rescue my opportunities to
' glorify [ms. p. 214] my Lord Jesus Christ, from the fine Devices of
' Satan to hurt them, yett I will hold on to glorify Him as much as ever
' I Can all my Dayes; Yea, tho' thou shouldest Leave me without Hopes of
' arriving to glory at ye Last.

While I was thus professing before the Lord, He Revived my broken,
drooping Spirit, with comfortable perswasions, That He would not Cast me
off, but that I should see a blessed Issue of all the dark Dispensations
that were Passing over me.

And, My Son, I have found it so! I have found it so!

§   I have Sometimes had my Mind awakened, with much Importunity to beg
Three Favours of ye Lord.

First, That CHRIST may appear to me the most Glorious of all objects.
Next, That SIN may appear to me, the most Odious of all objects.
Thirdly, That the Heavenly World may be as Real to me, as any thing

upon Earth.

These Things I also ask for you, My Son, and I Wish that you may ask them for yourself.

§   On a Certain Day of Prayer, Sitting as before ye Lord, and Thinking on the Purposes of Sovereign & Infinite Grace, to make me Happy, in the Fruition of God, & of His Christ, forevermore; I was Dissolved in Tears, and my Soul was Transported with Raptures of Love to God; and the Love and Joy of God So Raptured me, That I readily Consented [ms. p. 215] unto it, that if the Service and Interest of God, required my being Either Annihilated, or Miserable, it should be So; I was Willing, it should be so; I was wholly Sacrificed unto God in a Flame of Love; I was Willing to be Any Thing, Yea, to be Nothing, if the great God may be glorified.

And then, an astonishing Assurance Ensued upon it, That so far would my God be, from ordering my being Annihilated or Miserable, He would forever take pleasure, to glorify Himself, in heaping inconceiveable Blessedness upon me.

§   There were certain Wicked and Wretched people, (perhaps the Whole world could not have afforded a more horrid Spectacle,) With whom I took more than ordinary Pains, to bring them unto Saving Repentance, and Serious Religion.[45] I think, I never did in my Life, more Exercise ye true Spirit of Charity: I think, ye Lord was Glorified by the Charitable Essayes, thus Laboriously used upon this miserable Sett of people.

An Eminent person Sent me an Elegant Poem, written in the Latin Tongue, on that occasion; and the Stroke which most Comforted me in that Panegyrical Composure, was, That the People of God, had Seen Some Image of JESUS CHRIST, in my Labours and Expensive Compassion for those Miserables.

It ran thus.

Par nullus Domino, quicunqu negaverit, Ejas Anticyris rabies non Expur-
ganda duabus. [ms. p. 216] Sed Similes termi Mensura, Gratia Christi
Nonnullos reddit, Caelestis imagine Patris Fulgentes, quorum mihi Pars
non Parva videns. ἐπιλεγχιζεις Legitur Sponsor; Miserentis IESU Cernimus
Effigiem Claram, dum Viscera CHRISTI Exeris in Semet Perdentes, ut revo-
catis E Laqueo Satanae donetur Gratia Vitae.[46]

I thought, I was arrived unto the highest Pinacle of my Happiness, if I
might Represent and Exhibit, any Glory of my Lord JESUS CHRIST, unto the
world. No Glory, No, None, Like that of conformity to my Lord JESUS
CHRIST!

But then, I thought, that in this Instance, my Conformity had been
but Half carried through. For, when my Lord JESUS CHRIST had most Com-
passionately done for the people about Him, all the Good that there was
opportunity to do, they took Him, and Hang'd Him on a Tree,[47] after all.

Behold, Immediately after this, there were diverse Libels thrown at
my Gate, by Some horrid people, full of abominable Stuff, relating to
those Miserables, whom they foolishly thought, it was in my Power to have
rescued more than I did, out of their Temporal Miseries. And in One of
these Libels, they drew ye Picture of a Man, hanging on ye Gallowes;
They wrote my Name over it; and by the side of it, they wrote, This is
[Such an ones,] Desert.

Now, Now! my Soul was filled with unspeakable Joy! Now I had
Gain'd all my Point! Now my Resemblance unto [ms. p. 217] my Lord JESUS
CHRIST, had a Glorious Addition made unto it.

Oh! Token For Good![48] How can I be Sufficiently Thankful for such
a Token!

§ Being Engaged in the Duties of a Secret Fast before the Lord, I have been brought unto this Temper in them.

Full of Contritions and Amazements, has my Soul been; and anon it has arrived unto an astonishing Satisfaction.

I Considered the Afflictions, which had many wayes been Exercising of me. I considered ye Holiness of God, as Glorified in chastising me with all those Afflictions for my Sins against Him. I took Part with the Holiness of God against Myself. I think, I can truly say, That I found a Principle within me, inexpressibly Gratified and Satisfied, and Rejoicing that the Great God was Glorified, even by my own being Broken with miserable Circumstances. But then, I cannot Express ye Assurances, with which the Lord Irradiated me, That He would bring me near unto Himself, and not pour out His Wrath, but His Love, upon me forevermore.

§   One Day, upon o^e Singing in o^e Congregation, those words, Psal. 18. 23.

With Persons merciful that are

Thou Merciful thyself wilt show

My mind made this Reflection.

'   I see no person miserable, but my Heart [ms. p. 218] is very sen-
' sibly touched with their Miseries. I would, if I could, with all my
' Heart, help them in their Miseries. I have no pleasure Comparable to
' that of doing Acts of Mercy, Kindness, Goodness. I do them Every Day,
' & have an Heart Insatiably Disposed unto the Doing of them. I show
' Mercy to my very Enemies, & never decline doing them any Good, that I
' have an opportunity to Do. I beg of God, that He would show Mercy to
' them. When I see ye Glorious God Revenge upon them, with dreadful Dis-
' pensations, ye Wrongs which they have done to me, I am inwardly

' Troubled at their Confusions. If I should hear & see the Lord offering
' me, to Strike them for my Sake, I should Intercede for them, & cry to
' God, that He would Spare them, & make them Happy.

Then thought I. All this Mercy in me, is but a Faint Ray, from that
Vast and Bright Sun of Mercy that shines in ye Infinite GOD. And it is
upon me, a Token for Good, that the Great God, will be infinitely more
Merciful to me, than I can be to any of my Fellow-Creatures.

The Thought hereof, dissolved me into Tears, & filled me with Joy
unspeakable & full of Glory.

§   In the midst of ye Memorials, which I sett before my Son, for his
Imitation, or for his Encouragement, I dare not but mention one Article,
which I have Recorded, on a Day sett apart for ye Duties of a Secret
Fast before the Lord.

'   Some of my Bitterest Confessions and Confusions this Day before the
' Lord, were, That a vast variety of Successive Temptations [ms. p. 219]
' has Assaulted me. But I have always Miscarried under my Temptations.
' Tho' ye Temptations have not always gained ye Point pursued in them,
' yett my Miscarriages under them, have been great Provocations unto God.
' A Reflection upon the more Signally Temptational part of my Life, Ex-
' ceedingly Abased me before the Lord. It Caused me mightily to fly unto
' the Sacrifice, and the Righteousness of ye Lord JESUS CHRIST, who was
' Tempted, and never Sinned, but alwayes came off a Conqueror, and Glori-
' fied GOD.

§   I must observe it, unto the Glory of the Divine Mercy and Wisdome,
and you, My Son, may make a very Good Use of this observation; I have
rarely made it my Study, to be Exemplary in any One Thing, but the Lord
has Accepted me to Write something on that Thing, & have my Writings

Read, and Spred, and Priz'd among His People.[49]

But here, I must not be more particular.

§   This I can Testify for the Lord: That Cries to GOD, for Grace, to
Purify us, & Glorify Him, when made, with fervent Plea's, that such Grace
has been purchased for us, by the Blood of o^e Lord JESUS CHRIST, Alwayes
have Wonderful Answers, Often have Immediate Ones. [ms. p. 220]

§   A Considerable Part of my Study and Expense, has been, for the
Releef of the Poor. I Still do what I can, to find them & help them; and
when my own Little Stock of Money is Exhausted, I repair to the Richer
people in my Flock, (who on Such occasions readily hearken unto me,) &
Commend proper objects unto their Charity.

But Sometimes, I have been thus Encouraged by ye providence of
Heaven. At the very Time, When I have Laid out All I had, upon ye Poor,
& been Troubled & Grieved that I had no more, Some Gentleman or other,
altogether unto my Surprize has brought me a Summ of Money, with his
Desire, that I would Scatter it among such Poor, as I should judge proper to Receive it.

Oh! how ready do I find the glorious Lord in his Providence, to
assist my poor Intentions!

My Son, O^e Opportunities to do Good, would be more than they are,
if we were sett upon it.

§ Many and many a time, have Thoughts of this Importance been rolling in
my Mind; and my mind is, I hope, formed into a compliance with them.

There is an horrid Idolatry committed, when we take Notice of this
and that considerable in any Man, and Consider not at the same Time, the
great GOD, as ye Author and Fountain of all this Excellency. We must

Look upon Man, as Nothing, any further than what the Great GOD makes him to be; and when we Look upon any thing that Looks Great or Good in any Man, it must be with sensible Acknowledgments, That all this comes from God.

The most of men will celebrate the [ms. p. 221] Learning, the Vertue, the Conduct, of an Eminent person, without ye Least observation of the Great GOD in all; Much less do they give All the whole glory of All, to GOD, and behold Man, as no other than a Vessel chosen by the Sovereign Grace of GOD,[50] for to Exhibit something of His own glory, in the Points which render the Man observable.

I tremble, I tremble, at the Thoughts of having a Great Name in the world, or being admired & applauded & mightily Talk'd of. The only Reason of this Regrett on my Mind, is, Because they who Talk of me, Will not have the Piety to Look further than me. My Sorry Name, will have Sacrilegiously Lodg'd upon it, some Regards that should be Transferred unto the glorious Name of GOD alone. Indeed there will be no Iniquity charged on me, for the Sacriledge, which Others will thus fall into. But yett, it will be an Infelicity: I shall reckon myself Unhappy in being the Object, upon which any shall Sinfully terminate ye Honours and praises, which belong only to GOD: I abhor it wonderfully.

I shall Rejoice in it, if any Lovers of God shall say, The God of all grace has disposed that Servant of His, to do Vertuously! or, The Power and Wisdome of God, has carried that Servant of His, well thro' Labours and Sufferings! But I do not approve of it, That any people should Say of me; He is a man of Such and such Accomplishments; or, He has accomplished Such & such, notable matters, and acquitted himself bravely in them; --and Stop there; and see not GOD in all, Yea, See not that GOD is all. Now [ms. p. 222] the people who so Stop in the Creature,

are almost all the world. And for this Cause, I even Deprecate, as well
as Depreciate, a Great Fame in the World; I cannot with Pleasure think
of it; It is with Horror that I think of it.

I am Glad, my very Spirit is full of Gladness, that there is no more
Notice taken of me. And when I have had a Prospect of Easily doing Some
Things, that would have Contributed not a Little, unto my having a Name
among the Learned Men of the Earth; but I could not See any direct Sub-
serviency to the Name of the Great GOD, and of His glorious CHRIST, in
ye matters, I have therefore, Even for that very Cause, declined them.

{ Yea, My Spirit has proceeded thus far in this Exercise of Piety;
that I have been able to Enter this among my Memorials.
' My Dear SAVIOUR, what a Frame hast thou brought my Soul unto: I am
' willing to be Slandered, Reviled, Lessened: Patient of being Despised
' & Rejected of Men. This proceeds, not only from an Acquiescence in y^e
' Divine Sovereignty, & from a Submission to ye Just Punishment of my
' Iniquity; but also from a Secret Pleasure in Conformities to my SAVIOUR
' and from an Horror of being thought a Considerable Man, by people who
' terminate in Man, & Sett Man up in ye Throne of GOD, and make an Idol
' of whatever Man, they after be any Guardeins to. }

§   I have Seen and Read, how some very Little Men, have been the First
occasions and Instruments of Great Things in the world;[51] As, a Single
Hair applied unto a Flyer, that has other wheels depending on it, may
pull up an Oak, or pull down an House. This Consideration has Encouraged
me, who am among the most Inconsiderable persons upon Earth, to be alwayes
Watching, and often Thinking, What Good may I do in the World! I have
made it an Encouragement unto me, to be Continually Looking after Opportunities to be serviceable unto ye Interests of a glorious CHRIST, and
of His people, yea, and of All people in the world.

I have more particularly Seen, how Indefatigable Some are, to Do Mischief, in the world, and Embroil Mankind, [ms. p. 223] and pursue their own Sorry and Sordid Interests; and how much Hurt One Little Wretch may do. I have concluded upon it, That I ought to Do more for the Interests of my glorious LORD, than any Carnal Men can do for their own; and that it might be possible for me, to do as mucn Good, as One Little Wretch not beyond my own Dimensions, may do Hurt, unto o^e Fellow-Creatures.

This has done much, to Inspire my poor Activity. My Son, If you should Live to any Capacity, Lett it have as much Influence upon You.

§   If I hear that any person has done me Wrong in Word or Deed, I find, it is Often, (perhaps, not Alwayes,) the best way in the World, Not to Lett them know, that I have any knowledge of it. The best way is, to Forgive and Forgett the Wrong, and bury it in Silence. For, besides the Consideration due to ye Internal Advantage, reap'd by such christianity, there is this to be Considered: Such is ye Malignity in the most of Men, that they will Hate You, only because You know that they have wrong'd you. They will, as far as they Can, Justify the Wrong they have done; and because their Wicked Hearts Imagine that you must needs beat a Spite unto them, for the Wrong you have received from them, they will bear a Confirmed Spite unto you, on that Vile Account. Whereas, I have often found, That my Concocting with Patience and Silence, a Sleight, or an Hurt [ms. p. 224] that has been offered unto me, has been Followed (and Rewarded by God) with this Consequence; That the Very Persons who have wrong'd me, have afterwards been made Instruments of Signal Service unto me.

§ When any Remarkable Affliction befalls me, I sett myself to Consider,

What Advantage I may Contrive to my Flock, and to the People of God, out
of this Affliction? The Affliction awakens me to Preach, and perhaps to
Write, those things, which may be of General Advantage. I think with myself, It may be the Lord intends now to make me bear Some Special Fruits
for His Glory and Service in His Churches, which else would never have
been found upon me. And I can truly say, That tho' Affliction be not
Joyous but Grievous,[52] yett the very Prospect of this Effect, while I
have been but Entring into the Darkness, which I saw coming upon me, and
while I have been yett in the Dark, as to the particular Benefits &
Revenues, for the Service of Religion, which could arise from it; It has
caused my Spirit Exceedingly to Triumph over Troubles; I have, with a
Triumphant Satisfaction Rejoiced in it, that the Lord would please to
send Sorrowes, with Such admirable Designs upon me.

§   When I have been persecuted with any Calumny, or Calumnious Malignity, wherein I could plainly perceive Satan seeking to Damnify my
Opportunities to be Serviceable; Or, When any furious Temptations of
Satan, have in a more Internal [ms. p. 225] way assaulted me; I have sett
myself to Consider, How to Prosecute a Revenge upon Satan? It has been
a Contrivance of Great Consequence in my Ministry; By the Devices of
Satan against me, to be provoked unto the Taking of Such Steps, and the
preaching and writing of such Truths, as may render the Divel remarkably
a Loser, by going to meddle with me. The God of Peace has given me
astonishing Experiences of His Favour to me, in this Matter.

§   My Son, I know not whether ye Lord will accept you to Serve Him in
the Evangelical Ministry. Tis my Desire, that He may; and if He should,
I am Desirous, that you may do a thousand times better than your poor
Father has done.[53]

If any thing in my Experience, may be useful to You, Behold, how ready I am to Communicate it!

I will here mention Several Points, of my Conduct, relating to ye Flock, whereof I have y^e <u>Pastoral Care</u> Committed unto me.[54]

1. Tis my Watchful and Constant Study, that never any person of my Flock (or indeed any other) Comes fairly in my way, but I Lett fall Some <u>Word</u> or another, that I design to prove some way Serviceable to them.

2. I Endeavour generally to Sett apart One Afternoon in a Week, for <u>Pastoral Visits</u>; and in these, I address all sorts of Persons, Good and Bad, Old and Young, with as Exquisitely Contrived <u>Admonitions of Piety</u>, as ever I can. I find a [ms. p. 226] marvellous Presense and Blessing of God, in these <u>Pastoral Visits</u>.

3. Whenever I make any <u>Occasional Visit</u> I do not know, that ever I miss of Contriving, how to make my <u>Visit</u> Profitable, Serviceable, Edifying unto those to whom I make it.

4. I am Continually Scattering <u>Books of Piety</u>, into the Hands of my Flock; and often do it with this Advice, <u>Remember that I am Speaking to You, all the while you have this Book before you</u>! So there is not a Day in the year, in which I am not preaching to many of them.

5. It is a Rule with me, rather to <u>Suffer</u>, & bury in Silence, any manner of Injuries and Abuses, from <u>Absurd People</u> in ye Flock, than to manage any <u>Contention</u> with any of them on any occasion. Lett ye Matter or Issue of ye Controversy be what it will, I shall gain more in regard of the Great Interest, by <u>Remitting</u> of my Right, than by <u>Pursuing</u> of it.

6. And in the Services of Christianity, I make no Manner of Difference, between those that <u>Abuse</u> me, and those that <u>Value</u> me. If I

make any Difference, tis by being Readier to Serve ye Former, than the Latter.

Tis admirable to see, how this Conduct, will conquer ye Follies and Humors of unreasonable People.

7.   In my Public Ministry, if at any Time, (as I do Often times) I go thro' a Course, Either of Themes depending on one another in ye Body of Divinity, or of Texts as they Ly together in any paragraph of the Scripture; I make [ms. p. 227] much Prayer before the Lord, (even with Fasting,) for His Direction and Assistence before I undertake it. But still I Reserve myself a Liberty, usually every other Lords-day, to Discourse on Occasional Subjects; and for my Direction in these, I Consider ye particular Conditions, Occurrences, Temptations, of the Flock, and Endeavour as well as I can, to suit them with the Word of God.

§ I am Willing to recite Some Special Points of Conduct, which I have after my poor & weak Measure observed in the Education of My Children.^55

You, My Son, have been an Object and Witness, of almost all that I am going to Write. And I write it with ye more of Satisfaction, in hopes, that the Remembrance of it may have a blessed Effect upon you.

I. I pour out Continual Prayers and Cries, to the God of all Grace,^56 for my Children, That He will be a Father to them, and bestow His Christ and His Grace upon them, and guide them with His Counsil and bring them to His glory.

And in this Action I mention them Distinctly, Every one by Name, unto ye Lord.

II. I begin betimes to Entertain them with Delightful Stories, Especially Scriptural Ones. And I Still Conclude, with Some Lesson of

Piety; bidding them to Learn that <u>Lesson</u> from the <u>Story</u>.

And thus, every Day at the <u>Table</u>, [ms. p. 228] I have used myself, to tell a <u>Story</u> before I Rise; and make the <u>Story</u> useful, unto the <u>olive-plants about the Table</u>.[57]

III. When the Children at any time accidentally Come in my way, it is my Custome, to Lett fall Some <u>Sentence</u> or other, that may be Monitory and Profitable to them.

This Matter proves to me, a Matter of Some Study and Labour and contrivance. But who can tell, what may be the Effect of a <u>Continual Dropping</u>?

IV. I essay betimes, to Engage the Children, in Exercises of <u>Piety</u>; and Especially <u>Secret Prayer</u>: For which I give them very plain and brief <u>Directions</u>, and suggest unto them the <u>Petitions</u>, which I would have them to make before the Lord, and which I therefore Explain to their Apprehension and Capacity. And I often call upon them; <u>Child, Don't you forgett Every Day to go alone, and pray as I have directed you!</u>

V. Betimes I try to form in the Children a Temper of <u>Benignity</u>. I putt them upon the doing of <u>Services</u> and <u>Kindnesses</u> for one another, and for other children. I <u>applaud</u> them, when I see them Delight in it. I <u>upbraid</u> all Aversion to it. I caution them Exquisitely, against all <u>Revenges</u> of <u>Injuries</u>. I instruct them to Return <u>Good</u> Offices for <u>Evil</u> Ones. I show them, how they will, by this <u>Goodness</u> become Like to the Good GOD, and His glorious CHRIST. I Lett them Discern, that I am not Satisfied, [ms. p. 229] Except when they have a Sweetness of <u>Temper</u> Shining in them.

VI. As Soon as tis possible, I make the Children Learn to <u>Write</u>. And when they can <u>Write</u>, I Employ them in writing out, ye most Agreeable and profitable Things, that I can Invent for them. In this way, I

propose, to fraight their Minds with Excellent Things, and have a deep
Impression made upon their Minds by such Things.

VII. I mightily Endeavour it, That the Children may betimes, be
acted by Principles of Reason and Honour.

I first begett in them, an high Opinion of their Fathers Love to
them, and of his being best Able to Judge, what shall be Good for them.

Then I make them Sensible, Tis a Folly for them to pretend unto
any Witt or Will of their own: They must Resign all to me, who will be
sure to do what is Best; My Word must be their Law.

I Cause them to understand, That it is an Hurtful and a Shameful
Thing, to Do Amiss. I aggravate this on all occasions; and Lett them
See, how Amiable they will render themselves by Well-doing.

The First Chastisement, which I inflict for an ordinary Fault, is,
To Lett ye Child See and hear me in an Astonishment, and hardly able to
Beleeve, that the Child could Do so Base a Thing; but Beleeving, that
they will never do it again.

I would never Come, to give a Child a Blow, Except in Case of ob-
stinacy, or Something that is very Criminal. [ms. p. 230]

To be chased for a while out of my presence, I would make to be
Look'd upon, as ye sorest Punishment in the Family.

I would, by all possible Insinuations, gain this Point upon them;
That for them to Learn all the brave Things in the World, is the bravest
Thing in the world. I am not fond of proposing Play to them, as a Reward of any Diligent Application, to Learn what is Good; Lest they should
think, Diversion to be a better and a nobler Thing than Diligence. I
would have them come to propound and Expect at this rate; I have done
well, and now I will go to my Father; He will teach me some Curious Thing
for it. I must have them count it, a Priviledge, to be Taught; and I

Sometimes manage ye matter so, that my Refusing to Teach them Something, is their Punishment. The Strain of my Threatenings therefore is, You shall not be allow'd to Read, or to Write, or Learn such a Thing, if you do not as I have bidden you!

The Slavish way of Education, carried on, with Raving, and Kicking, and Scourging, (in Schools as well as Families;) Tis Abominable, and a dreadful Judgment of God upon ye world.

VIII. Tho' I find it a marvellous Advantage, to have the Children Strongly Biased by principles of Reason and Honour, (which I find, Children will feel sooner than is commonly thought for:) yett I would neglect no Endeavours, [ms. p. 231] to have Higher Principles infused into them.

I therefore Betimes Awe them, with the Eye of GOD upon them.

I show them, how they must Love JESUS CHRIST, and Show it, by doing what their parents require of them.

I often tell them of the Good Angels, who Love them, & Help them, and Guard them; and who take Notice of them; and therefore must not be Disobliged.

I do not Say much to them, of the Evil Angels, because I would not have them under frightful Fancies about the Apparitions of Divels. But yett, I Lett them know, that there are Divels, who tempt them to Wickedness, & who are glad when they do Wickedly, & who may gett Leave of God to kill them for it.

Heaven and Hell I sett before them, as the Consequences of their Behaviour here.

IX. When the Children are Capable of it, I take them Alone, one by one; and after my charges unto them, to Fear God, and Serve Christ, and Shun Sin, I Pray with them in my Study, and make them ye Witnesses of the Agonies, with which I address ye Throne of Grace on their behalf.

X. I find much Benefit, by a Particular Method, as of <u>Catechising</u> the Children, so, of Carrying on the <u>Repetition</u> of the public Sermons unto them.

The Answers of the <u>Catechism</u> I still Explain, with abundance of brief <u>Questions</u>, which make them to take in the meaning of it; and I See, that they do so. [ms. p. 232]

And when the <u>Sermons</u> are to be <u>Repeted</u>, I chuse to putt Every <u>Truth</u> into a <u>Question</u>, to be answered Still with, <u>Yes</u>, or <u>No</u>. In this Way I awaken their <u>Attention</u>, as well as Enlighten their <u>Understanding</u>. And in this way I have an opportunity to ask, <u>Do you Desire Such or Such a Grace of God</u>? and the Like. Yea, I have an opportunity to <u>Demand</u>, and perhaps to <u>Obtain</u>, their Early and Frequent, (and, why not, <u>Sincere</u>?) <u>Consent</u> unto the glorious Articles of the <u>New Covenant</u>. The <u>Spirit of Grace</u> may fall upon them in their Action, [I hope, He <u>has</u> done So!] and they may be Siez'd by Him, & held as His <u>Temples</u>, thro' Eternal Ages.

§ Ah, My <u>Sloth</u>, My <u>Sloth</u>! I have often made this Complaint, My <u>Sloth</u> has done me more mischief, than all the <u>Devils</u> in ye whole Kingdome of Darkness. To Exorcise this <u>Evil Spirit</u>, I have Cryed much unto ye Lord, that this my <u>Enemy</u> may not Prevail against me. A <u>Diligent Hand</u>, is a thing which I have <u>Diligently Sought</u> unto ye GOD of all grace for ye Bestowal of. And I often, often turn upon myself with that Pungent Question: <u>Do I now So spend my Time, that I may give a Good Account of it</u>? And, <u>Am I now at ye work in which I ought to be</u>? [ms. p. 233]

§ When I have been Lying prostrate in the Dust before the Lord, I have comfortably found my Spirit, not only <u>Desiring</u> of, but also in some desireable Degree <u>Arriving</u> to, these <u>Attainments</u>.

I. The Great GOD, and His Glorious CHRIST, have swallow'd me up.

I would be alwayes <u>Thinking</u> on Him; alwayes <u>Acting</u> for Him, and Relish nothing any further than I find it Assist me in <u>Acknowledging</u> of Him.

I can cheerfully Refer myself to Him, and be Satisfied in His Most Wise Dispensations towards me; because I am Sure, whether I see it or no, that His <u>Wisdome</u> does Consult His <u>Glory</u>, in all that befalls me.

Hence my Own <u>Will</u> is now very much Abolished; I find the <u>Will</u> of God wonderfully Extinguishing of it. And I grow towards an Extinction of all my <u>own Interests</u>; to know no <u>Interests</u> but the <u>Lords</u>.

II. My <u>Love</u> to my <u>Neighbour</u> improves to a very Sweet Serenity. I take an unspeakable Pleasure in all manner of <u>Beneficence</u>; no pleasure Comparable to it. If I can see <u>Opportunities</u> to <u>Do Good</u> unto any, I need no <u>Arguments</u> to move me to it. I do it Naturally, Delightfully, with Rapture. I seek for Such <u>Opportunities</u>, even <u>as for Great Spoil</u>. I am ambitious of nothing so much, as to be universally <u>Serviceable</u>.

I Rejoice in the <u>Prosperity</u> of others; It is a Refreshment unto me, to see the <u>Smiles</u> of God upon them.

I am afraid of allowing in myself, the Least <u>Ill Wish</u> towards my <u>Personal Enemies</u>, or such as have <u>Done Ill</u> unto me. It would be an <u>Affliction</u> unto me, if I should see God Afflicting of <u>Them</u>, for my Sake. It is an Easy Thing for me, to Forgett how Unkind and unjust they [ms. p. 234] have been, and to Load them with Kindnesses.

III. There is this Enjoyment added unto the Rest.

As I am <u>Nothing</u> before God, so I am Willing to be <u>Nothing</u> among <u>Men</u>. I have no Fondness for <u>Applause</u> and <u>Honour</u> in the world. It is with a sort of Horrour, if I perceive myself <u>Applauded</u>; I have a Dread of being <u>Honoured</u>. I am gott above <u>Anger</u> at those, who think or Speak meanly of me.

I take abundance of <u>Shame</u> to myself; I can bear with Submission, the <u>shaming Rebukes</u> that Heaven Smites me withal. I can Submitt unto it, to be <u>Despised of Men</u>.[58] If I am grossly <u>Reproached</u>, I hardly durst appear in my own Vindication, against the Falsest <u>Reproaches</u>, because I am sensible of so much <u>Evil</u> that might be truly Spoken of me.

These are Works of God, produced by y[e] Almighty Spirit of Grace. I noted them down, that I might Look upon them with advantage; Especially, when I should find the Vigour of them at any time abated in me.

§My Heart has been very Singularly Comforted in Meditations on that word; Joh. 15. 7,8. <u>If yee abide in me, and my words abide in you, yee shall ask what yee will, and it shall be done unto you. Herein is my Father Glorified, that yee bear much Fruit</u>. I have thought, That if I took Delight in <u>Serving</u> of God, it was an happy Omen of His Taking Delight in <u>Hearing</u> and <u>Helping</u> and <u>Saving</u> of me. I have thought, That if I were a man alwayes <u>bringing forth Fruit</u> unto God, and thereby giving Demonstration of my <u>Abiding in His Christ</u>, and having <u>His Words alwayes with me</u>, it was an Happy Symptom, that my [ms. p. 235] <u>Prayers</u> would be Accepted with Him.

Now, I have hoped, that the Lord has brought me to something of character.

I can't think on this Word, without a Thousand Heart-melting Astonishments!

§I have all this while Omitted the Mention of y[e] Various Intentions and Contrivances, with which the Dispensation of y[e] <u>Alms</u>, that have even filled my Life, have been Carried on. The Reason of the Omission has been; Because I thought an <u>Eternal Concealment</u> most proper for them; a

Concealment even from a <u>Son</u>, that is to be as my very Hand unto me.
But, inasmuch as ye Design of these memorials, is to instruct You, <u>My</u>
<u>Son</u>, in ye Methods of <u>Godliness</u> and <u>Fruitfulness</u>, I will rescue from y^e
midst of that <u>Concealment</u>, at Least one way to <u>Devise</u>[59] <u>Good</u>, which has
been Sometimes practised with me.

I have Several times, taken Little Parcels of <u>Money</u>, (<u>Seven</u> perhaps
at a time,) containing about Half a Peece of Eight in a Paper; These
Parcels of <u>Money</u>, I have accompanied, with so many <u>Books of Piety</u>. I
have Sent y^e <u>Packets</u> unto <u>Ministers</u> abroad, in Such Towns as I have
Convenient; and Sometimes, (that Grace might herein have ye more Triumphant Exercise,) I have Sent them to Such Ministers, as have treated me,
not so well as they might have done. I have Directed a <u>Nameless Letter</u>
unto them, in Such as way, as they might not know, that I was ye Person
with whom they were now concerned. I have desired them, to find out so
many <u>Poor</u> and <u>Bad</u> people, in their Flock, & ⟨⟨ Visit them, ⟩⟩ bestow
these <u>Alms</u>, and [ms. p. 236] <u>Books</u>, in their <u>own Names</u>, (if they pleased)
upon them; With their own Holy Counsils and Warnings Unto them, to Lay
hold on Eternal Life. In this way, I proposed, not only to <u>Do Good</u> unto
the Elect of God, but also to Awaken y^e <u>Ministers</u> themselves, unto a more
flaming Zeal to <u>Do Good</u>. But that I may more Exactly Describe, what I
would be at, I will Transcribe, One of ye Letters, which I Sent, (copied
by a <u>Female</u> Hand, for my being the better under <u>Covert</u>,) on these
occasions.[60]

' Syr. From an Unknown Hand, there is a Small Trouble now impos'd upon
' you. A Little <u>Silver</u> is, with the propriety thereof, devolved into
' your Hand. It is now no Longer any mans Else, but <u>Yours</u>; nor is any
' other Name now to be used on this occasion, but <u>Yours</u>. But it is de-
' sired, That you would find out as many persons in Your Flock, who are

' in very poor circumstances, both on Temporal and Spiritual Accounts,[61]

' as you find the Summ divided into Parcels; and Distribute ye Parcels

' unto them. At ye same time, it is desired, That you would bestow your

' Holy Counsils and Warnings upon them; and not Leave them, until they

' have Resolved upon ye practice of Serious Piety. If then you Lodge

' with them the Little Books, with which you are now also for that pur-

' pose furnished, Your Advice will be Rimembred ye better with them.

' Who can tell, but under an Angelical Conduct, you may now find out

' Some of the Elect of God, among the Poor, who thus have the Gospel

' preached unto them?[62] Your own Ministry will also be rendred very

' acceptable, among a People, to whom you make such Pastoral Visits.

' Lett not a word be Spoken, about the Original of this Action: For

' there is but one Man in the world, who knowes any thing of it, or is

' Like to know. A glorious CHRIST be with You! ---- ------ [ms. p.

' 237]

§ I have had my Mind Strangely and Strongly buffeted, with Temptations of
this Importance.

I have now for many, and weary years, been Leading a Laborious Life,
in ye wayes of Religion. I have Lived in a continual Flame. The Care
to carry on Ordinary and Extraordinary Devotions, & to have my Heart
filled with perpetual Thoughts of a Devout character, & Tendency; and
Suppress and Destroy all the Corrupt Inclinations of my Soul; and my
Watchful, Various, Numberless contrivances to Do Good, unto all that I
converse withal, and abroad in the world; and my perpetual Warfare wth
successive Temptations; whereof my Course of Living ever now and then Renewes a Tempest upon me: All these things together, fill my Life with
Labours and Sorrowes. I gett nothing of this world by these Labours;

There is no worldly profit of y^m. I miss many Advantages to come at worldly Riches, by reason of them. If there be any one point, wherein above the rest, I may pretend unto any shadow of a Vertue, it is ordered, that in that very point, I am singularly misunderstood & Calumniated. My Serviceableness does but Expose me to Malignity. My very Essayes to be Serviceable, are made my Blemishes and Reproaches. The Blessedness of the Future State, who can tell, What it is? And it may be, tis uncertain, whether I shall arrive to any such Blessedness. Why then should not my Weary Mind, abate of this Flame? I don't propose to turn a Profane & a Debauch't sort [ms. p. 238] of a Divel; But why may I not Leave off ye Labours of my Flights in Piety and Usefulness? Why may I not Suffer myself, to sink down, into ye Low, Dull, Slothful Measures, of ye Common and Barren Christianity? Why may not I Content myself, to Jog on, as the Christians of ye Lowest Form, who, if they can but just Creep along, in some Formalities, and keep clear of Grosser Scandals, do not Seem to Care for any more: How Easy should I make myself by such a Conduct! Why should I be an Enemy to such a Grateful Easiness? To what Purpose will be my Perseverance?

But now, to those Hellish Temptations, I have still my Answer, from that Oracle of Heaven: 1. Cor. 15. 58. Be yee Stedfast & unmoveable, alwayes abounding in the Work of ye Lord: forasmuch as yee know, that your Labour is not in Vain in ye Lord.

And Looking up to ye Lord, for the Aids of His Grace, I have then found my Resolutions fixed more than Ever in my Life, to Live unto Christ, & bring forth much Fruit unto Him, & never to be Weary of well-doing.
[ms. p. 239]

§ My Son, I am now going to Leave with you certain Memorials of Manly

Christianity, Which, if they may make a Suitable Impression upon you, will be more Enriching and Ennobling Things unto you, than if I had Left you ye fairest Estate in this world.

I gave you Lately a Description of Manly Christianity, in Three Essayes of it. But it was not Long before ye Lord show'd me, That I had not yett enough of a Glorious CHRIST, in my Essayes. The Strains and Flights of Real CHRISTIANITY in them, needed a further Improvement. I could not be at Rest, until I went over my Three Points again, and brought a Lovely JESUS, a Precious JESUS, under a more Explicit Consideration, in every one of them all.[63]

The First Thing I Saw necessary, was to fix ye Idea which I was to Live upon. Wherefore, I considered, That my Lord JESUS CHRIST, is God manifest in o^e Flesh;[64] ye Son of God Incarnate.[65] It is in Him that GOD Exhibits Himself unto ye world; It is thro' Him, that we Draw near to GOD; render o^e Devotions to GOD; & Enjoy o^e Communions with GOD. The Son of GOD, Assuming ye Man JESUS into One Person with Himself, is to be ye next Object of Considerations, in my Acts of Piety; But at the Same Instant, I would always take in this Consideration; That ye GOD, who in His own Second Person, Condescended unto an Incarnation, is the very Same GOD, who is also the Father, and the Spirit; the Infinite ONE, who is the First Cause and the Last End of all things. [ms. p. 240]

Provided of this Idea, I then proposed and pursued, these Attainments.

I. Not a Day must pass me, in which I do not fly, to the Sacrifice of a Glorious CHRIST, as the Only Atonement for my Sins; and to His Righteousness as my only Title to Blessedness.

Whenever I perceive I have done Amiss, I would fly Presently to that Sacrifice. Whenever I have made any Effort at Well-doing, I would presently fly to that Righteousness.

I must Zelously Seek the Death of Every Irregular Lust in my Soul.
But my great way to come at it, must be, by pleading ye Death of a Glori
ous CHRIST, as purchasing for me, such a Blessing of God. This I must
plead, with Strong Cries & Tears,[66] till an Efficacious Order come forth
from ye Throne of Heaven, That my Sin shall Dy.

My Mind must be assiduously Engag'd in Contemplations on a Glorious
CHRIST; until I feel myself Sweetly affected, and Even ravished, with some
Apprehensions of His Glory.

When I am Engaged in any fixed Meditations on the Words or Works of
God, E're I dismiss them, I must Enquire, What there is of a Glorious
CHRIST, that I am Led now to think upon; and Rejoice when I have Litt up-
on that Honey of the Rock.[67]

In my Public Discourses, I must Continually Sett a Glorious CHRIST
before my Hearers, and show them, the Truth as it is in Him,[68] and as it
Leads them to take Notice of Him.

In my Private Conversation, as it must be my perpetual Study and
Concern, [ms. p. 241] to talk Profitably, So I must Watch all Occasions
decently and Properly to introduce ye Mention of a Glorious CHRIST, and
Lay Something of His Incomparable Glory before ye Company.

Whenever I Write a Letter, I must use the best Ingenuity I can, that
Some Glory of a dear[69] CHRIST, may therein be handsomely Insinuated.

I must make unto a Glorious CHRIST, a Tender of all that I have;[70]
Inventing as Exquisite wayes as I can, How He may have Revenues out of
all; That is to Say, How I may fetch Acknowledgments to Him, even from
Others as well as Myself, out of all my Enjoyments. Yea, I must make Him
a Tender of what I have not, as well as of what I have; & pray and weep
unto Him, that the Whole World may be brought under the Golden Yoke of

Obedience unto Him; & Contribute all ye Assistences I can devise, to bring the World, so into the Possession of ye most Illustrious Lord of all.

And the Measures which I take for my Relish of any thing, must be from its Usefulness to me, in producing Acknowledgments of my Lord JESUS CHRIST: Examine this Continually, upon all my Delights, and have my Sentiments of them accordingly. I must Relish nothing, but what shall be Useful, to make me more Sensible of Him, and more Serviceable to Him; And so Regulate and Subjugate my Appetites, as to Relish Every thing, more or less, according as I find this Use to be made thereof. [ms. p. 242]

When I See any Sin Committed, it must bring me to think, with Love, and Holy Fear, on ye Holiness of my Lord JESUS CHRIST, who Hateth all such Wickedness: And think with Wonder, on the wonderful Merit and Vertue, in the Blood of the Son of God, which Cleanses from all Sin.

When in any Man, there is observed any Thing that is Excellent, I must presently Look off to a glorious CHRIST, and See that Excellency in Him Originally, in Him Transcendently, in Him Infinitely.

When I See myself or others, in any Circumstances, which carry Meanness, or Frailty, or any Abasements in them; as Eating, Drinking, Sleeping, or Weariness, or any Calamity whatsoever; it must raise in my Mind, some Thoughts of ye Abasing Circumstances, nearest unto them, which my Glorious CHRIST, underwent in ye Dayes of His Flesh.[71] But these Thoughts must alwayes be, with Rapturous and Admiring Praises, That ever ye Great GOD becoming a Man, should Submitt unto Such Diminutive, Such Vilifying Circumstances.

When I am called unto any Services, which would Else be very unacceptable to me, for ye Troubles and Fatigues attending of them, I sett

me gett attend them with all possible Alacrity; Because they are Services to a glorious CHRIST: They are Part of the Work which He has assign'd unto me: And, Oh! what uncomfortable Work, did He go through,
on my Account!

I must very, very often have in my View, the Example of a Glorious
CHRIST; Often think, What His Conduct and Carriage was on all occasions:
Take my Directions for my [ms. p. 243] Behaviour, towards all my Rela-
tives, towards all my Enemies, under all my Afflictions, from what I can
See in His way of treating such Objects on all occasions.[72]

I must Conscientiously and Industriously Practise the Duties of
Christianitie; the Duties of both Callings; the Duties which I owe to
all objects. But the Motive that shall Wing me for Every Duty, must be
this; This Duty is required & Expected of me, by GOD appearing in the
Nature of Man, & Subjecting Himself to the Law of God on my account; &
now from ye Throne of God, giving out this Law unto the World: And I
shall Please and Honour and Obey a glorious CHRIST, in my Rejoicing to
Work this Righteousness.

My Conversation with my Consort, must have this Thought Rectifying
and Sanctifying and Animating of it: How does a glorious CHRIST Love
His Church; What is His Tenderness for it!

My Conversation with my Children, must often, often Excite me to
prosecute a Thought of this Importance; A glorious CHRIST has made me a
child of God, What will He do for me; How must I place my Fear, & Love,
& Hope on Him, as the Fruit of this Adoption!

When I See an Infant, it should often raise in me, an Astonishment
at this thing; That ever the Son of GOD, becoming a Man, should putt
Himself into the poor State of Infancy!

When I Look over my Comfortable [ms. p. 244] Enjoyments, I must Look
upon the Sufferings of a Glorious CHRIST, and see, how far what I Enjoy,
was Deny'd unto Him. Unto those amazing Sufferings of my Lord, I must
ascribe the purchase of all those Blessings and Benefits, wherewith I am
daily Loaded by ye Lord.

The Felicity of being the Instrument in & by which a glorious CHRIST,
may One way or other Come to be Understood and Adored, must appear to me,
as the very Top of all Felicities. When I perceive myself So Improv'd
of Heaven, it should fill my Spirit with Triumphant Satisfactions; My
Spirit should be so Satisfied, & so Transported at it, as to Cry out;
O My Lord; I have All! I have All! I can ask for no more! O my Soul,
Return to thy Rest. The Lord has now dealt bountifully with thee![73]
II. Because a Glorious CHRIST has Ennobled the Name of MAN, by becoming
a MAN, This is the Consideration, that must Endear Mankind unto me. And
what He has done for Man, must Sweeten my Disposition to take pleasure
in all Acts of Beneficence, towards all ye children of Men.

I must Watch all Advantages to Do Good unto Men; because these Men
have that Nature on which a glorious CHRIST has putt a Marvellous Dig-
nity; and because He has not only Instructed me by His Pattern, but Commanded me by His Precept also, to Love them. I must Every Day continually
Do Good unto all sorts of Men; but still I am to [ms. p. 245] Do as unto
a glorious CHRIST all that I do.

Wherever I see the Image of a Glorious CHRIST, in Evangelical Endeavours to keep a Conscience Void of Offence towards God & Men,[74] I must
value that person on that Account, Exceedingly. That Holy Image must produce in me, a Singular Value and Kindness for any Person, and Swallow up
all other Things in him, that may have a Tendency to disaffect me to him.

Yea; The Regards that I Pay to any persons, that challenge any

Honours from me, on the Score of <u>Power</u>, of <u>Wisdome</u>, of <u>Riches</u>, or of any
other Accomplishments, must be founded in this: I See some <u>Image</u> of a
Glorious CHRIST, in those Excellencies: They give a faint Intimation of
<u>His Power</u>, and <u>His Wisdome</u>, and <u>His Unsearchable Riches, & Beauty</u>.

{ I will add. The matter of the greatest <u>Horror</u> among men, shall
drive me to Seek some Revival in the <u>Glory</u> of my Saviour; I see Mankind
Sunk into a fearful Degeneracy; Whole Nations of Men Degenerate and De-
praved beyond all Expression; Sometimes a Particular Man turn'd into a
Bruit, a Sott; or perhaps a very <u>Demon</u> of Malignity. I Shiver at what I
See: <u>Lord, What may Mankind be Sunk into!</u> But then, I will turn about;
I will Behold that MAN, whom the Son of God has taken into His own glorious Person, & filled Him unto the uttermost. Then I will think: <u>Lord,
What has mankind been Rais'd unto!</u> Another Thought shall take hold on
ye Heel of That; <u>Oh, Glorious JESUS, --Thou art Able to take these for-
lorn Creatures, and make Angels of them!</u> The <u>Faith</u> of ye Son of God
must fetch me to Life, on ye most killing Sight in ye world.}

Because a Glorious CHRIST made it His Work, to Releeve the <u>Miser-
able</u>, I must, according to my poor Capacity, do so too; and Like <u>Him</u>,
I must <u>Sympathize</u> tenderly with them in all their <u>Miseries</u>; Be <u>afflicted
in all their Afflictions</u>.[75]

Such wayes to <u>Do Good</u>, as were taken by a Glorious CHRIST, I must
also take, as far as I can, to Imitate them.

I must count it wondrous Agreeable, to Do Such <u>Offices</u> for <u>Poor
People</u>, as may Seem <u>too mean</u> for one of my Condition to do. I must Sett
myself to Seek and find out <u>Poor People</u>, & Enquire, What <u>Offices</u> I may
help them in. I must Esteem it the [ms. p. 246] Delicatest Refreshment
of my <u>Table</u>, to have a <u>Poor Person</u> at it, and I must often have so. I
must use all the <u>Artifice</u> imaginable, that with my <u>Alms</u>, I may convey

Something of a glorious CHRIST, unto those that shall be ye Partakers of them. I must Excogitate more Wayes of Helpfulness to the Sick, than I have yett Litt upon, and make their Bed Easy & useful to them.

Where I perceive Animosities in people against One another, I must use the best policies of a Peace-Maker; I must, with as Good Skill as I can, employ such Mollifiers, as may incline them to lay aside their Animosities, & Lett ye Spirit of Charity direct their mutual condescensions.

I must Forgive and Forgett ye most provoking Injuries. My Inducement unto it must be this; My Glorious CHRIST Pray'd for His Murderers;[76] Dy'd for us, while we were yett His Enemies: And after we have Injured Exceedingly, He Forgetts all; He Receives us into His Heavenly Places.

I must have deeply imprinted on my Mind, the Notion of my being but a meer Steward of all that I have in this World: And with as discrete and faithful a Stewardship as I can, dispense all, to just such uses, as a Glorious CHRIST has proscribed for all; Think, What would my Lord JESUS CHRIST have me to do with this? But Especially, Do Good with what I have; and therewith Succour the wants, both Temporal and Spiritual, of those, whom a glorious CHRIST has appointed, as His Receivers. [ms. p. 247]

I must use all Possible Devices, to do all manner of Good unto all sorts of Persons; but I must Endeavour no Good for them, so much as this, That a Glorious CHRIST, may be Theirs; That they may Obey Him, & have Him[77] for the Author of Eternal Salvation to them.[78]

III. If I pursue, and in any measure Attain, the Happiness, thus to glorify GOD in His CHRIST, I must be greatly Exposed unto the Envy and Hatred of a Malignant World: I must Look to be, as He was, Despised and Rejected of Men.[79] Satan operating on the Minds of men, will procure me a vast Encumbrance of Prejudice from the World. Men will have a Strange

Aversion for me. Yea, many that make a fair profession of Christianity, and pass for Good men, will have so: and yett not be able to give any good Reason for their Aversion.

I must Cheerfully undergo, all the Neglect, all the Contempt, all the Obloquy, that shall be cast upon me. My Love to a Glorious CHRIST, and my Hope of being Lov'd by Him, and Like to Him, is to carry me cheerfully thro' it all; yea, tho' I should be treated as the oftscouring of all things.[80]

I must be willing, that the Providence of God, and the Disesteem of Man, should make a Very Nothing of me; and this, not only from a Mind really Convinced, That I am nothing; but also from ye marvellous Exinanition [ms. p. 248] of my Glorious CHRIST, when He came into ye world.

I must have my Spirit Sweetly Composed, when I see those things ordered for me, wherein my God will Humble me:[81] From a View of the Humiliations, whereto a Glorious CHRIST Consented, when they were ordered for Him.

When I meet with any Uneasiness, in regard of any Wants, or any Griefs, or any Pains, or any unkind and unjust Relatives, or Neighbours not Easily brought over to Knowledge and all Goodness, or Expressions of black Ingratitude from those to whom I have shown abundance of Kindness; I must call to mind, what uneasy Things a Glorious CHRIST mett withal. Think, was my dear CHRIST more Easily Circumstanced in this Point than I am? This must Quiet me, Powerfully, Wonderfully!

If at any time, I have been or done any thing that may be accounted Good, I must never imagine myself, as any more than a Poor Chrystal, thro' whom a glorious CHRIST, with an unaccountable Display of Sovereignty, shines down upon those, who feel or see that Good; And I must use all the Means imaginable, That my observers, may not Stop at y^e

Chrystal, but make all their Acknowledgments of the Good pass thro' it, up unto the Lord.

I must maintain a Great Indifferency towards all Worldly Greatness; And that which Crucifies and mortifies me unto it, must be my having a Crucified CHRIST alwayes before my Eyes; The Messiah, who was [ms. p. 249] Cutt off, and had nothing.

I proposed, That I would thus have a Glorious CHRIST Live in me; and that ye Life which I now Live in ye Flesh, might be thus by ye Faith of the Son of God. [82]

And I must bear this Testimony, That this way of Living, has a very Purifying Efficacy, on ye Mind that keeps fixed in it. A mind repairing to the Impressive Thoughts of a glorious CHRIST continually, and replenish'd with them, will Scorn to Do, or so much as to Think, a Base Thing.

O Blessed JESUS; I Beleeve, and am Sure, That thou art ye CHRIST of God, and the Saviour of the World: Else the Thoughts of thee, would not so much Purify and Sanctify the Sinful Children of Men!

Behold, a most Compendious, and a most Effectual Method, of Coming at all ye Holy Purposes of Christianity!

This Way of Living proves an Incomparable Anodyne unto my Spirit, under all my daily uneasinesses.

It Strangely fetches in a Light from Heaven upon my mind; A Light which Revives me, Comforts me, Directs me, and not with meer Inferences of Reason, but in ye way of a Vital Touch, fills me with Pleasures that Cannot be uttered.

And tho' it Layes me Low, and makes me Little, and willing to be Any Thing, Yea, to be Nothing, yett it Raises me up; it Greatens my Spirit, for Services and for Intentions, which Ly only in ye Way that is Above. [83] [ms. p. 250]

§   I will go on to describe unto you, My Son, one Special Article of

my Study and Practice which I would Commend unto you, with the greatest

urgency; It followes most agreeably on ye former.

REPENTANCE! Oh, What a Continual Strain of it, ought there, to run

thro' the Life of a Christian! I have therefore been Willing to come

under ye Character, which ye Ancient assumed, Nulli rei natus nisi poeni-

tentiae.^84 A Desire to fill my Life with Repentance, has filled my Soul.

I have been desirous to take Every occasion for the Exercise of Repent-

ance, that a Watchful, Thoughtful, Self-abasing Mind, might lay hold

upon; On Every occasion to cry out, Lord, I Abhor myself, & Repent before

Thee, and Entreat a Pardon, thro' the Blood of ye Lamb of God.

More Particularly,^85

I would frequently Attend, frequently Perform, Solemn Acts of Re-

pentance. I would frequently Sett apart a Time on purpose, to go thro'

a Process of Repentance, in all the Parts of it, all the Acts of it.

This Time I would Employ after this manner.

Having first implored the Assistence of Heaven, I would then go on,

to take a View of my Original Sin. Therewithal I would Sett before me

an Exposition of ye Ten Comandments; What is Forbidden, what is Required

in them. I would Examine the Faults of my Life by that Holy Glass. I

would Acknowledge ye Faults with Bitterness before the Lord. I would

then glorify the Justice of God, in the worst of Punishments, which I

have undergone, or can undergo, for my offences. I would weep to the

Lord, for a Pardon, thro' the [ms. p. 251] Propitiation of ye Lovely

Jesus: Lay hold on the pardoning Mercy of God. I would hereupon take

up agreeable Purposes of Living more Carefully, more Fruitfully, more

Holily. I would Record my Purposes; make & keep a Record of them. Such

Solemn Acts of Repentance, I would Endeavour; Especially on my Dayes of

Humiliation; and in my Preparation for Approaches to ye Table of the Lord.

Every New and Gross Fall into Sin, [Alas, that ever I should be obnoxious to such!] It Shall immediately putt me upon a New and Fresh Act,
of ye most Explicit Repentance. If Temptation has gain'd at any time
upon me, and has drawn me into any Miscarriage, for which my Heart Con-
demns me, Now it will be a Time for me Immediately to Retire and Repent
before the Lord, and Lament my Foolishness, and beg of the Glorious Lord,
That He would Forgive my Iniquity, and Preserve me from falling again
into the Like Iniquity. I would have my Soul, in as much Pain, as a Bone
out of Joint, until this Repentance has Restored me.

Whenever I think on any Sin, which I Long ago fell into, Oh! Lett
it never be with Delight; Lett me not Renew the Sin, by a New Thought of
Delight upon it. But Lett it be with a fresh Lamentation & Indignation.
I would have the Remembrance thereof, be ye Wormwood & ye gall,[86] at
which I would have my Soul to be Humbled in me.

Every Evening, before I go to my Lodging, I would go to my Study;
There I would Call to mind, as, what Special Mercies of the Day past, I
have to be Thankful for, So, what [ms. p. 252] Special Evils of the Day
past, I have, to be Humbled for; All my Unwatchfulness, my Unfruitfulness, my Foolish Behaviour; I would mention it on my knees before y^e
Lord, and Beg, That He would Pardon it, for ye Sake of ye Only Sacrifice, and Assist me, that I may no more so Sin against Him.

Whatever Errand I go to Heaven upon, Whenever I make any Supplica-
tion to God, for a Mercy; I would not only Consider & Acknowledge y^e
Sins, that render me unworthy of all Mercy, but also more distinctly
Consider the Sins, that render me more notoriously unworthy of that
Mercy. I would make a Distinct Acknowledgment, That for Such a Sin,

& for <u>such a Sin</u>, I deserve, that the Petition, which I am now prosecuting, should be Rejected of Heaven. My <u>Repentance</u> will be a Necessary, and Agreeable <u>Introduction</u> unto ye Favours of ye Lord.

When I converse with y^e <u>Truths</u> of the <u>Gospel</u>, I would bear in Mind, That it is a <u>Gospel of Repentance</u>. When I hear a <u>Vertue</u> commended, it shall Cause in me this Reflection, <u>Lord, I am Sorry, that I have so Little of this Vertue in me</u>! When I hear a <u>Duty</u> propounded, it shall Cause in me this Reflection; <u>Lord, I am Sorry, I have been so Defective in doing this Duty</u>! When I hear a <u>Sin</u> Reproved, it shall raise this Reflection in me; <u>Lord, I mourn for a degree of that Sin found upon me</u>! Every <u>Sermon</u> I hear, must putt me in mind of <u>Something to be Repented of</u>. When I have been <u>Meditating</u> on any Truths of the Gospel, I would have my <u>Meditation</u> to Expire with Something of this importance; <u>What can I now find in myself to be Repented of</u>? Especially, [ms. p. 253] if the Glory of GOD and CHRIST, be at any time Sett before me, Oh! the <u>Self-abhorrence</u> which I would thereupon be filled withal! When I have seen the <u>Holy, Holy, Holy Lord</u>,⁸⁷ I would Cry out wth <u>Repentance</u> and Amazement, <u>Ah, Wo is me</u>! I am an Unholy Creature! How unlike to ye Holy One! Oh, how unfitt to hold communion wth Him!

As often as I See any person <u>Baptised</u>, I would Reflect: <u>I See, I See, That we all bring Sin into the World with us; A Sinful Nature. deeply to be Repented of</u>! And so often would I call to mind, my own <u>Forgetfulness</u> of my own <u>Baptismal Vowes</u>; A <u>Forgetfulness</u> that cannot be too often, or too Sadly <u>Repented</u> of.

I would not only come to the <u>Lords Table</u>, with some Solemn <u>Renewal of Repentance</u>, every time of my Coming; but I would also from the Exhibition of a <u>Pierced</u> JESUS there, Excite and Renew the work of <u>Repentance</u> in my Soul, & <u>mourn when I Look upon Him</u>.

I would hear a Call to Repentance, in Every Dispensation of God;
Whether it be a Comfortable Dispensation, or a Calamitous.

The Goodness of God must Lead me to Repentance. Upon all my Enjoyments, I would pause and think; What, What have I been & done, to Forfeit such Enjoyments? How gloriously does the Sovereign Grace of Heaven
triumph over an Ill-deserving Sinner in such Enjoyments? If God Smile
upon me, I will Repent, and Wonder that I do not Perish. Every Morsel
of Meat on my Table, I would Eat, with the Bitter Herbs[88] [ms. p. 254] of
Repentance. I would have my Diet Sauced with such Thoughts; Lord, My
Sins have rendred me unworthy of This! Yea, Lett me take a Catalogue of
my more Conspicuous Enjoyments, and upon Each of them, with much Confusion before the Lord, Confess the Remarkable Points of my Unworthiness
for them.

Oh! Lett all my Afflictions drive me to Repentance! Lett me Look
upon This, as the very Errand of them! Lett them Still cause me to think;
What, What are the Iniquities, that have procured me these Afflictions?
Wherein have I rendred myself Worthy of such Afflictions?

This would I do, upon Every one of my Afflictions; Do it with much
Deliberation, with much Impartiality: Willing to know the worst.

Especially, I would impose this, as a Law upon myself; If I hear
that I am Defamed in any point whatsoever, I would presently Sett myself
to think; What Fault in myself would the Holy Lord, by His permitting
this Defamation, awaken me to take Notice of? By Such Repentance, as I
would Shake off y[e] Viper, So I would fetch a Treacle out of a Viper.[89]
When I have to do with a Reproachful Man, I would not Forgett that I
have also to do with a Righteous God; who had Bidden him. And my Business now will be, to find out, Why God has Bidden him; and Repent of
the Sin, which has provoked my Father, to Employ the Scourge of the

Tongue[90] upon me. The most <u>cursed Slander</u> I would thus turn into a <u>Blessing</u>; By Setting myself <u>to think; How far am I to blame, in that thing, for which I am Evil Spoken of?</u> If clear of that, however I may <u>be sure, I am to blame for Something.</u> [ms. p. 255] <u>What, What is it, that the Glorious Lord Sees Blameworthy in me, for which He chastises me with such Reproaches?</u> I would not Leave off, till the <u>Lies</u> of Ill-minded People, have helped me to discover Something that is <u>truly</u> to be <u>Repented</u> of.

If I attempt my own <u>Vindication</u>, I would manage it with much <u>Humility</u>. I would have the <u>Spirit of Repentance</u>, to Dictate, and Mollify and Lenify, all that I Say, when I <u>Vindicate</u> myself.

When I See the <u>Sins</u> of <u>Other Men</u>, What Work they make for <u>Repentance!</u> I would think, <u>Was I never myself Guilty of such a thing?</u> If I find, that I have been Guilty of any thing Like it, I would <u>Repent</u> over again <u>in Dust & Ashes.</u>[91] Be that as it will, whatever <u>Wickedness</u> I know or hear to be committed in the World, it shall Cause me to Reflect on my own Vicious & Wicked Nature; It shall cause me to <u>Abhor</u> myself, and Say, <u>Alas, If I were Left unto myself, I should soon fall into that Wickedness.</u>

If I See a <u>Dismal Thing</u> befall any person, it shall quicken me to think; <u>Wherein have I deserved such a dismal Fate?</u> And I would thereupon <u>Repent</u>, Lest I <u>Likewise perish.</u>[92]

In a Time of <u>General Judgments</u> on ye world, & on ye place where I Live, I would sett myself penitently to think; <u>What share has my Sin had in pulling down these Judgments? What have I done, to increase that Heap of Wrath, which overwhelms</u> ye world?

Yea, I would Carry on the Matter, to So much of <u>Watchfulness</u>, in my apprehending <u>Opportunities</u> for Thoughts of <u>Repentance</u>, that the

Provocations [ms. p. 256] which may happen to be given unto my Bodily
Senses at any time, shall provoke such Thoughts in my Soul. If I Smell
any thing, that is Lothsome, or Taste any thing that is Bitter, My Soul
Shall fly away to some Thoughts on the Lothsomeness and Bitterness of
Sin immediately. A fresh Abhorrence of Sin shall be awakened in me.

If I happen to Lodge, where any Vermine, as, a Flea, or a Bug,
assaults me, it shall Humble me. I will think; I have been one among
the Enemies of God in the world. These uneasy Creatures, are part of y^e
Armies which ye Lord of Hosts employes, ⟨ and with Some contempt, ⟩
against His Enemies.

But in a peculiar manner, Oh! Lett Every SERMON that I preach, be
to me myself a Sermon of Repentance, and bring forth many an Action of
Repentance. Besides the penitential Frames to be raised in me, When in
Studying my Sermon, I make a Pause on Every Paragraph, to bring about an
Impression thereof, upon my own Soul; After my Sermon is prepared, before
the preaching of it, I would humble myself most Explicitly before y^e
Lord, for all ye Miscarriages I can discover in myself, relating to y^e
Subject handled in my Sermon; and Confess & Bewayl those Miscarriages
before ye Lord; & obtaim ye pardon of them, thro' ye Blood of the Great
Sacrifice; with Grace to Resolve Better Obedience, & maintain my Resolutions. In my going forth to preach a Sermon, I would also first of all,
in secret, Acknowledge before ye Lord, my great Unworthiness to be Employ'd by Him, in ye Holy Ministrations among His people. The Greater
the Service is, that I have before me, the more would I Lay myself in the
[ms. p. 257] Dust, with Such Acknowledgments. And after my Work in the
public is over, I would Lament before ye Lord, all the Sloth, all y^e
Pride, all ye Indifference of Soul, & want of Compassion towards the
Souls of others, & whatever Discomposure of Mind, that has attended me;

All my <u>Negligence in doing the Work of ye Lord</u>.

O my Soul. This <u>Life of Repentance</u>, tho' it be a <u>Grievous</u> one, yett it will be a <u>Joyful</u> one. God will <u>Dwell</u>, With the <u>Repenting</u> Soul; ye Humble & y^e <u>Contrite</u> One. But then, y^e <u>Harvest</u> of these <u>Tears</u>, What will that be, but interminable <u>Joy</u>!

My Son; This is y^e <u>Life of Repentance</u>, which I have pressed after. And I may tell you, I have not been altogether a Stranger to it. What I have here Expressed, in ye Form of <u>Wishes</u>, (as at first, they were no more than so!) I have happily arrived unto y^e <u>doing</u> of; at Least, very much of it, and very, very often. As having actually found it attainable, I recommend it unto you, <u>My Son</u>. Such Things, they <u>may</u> be done; I tell you, they <u>have</u> been done.

§ <u>My Son</u>, I would not Say to You, That <u>Serviceableness</u> has been the Ambition and Character of Your Fathers Life, if I did not hope, that my Saying of it might have a Tendency to bespeak & produce the Same Character for Yours; nor would I do it, without Laying hold on ye same opportunity, with all possible Sincerity, to Lament the horrid <u>Slothfulness</u> & <u>Sottishness</u>, which has rendred me So very much <u>Unserviceable</u>. [ms. p. 258] I will now go on to tell You; That this Question, <u>What Good may I do</u>? has been the Subject of my <u>Daily Thoughts</u>, ever since I was a Lad; And besides my Custome, to Sett apart now and then a Time on purpose, <u>To Devise Good</u>, I have Seldome come into any agreeable Company, without some <u>Explicit Consideration</u> upon it. Indeed, I have thought, that it would be but a Loss of Time, & otherwise Needless & Useless, to <u>Record</u> Thousands of Designs to <u>Do Good</u>, which have been Contrived in my (<u>Yett, alas, too barren!</u>) Mind. But that I may not be altogether Wanting to that Education, and Edification of You, <u>My Son</u>, which I propose in these <u>Memorials</u>, I am

willing here to give You a Little Recollection of the Method, ⁅(93)⁆
which anon I came to observe, in carrying on this Manner of Life, and
Purposing, & which it will not be amiss for you to know fully; that so,
Learning from a Father (herein, I hope, Taught of God)[94] You may, when
your Circumstances will allow of it, Go and Do Likewise.[95]

I found, That I could Every Morning Redeem the Time, while I was
Dressing myself, to take my Grand Question, What Good may I do? into
Consideration. Accordingly, the Week was divided by and into as many
Subjects of Consideration, as there be Dayes in the Week: And the Result
of my Thoughts on Each of them, I noted Still, as soon as I came into my
Study, in my Book of, Hints for things to be Spoke or done;[96] but with
such [ms. p. 259] very Brief Hints, that they Served only to Preserve
in my own Mind, the Remembrance of my Purposes, till I should have opportunity to prosecute them & Execute them.

I will now Recite, in the order thereof, The Question of the Morning;[97] But you may not imagine, that I will now Transcribe yᵉ multitudes of Answers to Each Question, which I have thought upon. However,
that I may Illustrate the Manner and Process of my Operation upon it, I
may insert a Few of my Brief Hints; from which, My Son, you may form an
Idea, how to proceed upon such a Question, when You shall have it Lying
before you.

The QUESTION for the Lords-Day Morning, Still was; (and is;)

What Shall I do as a Pastor of a Church, for the Good of the
Flock, wᶜʰ I have under my Charge?

Here, I rank'd the People of the Flock into their Several Classes; I distinctly considered, what they were, and what is to be done for them. I
Considered what Subjects were most Seasonable, & Agreeable to be handled

in my {{Public}} Sermons; What would most Suit, & best Serve, Each of y^e
Classes. { I considered how I might make my Prayers in ye Congregation,
as well as my Sermons, to Leave Good and Strong impressions on ye Auditory; And, } I Entreated the Neighbours, associated for Exercises of
Religion, to Send me in their Advice, What Things[98]they might want or
wish to hear treated on; and I accomodated them. I considered how to
make my Public Ministry more Lively, more Useful, more Acceptable. I
considered, who were to be Privately Address'd with my Visits, and on
what Intentions. I considered how I might Visit the [ms. p. 260] Schools
unto the best Advantage: {Particularly Some Charity-Schools, which I
procured to be Erected. I considered,} how I might Carry on Evangelical Designs, in Concert with the Physicians in my Neighbourhood; Whom I
particularly desired, That they would Lett me know ye Necessities of y^e
Sick, if I were at any time Ignorant of them; & unto whom I Still comuni-
cated Rich Notions or Medicines, which in my Reading I mett withal. And
many, many more such things as these, have been thought upon!

As belonging to this Head of Considerations, I will take particular
Notice of One thing among my Purposes and Practices.

I obliged myself unto this Method in Studying a Sermon. On Every
Paragraph I made a Pause; & Endeavoured with Acknowledgments and Ejaculations to Heaven, and with Self-Examinations, to feel some Holy Impressions of the Truths in that Paragraph, on my own Soul; before I went any
further. By means hereof, the Seven Hours, which I usually take, to make
& write a Sermon, prove but so many Hours of Devotion with me. The Day
in which I have made a Sermon, Leaves upon my Mind, just Such a Flavour,
as a Day of Prayer uses to do. When I come to Preach the Sermon, I do
it now with the more Liberty and Assurance; and the Truths thus prepared
are Like to come with a more Sensible Warmth and Life upon ye Auditory.

But I proceed.

The QUESTION for Munday-Morning, is,

What Shall I do in my Family, & for the Good of my Family? Here I Considered myself, as an Husband, and as a Father, and as a Master. [ms. p. 261] I asked my Wife to think, What Proposals there are, that she would make to me, in her own Service. I projected, how the Prayers which I made with her aloud in my Study, might be very much for her Service. I chose out Books to be Read by her, that might be so. I Contrived how to mention Some Instructive Thing to her, alwayes both at going to Sleep & Rising from it. And many, many more Such things, have been[99] thought upon!

I considered, What Points of Education were Still wanting, to any of my Children, and I pursued them in the best wayes I could. I Caused them to Read, and Write, such things, as I found out, for their best Advantage, & most Suitable Entertainment. I took each of them alone Successively, on the Satureday Evenings, and having obtained a knowledge of their Interiour State, and ye Declared Resolutions of their Souls for Early Piety, I pray'd with them. I caused Some of them to compose Prayers with their Pens, and bring them to me, that I might See their Temper and progress in Religion. I obliged them to Retire and Ponder on that Question, What should I Wish to have done, if I were now a dying? And Report unto me, their own Answer to the Question; Of which I took advantage to inculcate ye Lessons of Godliness upon them. And, many, many more such things have been thought upon!

I considered, how to drop Useful Admonitions on my Servants, as they were waiting on me; --if the Action afforded any Time for it. I provided for their Instruction, in Every thing, that I Supposed might be for their

Good. I putt Such [ms. p. 262] Treatises into their Hands, as might be
most profitable unto them, in their perusing thereof. And many, many
more such things have been thought upon! (Yea, as a Sort of Crumbs
falling from ye Table of my own Servants, I hired a Mistress, to keep a
School, where Poor Negroes might Every Evening, Learn to Read, & be
taught their Catechisms and I myself bore ye Whole Expence of this Charity Schole, Every week paying the Mistress her wages.)

The QUESTIONS for Tuesday-Morning are Two.

First, I Enquire;

What shall I do for my Relatives Abroad?

Here, I took a Catalogue of them; which begins with my Parents, but Extends as far as the children of my Cousin-germans. With ye Help of this
Catalogue, I propounded, that I would at proper Times, Pray for Each of
them distinctly by Name. And, that every Week, I would Single out, at
Least One of them, to consider, What Good may I do for them? or, Wherein may they be the Better for me? And, that I may address Every one of
them Successively with Faithful Admonitions, concerning their Interiour
and Eternal Interests; Either by personally Speaking to them; or by writing to them; or, by putting Books of Piety into their Hands. I propounded, in this way to glorify my Great Saviour, and Endeavour a Conformity to Him, who Even on His Cross took peculiar Care of one that was
nearly Related unto Him. I did not confine these Essayes of Good, unto
ye Relatives within ye Limits of my Catalogue. I made them reach as far
as ever I could find out Opportunities.

I need not any further Explain this Article. Only, One-Instance may
[ms. p. 263] do no hurt, unto You, My Son.

My Father being become Aged, and in continual, Yea, (tho' in a State
of Health & Strength & Vigour, much beyond mine,) Desirous Expectation

of his Call out of this World, I Resolved, That every Interview I had
with him, (which was almost Every Day,) should have in it, Something or
other that should refer to the Heavenly World, & assist his & my preparation for it; Not knowing, but it may prove ye Last Time of my Speaking
with him.

Many, many Such things have been thought upon!

But then, (When such an occasion for it has occurr'd, I have inter-
mitted this Question, & been concerned for My Enemies, (whom God makes
Instruments of much Good unto me;) as for my Relatives.) [100] I have
Enquired;

> What Good shall I do for my Personal Enemies; & how shall I over-
> come Evil with Good?[101]

My Public Circumstances; My Faithfulness, and I have Reason to think,
that many times my Foolishness also, in my Discharge of my Duty; and the
Power of Satan over ye Minds of many People; and ye Envy of some Ill
Spirits at my Improvement and Acceptance in ye world; And, finally, the
Just Judgment of GOD upon me, for my miscarriages; has procurred me a
Number of Personal Enemies, or of Such as treat me Abusively and Injuriously. Each of these persons, as far as I can come to ye knowledge of
them; I have Sett myself distinctly to Consider, What Good Offices I may
do for them? Accordingly, Be sure I Pray'd for Each of these by Name;
And if I could perceive or Invent any other opportunity to do [ms. p.
264] them Good, I have done it; tho' many times, I have done it so, that
they Know not whence it comes.

I hope, to be able to Say, That I know not any person in the world,
that has done me an Ill office, but I have done him a Good One. Yea, I
can say so; (and I have Left off the Alternation of this Question, till
there may recurr opportunities for my Thoughts upon it.)

The QUESTION for <u>Wednesday-Morning</u> is this;

<u>What Shall I do for the Churches of ye Lord, and ye more</u>

<u>general Interests of Religion in the world?</u>

Here I considered, What <u>Proposals</u> to make unto other <u>Ministers</u> of my

Acquaintance. I considered, What <u>Books</u> I might Compose & publish, to

advance ye Kingdome of my Saviour. I considered, how to disperse & to

diffuse y^e <u>Engines</u> of Christian Knowledge & Vertue, unto distant places.

{ I have many <u>Correspondences</u>; But I make 'em all Subservient unto the

main Design. } My poor Endeavours to Serve ye general <u>Interests of</u>

<u>Religion</u>, have reached unto Each of the <u>Three Kingdomes</u>. They have

reached unto Several other Nations of <u>Europe</u>. They have reached unto

all y^e <u>English Plantations</u> in <u>America</u>. And particularly; into Every

Town of the <u>New English</u> Colonies to which I am under some Special obli-

gation: <u>Negros</u> and <u>Indians</u>, whole Nations of them, as well as other

peoples, have been reached by them. Nor has y^e <u>Jewish</u> Nation been Left

unconsidered; nor y^e <u>Greek Churches</u>.

I will on this Occasion mention to You, <u>My Son</u>, One pretty Strange

Experiment. I have rarely had upon my Mind any Strong <u>Impulse</u> to ad-

dress <u>another Nation</u> in their <u>own Language</u>, but I have had a Scarce

accountable Assistance, in a <u>few Dayes</u> to come at that <u>Language</u> [ms. p.

265] So far, that I have with my own Hand, and Skill, Written Books in

it, which have been printed for the Intended Services. I have Books Ex-

tant in more than Two or Three of the <u>Living Languages</u>; the Good Effects

whereof I am Waiting for. But then, by Disuse, and for want of Conver-

sation, I have Soon Lost some of these Languages.

The QUESTION for <u>Thursday-Morning</u> tis this;

<u>What shall I do, in the Several Societies, to which I am Related?</u>

I am Related unto above <u>Twenty</u> Several <u>Societies</u>, of a <u>Religious</u> Character and Intention. I must have my Times to <u>Visit</u> Every One of these; Alwayes to <u>Do Something</u> in them, & for them. I must keep a Watchful Ey over them; and make them, as far as I can, to become <u>Engines of Good</u>, in my Town & Land.

Some of the <u>Societies</u>, which I have Produced and Cherished, are a sort of <u>Reforming Societies</u>, or, <u>Societies for ye Suppression of Disorders</u>. I have Contrived, & Proposed, that ye other <u>Societies of Religion</u>, may bear their part, as far they can, in pursuing the Design of these. But for <u>these</u>, I generally Every Week, Endeavour to be present at them; and Still to Lett fall Something or other, that may be for their <u>Direction</u>; and Something also for their <u>Encouragement</u>. I drew up, certain <u>Points of Consideration</u>, to be with due pauses, Read in the <u>Societies</u> Every time they mett; for any one [ms. p. 266] to offer what proposal he pleased, upon any of the Points, at the Reading of it.

I will here Transcribe those <u>Points of Consideration</u>;[102] And you may guess, <u>My Son</u>, whether they don't Supply me, as well as others, with matters wherein I may be a Little [<u>Ah, Lord, I am ashamed, I am asham-ed, When I See how Little!</u>] Serviceable.

' I. Is there any <u>Remarkable disorder</u> in the place, that requires our
' Endeavour for the Suppression of it; And in what Good, Fair, Likely
' Way, may we Endeavour it?
' II. Is there any <u>Particular Person</u>, whose <u>Disorderly Behaviours</u>, may
' be so Scandalous and so Notorious that we may do well to send unto the
' Said Person o^e Charitable <u>Admonitions</u>? Or, Are there any <u>Contending</u>
' <u>Persons</u>, whom we should Admonish, to Quench their <u>contentions</u>?
' III. Is there any <u>Special Service</u> to the Interests of Religion, w^{ch}

' we may conveniently desire o^e <u>Ministers,</u> to take notice of?

' IV. Is there any thing, which we may do well to mention and Recommend

' unto the <u>Justices,</u> for the further promoting of <u>Good order</u>?

' V. Is there any sort of <u>Officers</u> among us to such a Degree unmindful

' of their Duty, that we may do well to mind them of it?

' VI. Can any further Methods be devised, that <u>Ignorance</u> and <u>Wickedness</u>

' may be more chased from o^e People in general? And, that <u>Houshold-Piety</u>

' in particular, may may flourish among them? [ms. p. 267]

' VII. Does there appear any Instance of <u>Oppression,</u> or <u>Fraudulence,</u> in

' the Dealings of any Sort of People, that may call for o^e Essayes to

' gett it Rectified?

' VIII. Is there any Matter to humbly Moved, unto the <u>Legislative Power,</u>

' to be Enacted into a <u>Law</u> for Public Benefit?

' IX. Do we know of any person Languishing under Sad and sore <u>Affliction</u>;

' And is there any thing that we may do for the Succour of such an

' Afflicted Neighbour?

' X. Has any person any <u>Proposal</u> to make, for o^e Own further Advantage

' and Assistence, that we o^{e}selves may be in a Probable and Regular

' Capacity, to Pursue the <u>Intentions</u> before us.

Numberless Things I have Started in the <u>Societies,</u> upon these Points.

The Registers of ye Societies are fill'd with them. I will only add;

That once a year, they have used, all of them to meet in one Place to-

gether, and have a <u>Day of Prayer</u>; in which they humbled themselves for

doing so Little Good; & besought ye Pardon of their unfruitfulness, thro'

ye Blood of the Great Sacrifice; and implored, the Blessing of Heaven,

on ye Essayes to Do Good which they have made, & ye Counsil of & Conduct

of Heaven, for their further Essayes; and Such Influences of Heaven as

may bring about those <u>Reformations</u>, which tis not in o^e Power to accomplish. On these Dayes, I with another Minister, have Still carried on
ye Exercises.[103]

    At Length, I found it Expedient for me, Every other <u>Thursday</u> Morn-
ing to change my ⟨ <u>Question</u>. So I then made this the Alternate One;

    <u>Is there no particular Person, able to do the Good, which lies out</u>
<u>of my more immediate reach; to whom I may offer Some Good Proposal</u>?
By answering this Question, I made my Conversation Still more useful.
And I was very often a Doer of Good at y^e <u>Second Hand</u>; and often had y^e
pleasure to be not known to have any Hand at all in what was done. This
is a matter, <u>My Son</u>, that needs no Illustration. ⟩ [ms. p. 268]

    The QUESTION for <u>Friday-Morning</u>, has Long been This.

    <u>What Special Subjects of Affliction, & Objects of Compassion, may</u>
    <u>I take under my Particular Care; and what Shall I do for them</u>?
Here, I took a Catalogue of the <u>Poor</u>, in my Numerous Flock; yea, I extended my Care further than so; whenever I saw any miserable. I minded
also, who <u>Wanted Employment</u>; I minded, who were under any <u>Peculiar Exer-</u>
<u>cises</u>; I minded, What Souls were by particular Addresses, to be <u>Pull'd</u>
<u>as brands out of the Burning</u>,[104] because of their being abandoned into
flaming Wickedness. I Still have Singled out, Some or other of these,
this Morning to be considered.

    <u>My Son</u>, I will add only this one thing upon this Head.[105] I con-
sidered, That tho' the <u>Wind</u> will not fill the <u>Hungry</u>, yett it will turn
y^e <u>Mill</u>, that will grind the <u>Corn</u>, that will fill the <u>Hungry</u>. I have my
<u>List of Miserables</u> alwayes about me: Now, in Company, I often, often
make it a Subject of the Conversation; <u>What shall be done for such an one</u>
<u>in my List; & for such an one</u>? Thus, besides ye Innumerable kindnesses

which I have myself more Immediately done for them, I have procured multitudes of Kindnesses for them from others; & ye first Spring in ye Motion
has been unknown to them. Very much of ye Spirit, & pleasure of my Life,
My Son, has been in such things as these. Yea, I may tell you, I Lett
not ordinarily one Day in the year pass me, without Something Expended on
Pious Uses, besides my other Continual Kindnesses & Services to Afflicted
people. [ms. p. 269]

At Length I arrive to my QUESTION for Satureday-Morning. Tis,

What more have I to do, for the Interest of God, in my own Heart
and Life?

You are Sensible, My Son, That very much of the Book now in your Hands,
is but an Answer to this Question.

But that I may a Little more Illustrate my way of Thinking on it, I
will tell you; That I Thought often on Sacramental Errands; I mean, For
what Points of Salvation, I should in ye Methods of the Lords-Table from
time to time, apply myself to my Strong Redeemer.

I Sett myself more distinctly to Consider, What were the more Special Sins and Crimes of my Youth; And thereupon, What more Special Service I should now do for the Kingdome of God, in ye greatest Contrariety
and Contradiction to my Former Miscarriages.

I Sett myself then to Consider, What Reproaches I had mett withal;
And thereupon, What Services I should be Awakened thereby to do for y^e
Kingdome of God.

I Considered; I am favoured with Surprizing and uncommon Opportunities to Publish many Books of Piety. There is nothing of so much concernment for me, as to take Effectual Care, that my own Books, do not
prove at-Last, my own Condemnation; by my failing in those Points of
Piety, which I commend unto others. Wherefore (with Prayers to be

delivered from so great Confusion) I would Sometimes, on a Lords-day
Evening, Read over my own Books of [ms. p. 270] Piety; and Work them over
again upon my Heart; until my Soul be Exquisitely Conformed unto them.

I Resolved, That whatever Bodily Infirmities, I do Labour, (or may
call to Mind, that I have Laboured) under, I would make them the Occasions and Incentives of some Agreeable Dispositions in my Soul; And I
would sett myself, To consider, What?

Many, many more such Things have been thought upon. I will Mention
Comprehensive One, which must needs bring on very many more.

I demanded it of myself, That I would usually on the Lords-day Evening, take a Time, to Sett myself in Dying Circumstances; To Realize my
Approaching Death; To apprehend myself as having the Last pangs of Death
upon me; Then to Think; What would I at this Time chuse or Wish? And
what is there that I should be Sorry to have Left undone at such a Time
as this? To Note my Impartial Thoughts on this occasion; and Immediately
go do, what my Hand finds to do.[106] This Weekly Action, has a great Influence on ye Affairs of my Life.[107]

(I conclude this Article, with Transcribing one humbling Passage
out of my Memorials.

' Ah, Such is my Wretched Barrenness, that I am compelled Sometimes
' to think a considerable While, before I can invent any further Design
' to do Good, besides those, wch my Method of Living daily Leads me to.
' In this case, is it not Sometimes Enough, if I should then fall into a
' Lamentation over my own Sinful Barrenness, & humble myself before y^e
' Lord on ye Account thereof, and confess how worthy I am to be Cutt down
' for my Unfruitfulness, & Entreat for a Pardon thro' that Blood that
' Cleanses from all Sin, and for ye Grace that may render me a more
' Fruitful Christian.

However, I don't Remember that I ever did above once in many years content myself with no more than this Lamentation. ⟩

My Son, If I should Live to insert no more Memorials of Piety in these my PATERNA, here may be Enough, to furnish you, for very many purposes of Christianity, and Serviceableness. Your Dying Father charges you to make a Good Improvement of them! [ms. p. 271]

§ My Son, There is a Disposition and an Experiment, which your Father is able thus to declare unto you.[108]

I am not unable, With a Little Study to Write in Seven Languages; I have written and printed in them. I feast myself with the Swiets of all the Sciences, which the more Polite Part of Mankind ordinarily pretend unto. I am Entertained with all kinds of Histories Ancient and Modern. I am no Stranger to the Curiosities, which by all sons of Learning are brought unto ye Curious. These Intellectual pleasures, are beyond any Sensual Ones. Nevertheless, All this affords me not so much Delight, as it does, to Releeve the Distresses of any one Poor, Mean, and Miserable Neighbour; and much more, to do any Extensive Service for the Redres of those Epidemical Miseries, under which mankind in general is Languishing, and to advance ye Kingdome of GOD in ye world.

§ In those Opinions which I take to be Erroneous, I have proposed unto myself such a Rule as this. I would Consider, What may be the Duties, which the Honester Men, who hold the Errors, design to Support by them. If they are unexceptionable Duties, Lett me close with the Duties; and first of all try, whether the State of Things in my Hypothesis, may not Encourage them; or then, whether there be not such an Incomprehensible Transcendency of Things in ye Infinite God, as to render some Things very Consistent in Him, which in o^e Shallow understandings, will imply Inconsistencies. However, Where the Errors of any, are attended with a Consciencious Regard unto Duties, Lett me have much Tenderness, much Deference, for these, from whom I must nevertheless dissent in Judgment.

[ms. p. 272]

It will a Little Serve the Intention of these Memorials, if I should here mention Several Projections; which I have had, for ye more fruitful & useful Discharge of my Public Ministry. They have been,

To Suit ye Various Afflictions of the People, & make them the Handles by which to Manage ye Cause of Piety, & show them distinctly how to make pious Applications unto God under all.

To Spread the Netts of Salvation[109] for my Hearers, in ye way of their own Business & Language; Observe ye Callings which they follow; Adapt ye more notable Callings, with agreeable Texts of Scripture; and Employ on fitt Occasions as far as will Correspond well with ye Gravity of the Ministry, such Phrases as are most near to their Affaires; and hereby make the Truths have a more durable Impression on ye minds of ye people, whom I have nextly intended in y^m. I Hope to come at ye minds of my Neighbours, & board them with ye Maxims of Piety in their own way, & in such Terms, as may be most Likely to Engage, their Intention and Affection.

To Conclude my Sermons, often with certain proper and pungent Questions, which being Left with the Hearers, may compel them to consider ye Things of their peace, and Spend the Ensuing Evening in such Exercises as may be for their Everlasting peace.

My Son, you shall shortly have more Things of such a Tendency.

§ There are Three Points of my Conduct relating to my Flock, that have been useful to me.

First: I have thought it needful, to cry mightily unto the Lord, that He would give me a Goodness, a Patience, a Long-suffering and Condescending Spirit, with which I may Resemble and Imitate [ms. p. 273] my Admirable Saviour, in treating such people of my Flock, as are Foolish & Froward and unreasonable.[110]

Secondly, I have been desirous to Entertain an high opinion of the Personal Worth, Wisdome, and Goodness, and Accomplishments, of many in the Flock, and the unspeakable Worth of the Souls of all of them; and by this Opinion, to be quickened in my Studies for my Sermons, that they may be as Able and as useful Composures, as I can possibly render them.

Thirdly.. I have Endeavoured with Explicit Considerations, that all the Temporal Benefits I enjoy by the Salary which ye Flock allowes me, may be answered & Vastly Exceeded, in ye Spiritual Benefits wch my ministry may make them ye partakers of. Their Salary Feeds me. I will prepare as rich a Food for their Minds as ever I can; even Angels Food.[111] It cloathes me. I will do my best, in showing them, how they shall Putt on Christ,[112] and become Defended and Adorned with ye Garments of Salvation. It warms me. I will Endeavour to Speak Things unto them, that shall make their Hearts burn Within them,[113] & keep Alive ye Flame of Piety among y^m.

§ Not knowing how soon I may be called away, & Leave a Number of Orphans in an Evil World, among other Points of Provision for them, I Made, Wrote, and Sign'd, An Instrument of Betrustment & Resignation for my Orphans, which I Spred before the Lord, prostrate in the Dust; & then gave it unto ye children for such of them as were old Enough to use their pens, for them to Transcribe it, and preserve it, and afterwards on fitt occasions to have Recourse unto it. It ran in these Terms. [ms. p. 274]

' O My Great and Good Saviour; and thou SON of GOD, in my Glorious JESUS;

' and the Lord, in whom the Fatherless find Mercy.[114]

'   The Principal Satisfaction and Consolation, with which I receive

' the Children, which the Lord graciously gives unto me, at their Birth

' into the world, is, The Prospect of more Subjects for my Saviour, and

' the Propagation and Continuation of His Kingdome in the World. For

' this Purpose, tis my own Strong and Full Purpose, to do my Part, that

' my children may know their Saviour, & Serve Him with a Perfect Heart

' & a Willing Mind.[115] And I will Earnestly cry unto Him, to Produce a

' Work of His Grace in their Souls, and to take them under ye Perpetual

' Conduct of the Spirit of Grace, that they may do so.

'   Now, I firmly Beleeve, That the world is under the Government of my

' Admirable Saviour; and that He sitts at the Right Hand of God; and that

' the affayres of the Divine Providence are under His Administration.

' He does particularly Employ the Ministry of His mighty ANGELS, in Gov-

' erning the Children of Men; and yett more particularly, make them the

' Guardians of His Little Ones: Most of all, when in His Providence, He

' makes them Fatherless Children. Oh! Orphans well-provided for!

'   Wherefore, O my Saviour I committ my Children into thy Saviourly

' and Fatherly Hands. I pray to thee, that thy Gracious Providence may,

' and I trust in thee, that it will, be concerned for them. Oh! Lett

' nothing be wanting to them, that shall be Good for them. Oh! Cause

' them to, Fear thee, to Love thee, to [ms. p. 275] Walk in thy Wayes;

' and make use of them to Do Good in their Generation. Oh! Be thou

' their Friend, and Raise them up such as may be Necessary for them; And

' in a Convenient Manner Supply all their Necessities. Give thy ANGELS

' a Charge of them; and when their Father and Mother forsake them, then

' do thou take them up.[116]

'   This is the Supplication, this the Resignation, this the Dependence, ' of-----

My Son, This Instrument is not the Least Legacy, that I have to Leave you. Take it, Look on it, Think on it. Yea, When you come into Difficulties, plead before the Lord, Produce it, as a Plea with the God of your Father,[117] to deal with you, as He uses to deal with the children of them that have with a Lively Faith bespoke His Fatherly Care, for their Fatherless and Forsaken Families.

§   I am Entring into a very Large Paragraph of Christian Asceticks. It shall contain many Occasional Thoughts and Prayers, of a Mind Conversing with God, & preparing for Heaven. My Son, I will tell you, what My perswasion is, concerning Holy Thoughts, and such as Carry in them agreeable Acknowledgments of my Glorious God and Saviour, produced in my mind on all occasions. I Judge, That while I form such Thoughts, I am answering, directly, nearly, Sweetly answering, ye Grand End of my Life; Which is to Acknowledge God, & glorify Him.[118] I am also therein Rectifying my Soul, and Ripening it for ye Employments and Enjoyments of the Heavenly World. [ms. p. 276]

I Will proceed now to tell you Some of the Rules which I have prescribed unto myself, to Awaken ye Thoughts and Prayers of a Religious Mind, on ye Occasions, which are of a very frequent occurrence with me.

When I hear a Clock Strike, I would Commonly accompany it, with a Wish of my Soul, Sent up to Heaven, of some Such importance as this: Lord, Help me so to Spend every Hour of my Time, that I may give a Good Account of it, at the End of my Time! or, Lord, Prepare me for my Last Hour! or, Lord, Pardon my mispence of so many Hours! and, Oh! Teach me so to Number my Hours, that I may apply my Heart unto Wisdome![119]

At Winding up of my Watch, I would Bless God for another Day added
unto my Life; and beg of Him the Grace to Spend the Next, in Watchful &
Fruitful Endeavo^e s to glorify Him.

Whatever Comfortable Thing I see Enjoy'd by any other people, I will
in this way sweetly take the Comfort of it; O my God, I glorify thy Goodness to this my Neighbour! Oh! That he may also Glorify thee, and thy
Goodness!

My Life is full of Services; I am ashamed they are so few, & such
mean ones! But on Every Service ordinarily, I would have my Thoughts
distinctly Employ'd unto this Purpose. Lord, I do this out of obedience
unto my Saviour; to Glorify Him; to Imitate Him. And I renounce all
Vain Imaginations of the Least Merit in all that I do.[120] After all, I
am an unprofitable Servant![121]

When I dispense any Kindness to any Person, I would at ye Same time
Lift up a Prayer to God, for them, that they may not be unmindful of such
Duty to Him, as this Kindness of His to them, thro' my Hand, may invite
me and them, to think upon. [ms. p. 277]

⟨⟨ I [Receive?] presents of many lots. When upon my [Receipt?] of
any I would make it my Custome, Still to think; To what Good Thing should
my Mind be awakened on this occasion? or, To what Service of God, shall
this Favour of His Encourage me? ⟩⟩

I have oftentimes an Opportunity to Express a Benignity unto Bruit
Creatures; Either to Feed them, or to make their Condition Easy unto them.
I would Still do it With Delight; and thereat have Two Meditations raised
in me. The One; I am now an Instrument of God unto these Creatures; His
Kindness Passes thro' my Hands unto them. The Other; Will not the Blessed
God be as Beneficent unto me, as I am unto these Creatures? Especially,

if, as they Sometimes Look unto me, to be kind unto them, I alwayes Look up unto Him!

When I knock at a Door, I would have it Awaken in me, the Faith of that word of o^e Saviour; Knock, and it shall be opened unto you![122]

{ When I mend my Fire, I would form Some such Desire as this upon it. Lord, Lett what is out of order in my Heart, & Life, & any of my Affairs, be rectified. Or, Lord, Lett my Love & my Zeal, Burn more agreeably, thro' ye Emendations of thy Grace passing upon me! }

When I putt out my Candle I would putt up a Prayer unto the Father of Lights;[123] Lord, Lett not Sin ever, nor Death as yett, putt out my Light in Obscure Darkness! or, Lord, when I go out by Mortality, Lett me Enter into Everlasting Light![124]

As I taste of the Several Fruits, which ye Summer produces, I would Still sett myself to think on some Special Glory of our admirable JESUS, which I may be thereby Led, unto ye Contemplation of; and address him with a Rapturous Confession of it.

In drinking a Dish of Tea, I would make it an occasion of those Thoughts; Especially with ye Ingenuity of Occasional Reflection, & Agreeable Similitudes, that shall have many sweet Acknowledgments of my Glorious Redeemer in y^m. Yea, whatever Delight any of my Senses Enjoy, it shall soon be Sanctified [ms. p. 278] and be made much more Delightful, by my making such an Improvement of it.

The Servant of the Lord could Say, Mine Eyes prevent the Night-Watches, that I might Meditate in thy word.[125] I often wake in ye Night. I would impose it as a Law on myself, That Whenever I wake; before I fall Asleep again, I will Endeavour to bring some Glory of my admirable Saviour into my Meditation, and have some agreeable Desire of my Soul upon it.

When I pay what I owe at any time, I would make it an occasion for that Acknowledgment; O my glorious JESUS, How infinitely am I Endebted unto thee, who hast paid my Debt unto ye infinite Justice of God! And for that Supplication, O My God, grant me this Blessing, that I may owe no man any thing but Love! [126]

I Resolved, that my Attendence on the Excretory Necessities of Nature, should be Still accompanied, with some Holy Thoughts of a Repenting and an Abased Soul. Unto that projection of Piety, I made this Addition. The Urinary Excretions occur often Every day. I have seen such Tragical Instances of Nephritic and Ischuriac Miseries in others, that I cannot be enough Thankful for my own Deliverance from such Maladies. And then also, an Action that carries Humiliation with it, how justly may it Lead me, to think with wonderment, on what my Saviour will do for me, in ye Advancements, ye Dignities, of ye Future State! Wherefore, when I am obliged at any time, unto ye Urinary Discharges, I would have Thoughts of these two Tendencies formed in my mind, on that mean occasion. My God, I bless thee for Saving me from ye terrible Diseases of the Wheel broken at the Cistern! [127] And, O my Dear [ms. p. 279] JESUS; Wilt thou ever bring this Vile Body, to the glories & the Blessings of the Heavenly places!

Among the Occasions for the Expressions of Piety and Thankfulness, I would most affectionately take notice of one, that often occurs to me, in ye mean Employments wherein I see many other People occupied. When I see those, whose Business it is, to Dig in ye Earth, to Sweep ye Chimney's, to cleanse the Kennels, to drive ye Coach, ye Cart & ye Wheelbarrow; and carry Burdens; or ye Like Things of a Low Degree, I would have my Heart raised in Praises and Wonders, for the Sovereign Grace of

God, which has distinguished me, with much nobler & higher Employments.
I would also Lift up a Prayer for ye Neighbours whom I See more meanly
Employ'd, at ye Time of my Seeing them; That God would help them to do
what they do, out of Obedience unto Him; and also Bestow upon them some
Suitable Blessing, which I may be Led from ye Circumstances of what I
see them doing, to think upon.

When I Visit a Sick Person, I would use to fetch an Admonition relating to the Moral Distempers in my own Heart and Life, analogous to
something that I may see in the Circumstances of the Sickness on the person, whom I go unto. I would think; What thing amiss in my own Soul and
Walk, should I be Led now to deprecate? I would make this Deprecation,
an Article of my prayers to God. And why not an Article of my prayers
with the Visited person? And of my Discourses also, my Addresses to the
person? The Diseases that Sin has brought on o^e Spirits; worse them any
on o^e Bodies: And ye Releef we may find in o^e admirable Saviour! [ms.
p. 280]

When any thing begins to raise any Ebullition of Anger in me, I
would Endeavour to allay it, with one or both of these Considerations.
First; What provocations have I given to ye Great God, Like those, but
infinitely greater than those, which I receive of them that are about me?
And then; What was the Meekness & Wisdome of my Blessed JESUS, when He
was provoked by the Contradiction of Sinners?

When I Wash my Hands, I would Lift up my Soul unto ye Lord, with a
Wish of this Importance; Lord, Give me ye Clean Hands, & the Pure Heart,
of them that are to Stand in ye Holy Place of the Lord![128] or, Lord,
Deliver me & Recover me, from all Sinful Pollutions!

⟨ Yea, when I do so mean an Action, as that of Paring my Nails, I
would have it accompanied with a Stroke of this importance, Lord, Help

me to Lay aside all Filthiness and Superfluity of Naughtiness. }

Sometimes I have had kind presents made unto me; and I must therein
See the Kindness of God. But I would thereby alwayes be drawn to more
particular Acknowledgments and Resolutions; & such as may be most agreeably awakened by the Quality of the presents. I would think; What Good
thing should that man Wish, and what good thing should he do, whom God
obliges, by bestowing such things upon him? And I would alwayes add a
Reflection on ye Humiliation of my dear JESUS, who wanted such things, &
mett with barbarous Ingratitude from an Evil world.

Tho' my Life be filled, (after my poor manner) with Continual Services, yett I have now Litt upon a Noble Way, very much to increase y^e
Number of them. When I behold any Services to the Kingdome of the glorious One, done by any one whomsoever, I will Rejoice in them; and I will
give Thanks to Him for them; and I will be pleas'd with, and glad of,
the use He makes of other men. As a Complacency will involve men in a
Fellowship with the Sins of other [ms. p. 281] Men; their Unfruitful
works of Darkness; thus, Complacency will interest men in the Services
done by other Men; in the Consolations thereof; Perhaps in ye Recom-
pences.

Whenever I encounter with any thing that is not as I would have it,
(any Crooked thing) I would Look on it as a Call from Heaven, to Entertain a Thought of this Importance. My Will is Crossed; but what particular Instance of my Contradiction and my Disobedience to the Will of
God, should this Affliction Lead me to Consider of? Both Repentance and
Patience, may be produced by this Consideration.

The Disposition with which I enquire after Newes, needs a Little
more of Regulation & of Sublimation. I desire, that when I make that

Enquiry, <u>What occurs Remarkable</u>? it may be with a Disposition and a Resolution, to form, if it may be, some <u>Lesson of Piety</u>, upon the Answer; and Putt this Lesson into a <u>Wish</u>; presently and Silently sent up to Heaven. And, if it be Proper, to mention unto ye Company, that <u>Reflection</u>, which I would have to be made upon it.

When I read or see any <u>New Book</u>, wherein the Truth and Church and Cause of God, has any Notable Service done for it, I would offer up my Solemn Thanks unto the glorious <u>Head of ye Church</u>, for His thus Expressing His Care of it, and His Dispensing such <u>Gifts</u> unto ye Children of Men.

When I putt on y^e <u>Civilities</u> (of a <u>Glove</u>, or a <u>Ring</u>, or a <u>Scarf</u>) given me at a <u>Funeral</u>, I would Endeavour to do it, with a Supplication of this importance; <u>Lord, Prepare me for my own Mortality</u>. And, <u>Lord, Lett me at my Death be found Worthy of a Remembrance among ye Living</u>.

A <u>Morning Cough</u>, a Little tussient Expectoration, at my first Waking and Rising in a Morning, has these many years attended me. ⟨⟨129⟩⟩ [ms. p. 282] It ought to raise a <u>Disposition of Piety</u> in me. I would have it Still accompanied with a Thought of this importance; <u>Oh! that I may alwayes cast up, & throw off, whatever may be inimical to ye Health of my Soul! Every Lust, which Like this Flegm, should be Parted with Lord, help me to Part with it; Yea, to take Pains, that I may do so!</u>

{ When I am called out of my Study, (a most frequent occurrence) to Speak wth any one in my Parlour, I would have Such Wishes as these going up to Heaven, as I am going down to them. <u>Lord, prepare me for, and assist me in whatever Service may be now before me. And if I am going to Encounter any Sorrow, Lett me be prepared for that also.</u> }

⟨⟨ Here is a great Point of Religion with me, to keep out of <u>Debt</u>, so, when I <u>pay</u> any thing that I owe, be ye Summ Larger or Smaller, I would have this Thought well raised in my Mind, <u>O my dear Saviour, Thou hast paid my Debt unto ye Justice of Heaven, Oh! Help me to Love thee, and Praise thee, & Serve thee for thy Goodness.</u> ⟩⟩

In managing my Correspondencies, having used myself, when I wrote a Letter, still to think; <u>What Honourable Mention can I make of my dear Saviour here?</u> And carried on my Consideration to that further Point; <u>What Service may I do for ye Kingdome of my dear Saviour on this Opportunity?</u> I added afterwards Three Resolutions more. First; When I am <u>Sealing</u> a <u>Letter</u>, and Sending it away, I would, with an Act of <u>Resignation</u>, putt it over into ye Hand of y^e <u>Divine Providence</u> for ye Safety & Success of it. Secondly; When I am going to <u>Open</u> any <u>Letter</u>, that arrives with a Direction to me, I would Lift up my Heart unto God, That He would <u>Prepare me</u>, for whatever matter, Grievous or Joyful, I am therein to Encounter withal. Thirdly; In my <u>Last Prayer</u> in my Study, before I go to my Rest, I would Call to Mind, from whom I have received any <u>Letter</u> this day; and make a <u>Particular Mention</u> of that person unto ye Lord, with Supplications for Suitable Mercies to Him. [ms. p. 283]

There is a Thought, which I have often had in my Mind: But I Laid upon my Mind a Charge to have it yett oftener there: That ⟨ <u>Reason</u> in us, is y^e <u>Work</u> of GOD; A <u>Ray</u> from GOD: ⟩ ye Light of <u>Reason</u>, is the Work of GOD; The Law of <u>Reason</u>, is the Law of GOD; The Voice of <u>Reason</u>, is the Voice of GOD; We never have to do with <u>Reason</u>, but at the Same time We have to do with GOD; O^e Submission to the Rules of <u>Reason</u> is an Obedience to GOD. How much will this Expedient Contribute, unto a <u>Life of Obedience</u> to God! Lett me, as often as I have Evident <u>Reason</u> sett before me, think upon it; <u>The Great GOD now Speaks unto me!</u> And Lett me from this, yeeld a present Compliance: Alwayes <u>Hearken to Reason</u>, from this Consideration.

It is a practice that I am not unus'd unto, When I perceive an <u>Ill</u> <u>Thought</u> arising in my Mind, I Extinguish it, and Contradict it, with forming a <u>Good Thought</u>, that shall be directly Contrary to it. More Particularly. Upon a <u>Proud Thought</u>, I would immediately form a Thought, that shall carry ye greatest <u>Self-abasement</u> and <u>Self-abhorrence</u> in it. Upon an <u>Impure Thought</u>, I would immediately form a Thought, that shall carry in it a Resignation of myself unto y^e <u>Spirit of Holiness</u>, & an Invocation of Him to take possession of me. Upon an <u>Envious Thought</u>, I would immediately form a Thought, that shall carry in it, some ardent Wish for y^e <u>Prosperity</u> of the Person whom I had in my View. Upon a <u>Revengeful Thought</u>, I would immediately form a Thought, that shall carry in it, some Sincere Desires for <u>Blessings</u> on ye person that has injured me. Finally, Upon a Thought of <u>Discouragement</u>, from y^e <u>Labour</u> of being Serviceable, or from ye Malice, & ye Number, & ye Power of them that are <u>Enemies</u> to my Serviceableness, I would immediately form a Thought, that shall carry in it, a cheerful Dependence on ye Assistence & Protection of ye glorious Lord, & an <u>unfainting Resolution</u> to be <u>always abounding</u> <u>in ye Work of ye Lord</u>. I usually putt these Thoughts into ye form of Ejaculations, & so Send them up to Heaven. [ms. p. 284]

I grew afraid, Lest while I am conversing with my Neighbours (tho' it be alwayes with ye Intentions of <u>Doing some Good</u> unto them,) I may, Ere I am aware, be betray'd into some Degree of <u>Slothfulness</u>, which may be a prejudice unto my greater <u>Usefulness</u>. Wherefore, When I am abroad among my Neighbours, I often putt that Question to myself: <u>Would it not</u> <u>be more pleasing unto my Glorious Lord, that I should be in my Study at</u> <u>this time?</u> If I find myself in a Temper and Vigour, to be carrying on <u>Greater Services</u> in my Study, I would break off the most agreeable

Conversation, & flee thither, with a Zeal of Redeeming ye Time, upon me.

I became very sensible, That Envy is a very considerable part of the Satanic Image in the Soul; & the working of it very Displeasing to the Good Spirit of God. The Love[130] that Envies not,[131] is a very Vital and Lovely Stroke, in ye Image of my Sweet Saviour, after which I ought to aspire Exceedingly. And how far it may Engage the Good Providence of ye Holy One, to Look favourably upon me, tis with Him. I grew desirous, to have One Stroke more at this matter, by more distinctly forming these Resolutions, with an Eye unto my dear Saviour, to form in me ye Dispositions proper for them, & to help me in the Executing of them. First; The first and Least Ebullition of an Envious Thought at the Prosperity of another Man, I would Rebuke it, & Suppress it immediately, with all possible Imagination; & in a way of ye most Expressive Contradiction to it, Lift up my Heart unto God, with my Thanks to Him, for ye Good He has Done to that Man, & my Prayers and Hopes for the [ms. p. 285] continuance of it. Secondly; Upon all Occasional Views of the Blessings and Comforts Enjoy'd by Other Men, I would shape a Thought of Satisfaction in ye Sovereignty, and the Wisdome and the Goodness of the Glorious GOD, which is Exercised in it; and make that Article of their Prosperity, a particular Article of my Praises unto ye Lord on their behalf; with my Wishes, that they may improve it for His glory. Thirdly; When I am Sitting with my Friends in their Houses, and Walking the Streets where I may see some of their most Visible Possessions, I would Employ ye Ejaculations of my Mind unto ye Blessed GOD, in as Real and Sincere Acknowledgments of His Granting this Prosperity unto them, and with as true a Pleasure of Soul at the Prospect, as if it were All my own. Yea, and I would obtain a Liesure, to Walk about ye place, & Go round ye Neighbourhood, & tell the Smiles of God upon it, Mark well their Enjoyments, and Consider their Consolations, & upon Each of them gett my Soul raised into those Dispositions of Joy, which I ought to have, when I See ye Goodness of the Blessed GOD shining forth in so obliging a Manner; With Supplications for my Neighbours, that they may bring forth much of that Fruit, by which He may be glorified.

I will Conclude this Long paragraph, with a Resolution to which my Saviour brought me: That I will frequently Reflect on ye Condition and Employment of my Mind (often in a day,) and if I perceive no Tendency to a Good Thought in ye Operations of it, I will be Angry with myself, and Labour to form some Good Thought immediately. The Apprehension [ms. p. 286] of having my Heart alwayes under the View of the glorious God, & ye Thoughts thereof afar off known unto Him, Exceedingly Quicken me & Comfort me, in these Exercises of Piety. And the Thoughts which I therein fly unto, are ordinarily putt into ye Form of an Address unto ye Lord, who Considers my Meditation.

If I Live to make any further Additions to these Memorials, there will occur many things of ye Same importance with these, in some of ye Ensuing Paragraphs.

§   When a Winter has arrived, I have been from the Circumstances of ye Winter awakened unto many Strokes of Winter-Piety.[133] Particularly to Consider and Acknowledge the Sufferings of my dear Saviour, as Purchasing for me the Comforts, that Succour me in, & Shelter me from, the Difficulties of ye Winter. I have gone on to form certain Supplications Hyemales, or Winter-Desires and Prayers, which from ye Several Accidents of the Winter, I would be quickened, both to insist upon myself, & also to draw my Friends with me to take notice of. E. g.

On the Distance of the <u>Sun</u> from us.

<u>Oh, Lett not my Soul, nor the World, Languish in a miserable Distance from o^e Saviour.</u>

The <u>Snow</u>.

<u>Lord, Thro' ye Blood of my Saviour applied unto me, render my Guilty and Stained Soul, Whiter than ye Snow.</u>[134]

The <u>Frost</u>.

<u>Lord, Lett not my Capacities & Activities for thy Service, Ly under any Congelation.</u> [ms. p. 287]

The <u>Ice</u>.

<u>Lord, Save me from the Fate and Fall of them whom thou hast Sett in Slippery Places. Glory be to Him, who is able to keep me from Falling.</u>[135]

The <u>Vermine</u> Suppressed.

<u>Lord, Lett the Lusts in my Soul, which are worse than ye worst, & ye most noxious of all Creatures, be destroyed, without being Revived any more.</u>

The <u>Fruitless Face</u> of the Earth.

<u>Lord, Tho' my Life be too much without Good Fruits, yett thou Canst bring me to be Fruitful in Good Works. And tho' the Face of the World at this Day be horribly Barren & Wretched, yett I will hope in thee, to give it a better Face, and bring on a better Time.</u>

My <u>Garments</u>.

<u>Lord, I am not afraid of ye Winter, because of my Double Cloathing. But, oh, putt upon me ye Righteousness of my Saviour.</u>[136] <u>Lett me be also cloathed with thy Spirit; under such Influences of the Spirit, that none other shall be seen upon me: O Glorious, O Durable, Cloathing!</u>[137]

My <u>Fuel</u>.

Lord, Enable me to Warm all that are about me, with Holy Dispositions, & to Speak those Words unto them, which may Cause their Hearts to burn within them. And, oh, Save me & Mine from Eternal Burnings, & from the Fiery Indignation which is to devour thine Adversaries.[138]

As a further Essay of this Winter-Piety, When I have been at the Proper Season of the year, putting on my Garments for the Winter, I have at the doing of it, pressed after these Dispositions and Resolutions.

First. I would heartily Bless the Glorious God, for supplying me with Suitable and Sufficient Garments. I would Bewayl my Sin in my First Parents, that Sinn'd away the Garments of Glory, with which we were at first accommodated, & brought a Wretched [ms. p. 288] Nakedness upon us. I would Confess my Obligations to my dear JESUS, who by Submitting to the Sufferings wherein He was Disrobed, Purchased the Comforts of my Garments for me.

Secondly. I would Putt on the Lord JESUS CHRIST by a New Consent of my Soul, to be found in His Righteousness; and by fresh Contemplations and Resolutions, of such a Conformity to Him, that they who see Me, may see much of Him.

Thirdly. I would come into a further Degree of Sollicitude, that I may be Cloathed with ye Spirit; & Possessed by the Holy One, Evidently resting on me, in ye Inclinations of Holiness & Usefulness.

Fourthly. I would be Sollicitous, to provide Clothing for the Poor, that want it, & Convey some Garments unto those, who in ye Cold, may Want a Covering.

Thus for ye Winter.

And for ye other Three Seasons of the year, I have been awakened also by ye Circumstances of ye Seasons, to form Supplications, which might be both Privately & Publickly, at proper Times insisted on.

For the <u>Spring</u>.

Lord, <u>Lett the Sun of Righteousness</u>[139]<u>draw near unto me, & Lett me be</u>
<u>Quickened, & Revived, & made a New Creature, and made very Fruitful,</u>
<u>by His Benign and Blessed Influences.</u>

Lord, <u>Lett a Glorious CHRIST return, Like ye Sun, to a miserable world,</u>
<u>& bring a New Face upon it; Produce upon it a New Creation, & fill it</u>
<u>with the Fruits of Righteousness.</u>[140]

Lord, <u>Lett ye Hours of Darkness grow Shorter & Shorter with me.</u>

Lord, <u>Lett ye Time of ye Singing of Birds Come on. Lett thy Spirit fitt</u>
<u>me for & fill me with, the Songs of the Redeemed.</u>[141] <u>And Lett ye Songs</u>
<u>of Piety replenish ye Whole Earth, with an Heavenly Melody.</u> [ms. p. 289]

Lord, <u>Enable me with Diligence to Prosecute a Divine Husbandry; & with</u>
<u>Patience to Wait for a Good Harvest of my Endeavours to Serve ye King-</u>
<u>dome of God. Oh! Lett Light & Joy be Sown for me!</u>[142]

For the <u>Summer</u>.

Lord, <u>Lett me be as Fruitful as any of the Trees or Fields, which now yeeld</u>
<u>a grateful Spectacle. Oh, Lett me abound in the Fruits of Righteous-</u>
<u>ness.</u>

Lord, <u>Lett my dear JESUS, be to me as the Shadow of a Great Rock in a</u>
<u>Weary Land.</u>[143]
<u>And may I also drink of what flowes from that wonderful Rock.</u>[144]

Lord, <u>Lett me be Entitled to, & Prepared for, the Blessedness of that</u>
<u>world, in which no uneasy Heat will molest thy Children.</u>[145]

For the <u>Autumn</u>.

Lord, <u>Lett me see a Joyful Harvest of all my Poor Essayes to glorify thee.</u>
<u>Lett me Reap with Joy.</u>[146]

Lord, <u>Lett me arrive to my Grave, & thy Floor, as a Shock of Corn fully</u>
<u>ripe, in the Season thereof.</u>

Lord, <u>Affect me, & ye rest of Mankind, with a Sense of o^e own Mortality;</u>

<u>For we all fade as a Leaf!</u>[147] [ms. p. 290]

§   <u>My Son</u>, I don't Remember, that my <u>Method of Sabbatizing</u>, has been

described in these Memorials.[148] Now, this being a very Essential Article

in the <u>Christian Asceticks</u>, I ought to Endeavour Your Instruction in it.

But, as these Papers have hitherto instructed you purely from the Experi-

ence of a Father: they shall in this Article Continue to do so. I find in

my Reserved Papers, this Account, of my Spending One <u>Lords-day</u>; & in this

there is but an Intimation of ye Wayes, wherein I Endeavour to Spend y^e

rest. However, I Leave myself a Liberty to proceed herein with much

Variety. Which you may do; and indeed, the more various y^e <u>Sabbatizing</u>

<u>Exercises</u> are, so much ye better.

'   In the <u>Afternoon</u> that went before y^e <u>Lords-day</u>, I was desirous to

' have my Studies over, & Leave no affaires that might be any Encumbrance

' on me.

'   I charged my Family to make ye Like <u>Preparation</u>.

'   And I devoted y^e <u>Evening</u> unto the Exercises of Piety.

'   In y^e <u>Morning</u>, I awoke, blessing ye Lord for another <u>Lords-day</u>; and

' I arose a <u>Little Earlier</u> than on other Dayes.

'   I Considered my Usual <u>Question</u> for this Morning; <u>What shall I do for</u>

' <u>the Good of the Flock, which I have under my Charge</u>?

'   I Sang my <u>Morning-Hymn</u>.

' Coming into my Study, I wrote down my <u>Answer</u> to my Question.

'   I applied myself unto ye Lord, as for y^e <u>Pardon</u> of my former Tres-

' passes on ye Holy <u>Rest</u> of His Day, thro' y^e <u>Blood</u> of Him, who is y^e

' Lord of it, so, for <u>Grace</u> from Him now to Sanctify the Day; Without

' which <u>Grace</u> I can do nothing. [ms. p. 291]

' Throughout all the Ensuing Day, I kept my Thoughts in an agreeable

' Employment, and under the necessary Government. When I was not Engaged

' in any Extended Exercise of Devotion, I was Continually forming Admoni-

' tions of Piety, from Occasional Objects and Occurrences; Every thing

' about me preached unto me; and I usually turned ye Lessons into Ejacula-

' tory Prayers. If I found my Mind began at any time to Ly fallow, &

' Empty of Good Thoughts, I presently Rebuked it, and Renewed them. If

' any Evil Thoughts began to make the Least Approach to my Mind, I pre-

' sently Bewayled it, and Rejected them, and raised Good ones, just Con-

' trary to them.

' I so took heed against Sinning with my Tongue, that I did not utter

' one Word all ye Day, (tho' I Spoke on many Occasions,) but what, I

' think, I may say, I, did well to utter it.

' I wrote an Illustration on a Text of the Sacred Scripture.

' I Readd a Suitable Portion of ye Old Testament, in the Hebrew Lan-

' guage. Another in ye French. And then, a Suitable Portion of ye New

' Testament in ye Greek. And I fetch'd a Note & a Prayer, out of Every

' Verse.

' Then I made ye Morning-Prayer of my Study.

' My Little Breakfast being brought me, my Food was receiv'd, With

' Praises to God, and Meditations on the nobler provisions, wch He has

' made for my Better part.

' With ye Like Dispositions & Meditations, I anon took the other Two

' Meals of ye Day.

' I went down to my Family, and Sang and Pray'd with them. [ms. p.

' 292]

' I gave New Charges unto my Family, to Remember the Sabbath-day, and

' keep it Holy. And I assigned unto the Little Children that were to

' stay at home, <u>Sentences</u> of ye Bible to be gott by Heart.

'   I returned unto my Study, & Pray'd, that y^e <u>Public Sacrifices</u>, to
' which I was now going, might be acceptably & profitably carried on.

'   I went unto ye Public, where my Venerable Parent performed ye pub-
' lic Ministrations. The very <u>Bell</u> putt me in mind of y^e <u>Joyful Sound</u>.[149]
' Here I gave Such Attention, that not one Passage of y^e <u>Prayer</u>, not one
' <u>Head</u>, or <u>Text</u>, and Scarce one Sentence in ye Sermon, passed, Without my
' Mind moving towards Heaven, with an adapted <u>Confession</u> or <u>Petition</u>,
' upon it. And Every Verse of the <u>Psalm</u>, I accompanied wth a <u>Note</u> & a
' <u>Prayer</u> Educed from it.

'   When all was finished, I Sett myself to form ye Desires for <u>all the</u>
' <u>Hearers</u>, & the Desires and Resolves for <u>my own Life</u>; & think on those
' <u>Improvements in Piety</u>; which ye Subject newly treated on, might Lead
' me to.

'   Returning to my Study, I Readd over some Holy Discourses, relating
' to the Great <u>Sabbatism</u>, which ye Church of God <u>is</u> to Look for, and the
' <u>Glorious Things which are Spoken about the City of God</u>, & the prophecies
' relating to ye Latter Dayes.[150] This I did, (usually do,) because I
' Look on the Sabbath, as a peculiar <u>Type</u> and <u>Sign</u> of ye Blessed <u>Millen-</u>
' <u>nium</u>.

'   Going to my <u>Table</u>, I fed the Souls of ye Company, with as profitable
' Discourses, as I could Entertain them withal.   [ms. p. 293]

'   And I also <u>drew out my Soul to the Hungry</u>;[151] I thought it a Day
' Proper to dispense Kindness unto the <u>Poor</u>; I was careful to have some
' such invited unto my <u>Table</u>.

'   After this, I went on, upon the Affaires of ye Great <u>Sabbatism</u>. I
' Readd a Paragraph of the <u>Scripture</u>, that refers unto it; with my Acutest,
' & most Penetrating Thoughts thereupon, & Suitable Ejaculations.

' And I Sang an Hymn relating to it. Then, prostrate in ye Dust, I

' Poured out a Prayer, for Zion in ye Dust; & for ye Hastening of the

' Day of God.

' Hereupon, I took the Sermon I was to preach immediately. And ran

' it over, so that my Mind was formed into proper Tempers & Wishes, on

' every Head of the Sermon.

' I then on my knees bewayled before the Lord, Such Sins as ye Sermon

' I was to preach, most call'd me to Repent of; & Pray'd for Grace to do

' Such things myself, as my Sermon was to Excite my Hearers to; and

' begg'd for the Help of Heaven in ye Work before me.

' I went unto ye Public, & Spent about Three Hours, in Carrying on

' the Services there, in a Great Assembly, with a Great Assistence from

' God.

' My Mind, between ye Conclusion of the Services, & my Visiting of my

' Habitation, was filled with Prayers, that what had passed might make

' due Impressions on ye People.

' Excessively tired, I drank my Tea, with Praises to the glorious

' Lord; and some Thoughts on His precious Benefits, which this Water led

' me to. [ms. p. 294]

' I made a Prayer, such a feeble one as it was, for such Blessings as

' I am daily to ask for.

' I went down unto my Family; Where I Catechised the Children; and I

' went thro' the Sermons of the Day with them, in ye way of a Dialogue;

' and Sang and Pray'd with them, & with the Neighbours that came in to

' join with them.

' Then I Caused Such of the Children, as could do so, to tell me, What

' new Matter of Prayer, they were now apprehensive of? And Charged them

' to Retire with it, before ye Lord.

'   I also ordered my Little Son,[152] to hear y^e <u>Negro</u>-Servant, say his

' Catechism.

'   I retired unto my Study, & Meditated on that Point; <u>What have I</u>

' <u>yett Left undone, that it would be for my Consolation & Satisfaction</u>

' <u>to do, before I dy</u>?

'   I Readd in a <u>Book</u> of Piety, a Sermon that might add unto ye Heavenly

' Tincture on my Mind.

'   I was called forth to <u>Pray with a Sick person</u>; unto which I went

' with Alacrity as unto a Duty of the <u>Sabbath</u>.

'   I went again unto my Family, and Satt with them, while Each of the

' capable Children, successively readd their Several Parts in a <u>Book</u> of

' Piety, to the whole Family. And I took occasion from thence to Renew

' my Instructions to them.

'   Then I Sang my <u>Evening-Hymn</u> wth the Family.

'   I retired now unto my Study, and in Prayer, gave Thanks for the

' <u>Mercies</u> [ms. p. 295] of ye Day past; and implored a Pardon for y^e

' <u>Errors</u> of ye Day past; both of which I Endeavoured Particularly to

' Enumerate.

'   I Committed all my Interests into the Hands of a dear Saviour; and

' actually Exerted a <u>Principle of Grace</u> in an <u>Act</u> that was an <u>Evident</u>

' <u>Token of Salvation</u>, that might assure me of my Safety, if I were to dy

' before to morrow.

'   Finally, I declared before ye Lord, That altho Some had observed,

' a Reward of <u>Temporal Blessings</u>, even in ye Ensuing week, to Encourage

' their <u>Sabbatizing</u>, I had now been <u>abounding in this Work of ye Lord</u>,

' without ye Encouragement of any such Expectation. If never so much

' <u>Affliction</u> should befall me this Week, or in ye rest of my Life, yett

' I would go on, in all the Holy <u>Labours</u> of <u>Sabbatizing</u> to Him; and as-

' sure myself that I should find my Account in y^e <u>Rest that remains for</u>

' <u>ye People of God</u>. But renounce all pretence to <u>Merit</u> in my own Per-

' formances.

'   So I went unto my Rest; & fell asleep Reading a Book of Piety.

'   This Variety of Duty, was all done, with ye Help of Heaven, on <u>this</u>

' <u>One Lords-day</u>. And tho' it Left me very <u>Weary</u>, yett my Spirit now

' found (and alwayes does) those unspeakable Consolations and Advantages,

' from such <u>Unwearied Sabbatizing</u>, as carry rich Compensations with y^m.

    Thus, <u>My Son</u>, I have been teaching you to <u>Sabbatize</u>. Do as far as

you can this way, and you will be yett better <u>Taught of God</u>. [ms. p. 296]

§   <u>My Son</u>. I know not, whether I am not now come to a <u>Finishing Stroke</u>:

And therefore do you give a great Attention unto it.

    My Poor Life has been full of <u>Sacrifices</u>; and by the <u>Things that I have</u>

<u>Suffered</u>, I have <u>Learn'd the Obedience of</u>, A SACRIFICER:[153] By which my

Title to the <u>Heavenly Priesthood</u>, is, I hope, a Little Cleared up.

    I will describe to you a part of the Christian <u>Asceticks</u>, which I

have been very much used unto.[154]

    I have Considered y^e <u>Providence</u> of the Glorious GOD in all that be-

falls me; And I have Seen, that If I am ever putt upon parting with any

Thing, it is ye Hand of GOD that putts me upon it. I have thought, <u>It</u>

<u>is what the Great GOD calls me to</u>!

    I have then considered, That the <u>Sovereign</u> God, may <u>Take</u> from me

what He pleases, and may <u>Break</u> me to peeces if He pleases. I Lay myself

& my All, at ye Foot of a God, whose <u>Dominion over All</u> is irresistible,

& unquestionable; and Say, <u>Lord, Thou takest nothing from me, but what</u>

<u>was of thy Giving to me. Whatever thou callest me to part withal, All</u>

is Thine, and thou mayst do What thou wilt with thy own!

I have considered herewithal, That a Righteous God Inflicts no more on me than I Deserve, if I be Stript of all that is Desireable to me, & the whole Desire of my Eyes be taken away with a Stroke.[155] I have Lain down under ye Bereavements that have been ordered for me, with such Confessions; Lord, I have by my Sins forfeited all my Good Things. Tis a Just Siezure which thou makest upon whatever thou callest me to Part withal. And I will bear the Indignation of the Lord, because I have Sinned against Him. [ms. p. 297]

To Produce that awful Silence, wherewith Sacrifices are to be carried on, I have gone on to Consider, That my Great SAVIOUR has been made, yea, has made Himself a Sacrifice,[156] for me. I must have gone down to ye Pitt,[157] if He had not Stept in as the Ransome of my Soul.[158] At ye View of this, my Soul has been filled with Gratitude; and Said, When I Wanted a Sacrifice, then my Great Saviour said, Lo, O Come. He offered up His Life, & Stript Himself of Every thing, & readily Entertained a most bitter Cup of Sufferings, that He might Reconcile me unto God.[159] Oh! What shall I render to So obliging a Saviour? My dear Saviour, Whatever Sacrifice I am now Call'd unto, I will cheerfully present it, as a Thank-Offering unto thee, for thy Glorious Benefits. What I have parted withal, I have brought under this Notion: A Sacrifice of Thanksgiving[160] unto a Great Saviour, who has been Himself Sacrificed for me. This Notion of it, has inspired me with a most Sensible Alacrity, in what Sufferings I have been Call'd unto.

At the Same time, I have Considered this One thing more: That ye Providence of God, which calls me to any Sacrificing, is what my Saviour has most Immediately under His Administration. It is the Son of God, in the Man upon the Throne, who Administers all the Affaires of the

Divine Providence, and has the Government of the World under His Glorious Management. Accordingly When I have been brought into Circumstances, wherein I have been Called unto Sacrifices, I have thought with myself, This is the Thing that is appointed for me by my Saviour; A Saviour, who has Loved me, & given Himself also for me: A Saviour, who has told me, He will do me no Hurt: A Saviour, who has [ms. p. 298] undertaken to bring me unto perfect Happiness in the Enjoyment of God: What I am Call'd now to part withal, tis my Wise, my Good, my Faithful Saviour, that calls me to the Sacrificing for it. It cannot be best for me to keep any thing that Such a Saviour will have me to part withal. I have seen infinite Cause for ever to Comply with ye Will of such a Saviour!

My Considerations are not over yett. I have Considered, That it is impossible for me to do any thing more Acceptable to God, than Willingly to Offer what Heaven Calls me to part withal; Willingly to Suffer what Heaven shall impose upon me. I have thought with myself; When the Great GOD & o^e Saviour, beholds a Beleever Sacrificing his All unto Him, & Willing to Be all that God Will have him to Be, & Willing to Bear all that God Will have him to Bear, it is unto the Holy Eyes of His glory, a most Acceptable Spectacle: It wonderfully gratifies Him. This Obedience to the Will of God, is Better than any Sacrifice of ye Ancient Paedagogy: And so to Sacrifice, next unto the Faith which Lives upon ye Great Sacrifice of o^e Saviour, I have Said, This also shall please the Lord better[161] than all o^e other Devotions. This Thought has mightily Inflamed me, & While I have been musing on it, the Fire has burned within me.[162] What? Will it be a thing very agreeable unto my God & Saviour, that I should part with whatever He calls for, & Sacrifice my All unto Him? Lord, I will do it; I will do it. Sacrifice unto ye Lord, O my Soul; And all that is within me. Give up unto Him all that is About me. To please my

God & Saviour, Oh, Lett me never know any pleasure upon Earth Comparable to it! [ms. p. 299]

Prepared with such Impressions, I have now gone on, to Look with a Sacrificing Eye upon all of my Enjoyments, and make a most hearty Oblation of them all unto the Lord. I have Successively taken a Distinct View of my Enjoyments; & very often, very often, cast a Look upon ye dearest & most Valuable of them, with a Sacrificing Thought of this importance; O My dear Saviour, If thou shalt be most glorified, by my having of This taken from me, I Resign it, I Forego it, I am Content & Willing to be without it. When I have had a more Special Relish in any of my Enjoyments, it has provoked me to a Fresh Act of Sacrificing. Upon the Provocation I have said; O my dear Saviour, As much as I prize this precious & pleasant Thing, if Thou say to me, Part with it, I shall part with it, and Consent unto its Leaving of me. If Thou Wilt have this Thing to be denied unto me, that so my knowing, & Loving, & Serving of thee may be the better accommodated, I Consent, I Consent, that it be denied unto me; I am Willing to be deprived of it. When it has happened, that I have thought on any Desireable, which I had not Sacrificed so Cordially & so Explicitly as I desired, my Rebuked Soul has fallen a Trembling at the Rebellion and Idolatry I have seen myself in danger of; and I have presently formed a Fresh Act of Sacrificing thereupon; Help me, O my Saviour, That this also may be given up unto thee! To finish the Matter, my very Life itself has come into my List of Sacrifices. I have not given over, till I could say, My Life is Continually in my Hand, and Ready to be [ms. p. 300] offered up. Such is the Submission that I have made unto ye Lord of my Life; O my God, Whenever thou shalt give order for my Death, My Life shall not be so dear to me, as to hinder my finishing of my Course, with Saying, The Will of ye Lord be done! [163]

Yea, I have gone on, without any Robbery for an Offering, to make Sacrifices of the Things which I have not Enjoy'd, as well as of what I did. Not only those things of which I once had ye Possession, but have then felt the Bereavement, have Come into my Offering; wherein I have said, The Lord has given, & the Lord has taken away;[164] Blessed be the Name of the Lord;[165] and Lett these things be now Sacrificed unto ye Lord! When God Said, I should be Without such Things, as had heretofore been ye very Salt and Solace of my Life, I have Said, O my Saviour, I am Willing to be Without, what thou Wilt have to be Witheld from me! But also, when I have beheld the Enjoyments of other Men; And such Enjoyments, as I would Gladly, if I might Fairly, have been myself the Owner of, I have Converted them into Sacrifices too, and Said, O my dear Saviour, I am Sweetly Satisfied in it, that thou hast not allowed unto me these Enjoyments!

Anon, I have Come to make Reflections on the Sacrifices, wherew^th I have glorified God; and I have Enjoy'd the great Consolations of God[166] in Reflecting on them. Tho' ye very Idea of having my Enjoyments taken from me, and much more the actual Enduring[167] of such Dissections, has been, for the present not Joyous but Grievous to me, yett Afterwards my Soul has been filled with Peace, in Looking back upon it. If my Enjoyments [ms. p. 301] have been continued unto me, I have beheld them with a Singular Flavour, in this Regard; This is One of my Sacrifices! And if I have call'd unto Remembrance the Wormwood & the gall of the Time, when I underwent the Loss of my Enjoyments, I have had my Mind presently & wondrously refreshed, in this Review of it; My God helped me then to glorify Him, & Offer Sacrifices that were well-pleasing to Him. I have had these rich Comforts of God, Exceedingly to Delight my Soul, in ye Multitude of my Thoughts within me![168]

In this Way, & with such Exercises and Sacrifices, I have been preparing for all Events: I have bound the Sacrifices with the Cords of Love; They have Stood Ready for the Stroke, whenever the Sign should be given for its falling on them. Nature indeed has deprecated the Blow upon the Sacrifices; I have Cried unto ye Lord, Father, I pray that the Cup which I am threatened withal, may pass from me! [169] Nevertheless Grace by 'nd by has gott the upper hand of Nature; and I have been armed for an Encounter with such things as have been waiting for me. Yea, Tho' I have not been without a Natural Horror of Afflictions; & I have humbly pray'd, & begg'd, & Wept unto Heaven to have my Enjoyments prolonged unto me, yett the Prospect of a Sad Thing a coming upon me, has had with it, a certain, Sacred, Secret Mixture of Joy, to think; Well, However my dear Saviour will now give me a precious Opportunity to glorify Him, With most acceptable Sacrifices. I have been in a Sort, Glad, Glad of it, That I should have an Opportunity to be a Spectacle, that my glorious Lord would have pleasure in. I have counted it a Joy, to fall into diverse Temptations, [170] that were to [ms. p. 302] Try, what the Lord would Enable me to do at Sacrificing. ⟨ Yea, I may truly say; The Approach of Great Calamities, has found a sort of a welcome with me, fro ye View it has given me, of Opportunities to glorify GOD with Sacrifices. I have had my Heart pleas'd at ye Thoughts of being putt upon Sacrificing. On this I have thought; Is not ye Love of GOD now Sensibly at work in my Soul? Yea, what will ye Glorious One do, with one whom He has thus made a Sacrificer! ⟩

I have reckoned, That my best Course to Preserve and Obtain Enjoyments, would be, to Sacrifice them. And sometimes, I have had ye Heart-melting Joyes of a Particular Faith for Enjoyments, born in upon my Soul, at My Sacrificing of them. Yea, I have Esteemed this a comfortable Token, That I shall be found in the Catalogue of Priests, & not be putt away from ye Priesthood.[171] I have been full of Sacrifices. While I have

been in ye midst of my Obedient Sacrifices, my mind has been wonderfully

ravished with such a perswasion as this: Now I know, That my dear Jesus,

to whom I am now Sacrificing, will one day give me to Walk wth Him, in

the White Robes of ye Royal Priesthood.[172] My Sacrifices are undoubted

Marks of such a Blessedness. The promised Blessedness of the Saints, is,

To Inherit all things.[173] If I can Sacrifice all things, I shall undoubt-

edly Come to Inherit all things! A Sacrificing Soul was never made for

to be thrown down into Hell. If Such a Soul could be sent into Hell, it

would make a Strange Alteration there; it would Even carry Heaven thith-

er![174]

    Finally; I have happily felt the Peace of God, ye Effect and Reward

of this Disposition.[175] My Poor Life has been thus Enlightened with Ex-

pressions of Love to God, in multiplied Repetitions of them. It has here-

upon been Sweetened with many Intimations from Heaven, Powerfully bring-

ing home the Love of God into my Soul, & shedding it abroad in my Heart.

{ When I have been preferring ye Will of GOD unto my own, I have had this

Joyful Thought, Shott into my Mind, If ye Will of ye great GOD be mine,

Shall not His Power be so too! So far mine, as to be Employ'd for my

welfare, so far as there shall be real occasion for it! } While my Soul

has been inclined & assisted unto Sacrifices, which have gone up in a

Flame of Love unto the Lord, it [ms. p. 303] proved a Demonstration of

His Love unto me. I have thought, If any Saviour had not Loved me, He

would never have made me so Love, and Strive and Wish to please Him with

Sacrifices. If He would have pleased for to kill me, He would not have

received my Offerings, nor have shown me how to make them. I have Often

Lived in ye midst of such Satisfactions: My Saviour has Loved me, and

will make all things Work together for my Good, & has reserved Strange

Blessings in His Heavenly Places for me!

My Son, Among all the Arts, that are understood and professed, or Studied, among the children of men, there will be none found Comparable to this Holy Skill of Sacrificing, in which I have now instructed you. And I Conclude with telling you; None of all o^e Enjoyments themselves, are so Valuable, as the Skill of Sacrificing All.

As an Appendix to this Article of the Asceticks, I will here only mention one Experiment in my conversation. ⟨ When any thing befalls me, that is Grievous to me, I immediately apply my Thoughts to Two Questions. The First, What is ye Sacrifice I am now call'd unto? The Second, How, and with what Frames am I now to offer my Sacrifice? ⟩

§ A Mighty Desire have I had working in my Soul, to be found among the Priests of the Creation, and be Initiated in ye Holy Priesthood wherein I propose my Everlasting Blessedness, by offering up unto the Glorious God, ye Praises, which arise to Him from all the Works of His Hands. I have made very many Essays, at a Philosophical Religion;[176] & made very many Visits to ye Creatures in their Several classes, and with much La-bour observed ye Astonishing Displayes of ye Divine Power and Wisdome and Goodness in them; And I have concluded my observations, [ms. p. 304] with proper Sentiments of Piety, & such Acknowledgments of ye Glorious GOD, as they have Led me to; and I have taken Care, that a Glorious CHRIST should not be Left unconsidered in these Acknowledgments. If the Collections which I have made, on this Noble Subject, were published, it would no doubt, afford unto ye Gentlemen of the Finer Heart-Strings, a grateful Entertainment. But I must be content, that when I have prepared Such Sacrifices for GOD, they be after all Sacrificed in this further consid-eration, of my Submission to it, that they should be buried in obscurity

& oblivion.

However, My Son, from ye many hundreds of Matters & Methods, for the Raising of Devout Things in the Exercises of a Christian Philosopher, which I have Studied, I will single out but One, in which this part of our Asceticks, will have a competent Illustration.[177]

I am Continually Entertained with Weighty Body, or, Matter tending to ye Center of Gravity: { or, Attracted by Matter. } I feel it in my own. The Cause of this Tendency; Tis the Glorious GOD! Great GOD, Thou givest this Matter such a Tendency; Thou keepest it in its Operation! There is no other Cause for Gravity, but ye Will and Work of ye glorious GOD. I am now Effectually convinced of that ancient confession, & must affectuously make it, He is not far from Every One of us![178] When I see a Thing Moving or Settling that way which its Heavy Nature carries it, I may very justly think, and I would often form ye Thought, It is the glorious GOD who now carries this matter such a way. [ms. p. 305]

When Matter goes Down-ward, my Spirit shall therefore Mount Upward, in Acknowledgments of the GOD who orders it. I will no longer Complain, Behold, I go forward, but He is not there; and backward but I cannot perceive Him: On ye Left Hand, where He does work, but I cannot behold Him: He hideth Himself on ye Right Hand, that I cannot see Him.[179] No, I am now taught where to meet with Him; Even at Every Turn. He knows the way that I take:[180] I cannot Stir forward or backward, but I perceive Him in ye Weight of Every Matter. My Way shall be to improve this, as a Weighty Argument for the Being of a GOD: I will argue from it, Behold, There is a GOD, whom I ought forever to Love & Serve & Glorify! Yea, and if I am Tempted unto the doing of any Wicked Thing, I may reflect, That it cannot be done without some Action, wherein ye Power[181] of Matter operates. But then I may carry on the Reflection; How near, How near am I to ye glorious

GOD, whose Commands I am going to Violate! Matter keeps His Laws; But, O my Soul, Wilt thou break His Laws? How shall I do this Wickedness, & therein Deny the GOD, who not only is Above, but also is Exerting His power, in the very Matter upon which I make my criminal Misapplications! [ms. p. 306]

§   I came to see, that there was one Point of Daily Conversation, which called for more of my Care to, be Employ'd upon it.

The Expressions of Civility, which we call o^e Complements, in Daily Conversation, must not be Empty Things. Empty complements, not only carry a contradiction in ye Terms, but also come too much under ye Guilt of ye Idle Words Condemned by o^e Lord.[182]

I desired therefore to press after those Dispositions of Piety and of Charity, which my Complements ought always to be uttered withal, & have Suitable Frames and Thoughts annexed unto them. E. g.

When I pull of my Hatt unto any one, Lett my Mind, be thus disposed: I See ye Image of GOD in that person, & pay Respect unto it. I have here also an Opportunity for the Benedictions which are very often wont Secretly to accompany my Salutations.

When I say, Your Servant, Lett my Mind be thus disposed, I will really be glad of doing any Service for this person.

When I say, I am glad to see you, Lett my Mind be thus disposed, I pray, I hope, that I may see this person yett better Circumstanced in ye Heavenly World.

When I say, How do you do? Lett my Mind be thus disposed, I shall be glad if they do Well; I shall be griev'd if they do Ill; I wish them the Grace to do all they ought to do.

When I Drink to any one, with, My Service to you, Lett my Mind be

thus disposed; <u>I heartily desire, that they may drink of</u> y^e <u>Living Foun-</u>
<u>tains which the Lamb of</u> [ms. p. 307] <u>GOD Leads His chosen to!</u>[183]

When in a Way of <u>Return</u> for any thing, I say, <u>I humbly Thank you,</u>
Lett my Mind be thus disposed; <u>My Thanks are first and most of all due,</u>
<u>to the glorious GOD, from whom all Good comes down unto me.</u> <u>I will also</u>
<u>be ready to Retaliate any Kindness that can be shown unto me.</u>

When I <u>take Leave,</u> and Say--<u>Fare You well.</u>--Then Lett my Mind be
thus disposed; <u>I most heartily desire the Welfare of this person, and</u>
<u>should Rejoice to contribute unto it.</u>

<u>My Son,</u> Tho' you can't <u>alwayes</u> have these <u>Thoughts</u> actually formed
on these Occasions, Yett you may gett your Mind <u>fixed</u> in the <u>Frames</u> for
them, and as the <u>Thoughts</u> will <u>often</u> be formed, so your <u>Complements</u> will
be rescued from ye Character of Meer <u>Impertinencies.</u>

§ Upon the Occasion of <u>Sickness</u> on myself and others, I sett myself to consider PIETY, and the Effects of it, under ye Notion of, <u>An Healed Soul.</u>[184]

That I might have the Symptoms and the Comforts of, <u>An Healed Soul,</u>
I proposed these Attainments.

First, Lett me come to Entertain the <u>Right Thoughts of the Right-</u>
<u>eous,</u>[185]concerning [ms. p. 308] the Infinite GOD; and Herewithal, by
Faith in the <u>Sacrifice</u> of my SAVIOUR become <u>Reconciled</u> unto Him.

Secondly; Lett me come to make it the <u>Chief End</u> of all my <u>Actions,</u>
that GOD may be Gratified & glorified in y^e <u>Acknowledgments</u> which He
sees, I pay unto Him.

Thirdly; Lett me come to make it the <u>Main Sweet</u> of all my <u>Enjoyments,</u>
that I may <u>see</u> GOD in them, and <u>Serve</u> Him with them.

Fourthly; Lett me Still have my Eye to GOD in all my <u>Expectations,</u>
and Look upon all <u>Second Causes,</u> as no more than such.

Fifthly; Lett me have my <u>Will</u> Entirely Swallowed up in y^e <u>Will</u> of GOD.

And, finally; Lett me be full of <u>Benignity</u> towards my <u>Neighbour</u>, and make it my Continual Study, <u>To do as I would be done unto</u>.[186]

Now have I an <u>Healed Soul</u> ⟨⟨ and an <u>Happy</u> one. ⟩⟩ And now, No <u>Events</u> can come amiss unto me. ⟨ The Cure of what I feel at any time amiss in my Condition, Lies <u>Within</u>. My Appetites <u>Within</u>, wch give me all my Disturbance, when any thing Seems <u>Amiss</u>, these are now cured. ⟩ Such a Soul, will be able to take y^e <u>Bitterest Cup</u> which ye Heavenly <u>Father</u> shall appoint for my <u>Portion</u>,[187] & find a <u>Sweetness</u> in it.

Yea, I have GOD now <u>Reigning</u> in my Soul. There is a Return of GOD unto His <u>Throne</u>, in my Soul, upon this <u>Healing</u> of it. And will GOD so <u>Disgrace</u> y^e <u>Throne of His Glory</u>, as to condemn it unto y^e <u>Flames</u>: or, a <u>Palace</u> which ye HOLY SPIRIT of GOD has prepared & Adorned for Him; Will He throw it among y^e <u>Dunghils</u> of ye Earth, and make it ye Fuel of His Indignation? It were an Impiety to imagine it! [ms. p. 309]

The <u>Healing</u> of my Soul, takes away from it, those <u>Maladies</u> of a <u>Carnal Mind</u>, which unfitt me for an Admission into that City of GOD, where <u>Nothing</u> w^{ch} <u>defiles may Enter</u>.[188] Yea, My <u>Healed Soul</u>, will have GOD forever <u>dwelling</u> in it; It Adheres to GOD; It Conforms to GOD; It Rejoices in GOD, at such a rate, that it has <u>Heaven</u> itself after some Sort, inwrought into ye very Temper of it! Were it possible for such a Soul to be sent down into y^e <u>Place of Dragons</u>,[189] it sould carry <u>Heaven</u> thither with it. O Soul Sure of <u>Heaven</u>! As fast as thou art <u>Healing</u>, so fast art thou <u>Ripening</u> for <u>Heaven</u>, so fast <u>Heaven</u> is <u>Descending</u> to thee: Verily, Thou <u>hast Everlasting Life</u>.[190]

Now, that I may come at the <u>Blessings</u> of such, <u>An Healed Soul</u>, my course must be, to repair unto a glorious CHRIST continually; A Glorious

CHRIST, who is, The Lord my Healer; and, the Sun of Righteousness, from whose Wings alone Healing is to be Looked for.

And among other Methods of applying unto my SAVIOUR, there are Especially Two, that I must make a Daily Improvement of.

There is, first, the Blood of my SAVIOUR; O Marvellous Word! The Blood of my Physician: A Sovereign Balsam for all ye Distempers of my Soul. I am to plead with the Great GOD; Lord, The Blood of my SAVIOUR has purchased for Me the Happiness of an Healed Soul; For the Sake of this Blood Lett me have an Happy & an Healed Soul. Upon Every Malady in my Soul, and upon Every fresh commission of observable Sin, [ms. p. 310] which is an out-breaking of a Malady there, Oh! Lett me make a New Flight unto the Blood of my SAVIOUR.

But then, Secondly; I Must Meditate much on my SAVIOUR, and Especially Employ Serious & frequent Meditations on ye Pattern of my SAVIOUR. This will be ye Changing of my Soul into His Image from Glory to Glory.[191] A Soul full of a CHRIST, and Like to a CHRIST, is an Healed Soul. That I may come at this, I must be much in Beholding ye Glory of ye Lord. Especially Lett me Behold Him, as Glorious in Holiness; & Behold Him in ye Exemple of all Goodness, which He has given me. For ye Cure of my Slothfulness in, & Backwardness to, ye Service of GOD, Lett me behold my Diligent SAVIOUR, Eaten up with ye Zeal of GOD. For ye Cure of my Inclination to Sensual pleasures, Lett me behold my SAVIOUR, A Man of Sorrows & acquainted wth Griefs.[192] For the Cure of my Disposition to Anger & Revenge, Lett me behold my SAVIOUR, ye Lamb of GOD, Oppressed & Injured, and not Opening His Mouth.[193] For ye Cure of Every Envious or Evil Frame towards my Neighbour, Lett me Behold my SAVIOUR Moved with Compassion for ye Multitude.[194] For the Cure of a Mind ⟨⟨195⟩⟩ Sett upon Earthly Enjoyments, Lett me Behold my SAVIOUR Willing to be among the Poor of the World. For y^e

Cure of my Pride, Lett me Behold my SAVIOUR Humbling Himself, becoming

of No Reputation, willing to be Despised & Rejected of Men. Tis Enough

Illustrated. [ms. p. 311]

§ Among my many projections, to Improve in PIETY, and obtain the

Blessings of An Healed Mind, I sett myself more particularly to Consider

the Several Articles of the Holy Pattern, which I find in ye Life of my

SAVIOUR. I Putt the Subjects into Order, and then, on ye Lords-day

Mornings, I successively Employ'd my Meditations and my Supplications up-

on Each of them, until I went thro' them, & felt a deep Impression from

thence upon me.

It would Swell this Poor Book into too Large Dimensions, for me to

Transcribe ye Thoughts on Each of the Subjects, which, are Entred in my

Reserved Memorials. But, My Son; It having been my Manner now and then

to Instruct you with an Instance, for ye Illustration of what I propose

unto you, I will here only Transcribe ye First Instance which I have

Entred upon this proposal.

'   This Morning that I may come at the Glory of ye Lord, and be Trans-

' formed into His Glorious Image, I Consider,

'   How did my dear SAVIOUR, Seek ye Glory of Him that sent Him?

' After I have Thought on ye Pattern of so Living unto GOD, which He has

' given me, with Resolutions of Imitation, I Cry to Heaven for the Grace

' to Conform unto it; And I plead the Purchase which His Blood has made

' of this Grace for me.

'   These were the Heads of my Desires.

'   My GOD, I Desire to consider myself, as being Sent-into the world by

' Thee, to be an Instrument of thy Glory. [ms. p. 312] And I heartily

' close with it, as the Chief End of my Life, to Render and Procure those

' Acknowledgments to Thee, wherein thou wouldest be Glorified. It shall

' be ye principal & Perpetual Business of my Life, thus to Conform unto

' ye Exemple of my SAVIOUR; And I will forever Abhor, Avoid, Rebuke, what

' would be a Dishonour to Thee.

'   O my SAVIOUR, Thou hast purchased this Grace of GOD for me.

'   O Holy SPIRIT of my SAVIOUR, Apply it; Bestow it; Enter me; and for

' this Purpose Take Possession of me.

After this manner, I distinctly went over a great Variety of Articles, found in ye Holy Exemple of my SAVIOUR.

§   I also at other Times, went over distinctly, ye Several Maladies of
my Soul, and contrived Methods for ye Cure of them all. I will only
single out One, for Illustration, wch I thus wrote upon.

' I am Exceedingly Sensible, that ye Grace of Meekness is very defective

' in me. I will Study to Excell in that Gracious Ornament, & Resolve on

' these MAXIMS for my Conduct.

' I. Upon a provocation to Anger, I would make a Pause, and Think; Is it

' a Sin that now calls for my Anger? And, How must I manage it, that I

' may not Sin in my Anger?

' II. I would then also think, I have the Eye of a glorious, Gracious,

' Righteous GOD now upon me.

' III. I would then Likewise think, What would my Patient SAVIOUR have

' done on such Occasions?

' IV. Every Night at my going to Rest, I would be able to say, My Mind

' is in an Easy Frame towards all ye World.

' V. I would Especially keep a Guard upon my Spirit, when I think on y^e

' Base Treats I suffer from ye Ungrateful & Abusive people in general,

' that I do not Speak unadvisedly wth my Lips. [ms. p. 313]

§   In Seeking after the Blessings of <u>An Healed Mind</u>, I have thought with myself, Am I not accommodated with a <u>Tree</u>, y^e <u>Leaves</u> whereof are for y^e <u>Healing of the Nations!</u>[196] In the <u>Sacred Scriptures</u> I am so. And now, I had been used unto y^e <u>Porismatic Way</u> of Reading y^e <u>Sacred Scriptures</u>, Making a <u>Pause</u> on Every Verse, and fetching <u>Lessons of Piety</u> out of Every clause. But I Stop'd not here; I did proceed unto what I may call, the <u>Affectuous Way</u>: which, My Son, I will now Explain unto you.

I considered, That the <u>Holy Men of GOD</u>, who wrote the <u>Sacred Scriptures</u>, were <u>moved by His Holy Spirit</u>,[197] in and for the writing of them; and the <u>Spirit of Holiness</u>, at ye Time of the Inspiration, made suitable <u>Impressions</u> on the <u>Affections</u> of His faithful Servants. The Good Men had their <u>Hearts</u>, Holily, Graciously, Divinely, and Suitably <u>Affected</u> with the <u>Matter</u>, which the Spirit of GOD Employ'd their Pens, to Leave upon their Parchments. There will be found <u>Evident Indications</u> of such <u>Affections</u> working in ye Minds of ye Inspired Writers; as,

A Flaming <u>Love</u> towards GOD; and then towards <u>Men</u>, for the Sake of GOD; <u>Love</u> the <u>Root</u> of all <u>Spiritual Affections</u>.

A Lively <u>Faith</u>, relying on the <u>Existence</u>, and <u>Perfections</u>, and <u>Promises</u> or <u>Threatenings</u> of GOD; and on the <u>Meditation</u> of o^e SAVIOUR.

A Longing <u>Desire</u> after such Blessings, as are in ye View of a Soul that would <u>Live unto GOD</u>; Joined with [ms. p. 314] an <u>Hope</u> of obtaining them.

A fervent <u>Zeal</u> for GOD, and for the Cause of His <u>Kingdome</u>, and the Enjoyments of His <u>House</u>, among ye Children of Men.

A Mighty <u>Hatred</u> of SIN; accompanied with, an <u>Abhorrence</u>, and yett a <u>Compassion</u> for, those who abandon themselves unto it.

A bitter <u>Sorrow</u> for SIN, and for y^e <u>Mischiefs</u> & <u>Miseries</u> which are brought by it, upon them that are guilty of it.

A noble Courage, Resolving upon an Adherence to GOD, in ye ways of Godliness; notwithstanding all Discouragements.

A total Despair to find that Help in Creatures, which tis no where to be found, but in their Great Creator.

A distressing Fear of ye Judgments, whereto all Wickedness does Expose those who are drawn unto it.

A triumphant Joy in GOD, and in His CHRIST, and in ye Favours which He bestows upon His people.

A rapturous Admiration of Him who is the Glorious Maker and Ruler of the World, and of His Glories; with a Magnifying of His Work which men behold.

All true PIETY is begun, by the Enkindling of such Affections in the Soul. It proceeds, it prospers, it Improves, as those Affections gain Strength & Vigour there. O Lord, By these things men Live, and in all these things is ye Life of my Spirit: So wilt thou Recover me, and make me to Live.

Accordingly,[198] I have Somewhat used myself unto this Exercise of Godliness; following my dear Spenser's [ms. p. 315] Direction, Praemissis pius precibus, Affectum Scriptorum Sacrorum devota Attentione observent, eninqu Affectum assumere Studeant.[199] I have made a Pause upon a Sentence of the Sacred Scriptures, to discover what Affections of Piety, might be most obvious and Evident: Restless until I found ye same Affections beginning to Stir in my Soul, and Marvellously to Harmonize and Symphonize with what ye Holy SPIRIT of GOD, raised in His Amanuensis, at ye Moment of His writing it: Not at Rest until I found My Heart-Strings quaver, at ye Touch upon ye Heart of ye Sacred Writer as being brought into an

Unison wth it, & ye Two Souls go up in a Flame together.

When I have had a Design to gett into the Best Frames that can be wished for, I have taken a Sentence or Two or Three, of ye Word by which men Live, & Looking up to Heaven for Influences from Above, I have considered, What Affections of Piety, were plainly Discernible in ye Word now before me. And then, with a Soul Turning unto ye LORD, I have made my Essays to obtain ye Biass, and Utter ye Language, of ye Like Affections. The Book of PSALMS has been of ye most Singular Use to me in this Exercise. My Son, The most Glorious Book of Devotions, that ever was in ye world!

And when I have been to preach a Sermon, I have been Studious, first of all to make sure, of those Affections in my own Soul, which I found in ye Text I was going to preach upon. [ms. p. 316]

In this Exercise, it had been an unspeakable Consolation unto me, to think, That if I became Affected as those Favourites of Heaven were, whom GOD chose for ye Vehicles, and Enkindlers & preservers of PIETY in His Church, thro' all succeeding Ages, it will be an Infallible Mark of GOD upon me, Assuring me of an Everlasting Mansion with Them in His Holy City. My Son, Tis impossible to propound an Exercise, that will more Prepare and Ripen you, to be a Partaker in ye Inheritance of those Distinguished & Exemplary Saints; or Assure you, that you shall be Associated with these Angelical Men in ye Future Blessedness.

§ As I have improved in PIETY, I have made a Sensible Improvement in my Sollicitude, that I might grow more Exact in my Conformity unto ye Golden Rule, To do as I would be done unto. It requires a Growth in Piety, to Conform well unto this Rule of Equity and Charity; And it is what has a mighty Tendency to prepare and Ripen a Soul for ye Kingdome

of GOD. I therefore Sett myself to Study the Meaning and Extent of this
Rule; and in ye Midst of my Conduct towards my Neighbour, often make this
Reflection; Am I now doing as I would be done unto? And [ms. p. 317] I
have a little, [Alas, that no more!] applied my Endeavours, to observe
this bright Maxim of Goodness, not only in the Negative Way; By avoiding
what my Conscience tells me, I should think Injurious and Unrighteous in
another; but also in the Positive Way; By dispensing those Kindnesses,
which my Reason tells me, I should Expect from Others, if I were in their
Circumstances.

I Resolved, Whatever Self-denial I am in the Exercise of this Goodness call'd unto, I will reckon to be Sufficiently Compensated in the
Satisfaction of Mind, which is to be found in ye Exercise.

As a further Exemplification of this Disposition, I will here also
transcribe this Passage out of my Reserved Memorials.

'   As I grow towards ye more Perfect Work of Christianity, I find a
' Sensible Growth in my Concern for the Duties of Good Will towards Men.[200]
' One Instance I will here take Notice of. Every Night, just before my
' Retiring to my Rest, I give Thanks to GOD for ye Blessings in the Day
' past bestowed upon me; whereof I make a brief Recapitulation. But now
' I would make a further Article of Thanksgiving. If I can call to Mind,
' any Singular Blessings which I have Seen or heard bestow'd upon Others
' in ye foregoing Day, I would heartily give Thanks to GOD, for Them also.

Indeed,[201] it has been a Pleasure unto me, to see, what a Preacher I
always have accompanying and accommodating of me, with his Instructions,
if I would but hearken to him. SELF is ye Preacher; SELF, [ms. p. 318]
in which I have, as my dear Arndt Expresses it, Speculum Infallibile,[202]
wherein I may See my Duty to my Neighbour, Yea, (as You shall presently
See,) to my Maker too. Oh! That I could oftener & better use this Glass,

and Beholding my SELF, go my way, and not forgett what Manner of Regards
I owe to all about me.

Truly, Thus far have I carried on the Matter. That I might make My
self ye more Sensible of ye Regards which I owe unto ye glorious GOD, I
have made my SELF to be My Monitor. At this rate I have argued.

' O My Soul, What Regards does thy Self-Love incline thee to demand
' from Other Men? My Self-Love sais, Lett my Will never be Contradicted.
' Then, Lett ye Love of GOD restrain me from offering any Contradiction
' to the Will of GOD. My Self-Love makes me Willing to be Honoured by
' all the World. Then, Lett ye Love of GOD make me concerned, that GOD
' may have Honour from all ye World. Those by whom I am Contemned, my
' Self-Love causes me to be displeased at. Then, Lett ye Love of GOD
' render offensive unto me, all ye Contempt that is any where cast upon
' Him. Self-Love makes me Expect that Every one should Rely upon my
' Faithfulness. Then, Lett ye Love of GOD cause my Lively & Constant
' Reliance on my Faithful Creator. [ms. p. 319]
Thus I have been Willing to fetch a Treacle out of a Viper. My Self-
Love is the Vice, to which I owe all the Self-Destruction which overtakes
me, and overwhelmes me, in my Departure from GOD. But from this very
Self-Love I have been instructed, how to Return unto the GOD from whom
I have departed. I desire, That SELF may be Dethroned, and GOD be Re-
stored unto His Throne; And what has been Paid unto SELF, I would now
pay unto GOD.

§   Some of the Dispositions, with which My Prayer for Pardon, has been
managed; These, My Son, are what I am now going to Sett before you. Oh!
That you may Come into them!

At one time, I find this passage Entred in my Memorials.

'   When I was prostrate in ye Dust before the Lord, I declared unto
' Him, That tho' I had my <u>Life Sweetened</u> many ways unto me, yett my <u>In-</u>
' <u>dwelling Sin</u>, and my <u>Disposition to do amiss</u>, made me <u>Weary of my Life</u>.[203]
' It was, what I was not able to bear; a <u>Burden too heavy for me</u>![204]
' Wherefore, if my <u>Death</u> might forever deliver me from the <u>Burden</u> under
' which I groaned, [ms. p. 320] and bring me into a <u>Complete Conformity</u>
' to His Will, I should cheerfully Resign my <u>Life</u>, and Submitt unto an
' <u>Immediate Period</u> of it. I was <u>Willing to Dy this Hour</u>; Content, tho'
' I should be Struck <u>Dead on ye Spott</u> where I was now Abasing myself be-
' fore ye Lord: The <u>Mortal Stroke</u> would be welcome to me.

'   It presently darted into my Mind, That if I could be Willing to <u>Dy</u>,
' for a <u>Deliverance from Sin</u>, this was an Infallible Token and Effect of
' my Claim to the Benefits of my SAVIOURS <u>Death</u>. <u>Now</u> I know, That when
' my SAVIOUR <u>Died</u>, it was to Purchase this <u>Deliverance</u> for me. <u>Now</u> I
' know, That y^e <u>Death</u> of my SAVIOUR has obtained <u>This</u> for me, That my
' <u>Sins</u> will be all Forgiven, all Forgotten, all Covered; <u>That</u> I shall Ere
' Long arrive to a State, wherein my <u>Sins</u> will be no more present with
' me, but I shall be <u>filled with all the Fulness of GOD</u>;[205] <u>That</u> I shall
' be mightily Assisted in my Conflicts wth y^e <u>Sins</u>, & <u>Lusts</u> that <u>War</u>
' <u>against my Soul</u>; and that whatever foils and falls I may suffer, they
' shall serve as only <u>Scaffolds</u> for ye Triumphs of that Glorious Grace,
' which is to be display'd upon me. Yea, If my SAVIOUR has <u>died</u> for me,
' the Consequences of it will be, <u>Wonderful! Wonderful! Wonderful!</u>

   At other Times, in my cries to Heaven, that y^e <u>Blood</u> of my SAVIOUR
might <u>cleanse me from all Sin</u>, I have been mightily revived with this
<u>Consolation of GOD</u>. If I am well assured, That y^e <u>Blood</u> of my SAVIOUR
has been <u>Applied</u> unto me, for all y^e <u>Cleansing</u> and [ms. p. 321] Saving
Purposes of it, if I feel that--<u>Blood running Warm</u> in ye Veins of my

Soul. Now what is it, but that Precious Blood so Quickening of my Soul,
[This Blood is my Life!]²⁰⁶when I feel my Soul Setting a most High Price
upon this Blood! When I feel my Soul become Zelous of those Good Works,
which this Blood has been shed that I might be brought unto! When I
feel my Soul breathing and longing after yᵉ Image of Him, whose Blood I
thus Rely upon; and Wishing,

' Oh! That I were an Hater of Wickedness, and a Lover of Righteous-
' ness like my SAVIOUR! Oh! That it may be my Meat & my Drink to do yᵉ
' Will of GOD, as it was my SAVIOURS!

' Oh! That I were alwayes doing of Good, as my SAVIOUR was! Oh!
' That I could Endure Afflictions, and Forgive Injuries as my SAVIOUR did!

' Oh! That ⟨⟨207⟩⟩my Will, were Entirely Swallowed up in yᵉ Will of
' my Heavenly Father, as was my SAVIOURS!

I have at Length carried yᵉ matter into this Operation.

In my Vehement Cries from yᵉ Dust unto yᵉ Lord, for yᵉ Pardon of my
Crying Sins against Him, I consider the Dispositions in the Mind of my
dear SAVIOUR, at the Time when He was Enduring yᵉ Punishment of my Sins,
and making Himself a Sacrifice for them. I find, That He was Willing to
take whatever Cup His Father should give unto Him; That He Lamented the
Distance of GOD from Him; That He was Concerned for to have whole Will
of GOD finished; That He was Thoughtful [ms. p. 322] for yᵉ Welfare of
those whom He bore some Relation to; That He Wished the Mercies of GOD
unto His Enemies; That He Resigned His Immortal Spirit unto His Father,
for Him to do as He pleased with it.²⁰⁸ Now I Strive, till I find the
Holy One Working in my own Soul, Something that answers these Dispositions
of my SAVIOUR. Thus Disposed, I beg with Agony, for yᵉ Pardon which my
SAVIOUR so Disposed, has with His Precious Blood purchased for me. And
herein, I do not aim at Recommending myself by any Good Thing in me,

unto ye Benefit of a <u>Pardon</u>: But my Aim is, to gett a <u>Comfortable Evidence</u>, that it is a <u>Faith of ye Right Sort</u>, with which I now fly to ye Blood of my SAVIOUR, and Pursue and Receive a <u>Pardon</u>. Yea, These <u>Dispositions</u> assure me, That I am Actually <u>Alive</u>, and have <u>Passed from Death to Life</u>, and So a Sentence of <u>Life</u>, (<u>Justification of Life</u>,) is, with a <u>Pardon</u>, passed upon me. [ms. p. 323]

§ To animate my Endeavours to <u>Pray Without Ceasing</u>,[209] I have Cherished a marvellous Consideration, which comes with Power upon me.

All my <u>Prayers</u> made according to the Will of GOD, are the Dictates of His Holy SPIRIT. Tho' I forgett the <u>Prayers</u> which I have made, and I receive not Immediate Answers to them, Yett that Infinite One perfectly <u>Remembers</u> all that He has dictated. When I arrive to the Heavenly World, where I shall Reap the <u>Rich Harvest</u> of all my Devotions here, the Holy SPIRIT having all my <u>Prayers</u> in a most perfect <u>Remembrance</u>, will then heap in upon me the <u>Answers</u> of them, With <u>Blessings of Goodness</u>, far beyond <u>all that I can Ask or Think</u>.[210] Oh! Lett the <u>Strong Faith</u> of This, produce in me, a very <u>Praying Life</u>, and give Life to my <u>Prayers</u>; and make my <u>Sowing Time</u>, to be very Diligent and Plentiful!

§ My Mind has come to be very much under ye power of this Consideration.

As far as I <u>Dy</u> unto creatures, just so far I <u>Live</u> unto GOD. I must be <u>Dead With CHRIST</u>, that so I may be sure to <u>Live</u> with Him.

In pursuance of this Consideration, I have pressed after these Points of a <u>Death</u> to the <u>Things that are seen & are Temporal</u>.[211]

I must Look on all things here below, with, the Eye of a <u>Dying Man</u>; and when I Look on all my Enjoyments, behold[212] them, as a <u>Dying Man</u>, and as one immediately going from them. [ms. p. 324]

I must be Ready to <u>Sacrifice</u> all these Things, and if GOD call for them, I must be willing to be Stript of them all, and be left as <u>Naked</u>, as a man that is <u>Dead</u>, who <u>carries nothing away with him</u>.[213]

If any of these Things invite me unto any thing, that may be a <u>Sin</u> against the Glorious GOD, their Invitation must make no more Impression on me, than a Speech unto the <u>Dead</u>.

Finally; To the Saints that are <u>Dead</u>, GOD is become <u>All in All</u>.

A Respect unto GOD, must be the Thing, that shall Influence me, in my Addressing to, and my conversing with, all of my Enjoyments.

I can't be Ready to <u>Dy</u>, and Leave the World, until I become thus <u>Dead unto ye World</u>.

Because it has a Relation to this Disposition, I will here Transcribe this passage out of my Memorials.

'   I behold myself in the Condition of one that is nailed unto a <u>Cross</u>.
' A Man that is <u>Crucified</u>, Endures very <u>Uneasy Circumstances</u>; and has
' all possible <u>Indignities</u> heaped upon him; and finds himself <u>Stripped</u>
' <u>of Every thing</u> he had in the World: I Live, or I may rather say, <u>I Dy</u>
' <u>Daily</u>, in a continual Expectation of all these things, I actually <u>Suffer</u>
' <u>much</u>, and am in a Condition that obliges me to <u>Expect More</u>, of these
' Things. My Spirit is Reconciled unto this Condition. Tis Welcome to
' me, in regard of the <u>Glorious Designs</u>, wch my SAVIOUR has, in ordering
' for [ms. p. 325] me, such a <u>Conformity</u> unto Himself. Am I not now <u>Cru-</u>
' <u>cified</u> with my SAVIOUR? But now, --Oh! the Wondrous Consequences!

I have hoped, that I have somewhat improved in the <u>Death</u>, which I have thus proposed, when I have been able to make this Remark.

'   My Dear SAVIOUR, what a <u>Trance</u> hast thou brought my Soul unto! I
' am Willing to be Slandered, Reviled, Lessened: Patient, of being <u>De-</u>
' <u>spised and Rejected of Men</u>. This proceeds, not only from an Acquies-
' ence to ye Divine <u>Sovereignty</u>, and from a Submission to the just

' punishment of my <u>Iniquity</u>; but also from a Secret pleasure, in <u>Conform-</u>
' <u>ities</u> unto my SAVIOUR; and from an Horror of being thought a <u>Consider-</u>
' <u>able Man</u>, by people who terminate in <u>Man</u>, and Sett <u>Man</u> in ye Throne of
' God, and make an <u>Idol</u>, of whatever Man they ascribe any Grandents to. }} [214]

And at another time, this Remark.

' I feel, I feel the <u>Death</u> of my SAVIOUR in me. I feel myself <u>Dying</u>
' <u>to the World</u>; grown very much <u>Dead</u>, both unto the <u>Comforts</u> of it, and .
' unto the <u>Troubles</u> of it: Willing to be <u>Stript</u> of all things, and Pass
' into the Condition of the <u>Dead</u>. In this, I enjoy a Disposition which
' the <u>Death</u> of my SAVIOUR has <u>Purchased</u> for me; And I endeavour a <u>Con-</u>
' <u>formity</u> unto His <u>Death</u>, and such a Sense of Things in this World, as
' He had in ye Hours of His Crucifixion. Is not this now a Sure <u>Sign</u>,
' that my [ms. p. 326] SAVIOUR has <u>Dyed</u> for me; and that I have a share
' in the Benefits of His <u>Death</u>? Most Certainly! --But, Oh! the
' Glorious Consequences!

My <u>Death to Creatures</u>, being the Point of PIETY, which I am now upon,
before I dismiss it, I will give a Little further Illustration of it, by
Transcribing Two passages more, out of My Memorials.

One is this.

' Oh! Blessed, Blessed be my Glorious Redeemer! There are many <u>Temporal</u>
' <u>Enjoyments</u>, which my Heart is Willing to ask of a Gracious GOD. But
' my Heart has now such a <u>Biass</u> upon it, and is now so <u>Weaned</u> from this
' World, and so <u>Turned</u> unto GOD, that instead of <u>Asking</u> for such <u>Enjoy-</u>
' <u>ments</u>, I <u>Much more</u> Ask for an <u>Heart</u> Willing to <u>Go without them</u>. There
' is not any one of those <u>Enjoyments</u>, but when I go to Ask for it, I pass
' rather to a <u>Sacrificing Heart</u>, and pray rather for an <u>Heart</u> Able and
' Ready to make a <u>Sacrifice</u> of it. This I esteem a <u>Blessing</u>, preferrible
' to any thing that can be denied unto me.

Another is this.

' I find in my Soul a Strange Experience. I meet with very <u>Breaking</u> and
' <u>Killing</u> Things, which are the <u>Chastisements</u> of ye Holy GOD upon me for
' my manifold Miscarriages. In the <u>Sad Things</u> that befall me, the Glori-
' ous GOD is <u>Gratified</u>: It <u>pleases</u> Him to behold His Justice thus in-
' flicting Strokes upon me. Now [ms. p. 327] Now Such is my <u>Love</u> unto
' my God, and so <u>United</u> is my Soul unto Him, and so far my <u>Self-Love</u> is
' killed in me, that I have a <u>Secret Pleasure</u> in my Thoughts of the
' <u>Gratification</u>, wch is done unto <u>Him</u>, in the <u>Sad Things</u> which tear me
' to pieces before Him. I fly away from Even my very <u>Self</u> unto <u>Him</u>,
' and I take part with <u>Him</u> against my <u>Self</u>; and it <u>Pleases me</u>, that <u>He</u>
' <u>is pleased</u>, tho' I my <u>Self</u> am dreadfully torn to pieces in what is done
' unto me. By this I know, that now my GOD will Return unto me, with
' astonishing Expressions of His Everlasting <u>Love</u>; and that y^e <u>Bruises</u>
' given to my dear SAVIOUR, are Accepted for me; and my GOD will no more
' delight in <u>Bruising</u> me; but y^e <u>Punishment</u> of my Sin having been Laid
' on my SAVIOUR, I shall now have my GOD Reconciled unto me, and Rejoic-
' ing over me to do me Good.

§   I have much proposed unto myself, That there are Especially Four
Exercises of PIETY, of which I would Every day that passes over me, make
a most frequent Repetition.

The First is; To form in the most Explicit Manner that may be, <u>De-
signs</u> for the <u>Serving</u> and <u>Pleasing</u> of GOD, in what my Hand finds to do;
and <u>find the Life of my Hand</u> in doing so.

The Second is; To Abound in <u>Sacrifices</u>; and while I am <u>Sacrificing</u>
[ms. p. 328] those Enjoyments, which my GOD calls me to part withal, to
Look upon a <u>Sacrificing Heart</u> as a Better Thing than any of those Enjoy-

ments.

The Third is; To be <u>Devising of Good</u> Continually; Pondering, <u>What Good may I do?</u> and Contriving, that all about me may be the Better for me.

The Fourth is; To Behold and Beleeve the <u>Love</u> of my SAVIOUR to me, in Every Thing that befalls me, and by this <u>Perswasion</u> to animate the Dispositions & Resolutions of <u>Love</u> to Him & my Essays to Glorify Him.

§ There is a <u>Way of Living</u>, how Sweet, how High, how Holy!

From a very <u>unlikely Hand</u>, thire arrived unto me ye first Clear <u>Idea's</u> of it. My SAVIOUR Sent ye first clear proposals of it, by a very <u>unlikely Hand</u> unto me. But, <u>My Son</u>, you shall now have this Life described & commended unto you, by an Hand, which you may with ye more of Likelihood Expect it from.

I thought with myself; That for me to Beleeve and Behold, the <u>Love</u> of GOD my SAVIOUR to me, in all ye Circumstances and Occurrences of My Life, Still as they arrive unto me; and Perswaded & Sensible of His <u>Love</u> unto me therein, for me thereupon to have my Heart Enflamed with <u>Love</u> to Him, and formed into Dispositions and Resolutions to Praise Him, & Please Him, & Serve Him, and Shun Every thing that may be offensive to Him, and Study what I shall do for His Kingdome and Interest: This would be a <u>Way of Living</u>, [ms. p. 329] how Desireable! Most certainly, There is no Consideration in ye World, more Sanctifying, and more Animating unto all the Temper and Action of PIETY, than That; Gal. II. 20. <u>The SON of GOD hath Loved me.</u> I Sett myself to gett into the way of Entertaining this Consideration upon all occasions; & Experiencing the Holy Efficacy of it in me; and as I have <u>hop'd,</u> so have I found, ye Force hereof upon me, to be Wonderful!

In order to such a Life, in a Way so much Above, I proposed in the
first Place, the Application of this perswasion unto my Soul, in a more
General Way; My SAVIOUR has Loved His people; and I, tho' most Unworthy,
am One of the people, who may hope for a Share in His Love. The LOVE of
my SAVIOUR to His people, I have made a Subject of my most affectuous
Thoughts: His Electing Love, His Redeeming Love, His Espousing Love; His
Pardoning Love: And that Love which carries thro' ye whole Course of o^e
Living to GOD, until He has brought us into the Strong City, ^{215}where His
Marvellous Kindness will be shown unto us. That I might assure myself of
my own share in this Love, I first Encouraged myself with Some Hope, that
my Loving to Think on my SAVIOURs Love, my Value for, and my Delight in,
ye Thoughts, of it, ye Meditation Sweet, would be some Sign of my Portion
in it. I also gave myself up unto my SAVIOUR, most Sincerely and with
many Repeted Acts desiring to be one of His People, & forever under His
Conduct; and by this I made [ms. p. 330] it evident, that I am one of the
people, whom His Eternal Father has given unto Him. And, finally, Upon
Each Article of my SAVIOURs Love unto His people, I attempted an Adapted
Stroke of PIETY, which might assure me, of my own part in ye Love. I
have heartily Said, O My SAVIOUR, I make Choice of Thee for my SAVIOUR,
& My Portion! So I thought, it would be Evident, That my SAVIOUR has Loved
me, & Chosen me. I have heartily Said, O My SAVIOUR, Thy Blood is beyond
all Expression precious to me. The Merit of it weighs down with me a
Thousand Worlds. Oh! That I felt it Quickening of me, in ye Life of GOD!
So I thought, it would be Evident, That my SAVIOUR has Loved me, & shed
His Blood for me. I have heartily Said, O My SAVIOUR, I Consent unto y^e
Offers of thy Covenant, & would fain be for Thee, & not for another! So
I thought, it would be Evident, That my SAVIOUR has Loved me, and said
unto my Soul, Thy Maker is thy Husband. ^{216} I have heartily Said, O My

SAVIOUR, I am Sorry, I am Sorry, I have Sinned: My Sin is now Lothsome
to me. Oh! Lett me not Sin any more! I had rather Dy, than Sin at y^e
old rate any More! So I thought, it would be Evident, that my SAVIOUR
has Loved me, and said unto me, The Lord has Putt away thy Sin; Thou shalt
not Dy. In fine; This is what I have Heartily declared; O My SAVIOUR, I
Rely upon Thee to do for me, all that Thou doest for all thy People:
Fulfill for me & in me, the Good pleasure of [ms. p. 331] thy Goodness,
& the Work that Faith would have to be done, With Power. Now I thought,
it would be Evident, That my SAVIOUR has Loved me, and Will do wonders
for me; Yea, Will Show Wonders to the Dead.[217]

I apprehended myself now Qualified, for Proceeding to the Application of this Perswasion, in a more Special Way, unto ye Dealings of my
SAVIOUR with me, in all the Dispensations of His Providence.

In order to a Life of such Holy Thoughts, I first gott my Heart
fixed in this perswasion, That Whatever befalls me, there is in it, the
Providence of my Great SAVIOUR, therein Performing the Thing that is
Appointed for me. I then went on, further to Secure the Tokens, which
might Encourage & Embolden this Perswasion in me, There is ye Love of my
SAVIOUR in all that His Providence dispenses to me. Now, I saw; First,
There are Glorious Designs of Love, which My SAVIOUR has, in all His
Dealings wth ye Children of GOD. He Designs, That Repentance may have
its perfect work in them, and Holiness be brought unto Perfection, in y^e
Fear of GOD.[218] He Designs, That all Idols may be dethroned in them, and
GOD assume His Throne in their Souls. He Designs, That their Diligence
in the Service of GOD may be Excited, and they be made more Fervent in
Spirit, Serving ye Lord.[219] He Designs, That their Conformity unto a Cru-
cified & an Exemplary JESUS, may come to its Consummation; And He Designs,
That their Faith, and Patience, and Goodness, and Resignation to ye Will

of GOD, may be Tried [ms. p. 332] unto the Uttermost. Now, I found my
Soul falling in with such Designs as these; And I said, O My SAVIOUR,
What Thou doest, is in Love to my Soul, if Those be thy Designs in what
Thou doest. Yea, my Soul knows it right well, That these are Thy Designs.
Happy, Happy am I, if Those Designs be once accomplished. This I esteemed
a Token for Good; That I might now venture upon this Perswasion about all
that befalls me: This Thing befalls me, because ye Son of GOD has Loved
me. I again, Considered, That if I saw ye Love of my SAVIOUR in all His
Dealings with me, my Love of Him would be mightily inflamed from it, and
be raised into ye Flames of ye Fire of GOD. I foresaw, The Love of CHRIST
would Constrain me, to Abhor that which is Evil,[220] and give Temptations
to Sin, that Repulse: How shall I do this Wickedness, and Sin against a
SAVIOUR who has Loved me! Constrain me, to Abound in ye Work of ye Lord;
and to treat with a suitable Benignity all that are about me; Constrain
me to Contrive ye Best Returns of Gratitude and Obedience unto Him, who
has dealt so well with me, and fetch Revenues of Praise to Him out of all
His Benefits: Yea, to Offer myself & my All up unto ye Lord in ye Flames
of Love, and bring my All under a Consecration[221] to Him. Now, I Conceived,
That if, when I was going to Refresh myself with a perswasion of my SAV-
IOURs Love unto me in all His Dealings with me, this were my Intentions;
O My SAVIOUR, I would apprehend thy Love unto me, that so I may Love Thee
more Vehemently [ms. p. 333] and Serve Thee more Vigorously, and Please
Thee more Studiously, from ye Fire which thy Love will give unto me!
This also would be a Token for Good, that I may Venture upon this per-
swasion about all that befalls me, That Thing befalls me, because the Son
of GOD has Loved me.

Hereupon, I formed ye Process of Taking and Using this perswasion,
on all Particular Occurrences: There is the Love of my SAVIOUR, in what

His Providence is now adoing to me.

I will Single out a few Particular Occurrences, on which, My Son, if you do, as your Father has done, you will be soon Taught of GOD, how to Animate & Regulate ye perswasion upon all occasions.

When I have been Approaching to GOD, in ye public or private Means of Grace, I have thought: It is because my SAVIOUR has Loved me, that He has written to me the Great Things of His Law, & that He setts open ye Doors of His House unto me.[222] I saw this Love, in ye End of it; which is, To bring me Near unto GOD, & fitt me for the Spiritual Blessings in ye Heavenly Places.[223] To putt it out of Doubt, that I might Safely take up this perswasion, I added upon it; O My SAVIOUR, I will take more Pains than ever, that thy End may be obtained upon me. I will attend upon thy Ordinances, with all Possible Industry, that I may meet with GOD in them, and grow more meet for the Inheritance of the Saints in Light.

Again; Being Surrounded with the Blessings of Goodness, in Temporal, [ms. p. 334] in Various, in Manifold Enjoyments; I have Thought, It is Because my SAVIOUR has Loved me, that He has bestowed Such Good Things upon me. I have made a Pause on my Several Enjoyments, to Taste ye Love of my SAVIOUR unto me in them. I Saw, The End of all was, To accommodate me in the Seeing & Serving of GOD, and Melt my Heart into Resolutions to Glorify a GOD, whose Goodness & Mercy follows me. To Putt it out of Doubt, that I might Safely take up this perswasion, I added upon it, O My SAVIOUR, I Desire, that I may Have more of GOD, and May Do more for GOD, being Help'd by what Thou hast bestow'd upon me. But then, I have made a Recapitulation of my Enjoyments, and Thought, What Special Exercise of Godliness would this Good Thing Lead me to? And, What Advantage to Do Good, is by this Good Thing Putt into my Hands?

Well; Adversity finds me out. But I have a SAVIOUR who tells me,

As many as I Love, I Rebuke and Chasten.[224] I saw, My Adversity comes to
Embitter ye Sin that is Chastend in it: And I Said, O My SAVIOUR, Tis
thy Love, which will this Way make My Sin Bitter to me! _Welcome, Welcome, ye most Bitter Thing, that will make my Sin more Bitter to me. I
saw, My Adversity comes, to Awaken my Prayer, to which I have been too
much Indispos'd. And I said, O My SAVIOUR, Tis thy Love unto me, which
will this Way Sett me a Praying to thee. Every Thing that brings me down
on my [ms. p. 335] Knees, & Setts me a Praying, is a Kindness to me. I
saw, My Adversity comes, to kill my Unchast Love of Creatures, and render
me Dead unto ye world before Death call me out of ye world. And I said;
O My SAVIOUR; Tis Thy Love unto me, that will not Lett me Love any thing
Else Irregularly, Inordinately. If Thou send Killing Things upon me,
only to take off my Heart from Lying Vanities, and render This world unto
me, as it is unto one that is Crucified; So to kill me, is to Love me
Wondrously! What makes me Dead with CHRIST, it is a Love, that brings
me into ye Life of GOD. In short; I have Thought, that Adversity would
Prove an Incentive to all PIETY; And whatever did so, would bring with
it, the Love of my SAVIOUR to me. So I sett myself to Think, What Fruit
of PIETY, Every Particular Thing that was not Joyous but Grievous to me,
should be followed Withal: And I have made it my Study and my Purpose,
to gett this Fruit produced in me. Now might I Safely take up this perswasion; O My SAVIOUR, Tis because thou Lovest me, that thou dost so
Chasten me.[225]

Yett more Particularly. When I have mett with Impoverishing Losses,
I have thought; Here is the Love of My SAVIOUR to me, that I may more
Effectually Seek after His Durable Riches. When they who have been the
Desire of my Eyes, have been taken from me, I have thought; Here is the
Love of My SAVIOUR to me, that I may now More [ms. p. 336] Acquaint

Myself with Him, who Lives forevermore. When I have had my Body Languishing or Uneasy under Maladies, I have thought; Here is the Love of my SAVIOUR to me, that the Blessings of an Healed Soul, may be Convey'd unto me. And when Reproaches have been cast upon me, I have thought; Here I see the Love of my SAVIOUR to me, that He may make me & keep me Humble, & give me an Opportunity to Forgive Injuries & Enemies. I have Supposed, That if I Reckoned it a Love in ye Affliction which aim'd at such Things, & if I did Incline to pursue these Things, it was now Indisputable; I might Say, The Son of GOD has Loved Me in all the Sad Things that I have mett withal.

This has been my Way, to keep myself in ye Love of GOD, Looking for ye Mercy of my Lord JESUS CHRIST.

My Son, Try to Live so. Such a Life will be a Continual Walk in ye Light;[226] and a Bright Holiness in all Manner of Conversations, will be ye Consequence.[227] [ms. p. 337]

§ Some Very Singular Methods were used by my dear SAVIOUR, to awaken My Concern, That I might maintain that Life by ye Faith of ye SON of GOD, whereof I had Some years ago prescribed the Methods, in ye Most Lively Vigour imaginable. And now, My Son, I can bear a Testimony for my Glorious LORD, which, I hope, will make a mighty[228] Impression on you.

Having Entertained a Right & Clear Apprehension of my Great SAVIOUR; and His Glorious Person, as the Eternal SON of GOD, Incarnate and Enthroned in my JESUS, being Somewhat Understood with me; ⟨ and Beholding ye Infinite GOD, as wining to me, & Meeting with me in this Blessed Mediator: ⟩ the THOUGHTS of HIM are become Exceedingly Frequent with me. I Count it a Fault, if my Mind be many Minutes together, without Some Thoughts ⟨⟨ of Him ⟩⟩ that have in them a Tincture of PIETY. But I have Learnt the

Way of Interesting my SAVIOUR in these Thoughts; And I feel an Impatience raised in me, if I have been Many Minutes without Some Thoughts of Him. I fly to Him on Multitudes of Occasions Every Day; and am Impatient, if many Minutes have Passed me, without some Recourse to Him.

Ever now & then, I bestow a Rebuke on myself; Oh! why have I been so Long without some Thoughts on my Lovely SAVIOUR? How, How can I bear, to keep at any Distance from Him? I then Look up to my SAVIOUR; O My dear SAVIOUR, Draw near unto me; Oh! come down to dwell in my Soul, & help me, to form Some Thoughts wherein I shall Enjoy thee! [ms. p. 338] Hereupon I sett myself to form Some Thoughts, on My most Amiable SAVIOUR; His Glories, His Mercies, His Patterns, His Maxims, what He has done, and what He will do for us. I find ye Subject Infinitely Inexhaustible. And after I have been in ye Day thus Employ'd, I fall asleep at Night perpetually in ye Midst of a Meditation on some Glory of my SAVIOUR; usually on a Scripture, wherein that Glory is mentioned. So, I sleep in JESUS![229] And when I Wake in ye Night, I do on my Bed Seek Him that my Soul does Love: Still in ye Night ye Desires of my Soul, do carry me unto Him, in Thoughts on ye Subject which I fell Asleep withal. ⟨⟨230⟩⟩

I find, That where a CHRIST Comes, a Wondrous Light, and Life, and Peace Comes with Him; and a Strength to Go thro' Services and Sufferings. The Holiness and Happiness, whereinto I am introduced by this Way of Living, tis Better to me, than all the Enjoyments of this World. All ye Riches of this World appear Contemptible Things unto me, while I have the Unsearchable Riches of CHRIST thus brought into my possession. And all ye Glory of this World, would not incline me to forego this Way of Living.

O My dear JESUS; Now I know, I know; I have a Witness within, That Thou art the SON of GOD, and the SAVIOUR of the World. [ms. p. 339]

Concerning this Matter, I have had a Contemplation, which has had on me, a Most Heart-melting Efficacy.

' When the Cloud of Glory,[231] which was the SHECINAH,[232] that had o[e]
' SAVIOUR, with the Angels of His Presence[233] dwelling in it, came down,
' & filled the Temple of old, What a Grateful Spectacle was it, and what
' Acclamations did it raise in the Spectators! A Godly Man is a Temple
' of GOD;[234] A Living Temple; Dearer to Him, than any Temple of Meer
' Matter, tho', the most Splendid & Costly in the world. When o[e] SAVIOUR
' Comes into the Heart of a Godly Man, then the Glory of the Lord, Comes
' to fill a Temple, which He has Chosen for His Habitation.[235] And o[e]
' SAVIOUR comes into an Heart, which is Continually Instructing, and Re-
' forming, and Solacing itself, by Thinking on Him. O Heart Panting
' after thy SAVIOUR; So kind is thy SAVIOUR; So Kind is thy SAVIOUR, that
' Even at y[e] Call of a Thought, He will come in unto thee! A Temple so
' filled with the Glory of the Lord, is Unseen by the Standers-by; to
' Flesh & Blood, Standing by.[236] The Life of the Godly Man is Hid with
' CHRIST in GOD;[237] It is an Hidden Life. But GOD sees y[e] Temple with
' pleasure. The SAVIOUR, who knoweth all things, is pleased with the
' Sight.[238] His Angels make their Acclamation upon it. ⟨⟨239⟩⟩ [ms. p.
' 340]

But, that I may Sett this Important Matter, in yett a Fuller Light before you, I shall be in my Account of it, more Punctual and Instructive.

I Behold the Infinite GOD in His Eternal SON, assuming the Man JESUS, into Such an Íntimate and Conscious Union with Him, that in my SAVIOUR I now see a GOD-MAN, and a MAN who has the Fulness of the God-head Personally dwelling in Him.[240]

In this GOD-MAN I behold all Possible Provision for the Happy Return of Man unto GOD: And all Possible Encouragement unto Man to Seek and

Look for such an Happiness.

As this my SAVIOUR is very GOD, and my Hope and Joy in Him is all animated from that Consideration, So, being ONE-GOD with the FATHER and the SPIRIT who do thro' HIM Communicate Themselves unto me, I Consider my-self as Coming to GOD in HIM, and Conversing with the Whole GOD-HEAD in my more Immediately having to do with Him.

The First Thing I do, is, To accept the offers which this wonderful SAVIOUR makes to me, of being Mine, and bringing me to GOD.[241] I Hear Him graciously offering to Make me Righteous and Holy,[242] and Reconcile me to GOD,[243] and Quicken me to Live unto Him, and Work in me What shall be Well-pleasing before Him.[244] I feel Him so Apprehending of me, that He Dis-poses me & Enables me, to give an Heavy, Joyful, Thankful Consent unto these Proposals of His Grace; And in Consenting to [ms. p. 341] them, I entertain a Comfortable Perswasion of my kind Reception with Him; I think it my Duty, to be well-perswaded, That He will Surely do me Good.[245]

And now, What remains is, That as I Worship GOD in the Spirit,[246] so may I Rejoice in CHRIST JESUS.[247]

Wherefore, in the first place, I ask it of the Glorious GOD with the greatest Importunity, That having a CHRIST Concerned for me, I may also have a CHRIST Possessing of me: That I may have Skill and Will and Help from Heaven, to Converse with a Glorious CHRIST Continually; That I may be so Well of it[248] as to keep Continually Calling a Glorious CHRIST into my Thoughts, ⟨⟨ on all occasions, ⟩⟩ and feeding upon Him.[249] I have declared unto the Lord, That if He would grant me but this Felicity, I cared not what befel me; I am Willing and Ready to Encounter any thing, that He shall please to order for me.

My Life is full of Sacrifices. But that which carries me well thro' them all, is this Consideration: While I have a CHRIST, I have Enough;

I can Rejoice in Him, while I have nothing Else Left unto me![250]

Yea, I have by the Faithful Dispensations of GOD been brought unto This; That I feel myself Dead unto all Creatures! I have Employ'd the Sacrificing Stroke upon all of my Enjoyments; My Serviceableness to the Kingdome of my SAVIOUR, was the Last Thing, that in my Death to all things here below, I did Part withal; the Thing which I could Least of all Part withal. But this Darling have I also Sacrificed; the Darling which I would fain have had [ms. p. 342] Saved from the Power of the Dog.[251] I have submitted unto it, that the Ever-Blessed One, should not only make me Vile among His People, but also utterly Lay me aside from doing any more Services to His Kingdome in the World. I have been Entirely Dead unto Every thing else; and I have had Nothing but This One Thing Left unto me; That I may have a Glorious CHRIST, not only Doing for me, but also Dwelling in me; and Enabling me Perpetually to Feed and Live upon Him. This will be Enough. I Care not tho' I am Stript of Every thing Else, if I may but Enjoy this Felicity.

In Pursuance of this Felicity, tis not Easy for me to Delineate, or Enumerate, the Methods of Conversing With my Only SAVIOUR, wherein I have been Instructed of GOD. And it is impossible for me to Express the Satisfaction that Irradiates and Replenishes my Mind, upon the Discoveries of any New Methods for it. No Affluence of any Worldly Wealth, no, nor any Advances in my Sciences, Could so Transport and Ravish me!

The Blessedness of the Heavenly World Lies, in o^e Being with CHRIST; And by being With the Lord, and Beholding of His Glory in Precious Thoughts of Him here, I apprehend myself even in Heaven upon Earth. And indeed the Light, and Peace, and Joy, and Strength, and Purity, which it fills my Mind withal, Carries a Foretaste, and Earnest, of Heaven in it. [ms. p. 343]

I soar up to inexpressible Contemplation on my SAVIOUR, as the Wisdome of GOD, Who is the Archetype of ye whole Creation, and in Whom there are the Original Ideas of all that is produced by His Hand, in the World, even that Platform and Substance, whereof all Creatures are but the Issues and the Shadows.

I am hence Wondrously Reconciled unto my approaching Death; Inasmuch as going from Creatures here, I go to Him, on whom I shall find All that I Leave, and Infinitely More.

In the Mean time, I am sure, That whatever I find Amiable or Comfortable in any Creatures here, is much more to be found in Him.

Hence, when I see any Thing that is Amiable in any Creatures, I Commonly fly away from them to my SAVIOUR, and Think, How Great is His Goodness & His Beauty![252]

When I find any thing that is Comfortable in any Creatures, I Commonly hasten away unto my SAVIOUR, and Think, What Benefits will flow from Him unto me?

Upon the Withdraw of any Creatures, or When any Desireable Enjoyments are Witheld or Taken from me, I Think, What is it that would Recommend these things unto me? And I presently find my SAVIOUR Commended unto me, by such and more Desireable Qualities. In His being Mine, I find Every Loss repaired abundantly!

Dead unto Every Thing but my SAVIOUR; I thus Express my Sentiments. [ms. p. 344][253]

' For the Delights of This World.

'   Such Delights as I taste in the meer Tendencies of Nature, I would
' in the Taste of them think, The Will of GOD Expressed in the Nature of
' His Works, is thus Complied withal. But, Oh! What Shall I find in the
' Infinite GOD Himself, upon my Going back unto Him!

' Those Delights which are most Helpful unto Me in the Seeing & Serving of GOD, are those which I would have the Most Value for: And Even my Appetities for my Food particularly shall be so Regulated.

' But I know no Delights comparable to those which I take in Communion with my SAVIOUR.

' For the Riches of This World.

' I use no Labour, I have no Desire, to Obtain Temporal Riches: They appear to me very Contemptible.

' My Riches are my Opportunities to Do Good; And those Illuminations of my Mind, which furnish me for it.

' In my SAVIOUR I have Unsearchable Riches; And in my Fruition of Him, I have a Full Supply of all my Wants.

' For the Honours of This World.

' My Abhorrence of having the Great GOD robbed in my account, by People gazing on me, without being Led thro' me to Him, renders all the Honours in ye Praise of Men very distastful to me.

' I do nothing to gain Honours for myself: And if I do Secure any thing of Esteem or of Station, it shall be Purely for the Interest of GOD.

' If I may be Accepted with my SAVIOUR, and Employed in Work for His Kingdome, and have His Image imprinted on me; Here are all the [ms. p. 345] 254 Honours that I wish for.

I go over the Afflictive Things, with which my Life is at all Embittered, (and I make the same CHRIST-ward Salleys upon the Arrival of New Affliction). I Repair to a Glorious CHRIST. I Realize not only His Hand, but also His Love, in the sending of the Trouble. I See my SAVIOUR once Encountring the Same Trouble; and I am heartily pleas'd and glad at my Conformity to Him. I See how Patiently, and with what Views, He bore

the Trouble; and I Wish to be Like Him. I consider, What is that Good
which this Trouble deprives me of; and I see the Same Good, and what is
Infinitely Better, Laid up in my SAVIOUR; and I am Satisfied. The
Thoughts of my SAVIOUR I forever find Sweetening the Bitter Waters of
Marah[255] to me. I find Him the Comforter, that always releeves my Soul,
when I have Him near unto me.

How many, O Lord my GOD, are the Thoughts, which I form in my Mind
concerning Thee? And the Occasions on which, the Contrivances with
which, I cherish the Thoughts, Cannot be Reckoned up in Order.[256]

When I see any thing Excellent in any Man, it Leads me to Thoughts
on the Superiour Excellencies in my SAVIOUR.

Yea, when any thing that is Detestable, or, Despicable, in any Man,
appears unto me, it provokes my Thoughts to retire unto what is most
Wonderfully Contrary unto it, in my SAVIOUR.

The Qualities of the Various Animals, which I happen to have before
me, putt me in Mind of the admirable [ms. p. 346] Qualities, by which my
SAVIOUR is Endear'd unto me.

When I see People Miserable in any Point, it raises in me some
Thoughts on the Miseries, from which I am delivered by my SAVIOUR, and
my Obligations to my Deliverer!

What are the Uses of My Garments to the Parts that are covered with
them? Of such Uses is my SAVIOUR to my Spirit; With the Thoughts of
which I have adored Him.

What is there in the Diets of my Table, to render them agreeable
unto me? Analogous Properties I discern in my SAVIOUR; And the Thoughts
thereof give me an Exquisite Relish of Him.

I durst not Lett my Mind Ly fallow, as I walk the Streets. I Rebuke myself with heavy complaints, (and I make my Moan to Heaven) if I have gone many Steps, without Some Struggle, to pull down the Thoughts of my SAVIOUR into my Soul. I have Compelled the very Signs in o^e Streets, to Point me unto something in my SAVIOUR that should be Thought upon. When I have been at a Loss for fresh Thoughts on Him, it has been but casting my Eye towards the Shops on Either Side, and from the Varieties in them, I have had Something of my SAVIOUR Suggested unto me.

Enquiries after News are made with Frequency, with Eagerness. I am grown very Cold in such Things: My Concern for them, [ms. p. 347] and Pleasure in them, is very much Extinguished. Some New Thoughts of my SAVIOUR, Some New Sight of Him, Shall be the News, after which I shall be Still most Enquiring. Here I have my Curiosity gratified, a thousand times more, than in the News of ye Common Occurrences in the World.

I have Sometimes an Expectation of Some Satisfaction arriving to me; and a Little of Strength and Impatience in it. I retune it. I have done Expecting any Good Thing from This World. My Thoughts usually are; What is the Good of What is Expected by me? O My Soul, All of this Good thou hast already in thy SAVIOUR.

I have in My Study a very Easy Chair. When I am going to Repose myself in my Chair, it is a Common Reflection with me, Return to thy Rest, O my Soul: O my SAVIOUR, Thou art the Rest of my Soul.

On the Lords-day I would Enter into the Rest of GOD.^{257} That I may Sabbatize aright, I hear my SAVIOUR Inviting of me, Come to me, and I will give you Rest.^{258} On this Day, I try to make a Particular Application of that Invitation. I gett my Mind filled this Day with as Many Thoughts of my SAVIOUR as may be: which Thoughts in general have a Tendency to Convey a Sweet Rest unto the Soul that Entertains them. And more Particularly, if I happen to Think on any thing that may be Uneasy to me, I presently Seek a Sweet _Rest_ for my Soul, in a Glorious CHRIST, as being and as doing, What will be a Releef [ms. p. 348] of that _Uneasiness_. Yea, I Sometimes now Cast an Eye on the _Uncomfortable Things_, which give a Disturbance to my _Rest_, in this World, on purpose, that I may immediately take my Flights to Something in a Glorious CHRIST, that shall show me a _Plenteous Redemption_[259]from them. So, _I Rejoice in the Lord again & again_,[260] And so I find, _His Rest is Glorious_.[261]

Every Day I find in myself, Such Imperfections, Infirmities, _Miscarriages_, as Cause me to Humble and _Abhor myself_ before the Lord. Now I employ My own _Humiliations_, for _Scaffolds_ from whence I would raise the _Praises_ of my admirable SAVIOUR. Whatever I see _Mean_ and _Vile_ in myself, I would proceed from thence, to _Think_, How much the _Reverse_ of This, is to be Seen in my SAVIOUR. From the _Loathing_ of myself, I would pass on to the _Loving_ of my SAVIOUR. And So, among other Consequences, I Shall also affect myself, with the Only _Righteousness_, which I have to _Plead_, _that I may be Justified_ before the Glorious GOD.

The _Pagans_ had their _Many Gods_; and for One Blessing they hoped from one of their Gods; for Another from Another. Now, all the _Glories_ which I find them dividing among their _Many Gods_, I ascribe unto my SAVIOUR, who _is the True GOD, & Eternal Life_:[262] and Look for Every Blessing from Him alone.

In my Conversing with my SAVIOUR, I go thro' many Portions of the _Scriptures_, which _testify of Him_;[263] Especially the PSALMS; [ms. p. 349] Employing a _Verse_, or a _Clause_, at a Time, for the Subject of My _Meditation_, When Every Night I _fall asleep in JESUS_. Now, the _Psalms_ are filled with _Prayers_, wherein I find my own Condition so Suited, that I Cannot Express it better before ye Lord. But when I present such _Prayers_ unto the Lord, it proves a Vast Encouragement and Consolation unto me,

and therein I maintain a Most Sweet Fellowship with my SAVIOUR, when I
think; This Very Prayer was once presented by my SAVIOUR unto His Eternal
FATHER. My SAVIOUR once Pray'd at this rate, & found Acceptance. I Pray
but as my SAVIOUR taught me, and as He did before me. Certainly, Such a
Prayer will be grateful unto GOD.

Finally. In my admirable SAVIOUR accomplishing an Eternal Redemption for us,[264] I see glorious Transactions & Occurrences. Now I am
Sollicitous to feel the Heavenly Power of those things upon me, that I
may come into an Holy Fellowship with them, and with Him in them. This
I take for a Token to me, That my SAVIOUR has been Concerned for me, in
these Parts of His Potent Mediation.

I see GOD becoming a Man in my SAVIOUR. I feel the Power of it in
my Returning to GOD, and meeting with Him in my SAVIOUR.

I see my SAVIOUR Leading an Hidden Life, and Passing thro' Obscure
Circumstances, while He sojourned among us. I feel the Power of it, in
my being Willing to have my Walk with God carried on with all possible
Concealment upon it. [ms. p. 350]

I See my SAVIOUR doing illustrious Miracles upon the Children of
Men in their Distresses. I feel the Power of it, in my own Experience
of the Divine Works upon my Soul, answerable to what was in those ancient Operations of the Lord.

I See my SAVIOUR Dying for my Sin, Dying on the Cross. I feel the
Power of it, in the Death of my Sinful Dispositions; my Dying unto Crea-
tures; My having for This World the Sentiments of a Man hanging on a
Cross.

I See my SAVIOUR in a Marvellous Resurrection triumphing over the
Powers of Darkness,[265]and Entring into a New Life, wherein He Lives

forevermore. I feel the _Power_ of it, in my Rising & Getting up out of my _Lifeless Darkness_, and my Coming into a _New Life_, wherein I shall pursue the Designs of PIETY, _Quickened_ with an _Everlasting Principle_ of it, which I was once a Stranger to.

This may be Enough to illustrate the _Way of Living_, which the GOD of all Grace has brought me to. In this _Way of Living_, I keep Waiting for what my SAVIOUR has to do for me. I _go up from the Wilderness of This World_, thus _Leaning on the Beloved_ of my Soul. [ms. p. 351]

§ The Sentiments of a _Spirit Rejoicing_ in GOD my SAVIOUR, I thus now Express on Various Occasions; whereof indeed Some are but _Supposed Cases_.

I have a Glorious CHRIST Concerned for me; Whose _Providence_ Orders my Whole Condition, and Will surely _do me Good_; Surely _make all things Work together for my Good_.[266]

Should it be so, that my _Body_ were Languishing under _Grievous Diseases_; A Glorious CHRIST will bestow the _Blessings of an Healed Soul_ upon me; take away _the Worst_ of my Diseases, and make _the rest_ Wholesome to me.

Should it be so, that my _Name_ Suffered the Vilest _Calumnies_ and _Reproaches_; A Glorious CHRIST knows me by _Name_, and makes a kind Mention of me before His Eternal FATHER.

If it should be so, that in any Circumstances of my _Children_, I should See Heart-breaking ⟨⟨267⟩⟩ Spectacles; A Glorious CHRIST has brought me into an _Adoption_, and into an _Inheritance_, among the _Children_ of GOD: And while the SON of GOD makes me _His Own_, what tho' I should not be _Happy in Sons & in Daughters_?

Should it be so, that I have no _Friends_ in the World Left unto me; A Glorious CHRIST is my _Friend_; And in His _Friendship_ I have Enough to

Satisfy me, tho' all other <u>Lovers</u> were <u>Putt far from me.</u>[268]

Should it be so, that I must Conflict With <u>Wants</u> and <u>Straits</u> and a Pinching <u>Poverty</u>; A Glorious CHRIST is a <u>Fountain</u> that Will <u>Supply all my Needs</u>.[269] He Will allow me <u>Food Convenient for me</u>;[270] And if I am never [ms. p. 352] so <u>Poor</u>, I have in Him the <u>Bread of Life</u>;[271] I have in Him the <u>Garments of Righteousness</u>;[272] I have in Him a <u>Dwelling on High</u>,[273] a Lovely & a pleasant Habitation.

Should it be so, that I must meet wth many things <u>Uneasy</u> to me, and such as it may Vex me to think upon; A Glorious CHRIST is an <u>Inexhaustible Object</u> for my Contemplation. He will kindly come into my Soul, at y[e] Call of a <u>Thought</u>. When I begin to Think on <u>Him</u>, all my <u>Uneasiness</u> presently Vanishes; A Wondrous Light and Life and Strength and Peace and Joy Comes into my Soul.

§   I think,

If I were fastened unto a CROSS, and under all the Circumstances of a Crucifixion,

What would be My Dispositions, What My Exercises?

I should Look on my approaching <u>Death</u>, as Unavoidable; and the Approaches of it would now be Welcome to me, not having any Prospect of being any other way delivered from Numberless Uneasinesses.

I should Look on all the <u>Delights</u> and <u>Riches</u> and <u>Honours</u> of the World from which I am departing, as things of no <u>Use</u> and no <u>Worth</u> unto me.

I should have done Expecting of <u>Satisfaction</u> from any thing of <u>This World</u>; and no more propose a <u>Portion</u> in any thing that is done under the Sun. [ms. p. 353]

I should be Extremely <u>Sick</u> of a World, which I saw fitted with such Unreasonable, Unrighteous, Barbarous Things, Where the <u>Most Holy City</u> is full of Murderers.

I should Expect a Series and Succession of many Killing Things, to be with Repeted Strokes inflicted on me; And Mightily beg of GOD, that I may not be Left unto any Impatience or Miscarriage under them.

I should, as One Free among the Dead,[274] forbid any Disturbance of Mind upon it, if People treat me as if they had Free Liberty to do what they will to me, and Speak what they will of me; and as I should pursue no Personal Revenges on them, So, I should Pray for them, Father, For-give them.[275]

Tho' I should have done with This World, yett I should Express a Concern for the Relatives which I Leave behind me, in a Land of Pitts & of Droughts, & fiery flying Serpents.[276]

I should utter Words, that may be for the Instruction and Advantage of People that are about me; and Lay hold on Opportunities to say what I Could for the Advancement of Piety among them.

I should fly to Passages in the Word of GOD that may be Suitable for me; and fetch Support and Comfort from thence, in the Multitude of My Thoughts within me.

I should, with Continual Acts of Resignation, committ my Spirit into the Hands of my FATHER,[277] and my SAVIOUR; With Assurance of my Speedy Reception into a Paradise, where I shall be Comforted. [ms. p. 354]

I should Endeavour to Look into the Heavenly World; and Rejoice in the View of the Joy Sett before me[278] there, and count the Light Afflic-tions here which are but for a Moment, abundantly Compensated in that far more Exceeding & Eternal Weight of Glory.[279]

In these Things I should propound a Conformity to my Crucified JESUS. Thus Dying, Behold, I Live![280]

And finding myself brought into these Dispositions and these Exer-

cises, the Faith of what must most Certainly follow hereupon fills me
with Joy Unspeakable & full of Glory.

§   There is an Illustration of the glorious TRINITY in the Eternal GOD
HEAD,[281] which apprehends GOD propounding to Himself an Infinite Satisfaction: And here is GOD the FATHER. Then, GOD Reflected on Himself,
that so He may have that Satisfaction: And here is GOD the SON. Lastly,
Upon this Contemplation wherein GOD Beholds and Enjoys Himself, arising
a Love, a Joy, an Acquiescence, and a Satisfaction of GOD within Himself;
And here is GOD the Holy SPIRIT.

Now, I sett before me my Admirable SAVIOUR, that I may See GOD in
Him, and Live. From this View of GOD in my SAVIOUR, my Soul is filled
with Love to Him, with Joy in Him, with an Incomparable Satisfaction from
Him. What a Communion with the [ms. p. 355] Glorious GOD, and the Three
Subsistences in Him, is Dust & Ashes herein raised unto! What a Demonstration will this Exercise of Piety give of ones having the Holy SPIRIT
of GOD filling and acting of Him! Yea, What a Prelibation here have I
of that Final Blessedness wherein all the Gracious Designs of my SAVIOUR
for me terminate!

This is the way that I take. And in this way of Living by Faith of
the SON of GOD, I keep Looking for His Mercy to me in Eternal Life.[282]

Plancus being told, that Asinius Pollio had Written certain
Invective orations against him, that should not be published
until after Plancus's Death, to y^e End they might not be
answered by him. There is none, saith he, but Ghosts
& Goblins, that fight wth y^e Dead!

APPENDIX A

CHRONOLOGICAL SUMMARY OF AND RECORD OF DIARY SOURCES FOR PATERNA

The entries in the following table signify Mather's age as represented
in both the Paterna manuscript and the Diary, the years for which we have
information from Mather about his life from either the Paterna or the Diary
or from both works, and a page by page breakdown of Diary entries which
Mather incorporated into Paterna. When Mather's age is not specifically
noted in the Paterna, his age has been arrived at through reference to
Diary entries copied into the manuscript. It is important to note that in
the Paterna Mather treats the first thirty-five years of his life in groups
or "Lustres" of five years each, although the first three "Lustres" are
treated as a whole (pp. 3-9). After his thirty-fifth year, Mather discontinues this practice in "The Second Part," which is "No Longer Distinguished
into Lustres." All page references to the Paterna are from the manuscript.
With the exception of the references to the 1712 Diary all page references
to the Diary are from Worthington Chauncey Ford's two volume edition of the
Diary of Cotton Mather. All page references to the 1712 Diary are from the
edition by William R. Manierre II, The Diary of Cotton Mather for the Year
1712.

Mather's Age	Years	Pages in Paterna	Pages in Diary	Record of Located Passages	
				Individual Pages in Paterna	Individual Pages in Diary
1-15	1662-1677	3-9	---	---	---
16	1678	11	---	---	---
17	1679	11-17	---	---	---

301

Mather's Age	Years	Pages in Paterna	Pages in Diary	Record of Located Passages Individual Pages in Paterna	Individual Pages in Diary
18	1680	17-20	---	---	---
19	1681	20-42	I, 1-53	20	I, 1
				21	I, 1-2
				22	I, 9-10
				23	I, 10
				24-26	I, 3-5
				26	I, 13-14
				26-27	I, 24
				27-28	I, 15-16
				28	I, 16
				29	I, 16-17
				30	I, 17-18
				31	I, 18-19
				32	I, 19, 21
				33	I, 21-22, 24
				34-35	I, 28-30
				36-40	I, 36-41
				41-42	I, 44-45
20	1682	43-59	---	---	---
21	1683	61-77	I, 54-85	61-65	I, 81-84
				65	I, 62-63
				66	I, 63-64, 22, 203
				67	I, 64-66
				68	I, 66, 68-69
				69-71	I, 69-71
				71-72	I, 71-72
				73	I, 75-76
				74	I, 81
22	1684	77-80	---	---	---
23	1685	81-102; 130-132	I, 86-120	81-82	I, 88-89
				82-83	I, 92-93
				84	I, 94, 95
				85	I, 96
				86	I, 97
				87	I, 101
				90	I, 105
				91	I, 103
				91-92	I, 108
				92	I, 104
				93	I, 107-109
				93-94	I, 114
				94-96	I, 110-112
				96	I, 114
				99	I, 115

Mather's Age	Years	Pages in Paterna	Pages in Diary	Record of Located Passages	
				Individual Pages in Paterna	Individual Pages in Diary
				100-101	I, 106-107
				101-102	I, 109-110
				130-132	I, 86-87
24	1686	102-106	I, 121-136	102-103	I, 121-122
				103	I, 126-127
				104-105	I, 128-129
				105	I, 130, 133
				106	I, 135-136
25	1687	106-109	---	---	---
26	1688	111-112	---	---	---
27	1689	113-115	---	---	---
28	1690	116-121	---	---	---
29	1691	---	---	---	---
30	1692	73-74; 125	I, 144-159	73-74	I, 155
				125	I, 158
31	1693	127-130; 133-134	I, 160-180	127	I, 160
				128-129	I, 162-163
				130	I, 166-167 (The Paterna version lacks the colorful language used in this Diary passage.)
				133	I, 174
				134	I, 179-180
32	1694	135-148	---	---	---
33	1695	148-161	---	---	---
34	1696	165-174	I, 182-220	165-166	I, 199-201
				168	I, 194-195
				170	I, 185-186
				171	I, 189-190
				172	I, 195, 199
				173	I, 204
				174	I, 206-207
35	1697	175-184	I, 221-251	175-176	I, 221-222
				176	I, 224
				177	I, 224-225

Mather's Age	Years	Pages in Paterna	Pages in Diary	Record of Located Passages Individual Pages in Paterna	Individual Pages in Diary
				179	(Appears to be a paraphrase of I, 184, 188, 207, 233)
				181-182	I, 226-227
				182-183	I, 234
				183	I, 237
				183-184	I, 239
36	1698	188-193	I, 252-291	188	I, 255
				188-189	I, 257-258
				189	I, 261
				190	I, 269
				191	I, 272-273, 278
				192-193	I, 281-282
37	1699	186-187; 193-196	I, 292-334	186-187	I, 307
				193	I, 160, 292-293
				194	I, 297-298
				195-196	I, 333-334
38	1700	122-123; 196-199	I, 335-392	122-123	I, 354-355
				196-197	I, 345-346
				198-199	I, 372-373
39	1701	----	----	----	----
40	1702	197; 200-205; 209-210	I, 418-465	197	I, 421-422
				200-202	I, 440-441
				203-204	I, 426
				204-205	I, 427-429
				209-210	I, 425-426
41	1703	210-215	I, 466-507	210-212	I, 477-479
				212-213	I, 483
				213-214	I, 485
				214	I, 497
				214-215	I, 501
42	1704	----	----	----	----
43	1705	217-232	I, 509-544	217	I, 510
				218	I, 518-519
				218-219	I, 521
				219	I, 529
				220	I, 529
				220-222	I, 533-534
				222-223	I, 534
				223-225	I, 537-538
				225-227	I, 538-539

Mather's Age	Years	Pages in _Paterna_	Pages in _Diary_	Record of Located Passages Individual Pages in _Paterna_	Individual Pages in _Diary_
				227-232	I, 534-537
44	1706	232-236	I, 545-592	233-234 234-235 235-236	I, 559-561 I, 558 I, 580-581
45	1707	---	I, 593-598	---	---
46	1708	---	---	---	---
47	1709	258-265; 268-270	II, 1-34	258-265; 268-270	II, 24-29 (The _Paterna_ version is considerably more detailed.)
48	1710	---	---	---	---
49	1711	270; 273-275; 279-288	II, 39-168	270	II, 90-91 (The subject matter is the same; _Paterna_ version is vastly altered and abbreviated.)
				273-275 279 280 280-281 281 281-282 282 283 284 284-285 286-288	II, 59-60 II, 42-43 II, 46, 67-68, 71 II, 79 II, 80, 83, 92, 96 II, 121 II, 136, 141-142 II, 144, 125-126 II, 48 II, 123-124 II, 152-153, 131
50	1712	278-279; 282; 285-286; 288-295	1712 _Diary_	278 278-279 279 282 285-286 288-289 290-295	1712, 13 1712, 22 1712, 27 1712, 72 1712, 35 1712, 124-125 1712, 66-70
51	1713	---	II, 178-290	---	---
52	1714	---	---	---	---
53	1715	---	---	---	---

Mather's Age	Years	Pages in Paterna	Pages in Diary	Record of Located Passages	
				Individual Pages in Paterna	Individual Pages in Diary
54	1716	323-324	II, 334-403	323 323-324	II, 343 II, 384
55	1717	312-316; 324-325; 328-329	II, 434-510	312 313-316	II, 454 II, 479-480 (The Paterna passage appears to be an amplification of sentiments expressed in this brief diary passage, which Mather concluded as follows: "This Design must be elsewhere more largely Spoken to.")
				324-325 328 329 (329-336)	II, 475-476 II, 452 II, 492 (Appear to be taken from Mather's sermon preached on 8^d 10^m 1717; see Diary, II, 493, 510.)
56	1718	311-312; 321-322; 325-328; 339	II, 514-596	311-312 321-322 325-326 326 326-327 327-328 339	II, 551-552 II, 575-576 II, 529 II, 547 II, 533 II, 535 II, 571
57	1719	----	---	----	---
58	1720	----	---	----	---
59	1721	352	II, 601-681	352	II, 633 (The entry dated July 23 concludes: "My Answer to it, is written down on a separate Paper." The question to which Mather refers is the same as appears in Paterna, p. 352. However, Mather's numerous references in Paterna to other private

Mather's Age	Years	Pages in Paterna	Pages in Diary	Record of Located Passages	
				Individual Pages in Paterna	Individual Pages in Diary
					papers, pp. 44, 55, 172, 258, preclude the possibility of assuming Paterna to be the "Paper" to which Mather alludes in the Diary.)
60	1722	----	----	---	----
61	1723	----	---	---	----
62	1724	----	II, 696-790 (Mather's last extant diary)	---	----

APPENDIX B

A RECORD OF PASSAGES IN PATERNA WHICH HAVE BEEN LOCATED

IN MATHER WORKS OTHER THAN THE DIARY

The following table represents all Paterna passages which have been
located outside the manuscript. The first section of the table lists
those works which are sources for passages found in Paterna. The second
section of the table lists those works which contain passages for which
Paterna is a probable source.

I: Index to Mather works which are a source for passages found in Paterna

Title of and pages in source	Pages in Paterna manuscript
Bonifacius, ed. David Levin (Cambridge: The Belknap Press of Harvard Univ. Press, 1966), pp. 24-25; 43-52; 136-137	222-223; 227-232; 266-267
The Heavenly Conversation (Boston, 1710), pp. 7-30	239-249
Dust and Ashes (Boston: B. Green, for T. Green, 1710), pp. 16-34	250-257
Winter Meditations (Boston: Benj. Harris, 1693), pp. 29-38	286-289
The Sacrificer (Boston: Fleet, for Gerrish, 1714), pp. 28-45	296-303
Christian Philosopher (London, 1720), pp. 93-94	304-305
Valerius; or, Soul Prosperity (Boston: Fleet, for Gerrish, 1723), pp. 8-16	307-310
"Of Equity," in Piety and Equity, United (Boston: Allen, for Starke, 1717), pp. 37, 34-35	317-319

309

II: Index to passages located in Mather works for which Paterna is a

probable source

Title of and pages in work for which Paterna is a probable source	Pages in Paterna manuscript
Bonifacius, pp. 66-68; 85; 71-72; 75-77	8-9; 76-77; 88-91; 96-98
Manuductio ad Ministerium (Boston: for Thomas Hancock, 1726), pp. 90-96; 106-107; 74-75; 16-18; 23-24; 81-82	88-91; 96-98; 99; 210-212; 271; 314-315
Parentator (Boston: B. Green, for Nathaniel Belknap, 1724), pp. 189-191	119-125

APPENDIX C

BIBLICAL TEXTS USED BY MATHER IN PATERNA

I: Texts used in direct reference

ACTS

chapter	verse(s)	page(s) in Paterna
5	35	37
8	29	145
10	30, 32	145
16	9, 10	145
26	22	193

I CORINTHIANS

chapter	verse(s)	page(s) in Paterna
11	31	37
15	58	238

DANIEL

chapter	verse(s)	page(s) in Paterna
6	22	146
9	23	147

EXODUS

chapter	verse(s)	page(s) in Paterna
34		72
34	6, 7	37
35		72
36		72

EZEKIEL

chapter	verse(s)	page(s) in Paterna
31	3, 4, 5 7, 8, 9	131

GALATIANS

chapter	verse(s)	page(s) in Paterna
2	20	329

GENESIS

chapter	verse(s)	page(s) in Paterna
21	17, 18, 19	144
22	12	161
24	7	145
33	4	146

HABAKKUK

chapter	verse(s)	page(s) in Paterna
2	4	28

HEBREWS

chapter	verse(s)	page(s) in Paterna
1	14	147
11	17	161
13	17	152

ISAIAH

chapter	verse(s)	page(s) in Paterna
1	18	37
6	6, 7	145
26	13	41
44	3	7
55	7	37
59	2	41

JAMES

chapter	verse(s)	page(s) in Paterna
5	16	120

JOB

chapter	verse(s)	page(s) in Paterna
1	21	170
9	21	title page
14	1	127, 193

JOHN

chapter	verse(s)	page(s) in Paterna
2	1-11	103
5	4	146
6	37	72
14	6	42
	23	34
15	7, 8	234
16	21	186

II: Texts to which Mather alludes*

*Superior figures indicate multiple references on a given page.

APPENDIX D

WILLIAM PERKINS'S OUTLINE OF THE CONVERSION EXPERIENCE

The following selection is from William Perkins's The Whole Treatise
of the Cases of Conscience, in The Workes of That Famous and Worthy Minister
of Christ, in the Universitie of Cambridge M. William Perkins, 3 vols.
(London: John Legatt, 1612-13), II, 13.

"In the working and effecting of Mans salvation, ordinarily there are
two speciall actions of God: the giving of the first grace, and after that,
the giving of the second. The former of these two workes, hath ten
severall actions. I. God gives man the outward meanes of salvation, especially the Ministery of the word: and with it, he sends some outward or
inward crosse, to breake and subdue the stubbornnes of our nature, that it
may be made plyable to the wil of God . . . II. This done, God brings the
mind of man to a consideration of the Law, and what is not sinne. III. Upon
a serious consideration of the Law, hee makes a man particularly to see and
know his owne peculiar and proper sinnes, whereby he offends God. IV. Upon
the sight of sinne, hee smites the heart with a legall feare, whereby when
man seeth his sinnes, he makes him to feare punishment and hell, and to
despaire of salvation, in regard of any thing in himselfe.

"Now these foure actions, are indeede no fruits of grace, for a
Reprobate may go thus farre; but they are onely workes of preparation,
going before grace; the other actions which follow, are effects of grace.
V. The fifth action of grace therefore is, to stirre up the minds to a
serious consideration of the promise of salvation, propounded and published
in the Gospell. VI. After this, the sixt is, to kindle in the heart some
seedes or sparkes of faith, that is, a will and desire to beleeve, and grace

319

to strive against doubting and despaire. Now at the same instant, when God beginnes to kindle in the heart any sparkes of faith, then also hee justifies the sinner, and withall beginnes the worke of sanctification. VII. Then, so soone as faith is put into the heart, there is presently a combate: for it fighteth with doubting, despaire, and distrust. And in this combate faith shewes it selfe, by fervent, constant, and earnest invocation for pardon: and after invocation followes a strength and prevailing of this desire. VIII. Furthermore, God in mercy quiets and settles the Conscience, as touching the salvation of the soule, and the promise of life, whereupon it resteth and staieth it selfe. IX. Next after this setled assurance, and perswasion of mercie, followes a stirring up of the heart to Evangelicall sorrow, according to God, that is, a griefe for sinne, because it is sinne, & because God is offended: and then the Lord workes repentance, whereby the sanctified heart turnes it selfe unto him. And though this repentance bee one of the last in order, yet it shewes it selfe first: as when a candle is brought into a roome, wee first see the light before wee see the candle, and yet the candle must needes bee, before the light can be. X. Lastly, God giveth a man grace to endeavour to obey his commaundments by a new obedience. And these degrees doth the Lord give the first grace.

"The second worke of God tending to salvation, is the giving of the second grace: which is nothing else but the continuance of the first grace given . . . so in bringing a man to salvation, God gives the first grace . . . to beleeve and repent; and then in mercie gives the second, to persevere and continue in faith and repentance to the ende. And this, if wee regard man him selfe, is very necessarie."

APPENDIX E

ALTERATIONS IN THE MANUSCRIPT

Note: Without exception, all alterations in the manuscript during
its inscription and review by Mather are noted here. Deletions or mendings within a line or more of the manuscript that could not be read
have been noticed by a statement as to the exact number of lines or the
approximate number of words involved. Deletions or mendings of more
than one line of the manuscript that could be read have been given brief
notice here, for they have been incorporated into the edition in their
entirety, with notice taken to that effect there. In the descriptions
of manuscript alterations, above means "interlined," over means "in the
same space," and right-hand margin or left-hand margin indicates the
location of margin entries as found on the manuscript page. Further,
the phrase "several letter" is used to indicate an unreadable deletion
which may be a false start for the word that follows, an actual word
which has been deleted, or a misspelling later corrected by Mather. In
all instances in which "several letter" is used, the precise nature of
the deletion is unclear. Empty square brackets which appear within a
line of readable deleted text signify one or more unreadable letters
within that line. Finally, the presence of a caret is always noticed.

All page and line numbers below refer to those of this edition.

1.1	Paterna] written above deleted ' [ ] my son'
2.13	Book] second 'o' written over an initial, incorrect 'k'
2.17	Either] interlined above deleted 'Ether'
4.3	Nullus] followed by deleted 'tibi'

321

4.5   who]   interlined with a caret above deleted 'that'

4.8   Hopes]   followed by three unreadable deleted words

4.9   Somewhat]   followed by one unreadable several letter
                    deletion

4.14   Hopes]   followed by deleted 'and Faith'

4.17   it;]   followed by deleted 'and'

4.17   intimated in]   followed by one unreadable several letter
                    deletion

4.19   Advice unto]   followed by deleted 'persons'

4.20   Dead Parents]   'Dead': interlined with a caret

4.24   chosen to]   followed by one unreadable several letter
                    deletion

5.1-2   own Poor]   preceded by deleted 'poo'

5.10   Lately]   followed by one unreadable smudged word

5.13   Leave]   followed by deleted 'some'

5.17   Would]   'W' written over 'c'

6.5   as well as,]   interlined with a caret above deleted 'and'

6.7   would be Cautious]   preceded by deleted 'am [   ]'

6.9   Early]   interlined with a caret

6.10   Very]   'V' written over 'B'

6.14   going astray]   followed by two unreadable several letter
                    deletions

6.16   in which I]   'in': interlined with a caret

6.23-7.1   I read the Scripture . . . would Suffice me.]   written in
                    right-hand margin; position in text indicated with a
                    caret

6.24   for one while]   interlined with a caret above deleted 'once'

7.8   One thing that]   followed by deleted 'much'

7.9   the Distance]   preceded by deleted 'my'

7.10   caused him,]   followed by deleted 'to'

7.10	Weakly] 'a' written over doubtful 'e'
7.16	English] interlined with a caret
7.17	Cato] interlined with a caret
7.18	Made] interlined above deleted 'written'
7.23-25	And I was . . . mentioned.] written in right-hand margin; position in text indicated with a caret
7.26	Ran thro'] followed by deleted 'all'
9.13	now] interlined with a caret
9.14	Sweet] 'w' written over initial, incorrect 'e'
9.25	Moreover] 'ver' written over '[}r'
9.27	it had no worse Effects upon me.] written in right-hand margin; position in text indicated with a caret
10.12	Relation] written over 'Belonging'
10.19	(and other)] followed by deleted 'such'
12.2	here] interlined with a caret
12.4	Sixteen] 'Sixte' written over 'Fift'
12.10	wrote] followed by deleted 'the following'
12.14	I am] followed by one unreadable several letter deletion
12.25	one of my] followed by one unreadable several letter deletion
13.3	unto me,] followed by one unreadable several letter deletion
13.5	for ye Sin] followed by deleted 'my'
14.25	Fulfilment of that] followed by one unreadable several letter deletion
14.26-27	Opportunities, till] followed by one unreadable several letter deletion
15.3	advise you,] followed by one unreadable several letter deletion
15.10	I must] followed by deleted 'now'

15.13	any thing] preceded by deleted 'So'
15.16	I was, at] followed by one unreadable deleted word
15.23	had] 'h' written over initial, incorrect 'a'
15.25	I was] followed by deleted 'like'
15.26-27	pray, & mourn] 'pray': followed by one unreadable several letter deletion; '&': followed by deleted 'Cry'; 'mourn': interlined with a caret above deleted 'Cry'
16.17	raised unto] followed by deleted 'some'
16.23	I may] followed by one unreadable several letter deletion
16.24	mostly] interlined with a caret
16.25	occasion] 'io' written over 'on'
17.7	on this] 'on': written over 'In'
17.10	Soul is the] 'the': written over 'in'
17.18	desired] interlined with a caret above deleted 'chosen'
17.19	Then will] followed by one unreadable several letter deletion
17.19	Hallelujahs be] followed by deleted 'Eternally'
17.23	Design] interlined above deleted 'Study'
17.26	(successively)] interlined with a caret
19.23	Non-conformist] preceded by deleted doubtful 'non'
20.3	most Explicit] interlined with a caret above deleted 'conscious'
20.28	this Action] preceded by deleted 'th'
21.1	my Study] preceded by deleted doubtful 'So'
21.8	Still] 'S' altered from doubtful 's'
21.8	myself] followed by deleted 'in'
21.12-13	tho' at] 'at': written over 'I'
21.13	Such] interlined above deleted 'any'
21.14	Travail that I] followed by deleted 'sh'
21.17	I find] followed by deleted 'I'

21.24	my Lord for] 'for': interlined with a caret
21.24	Why] 'y' written over 'at'
21.26	Most] interlined with a caret
23.5	Punctually] interlined with a caret
23.9	About this Time,] followed by deleted 'I ha'
24.3	Contriving, What] followed by deleted 'may'
24.6	To Pray,] followed by deleted 'for'
24.24	of my] followed by one unreadable several letter deletion
24.25	have] 'ha' written over doubtful 'Fli'
25.12	heard: And] followed by deleted 'about'
25.13	afterward,] followed by deleted 'I [ ]ye Answer'
25.14	On] preceded by deleted 'And'
25.25-26.1	and even at an Age . . . in the Streets] written in right-hand margin; position in text indicated with a caret
26.1	very] interlined with a caret
26.6	PRIDE] preceded by deleted 'pride'
27.16-17	Tis not Seemly for such a Fool!] written in right-hand margin; position in text indicated with a caret
29.21	to] interlined with a caret
29.21	had] interlined with a caret
30.10	which] preceded by deleted doubtful 'f'
30.11	Me] 'M' written over 'a'
31.4	Special] 'Sp' written over doubtful 'M'
31.15	Teeth] 'th' written over 'eth'
31.17	Search] 'rch' written over 'ch'
31.20	Have] preceded by deleted doubtful 'I'
31.20	How?] 'H' written over half-written 'B'
33.6	But] followed by deleted 'I'

34.7	meaning of] followed by one unreadable several letter deletion
34.9	GOD] 'OD' written over 'od'
35.19	Eternal] 'nal' written over 'nity'
35.20	Argue] 'A' written over 'a'
36.1	in myself] followed by deleted 'in'
36.2	of y^e] 'y^e': 'y' preceded by attached, deleted 'm'
36.6	Methods] 't' written over doubtful 'd'
36.10	Workings] 'W' written over 'At'
37.5	If I] followed by one unreadable several letter deletion
38.2	charming] followed by one unreadable several letter deletion
41.9	for Some while] 'while': interlined above deleted 'years'
41.15	My] 'M' written over 'C'
41.19	Years,] followed by deleted 'as'
41.22	only] followed by two unreadable deleted words both of which are underlined and written within parentheses
42.7	away.] followed by one unreadable several letter deletion
42.13	had] written over 'was' and followed by deleted 'by'
42.15	thing,] followed by deleted 'of y'
42.17	did] first 'd' written over one unreadable letter; 'i' written over 'a'
42.17-18	I know not how many more] interlined with a caret above deleted 'more'
42.21	Books] followed by one unreadable several letter deletion
42.25	I shall] followed by deleted 'by'
42.27	now Surviving] interlined with a caret
43.9	Contributed,] followed by deleted 'more' which preceded the comma
43.13	My] 'M' written over 'm'

43.26	Desirous to] followed by deleted 'go'
44.3	as these] preceded by deleted 'th'
47.16	into] written over 'in'
47.26	thou,] followed by deleted doubtful 'now a'
48.1	'Ere] interlined with a caret above deleted 'Before'
48.2	received] preceded by deleted doubtful 'h'
48.8	upon] followed by deleted 'these'
48.27	Afflictive,] followed by one unreadable several letter deletion which, in turn, is followed by a second un-deleted comma
49.18	My] 'M' written over 'm'
49.26	Not-Employ'd] 'N' written over 'n'
50.25	Ask] followed by deleted doubtful 'on'
51.3	Shall] followed by deleted 'in'
51.10	should] followed by deleted 'my'
52.11	May] 'M' written over 'c'
53.2	Tho' in] 'in': interlined with a caret
53.6-7	I am now Twenty years Old!] originally deleted in the manuscript
54.7	this] followed by one unreadable several letter deletion
54.9	it has been] interlined with a caret
54.12	Imitation,] followed by deleted 'if'
54.12	only] followed by deleted 'a'
55.16	Lord, his] 'his': 'h' written over 'O'
55.23	for] 'or' altered from doubtful 'in'
58.4	and] preceded by deleted 'and'
59.2	made a Present of] interlined with a caret above deleted 'gave'
59.3	not go] preceded by deleted doubtful 'not'

59.6	Accept] 'A' altered from 'a'
59.13	But] followed by deleted doubtful 'to'
59.15-16	& Particularly, in your Tenderness for Your Mother, (if she Survive,) when I shall be gone to a better World.] preceded by a comma altered from a period; originally deleted in the manuscript
59.22	unto my] 'unto': interlined with a caret above deleted 'to'
60.5	Active] 'A' altered from 'a'
60.12	myself] followed by one unreadable several letter deletion
60.13	Notes;] followed by deleted 'to'
61.5	comes] interlined with a caret above deleted 'is'
61.23	myself] 'my' written over 'any'
62.7	Glorious] preceded by deleted 'Lord'
62.9	into] 'in' written over smudged 'un'
62.16	for the doing of] interlined with a caret above deleted 'to do'
63.4	for I] followed by deleted 'had'
63.10	Lords-Day] 'D' altered from 'd'
63.13	pious] interlined with a caret
63.17	than if it had been Left unmentioned.] written in right-hand margin; position in text indicated with a caret
63.21	Service] interlined with a caret above deleted 'Glory'
63.22	my] interlined with a caret
63.25	then] interlined with a caret
63.26	occurring,] followed by two unreadable deleted words
64.6-10	On the Exceeding Willingness . . . unto others] originally deleted in the manuscript
64.15	Saw, this] followed by deleted doubtful 'preach'
64.18	also] followed by either two deleted letters or one deleted punctuation mark and one letter

64.20   If you] preceded by deleted 'You'

64.24   sometimes] interlined with a caret

65.15   Stingless Death] written under two unreadable deleted
          words which were underlined only once

65.16   celebrate] preceded by deleted 'show'

65.24   that my Jewels are;] preceded by deleted 'greatly dear
          unto me'

65.25   Work,] interlined with a caret above deleted 'Church'

65.26   And Still accept my Prayer.] written under deleted 'To
          Speak and Write for thee.'

66.5   hateful] interlined with a caret

66.5   Temptations.] followed by five unreadable deleted lines

66.5-6   I found my Mind haunted with Ideas, on the occasion whereof,]
          written in right-hand margin; position in text in-
          dicated with a caret which was written into the fourth
          line of the deletion following 'Temptations.' (see
          above, 66.5 Temptations.])

66.6   Ideas,] preceded by one unreadable several letter deletion

66.10   of y^e] followed by one unreadable several letter deletion

66.15   in these Exercises of Piety,] interlined with a caret

67.4   Jest,] 's' altered from doubtful 't'

67.7   I had,] preceded by deleted 'It'

67.17   only] interlined with a caret

67.18   any thing,] followed by doubtful 'or'

67.19   how I] 'I': interlined with a caret above deleted 'he'

67.22   use to] interlined with a caret

68.7   for] followed by one unreadable several letter deletion

68.10   this] 'is' written over 'e'

69.7   That] followed by deleted 'there'

70.19   Resort,] followed by one unreadable several letter deletion

70.20   And,] preceded by deleted 'So'

72.9   conveniency]   preceded by deleted 'Ha'

72.21   doubtless more than to make a Thousand:]   interlined
                with a caret

72.22   Persons]   preceded by deleted 'than'

72.23   Assemblies]   'A' altered from 'a'

72.25   Impossible]   'm' written over doubtful 'n'

73.15   walking in]   'in': preceded by deleted doubtful 'on';
                written over 'a'

74.9   Testimonies]   first 's' written over doubtful 't'

75.10   and]   'an' altered from 'w'

75.12   my]   interlined with a caret

75.13   was]   'w' altered from 'c'

75.25   III. That if He]   preceded by deleted 'III. That I [   ]'

76.8   was now]   preceded by deleted 'now'

76.10   Over]   'O' written over 'o'

77.2   necessary]   interlined with a caret

77.2   Succours]   followed by deleted 'of Alsufficient Grace.'

77.4   Weigh]   'i' written over 'e'

77.5   for a]   'a': followed by attached, deleted 'ny'

77.7   Especially]   'Es' written over two unreadable letters

78.20   Rising]   preceded by deleted 'morning'

79.11   proved]   followed by one unreadable several letter deletion

79.27   it;]   followed by deleted doubtful 'very'

80.10   a]   interlined above deleted 'one'

80.11-12   afterwards]   'w' altered from 'd'

80.21   form]   interlined with a caret above deleted 'devise'

80.21   Christianity.]   followed by deleted 'They [   ]the [   ].'

82.22   Labours.]   preceded by one unreadable several letter
                deletion

84.8-10	Yea, I pray'd . . . for it.] written in right-hand margin
84.11	them] interlined with a caret
84.17	Recomend] preceded by deleted doubtful 'Cause'
84.24	frequently] followed by deleted 'add'
84.26	they have] followed by deleted 'done'
85.18	more than] followed by deleted 'Three or'
85.18	or Five] interlined with a caret
86.6	Disputation] 'n' followed by attached, deleted 's'
86.7	Heads of] 'of': 'o' altered from 'i'; 'f' written over 'n'
86.23	I] followed by an unreadable one letter deletion
87.13	Least] 's' altered from an unreadable letter
87.27	Who] 'o' followed by attached, deleted 'se'
87.27-28	might accompany me to] interlined with a caret above deleted 'company I might also at length have in'
88.14	Methods] followed by deleted comma
88.18	God] followed by deleted 'has'
88.18	made] followed by deleted 'Your Mother'
88.28	I did] followed by deleted 'not'
88.28	whole] interlined with a caret
89.6	my Consort] interlined with a caret above deleted 'your [ ] Mother'
89.7	One month] followed by deleted 'still'
89.7	years] followed by deleted 'old'
89.13	for me.] followed by three unreadable deleted lines
89.14	of o^e] 'of': 'f' altered from superscript 'e'
89.19	that Story] 'that': 'a' altered from 'e'; second 't' inserted closely between mended 'a' and 'S' of 'Story'
89.26	I might] followed by deleted doubtful 'Wri'

90.11   Promise,]   followed by deleted 'for'

90.18   it were]   followed by two unreadable deleted words

90.24   be glancing]   'be': interlined with a caret

90.26   for the]   'for': 'f' altered from 'i' and 'or' altered
          from 'n'; 'the': 'th' altered from doubtful 'm'

90.26   Perfecting of]   'of': interlined with a caret

91.4   out]   followed by deleted 'out'

91.19   then]   interlined with a caret

91.20   Text]   preceded by deleted 'Head'

91.21   meditation]   'm' preceded by deleted doubtful 'n'

92.1   in]   'i' altered from 'd'

92.3   What]   interlined with a caret above deleted 'All'

92.9   old,]   followed by deleted doubtful 'on'

92.27   was)]   followed by deleted 'Enl[ ]'

93.3   Heaven-ward]   interlined with a caret

93.12   Promise,]   followed by deleted 'Psa'

93.16   any]   'ny' altered from 'n'

95.2   I]   followed by deleted doubtful 'to'

95.3   to w^ch]   'to': interlined above deleted 'in'

96.1   years,]   interlined with a caret above deleted 'Lustres,'

96.1   Private]   originally deleted in the manuscript

96.23   Changes,]   originally deleted in the manuscript

96.24   Law]   followed by deleted comma and 'the'

96.25   Say]   followed by attached, deleted 'ing'

97.8   in this world]   interlined with a caret

97.19   Riches]   'R' altered from 'H'

97.22   Once]   'ce' altered from 'e'; followed by deleted 'Night'

98.12   all]   written over 'in'

98.22	came,] interlined above deleted 'am,'
98.24	had] 'd' altered from 'v' and followed by attached, deleted 'e'
99.20	<u>Tongue</u>] followed by one unreadable several letter deletion
99.21	so far] interlined with a caret
100.17	accept] 'a' written over 'p'
100.24	right] followed by deleted 'R '
101.5	successively, and] interlined with a caret
101.20	Indeed,]followed by deleted 'my Time'
101.24	that I] 'that': 'at' written over 'en'; 'I': either smudged or altered from one or two unreadable letters
101.27	many of] interlined with a caret
102.2	Bless] 'B' altered from doubtful 'to'
102.2	the Communications] 'the': 'e' followed by attached, deleted 'se'
102.2	Communications of those <u>other papers</u>] 'of those <u>other papers</u>': interlined with a caret misplaced after a comma following 'Communications'
102.25	Enjoyes that] 'that': 'at' altered from 'is'
103.3	God] followed by deleted 'has acc'
103.7	Lord.] followed by deleted 'that is'; period altered from a comma
103.11	So] preceded by deleted 'in'
104.6	you, that] followed by deleted 'the'
104.15	Expectation,] followed by deleted 'of'
104.18	<u>Faith</u>,] followed by deleted 'came'
104.19	were] followed by deleted 'not'
105.4	Which] followed by deleted 'was'
105.17	<u>Deceit</u>] preceded by deleted 'Delusion'
106.12-13	Yea, and for some Remarkable changes in the world,] interlined with a caret

106.15	which have] followed by deleted 'caused me to fall into'
106.18	y^e] 'y' preceded by attached, deleted 'm'
106.18	still been] followed by deleted 'from'
106.21	and] followed by deleted 'it'
106.22	into] followed by one unreadable several letter deletion
106.22	yea] originally deleted in the manuscript
106.26	an astonishing] 'n astonishing' originally deleted in the manuscript
106.27	go to] followed by deleted 'Embellish &'
107.1	Scarce] followed by deleted doubtful 'not'
107.16	may] followed by one unreadable several letter deletion
107.20	Lest you] followed by deleted doubtful 'pa'
107.24	invasit] first 'i' written over 'a'
108.1-19	But after . . . I now Sett before you.] written in right-hand margin and across bottom of the page; the absence of a caret leaves the intended position of this passage open to question
108.14	me,] followed by deleted 'on'
109.8-17	My Birth-day . . . they were so to others.] originally deleted in the manuscript
110.20	perceive] 'rc' written over doubtful 'a'
111.6	as] interlined with a caret above deleted 'Even'
111.8	and of] followed by deleted 'what'
111.20	Sick] 'i' altered from 'o'
111.20-21	I was] preceded by deleted 'And'
111.24	And] followed by deleted 'I'
112.1-2	not many months after the Day of Prayer above Said,] interlined with a caret
112.2	I am] 'am': interlined with a caret located between deleted 'kn' following 'I' and two unreadable deleted letters

112.5	Language] preceded by deleted 'Latin Tongue'
112.14	afferat] followed by one unreadable several letter deletion
113.1	unto him,] followed by deleted 'such'
113.5	hic] 'h' and 'c' written over two unreadable letters
113.6	praedictiones,] followed by one unreadable several letter deletion
113.13	Sure] followed by deleted 'that'
113.14	Holy Angels] preceded by deleted 'Good A'
113.18	has] followed by two unreadable several letter deletions
113.20	But] 'B' altered from 'I'
114.4	that,] followed by one unreadable two letter deletion
114.4	as] followed by one unreadable two letter deletion
114.6	On,] 'n' followed by unattached, deleted 'e' which suggests that the comma was added after the 'e' was deleted
114.17-18	(who is now, My Son, Your Eldest Sister,)] originally deleted in the manuscript
115.11	preached] followed by deleted 'on'
115.25	many whole Dayes] 'whole Dayes': interlined with a caret misplaced after a comma following 'many'
116.17	Soul] preceded by deleted doubtful 'H'
117.2	Paradise] interlined above deleted 'Kingdome' and preceded above deleted 'Kingdome' by one unreadable several letter deletion
117.11	That] followed by deleted 'all'
117.20	Things] followed by deleted 'most un'
117.23	Wofully] 'W' written over an unreadable letter
118.3	Dedicated] 'c' written over 'd'
119.3	Doing of] followed by deleted 'Some'
119.7	with] interlined with a caret above deleted 'unto'

119.12	hereof] followed by deleted 'proceded and'
119.12	into] 'i' written over 'u'
119.12	an uncommon Satisfaction] preceded by deleted 'what was Little [ ] of [ ]'
120.20	Marvellous] preceded by deleted 'Wonder'
120.21	the Lord] interlined above deleted 'HIM'
120.24	become] preceded by deleted 'Engage to'
120.26	one] interlined with a caret above deleted 'a'
120.27	more] interlined with a caret
121.1	Singular] 'S' altered from 'I'
121.5	That] 'T' altered from doubtful 'R'
122.2	But] 'B' altered from 'A'
122.6-7	the Properties,] 'the': interlined with a caret
122.21	in the Company of] interlined with a caret above deleted 'together with'
122.25	Sacred] originally deleted in the manuscript
122.27	Agency,] followed by deleted 'about'
123.23	me] interlined with a caret
124.8	But] 'B' altered from doubtful 'T'
124.25	Ready] 'R' altered from 'r'
125.5	of] 'o' altered from 'a' and 'f' altered from 'r'
125.18	man.] followed by deleted 'So I'
126.8	my own] 'own': preceded by deleted 'own'
126.16	out,] followed by deleted 'My Son'
126.16	to give] followed by deleted 'to give'
126.17	Such] interlined above deleted 'these'
128.8	Entitled] originally misspelled 'Etitiled' by Mather; corrected by him to 'Entitled' by writing 'n' over first 'ti'

128.22   That]   followed by deleted 'n'

128.25   Now]   'N' written over 'n'

129.3   there]   originally deleted in the manuscript

129.4-6   That Something should . . . coming of ye Lord]   interlined
           between and below two unreadable deleted lines

129.12   them,]   'm' written over 'ir'; followed by deleted 'charge'

129.14   which]   'w' written over 'I'

129.17   My]   'M' altered from 'y'

129.26   Say,]   followed by deleted 'I watched'

130.7   that]   preceded by deleted 'what'

130.11   Seasonably]   'y' altered from doubtful 'e'

130.23   y^e]   'y' preceded by attached, deleted 'm'

131.1   you]   'u' followed by attached, deleted 'r'

131.8   Designs]   'D' altered from 'd'

131.13   y^e]   followed by one several letter unreadable deletion

131.14   me]   interlined with a caret

131.22   now]   'n' altered from 'm'

131.22   Demand]   'D' altered from 'd'

131.23   Glorify]   followed by deleted 'Him'

131.28-132.1   and my Violation of Sin;]   written in right-hand margin;
               position in text indicated with a caret

132.7   Time]   'T' written over 't'

132.18   Son]   followed by deleted 'Son'

132.18   I]   altered from doubtful 'T'

132.20   uncapable]   'u' either smudged or written over an unreadable
           letter

133.3   a few]   interlined above deleted 'and ackno'

133.3   Passages,]   followed by deleted 'for Your'

133.14-15 Untolerable]   'U' written over an unreadable letter

135.17   will]   followed by deleted 'no'

137.4   Entred]   'E' altered from doubtful 'n'

137.11   as]   interlined with a caret

137.13   Sing,]   followed by deleted 'ye f'

138.7   Kind]   'K' altered from 'H'

138.14-139.7   In this Year, I oftentimes had my Mind Strangely Irradiated
                in my . . . next year of my life.]   originally deleted
                in the manuscript

139.8   On]   written over 'For'

139.8   that year,]   originally deleted in the manuscript

140.21   for]   'f' altered from 'y'

141.2   will]   followed by deleted 'here'

141.8   as]   followed by deleted 'pur'

141.9   Carry]   'C' altered from 'f'

141.13   You]   'Yo' written over 'mu', the 'u' of 'mu' appearing
                to be the top-half of a 'y'

141.14   Experiences]   'i' followed by attached, deleted 'n'

142.9   this]   'th' altered from 'in'

142.17-18   of Roses in Milk, which totally & forever delivered me.]
                written in right-hand margin;   position in text indi-
                cated with a caret

142.21   or perhaps with Chariots or with Coaches.]   written in
                right-hand margin;   position in text indicated with
                a caret

142.22   is,]   'is' written over 'A'

142.27   Mean]   'M' altered from doubtful 'F'

142.27   Journey,]   followed by two unreadable deleted letters

143.1   and]   followed by deleted 'This one'

143.2-10   My Cloak being Somewhat so Old . . . could not but Raise
                in my mind some Reflections.]   originally deleted in
                the manuscript

143.11	But these] preceded by deleted 'It was'
143.14	therein] interlined with a caret
143.16	contrary] interlined with a caret
143.23	Dead,] followed by deleted 'so suddenly'
144.26	begin to] interlined with a caret
145.9	more than] interlined with a caret
145.10	County;] followed by two unreadable deleted letters
146.8	Son,] followed by two unreadable deleted letters
147.26	obligations,] followed by deleted 'wh'
148.25	me] 'm' either smudged or written over an unreadable letter
148.28-149.1	upon France, and upon Great Britain] originally deleted in the manuscript
149.1-3	It will be so . . . for this glorious Matter.] originally deleted in the manuscript
149.8	this] followed by deleted 'world'
149.11	My Son,] followed by deleted 'I ha'
150.1	prostrate] 's' preceded by deleted 's'
150.6-8	And I Successfully Renewed my Cries . . . with a mighty Revolution.] originally deleted in the manuscript
150.24	Among] preceded by deleted 'One m'
151.4	very] interlined with a caret
151.12	passage,] followed by deleted 'w^{ch}'
151.26-152.2	It was then told unto me . . . and Glorified over the whole world with very marvellous Dispensations.] originally deleted in the manuscript
152.8-153.5	§ And now my Hand is in . . . that should be the Astonishment of the World.] originally deleted in the manuscript
153.18	USE] 'SE' written over 'se'
155.1	In] 'I' written over 'O'

155.11	Day] 'D' written over 'd'
155.18	first] interlined with a caret
155.18	Seven] followed by deleted 'fir'
157.1	The SECOND Part.] written below twice written and twice deleted 'The Eighth Lustre.'
157.4	Your] followed by deleted 'par'
157.7	Larger] interlined with a caret
157.9	of it.] followed by five unreadable deleted lines
157.15	Time,] followed by deleted 'should'
157.15	Coming] originally written 'Come'; 'e' subsequently deleted and 'ing' interlined with a caret above it
157.17	to be] followed by several unreadable deleted words
157.20	until] followed by deleted 'this many'
157.20	after Seven Lustres] 'after Seven': written in right-hand margin level with 'Lustres'
157.20-21	Life were Expired] 'were Expired': interlined with a caret misplaced after a comma following 'Life'
157.21	bestow'd] followed by deleted 'You'
157.21	upon] 'u' either smudged or written over an unreadable letter
157.21	unto an Age] interlined with a caret
157.23	he was] interlined with a caret above deleted 'You were'
157.24	my Consort,] interlined with a caret above deleted 'Your Excellent Mother'
157.25	A Son] followed by deleted 'You'
158.1	before;] followed by deleted 'your birth'; semi-colon added after and slightly below 'before'
158.1	and, in] 'in': interlined with a caret
158.2	kept,] followed by deleted 'for You'; comma added after and slightly below 'kept'
158.3	Meditation] preceded by deleted 'Discourse'

158.4   delivered,]   followed by deleted 'She'

158.8   midnight,)]   followed by three unreadable deleted words

158.8   Day]   followed by deleted 'Esuing'

158.12   Arise]   'Ar' written over 'R'

158.18   me!]   followed by six unreadable deleted lines

158.25   It may not be amiss for You to Remember That.]   originally
             deleted in the manuscript

158.26   One Son who]   'Son': interlined above 'who'; 'who':
             'o' followed by attached, deleted 'se'

159.3   Passages yett Unmentioned,]   'yett Unmentioned': inter-
             lined with a caret misplaced after a comma following
             'Passages'

159.4-5   are occurring]   interlined above several unreadable
             deleted words

159.5   that]   'a' altered from 'e'

159.5   part]   followed by deleted 'Lustre'

159.5   which is]   interlined with a caret

159.5   running;]   followed by one and one-half unreadable deleted
             lines

159.8   will]   interlined above deleted 'may'

159.11   in]   either smudged or written over 'an'

159.17   from an]   'an': interlined with a caret

159.22   SELF-EXAMINATION]   'X' altered from 'A'

160.2   Dispensations,]   followed by deleted 'towards'

160.8   Now]   'N' altered from 'S'

160.10   In]   followed by deleted doubtful 'N'

160.12   Exceedingly]   interlined with a caret

160.13   myself]   followed by deleted 'be'

160.13   Lest the]   'the': 't' written over 'I'

160.15   that the]   followed by two unreadable deleted letters

160.18   presence of]   followed by deleted 'God'

160.24   must]   followed by deleted 'make'

160.24   Sins in]   'in': interlined with a caret above deleted
          'of'

161.2   my Dying,]   'my': interlined with a caret

161.9   What]   'W' written over 'T'

161.15   Two]   'T' altered from 't'

162.8   within]   'w' altered from 'in'

163.6   not only]   interlined with a caret

163.6   Converse with]   followed by deleted 'Go'

163.7   Sacrifice and]   interlined with a caret

163.10   would]   written in right-hand margin level with deleted
          'is' which appears inside the margin

163.19   Agreeable]   'A' altered from 'T'

163.22   Birth-day,]   followed by deleted 'John'

163.23-24 Another time . . . this Year also.]   interlined above
          following paragraph

164.1-2   Another time . . . this Day.]   written in right-hand
          margin; position in text indicated with a double
          caret

164.13-16 Once I made my . . . unhappy Story.]   written in right-
          hand margin; position in text indicated with a triple
          caret

164.19   a Glorious]   interlined with a caret

164.23   thy]   preceded by deleted 'my'

165.4   yᵉ Repetitions of]   interlined with a caret above deleted
          'an'

165.8   wherein]   'er' written over 'ich'

166.8   When I]   followed by deleted 'Speak'

166.14   Aggravate]   'A' written over 'a'

167.25-26 withdrawn from a Lodging agreeable Enough with me;]
          interlined above one unreadable deleted line

170.7   Absolute]   'A' altered from 'a'

170.8   not under]   preceded by deleted 'un'

170.14   of oᵉ]   followed by deleted 'Lord JESUS CHRIST!'

170.14   GOD]   'OD' altered from 'od'

172.21   Glorify]   followed by deleted 'the'

172.26   [The Title of a Book, which I have published]]   written
         in right-hand margin; position in text indicated with
         a star

173.14   Young]   preceded by deleted 'Gracious'

174.3   to be]   followed by deleted doubtful 'no'

174.7   A Work]   'A' altered from 'a'

174.24   often]   followed by two unreadable deleted words

174.24   Recited]   'i' written over 'd'

174.24   New]   preceded by deleted 'an'

175.27   ONE]   'NE' written over 'ne'

177.25   to me,]   followed by deleted 'to'

178.7   home]   interlined with a caret above deleted 'in'

178.19   I had]   followed by deleted 'some'

178.20   to Spend]   'to': interlined above deleted 'of';
         'Spend': 'd' followed by attached, deleted 'ing'

178.26   Devotion,]   followed by deleted 'to'

178.26   which]   followed by deleted 'all the'

179.21   Astonishing]   preceded by one unreadable several letter
         deletion

180.8   for these]   followed by deleted 'Extreme'

180.11   That,]   followed by deleted doubtful 'I was'

180.11-12   as much]   interlined with a caret

180.17   I have]   followed by deleted 'Re'

181.6   Prayers]   'P' written over 'p'

181.10   Lord,]   interlined above deleted 'That'

181.15   I will]   followed by one unreadable several letter
              deletion

181.19   would]   preceded by deleted 'will'

182.15   pleasure,]   followed by deleted 'in'

182.21   Charitable]   second 'a' written over 'y'

182.23   person]   interlined with a caret above deleted 'minister'

182.25   Panegyrical]   interlined with a caret above an unreadable
              deleted word

183.1   It ran thus,]   followed by one unreadable several letter
              deletion

183.25   Addition]   interlined with a caret above deleted 'Perfected
              Occasion'

183.26   For]   'F' altered from 'f'

184.9   inexpressibly]   followed by deleted 'Graf'

184.18   mind]   followed by deleted 'had'

184.22   Mercy,]   'c' written over doubtful 's'

185.10   my Son,]   followed by deleted 'for his Instruction'

186.10   people in]   followed by deleted doubtful 'y^e'

186.14   Gentleman]   'a' written over 'e'

186.15   Money,]   followed by deleted 'wh'

187.5   men]   'e' written over 'a'

187.9   for to]   'for': interlined with a caret

187.13   Talk]   'T' altered from 't'

187.26   & such,]   followed by deleted 'matters'

187.28   Creature,]   followed by deleted 'have'

188.7   Men]   followed by deleted 'upon'

188.10-19   Yea, My Spirit . . . they after be any Guardeins to.]
              written in right-hand margin; position in text indicated
              with a triple caret

188.12	what a]	followed by deleted 'Fr'
189.6	Good, as]	followed by deleted 'a'
189.20	Wrong]	followed by deleted 'th'
189.22	my]	interlined above deleted 'by'
190.20	Satan]	followed by deleted 'to'
191.1	how]	'h' altered from 'I'
191.25	Interest,]	followed by deleted 'than'
192.17	Witness, of]	followed by deleted 'what I am going'
192.17	almost]	'm' altered from a second, incorrect 'l'
193.25	Shining]	'S' altered from 's'
194.14	me in an]	interlined with a caret above deleted 'my'
195.14	Show]	'S' altered from 's'
196.18	me]	interlined with a caret
198.14	Taking]	'T' altered from doubtful 't'
198.26	Life,]	followed by deleted 'had'
199.2	these	followed by deleted 'm'
199.4	one way]	followed by deleted (of devising'
199.4	Good,]	second 'o' written over initial, incorrect 'd'
199.6	Several times,]	interlined with a caret
199.8	I have]	followed by deleted 'Sent'
199.9	abroad,]	interlined with a caret
199.9	abroad, in]	followed by deleted 'as'
199.12	Directed]	'D' altered from doubtful 'd'
199.15	Visit them,]	originally deleted in the manuscript
199.16	Names,]	followed by deleted 'upon'
199.19	Awaken]	'A' altered from 'a'
199.21	copied]	interlined above deleted 'written'
200.1	in very]	'in': interlined with a caret

200.1   circumstances, both on Temporal and Spiritual Accounts,]
               interlined with a caret above deleted 'and not so very
               Good'

200.18   many,]   followed by deleted 'Ye'

200.20   Heart]   followed by deleted 'perpetually'

200.21   with]   interlined with a caret above deleted 'with'

200.21   perpetual]   'l' followed by attached, deleted 'ly'

202.7   Real]   interlined with a caret

202.8   went]   'w' written over 'h'

202.9   under]   followed by deleted 'a'

202.11   y^e]   preceded by attached, deleted 'm'

202.24   Not]   preceded by deleted doubtful 'To'

203.2   I must]   preceded by deleted 'My Mi'

203.6   Throne of]   followed by deleted 'God'

203.10   Meditations]   'a' followed by deleted 'ta'

203.22   Some]   'S' altered from 's'

203.22   of a]   followed by deleted 'precious'

203.28   may]   followed by deleted 'come unto'

204.28   I sett]   followed by deleted 'ge'

205.9   See]   followed by deleted 'of'

205.25   See]   interlined with a caret above deleted 'Look upon'

206.3   Lord,]   preceded by deleted 'Lord'; followed by one un-
               readable several letter deletion

206.8   myself]   followed by deleted 'brought [ ]'

206.28   Pay to]   followed by deleted 'any'

207.5-16   I will add . . . ye most killing Sight in ye world.]
               written in right-hand margin; position in text indicated
               with a triple caret

208.2   Sick,]   followed by deleted doubtful 'on'

208.10   His]   interlined with a caret

208.13 with as] 'as': written over two unreadable letters

208.14 as I] 'as': written over two unreadable letters

208.22 they may] preceded by deleted 'know Him & love Him'

209.22 Circumstanced] interlined with a caret

210.5 who was] followed by deleted 'Cutt'

214.5 Sovereign] 'g' written over an 'n' which preceded final 'n'

214.8 of Meat] 'of': interlined with a caret

214.17 myself] followed by deleted doubtful 'mo'

214.17 Worthy] 'W' altered from 'w'

215.23 Judgments] 't' written over an 's' which preceded final 's'

215.25 What have] 'have': 'h' altered from 'I'

216.3 Lothsome] interlined above deleted 'not Gratful'

216.3 Bitter] 'itter' either smudged or written over several unreadable letters

216.7 I have] 'I': altered from doubtful 'B'

216.7 one] interlined with a caret

216.8 in the world.] interlined with a caret

216.9 and with Some contempt.] written in right-hand margin; position in text indicated with a caret below an interlined unreadable several word deletion

216.13 When in] 'in': interlined with a caret

217.2 Grievous] interlined above deleted 'Bitter'

217.10 actually] first 'a' altered from 'f'

217.11 unto you,] followed by deleted 'you'

217.11 My] 'M' written over 'm'

217.16-17 with all possible Sincerity,] interlined with a caret

217.22 come into] followed by deleted doubtful 'an'

217.26 Wanting to] followed by deleted 'that [ ] Your'

217.26   to that]   'that': first 't' written over an unreadable
          letter

217.26   Education, and]   interlined with a caret

218.1-2   Method, which]   followed by one unreadable deleted line

218.4   You may,]   followed by deleted 'Cir'

218.8   and into]   followed by deleted 'as various'

218.18-19 I may]   'may': preceded by deleted 'wi'

218.25   into]   written in right-hand margin level with deleted
          'under'

218.27   most]   followed by deleted 'prop'

219.1   Public]   originally deleted in the manuscript

219.2-4   I considered . . . And,]   written in right-hand margin;
          position in text indicated with a caret

219.3   Sermons, to]   followed by deleted 'as'

219.5   Things]   interlined above deleted 'Subjects'

219.5   might]   interlined with a caret

219.6   and I]   followed by deleted 'ac-'

219.6   I considered]   followed by deleted 'What [ ] '

219.7   Public]   interlined with a caret

219.9   I might]   followed by two unreadable several letter deletions

219.10-11 Particularly . . . I considered,]   written in right-hand
          margin; position in text indicated with a caret

219.11   considered,]   followed by deleted 'And'

219.16   things as]   'as': interlined with a caret

220.5   asked]   interlined above deleted 'prayed'

220.10   Sleep]   'Slee' written over 'Rise'

220.11   have been]   interlined above deleted 'were'

220.14   as I]   followed by deleted 'then'

220.17   Declared]   interlined with a caret

220.18	Some of] interlined with a caret
220.22	own] interlined with a caret
220.24	have] interlined with a caret above deleted 'here'
220.25	Useful] 'U' altered from 'A'
220.26	on me] 'on': 'n' written over 'm'
221.2	thereof.] double caret smudged away following period (see below, 221.3-7)
221.3	have been] interlined with a caret above deleted 'were'
221.3-7	Yea, as a Sort of Crumbs . . . Every week paying the Mistress her wages.] written in right-hand margin; position in text indicated with a clear double caret
221.3	Sort of] followed by deleted 'an'
221.6	myself] 'self' interlined below four unreadable deleted letters
221.6	Whole] followed by one unreadable several letter deletion
221.11	of them;] followed by deleted 'Extending'
221.12	With] 'W' altered from 'B'
221.14	that every] followed by deleted 'We other'
221.15	or, Wherein] 'or,': written in right-hand margin level with 'Wherein'
221.23	Catalogue. I] followed by deleted doubtful 'went'
221.25	One] altered from 'Now'
222.2	should] 's' altered from 'I'
222.7-9	When such an occasion for it has occurr'd . . . as for my Relatives.] written in right-hand margin; position in text indicated with a caret
222.9	Relatives.] followed by deleted 'Every other Week'
222.9	have] interlined with a caret
222.20	have] interlined with a caret
222.22	could] interlined with a caret above deleted 'can'
222.23	Good, I have] 'have': interlined with a caret

222.23   I have done it so] 'I': written over one unreadable letter; 'have': written in right-hand margin level with 'done'; 'it': interlined with a caret

222.23   so, that] 'that': interlined with a caret

222.24   comes.] 'o' written over 'a'

222.25   I hope,] preceded by deleted 'A'

222.26   done me] followed by deleted 'any'

222.27-28   and I have . . . my Thoughts upon it.] written in right-hand margin; position in text indicated with a caret

222.27   I have] followed by deleted doubtful '&'

222.28   there may] followed by one unreadable several letter deletion

223.2   and y^e] followed by deleted '[　] Interests'

223.3   of Religion] followed by deleted 'of Relig'

223.7   distant] second 't' written over doubtful 'c'

223.8-9   I have . . . the main Design] written in right-hand margin; position in text indicated with a caret

223.9   general] interlined above deleted 'Conversion'

223.13-14   to which I am under some Special obligation] interlined with a caret

223.18   upon] 'up' written over 'my'

223.22   Services. I] 'I': followed by doubtfully attached, deleted 'n'

223.22   I have] followed by deleted 'written'

223.22-23   Extant] interlined with a caret

223.26   tis this;] interlined above deleted 'I am Related unto'

223.27   Related?] 'R' altered from 'r'

224.1   above] interlined above deleted 'more'

224.7   or, Societies] followed by deleted 'to'

224.7   for ye Suppression] 'for y^e': written in right-hand margin level with 'Suppression'

224.7   Suppression]   'on' written over 'di'; followed by deleted
                   'sorders.'

224.12   Encouragement.]   followed by one unreadable several letter
                   deletion

224.13   with due pauses,]   interlined with a caret above deleted
                   'often in'

224.14   any]   'a' altered from 'E'

225.12   any]   followed by deleted 'thing'

225.12   humbly]   'y' written over doubtful 'e'

225.22   used,]   followed by one several letter unreadable deletion

225.27   for]   followed by deleted 'for'

226.5   Question . . . Illustration.]   written in right-hand margin;
                   position in text indicated with a double caret

226.17   under]   interlined with a caret

226.20   have]   interlined with a caret

226.22   My Son,]   followed by deleted 'Take only this Thought'

227.5   ordinarily]   interlined with a caret

227.14   For]   interlined with a caret

227.19   of God,]   followed by deleted 'most contrary to my'

228.18-229.2   I conclude . . . this Lamentation.]   written in right-hand
                   margin; position in text indicated with a triple caret

229.19   GOD]   'OD' written over 'od'

230.6   Memorials,]   'M' altered from 'P'

230.14   Adapt]   preceded by deleted 'Sett'

230.18   Hope]   'H' written over 'i' and followed by attached,
                   deleted 'ng'

230.18   come at]   followed by deleted 'my Neighbour'

230.22   To Conclude]   preceded by two unreadable several letter
                   deletions

230.26   such a]   interlined above deleted 'this'

231.14   Spiritual]   followed by deleted doubtful 'Main'

231.15   partakers] either smudged or altered from an unreadable word

231.23   Made,]   'M' written over 'm'

233.11   many] followed by deleted 'of the'

233.12   you, what]   followed by deleted 'op'

233.15-16   answering,]   followed by deleted 'y^e'

233.18   it for] 'for': 'or' written over doubtful 'ro' and followed by deleted doubtful 'm'

233.23   I would]   followed by deleted 'use'

233.24   Soul]   preceded by deleted 'Soul'

234.18-21   I Receive? presents . . . this Favour of His Encourage me?] originally deleted in the manuscript

234.27   Especially,]   'E' altered from 'I'

235.5-8   When I mend my Fire . . . passing upon me!]   written in right-hand margin; position in text indicated with a caret

235.7   Zeal,] followed by deleted 'bu'

235.18-19   Agreeable] interlined with a caret

236.1   an occasion] 'an': interlined with a caret above deleted 'the'

236.14   Dignities,]   'D' altered from 'd'

236.15   Thoughts] interlined with a caret above deleted 'Those'

236.25   ye Coach,]   interlined with a caret

237.13   And] 'A' written over 'a'

237.27-238.1   Yea, when I do . . . Superfluity of Naughtiness.]   written in right-hand margin; position in text indicated with a double caret

238.3   more] followed by deleted 'more'

238.11   increase] 'eas' written over 'es'

239.16   attended me.] followed by two unreadable deleted lines

239.22-26	When I am called . . . for that also.] written in right-hand margin; position in text indicated with a triple caret
239.27-240.3	Here is a great Point . . . for thy Goodness.] originally deleted in the manuscript
240.19-20	Reason in us, is ye Work of GOD; A Ray from GOD:] written in right-hand margin; position in text indicated with a caret
241.4	would immediately] preceded by deleted 'immediat'
241.22	Ere] 'E' written over 'a'
242.4	Love] written in right-hand margin level with deleted 'Charity'
242.4	Vital] followed by deleted 'Stroke'
242.14	up] 'u' altered from 'm'
242.21	His] preceded by deleted 'the'
242.27	Liesure] 'i' written over 'e'
243.1	of God] followed by deleted 'of God'
243.7	Resolution] followed by deleted 'whi'
243.8	I will] followed by deleted 'often'
245.6	I have] followed by deleted 'done it'
245.7	pressed after] followed by deleted 'y^e'
245.13	Sufferings] followed by deleted 'of'
245.26	And] written over 'But'
245.26	Seasons] 'S' written over 'T'
245.27	also] interlined with a caret
246.2	Sun] 'S' written over 'R'
246.24	For the] 'the': 't' altered from doubtful 'A'
246.25	a Joyful] 'a': followed by deleted 'n'; 'Joyful': interlined with a caret above deleted 'Happy'
247.2	all] 'a' altered from doubtful 'f'
247.7	Father:] followed by deleted 'so'

247.8   & in] 'in': interlined with a caret above deleted
              'from'

247.18   I awoke, blessing yᵉ Lord for another Lords-day; and]
              interlined with a caret

247.18   Morning, I]   followed by deleted doubtful 'rise'

247.19   arose]   'aro' altered from 'ri'

248.20   Food]   followed by deleted comma

249.1   to be]   'be': written over 'H'

249.8   with an]   followed by deleted 'Ea'

249.17   Spoken]   'e' written over a second, incorrect 'k'

249.22   Entertain]   'Enter' either smudged or written over un-
              readable letters

250.14   & my]   followed by deleted 'Returning'

250.26   Then I Caused]   preceded by deleted 'I also cau'

251.1   ordered]   followed by one unreadable several letter de-
              letion

251.19   into]   'to' interlined with a caret

252.3-4   But renounce all pretence to Merit in my own Performances.]
              interlined between preceding and following sentences

252.9   from such]   followed by deleted 'Indefatigable'

252.20   If]   'I' written over 'i'

254.17   him]   'h' written over 'm'

254.23   than all]   followed by deleted 'the'

254.23   Inflamed]   'I' written over doubtful 'i'

255.14   Leaving]   'v' altered from doubtful 'd'

255.23   List]   followed by deleted 'Sa [ ]'

256.3   Possession]   'P' altered from 'D'

256.18   Enduring]   preceded by deleted 'Suffering'

257.9   & I]   'I': written over 'h'

257.17   were to]   preceded by deleted 'would'

257.18-23	Yea, I may truly say . . . He has thus made a Sacrificer!] written in right-hand margin; position in text indicated with a double caret
257.27	My] 'M' written over 'm'
258.17-20	When I have been preferring yᵉ Will of GOD . . . there shall be real occasion for it!] written in right-hand margin; position in text indicated with a caret
258.24	made me so] followed by one unreadable several letter deletion
258.25	If He would] 'would': 'w' written over doubtful 'c'
259.3	be none] followed by deleted 'Com'
259.8	mention one] followed by deleted 'hereof'
259.8-11	When any thing befalls me . . . am I now to offer my Sacrifice?] written in right-hand margin; position in text indicated with a double caret
259.10	Second,] preceded by deleted 'Se-'
259.13	Initiated] 'nit' written over several unreadable letters
259.15	from all] followed by deleted 'His [ ]'
259.26	Sacrificed] followed by deleted 'by'
260.5	have a] followed by deleted 'Suffic'
260.7	or, Attracted by Matter.] written in right-hand margin; position in text indicated with a caret
260.27	Power] interlined with a caret above deleted 'Weight'; preceded by one unreadable deleted word which is also interlined above deleted 'Weight'
261.12	desired] interlined with a caret above deleted 'wanted'
261.12	to press] 'to': interlined with a caret
262.13	be rescued] preceded by deleted doubtful 'not'
262.16	and the] followed by deleted ' [ ] B'
262.18	Entertain the] 'the': interlined with a caret
262.19	Herewithal,] interlined with a caret
262.21	Secondly;] preceded by deleted 'H'

262.22   may be]   followed by deleted 'Glor'

262.22-23   He sees, I]   'He sees,': written in right-hand margin
              level with 'I'

263.3   me be]   'be': interlined with a caret

263.5   and an Happy one.]   originally deleted in the manuscript

263.5   And now,]   interlined above deleted 'and an Happy one.'

263.5   No Events]   preceded by deleted 'Yea,'; followed by de-
              leted 'now'

263.6-8   The Cure of what I feel . . . these are now cured.]   writ-
              ten in right-hand margin; position in text indicated
              with a caret

263.10   my]   'm' written over 'th'

263.25   so fast]   followed by deleted 'is'

263.25   Heaven]   followed by deleted 'des'

263.27   Soul,]   followed by deleted 'I [   ]'

264.3   Methods]   't' written over 'd'

264.8   Me]   'M' altered from 'th'

264.10   observable]   interlined with a caret

264.15   Soul into]   followed by deleted 'the'

264.23   Griefs]   'G' altered from 'g'

264.23   Disposition to]   followed by one unreadable several letter
              deletion

264.27   For the Cure of]   followed by one unreadable deleted line

264.28   Behold]   'B' written over 'b'

265.20   I have]   followed by deleted 'so'

265.21   the Grace]   'the': interlined with a caret

265.25   would]   followed by deleted 'to'

265.27   Procure]   followed by deleted 'to Thee'

267.1   Mind, I]   followed by deleted 'th'

267.3   And now,]   followed by deleted 'as'

268.8	in His] preceded by deleted 'in'
268.21	Affectum] 'A' written over 'a'
268.21	upon a] followed by deleted 'Text of'
269.2	I have] followed by deleted doubtful 'learned'
269.2	have had] 'had': 'h' written over 'a'
269.3	taken a] followed by two or three unreadable deleted words
269.4	Above] 'A' written over 'a'
269.7	Essays to] followed by deleted 'utter ye Language'
269.11	have been Studious] 'have': interlined with a caret
270.13	also] interlined with a caret
270.24	with his] 'his': 'h' written over 'I'
271.1	Beholding] 'B' written over an unreadable letter
271.7	Men?] followed by deleted 'Thy S'
271.17	My] preceded by deleted 'By'
271.21	departed.] followed by deleted 'I have'
271.24	Prayer for] followed by deleted 'y^e'
272.27	unto me] followed by deleted 'unto me'
273.4	Blood] followed by deleted 'wa'
273.8	That it] 'it': interlined with a caret
273.10	That I] followed by deleted doubtful 'was'
273.11	Forgive] 'i' written over 'a'
273.12	Oh! That] followed by deleted 'I would Render Expressly'
273.13	Father, as] followed by deleted 'my'
273.21	He] interlined with a caret
273.22	those] preceded by deleted 'wh'
274.12	Remembers all] followed by deleted 'He once Dictated.'
274.20	As far] preceded by deleted 'In as'

274.20	so far] followed by deleted 'as'
274.25	behold] interlined with a caret above deleted 'Consider'
275.4	GOD, their] followed by deleted 'Impression'
275.8	and my] followed by deleted 'D'
275.25-276.4	'My dear SAVIOUR . . . of whatever Man they ascribe any Grandents to.] originally deleted in the manuscript
276.22	it, and] 'and': interlined above deleted 'as'
277.7	so far] followed by deleted 'as'
278.2	Continually;] followed by one unreadable several letter deletion
278.11	this Life] followed by deleted doubtful 'commend'
278.12	you,] followed by one unreadable several letter deletion
278.15	Circumstances] followed by deleted 'of my'
279.13-14	and with many Repeted Acts] interlined with a caret
279.16	Upon] followed by deleted 'Every'
279.19	make Choice of] one unreadable several letter deletion interlined above 'Choice of'
279.23	That] followed by deleted 'it'
280.6	for all] 'all': interlined with a caret
281.11	Evil, and] followed by deleted 'Repel'
281.14	treat with] followed by deleted 'an [ ]'
281.18	under a] followed by deleted 'Dedication'
281.23	more] followed by deleted 'cons'
282.17	Because] 'B' written over 'b'
282.20	Heart into] followed by deleted 'the'
282.26	And,] followed by deleted 'And'
283.3	thy Love] followed by deleted 'unto me'
283.20	I have] 'I': preceded by deleted caret; 'have': interlined with a caret

284.6   have]   interlined with a caret

284.7   aim'd at]   followed by deleted 'This'

284.17   Concern,]   followed by deleted 'for'

284.17   That I]   'I': interlined with a caret

284.19   Vigour]   'V' altered from 'v'

284.20   mighty]   interlined with a caret above deleted 'Great'

284.23-25   and Beholding . . . this Blessed Mediator:]   written in
             right-hand margin; position in text indicated with a
             caret

284.27   of Him]   originally deleted in the manuscript

285.2   Many]   'M' altered from 'm'

285.7   I then]   preceded by deleted doubtful 'H'

285.8   come down]   followed by deleted 'in'

285.10   Thoughts, on]   followed by deleted 'the Ben'

285.10   My]   'M' written over 'm'

285.11   Maxims,]   followed by deleted 'His'

285.18   withal.]   followed by two unreadable deleted paragraphs
             which are written in the right-hand margin and for
             which a position in the text is indicated by a deleted
             triple caret

285.24   thus]   followed by deleted 'made'

286.14   unto]   'un' interlined with a caret

286.15   Unseen by]   'by': written over 'to'

286.15-16   to Flesh]   'to': interlined with a caret

286.19   upon it.]   followed by deleted 'My Son [ ] with Wonder-
             ful Things.'

286.21   Matter,]   followed by deleted 'in'

286.27   Provision for]   followed by deleted 'y^e'

287.10   What]   'W' altered from 't'

287.22   Well of it]   interlined with a caret above deleted
             'Happy'

287.23   on all occasions,]   originally deleted in the manuscript

288.21   no,]   'o' followed by attached, deleted 'r'

288.24   And] 'A' altered from 'a'

289.14   find] interlined above deleted 'wish'

289.21   Loss] followed by deleted 'abundantly'

290.2   Most] 'M' altered from 'm'

291.16   Qualities] preceded by deleted 'For the Delights of This World & such Delights [ ]'

291.25   Properties I] followed by deleted 'discer'

291.26   Relish of] followed by deleted doubtful 'of Him'

292.13   in the World] 'the': 't' written over 'y'

293.2   doing,] followed by deleted 'of'

293.5   Flights to] 'to': 't' preceded by attached, deleted 'un'

293.7   I find] 'I': written over 'f'

293.25   asleep] 'p' either smudged or written over one unreadable letter

293.26   Prayers] 'yers' altered from 'ises'

294.22   I feel] 'I': written over 'f'

295.6   Grace] followed by deleted 'to'

295.10   indeed] interlined with a caret

295.16   the rest] 'the': 'e' followed by attached, deleted 'se'

295.22   Heart-breaking] followed by two or three unreadable deleted words

297.7   what they] 'they': 'th' written over 'w'

298.17   all the] followed by deleted 'Designs of'

APPENDIX F

WORD-DIVISION

I. End-of-the-Line Hyphenation in the Present Edition

Note: No hyphenation of a possible compound at the end of a line in the present text is present in the manuscript except for the following readings, which are hyphenated within the line in the manuscript.

10.13	Lords-/day
82.28	Free-/Grace
118.9	Lord-/Redeemer
193.3	olive-/plants
257.25	Heart-/melting

II. End-of-the-Line Hyphenation in the Manuscript

Note: The following compounds, or possible compounds, are hyphenated at the end of the line in the manuscript copy-text. The form in which they have been transcribed in the present edition, as listed below, represents the practice of the manuscript as ascertained by other appearances or by parallels within the manuscript.

6.14	astray	33.11	Morning-Thoughts
7.12	Church-History	40.2	THANKSGIVING
9.9	Loathsome	44.21	thereby
10.10	Sunrise	86.7	Common-place Heads
12.9	Self-Examination	87.19	Study-floor
12.11	Self-Examination	88.10	Loving-kindness
15.8	Betimes	91.1	THANKSGIVING
26.27	betimes	101.5	Gentlemen

114.5	Gravestones	158.2	Evening-Prayers
116.9	Study-floor	161.21	aforehand
116.11	Heart-melting	186.14	Gentleman
119.16	Loathsome	219.10	Charity-Schools
120.9	undervaluing	231.3	Long-suffering
125.17	Extraordinary	243.21	Winter-Piety
126.15	THNAKSGIVING	253.20	Thank-Offering
126.21	THANKSGIVINGS	259.24	Heart-Strings
149.5	Lords-Table	288.9	Ever-Blessed
157.28	off-spring		

III. Special Cases

(a)

Note: In the following list the compound, or possible compound, is hyphenated at the end of the line in the manuscript and in the present edition.

139.1   over-/turn   (i.e. overturn)

(b)

Note: In the following list the hyphenated compound appears at the end of the line in the present edition, but the hyphen is an editorial emendation not present in the manuscript.

286.26   God-/head   (i.e. God-head for MS Godhead)

Introduction

[1]A complete account of the "Mather Dynasty" with an emphasis on its intellectual attainments is the subject of Robert Middlekauff's The Mathers: Three Generations of Puritan Intellectuals, 1596-1728 (New York: Oxford Univ. Press, 1961).

[2]Cotton Mather, Paterna manuscript, p. 186. Hereafter all references to Paterna will be incorporated in the test by page number(s). All page numbers refer to Mather's own pagination as represented in the manuscript.

[3]Cotton Mather, The Diary of Cotton Mather, ed. Worthington Chauncey Ford, 2 vols. (Boston: Massachusetts Historical Society, 1911-12; rpt. New York: Frederick Ungar Publishing Co., 1957), I, 307. Hereafter all references to this work will be incorporated in the text as Diary followed by the volume and page numbers.

[4]In addition to those scholars identified later in the text, Paterna has been used by the following in their individual considerations of Mather: Sacvan Bercovitch, "Cotton Mather," in Major Writers of Early America, ed. Everett H. Emerson (Madison: Univ. of Wisconsin Press, 1972), pp. 93-149; David Levin, "The Hazing of Cotton Mather: The Creation of a Biographical Personality," in In Defense of Historical Literature: Essays on American History, Autobiography, Drama and Fiction (New York: Hill and Wang, 1967), pp. 34-57; Daniel B. Shea, Jr., "The Mathers," in Spiritual Autobiography in Early America (Princeton: Princeton Univ. Press, 1968), pp. 152-181. Although Shea's treatment of Paterna is the most comprehen-

sive of the studies cited, neither Shea nor Bercovitch or Levin corrects
the important errors concerning the circumstances of Paterna's composition
which have been passed down by scholars whom I later consider.

[5]See Barrett Wendell, Cotton Mather: The Puritan Priest (New York:
Dodd, Mead, and Co., 1891), p. 33, and Thomas James Holmes, Cotton Mather:
A Bibliography of His Works, 3 vols. (Boston, 1940), III, 1306.

[6]See William R. Manierre II, "A Description of 'Paterna': The Unpublished Autobiography of Cotton Mather," Studies in Bibliography, 18
(1965), pp. 189-193.

[7]Cotton Mather, Bonifacius (Boston in New England: B. Green, for
Samuel Gerrish, 1710).

[8]Manierre, "A Description of 'Paterna,'" p. 191.

[9]Cotton Mather, Bonifacius, ed. David Levin (Cambridge: The Belknap
Press of Harvard Univ. Press, 1966), p. 75. Because it is readily avail-
able to most readers, all references to Bonifacius are from this edition.
Hereafter all references to this work will be incorporated in the text as
Bonifacius followed by page number(s).

[10]Cotton Mather, The Diary of Cotton Mather for the Year 1712, ed.
William R. Manierre II (Charlottesville: The Univ. Press of Virginia,
1964), p. 9. Hereafter all references to this work will be incorporated
in the text as 1712 Diary followed by page number(s).

[11]Manierre, "A Description of 'Paterna,'" p. 191.

[12]The evidence that follows for the early date of Paterna's composition is based on the date of Abigail Mather's death. Interestingly, one of the few passages in the first part of Paterna which cannot be dated exactly but which was added some time after the original composition of the first part is the marginal note on page 125. There Mather cautions the reader against placing too much reliance upon "particular faiths." The failure of a particular faith which appears to have most affected Mather is that Abigail would not die (Diary, I, 431, 434, 441, 442). His response to her death indicates his shock at this particular faith's failure: "Has not the Death of my Consort, that most astonishing sting in it; a Miscarriage of a Particular Faith!" (Diary, I, 451). If the particular faith to which Mather refers in the marginal note on page 125 is that which he had concerning Abigail, then the note represents another proof that Mather had substantially finished Paterna's first part before the end of 1702.

[13]Although Abigail's death is attributed to "consumption," she was afflicted with a series of serious ailments for nearly the entire year before she died. During the week of May 25, 1702, Mather enters the following into his Diary: "My dear Consort, this Week . . . after previous Illness, unhappily miscarried of a Son, after being four or five Months with Child . . . She was brought into Languishments of extreme and threatening Sickness." "The next [week]," Mather writes, "made her State, very dangerous and dubious" (Diary, I, 430). Thus, Mather's caution in Paterna, "if she Survive," could be an indication that this section was written during the early months of 1702. However, it could also represent only another example of Mather's keen sense of mortality which is apparent throughout Paterna.

[14]See _Paterna_, "The Seventh Lustre," footnote 54, for another reference to Abigail Mather. This reference is, however, inconclusive for our dating of the manuscript.

[15]This passage must be read in its context in _Paterna_. It should be noted that all references to "Your Mother" were deleted in the manuscript and replaced by "my Consort" sometime after Abigail's death.

[16]Until his death in 1724 Increase, according to Mather's _Diary_, continued to be singularly unreceptive to all his father's pious efforts. By 1721 Mather's patience was exhausted. The final blow to this once promising father-son relationship is revealed in Mather's entry for April 4 of that year: "My miserable, miserable, miserable Son _Increase!_ The Wretch has brought himself under public Trouble and Infamy by bearing a Part in a Night-Riot, with some detestable Rakes in the Town" (_Diary_, II, 611). On April 11 Mather writes that he has decided to cast out this "ungodly, distracted, hard-hearted son": "My miserable son _Increase_, I must cast him and chase him out of my Sight; forbid him to see me, until there appear sensible Marks of Repentance upon him" (_Diary_, II, 612-3). Finally, on April 25, 1721, Cotton Mather relinguished all personal right to the control of Increase's spiritual welfare: "Ah, Poor _Increase_," he writes, "His Grandfather, and his Kinsmen and others, must labour with him" (_Diary_, II, 615).

[17]The _Life of the Very Reverend and Learned Cotton Mather, D. D. & F. R. S._ (Boston, 1729). Samuel made extensive use of _Paterna_ material in this biography. A record of passages from _Paterna_ which appear in Samuel Mather's _Life_ is provided by Manierre, "A Description of 'Paterna,'" pp. 201-3.

[18]Complete bibliographical information on the manuscript, including
a collational formula and a study of watermarks, is provided by Manierre,
"A Description of 'Paterna,'" pp. 194-5.

[19]To date there have been only three extended studies of autobiographical writing in America during the seventeenth and early eighteenth
centuries: Josephine K. Piercy, "Personal Records," in Studies in Literary
Types in Seventeenth Century America (1607-1710) (New Haven: Yale Univ.
Press, 1939), pp. 78-82; Kenneth B. Murdock, "The Personal Literature of
the Puritans," in Literature and Theology in Colonial New England (Cambridge: Harvard Univ. Press, 1949), pp. 93-135; Daniel B. Shea, Jr.,
Spiritual Autobiography in Early America. Unfortunately, none of these
studies extensively considers the motives for autobiographical writing
during the period. For confirmation of my view of the Puritans' motives
for autobiographical writing the reader is directed to the following primary sources which, along with Paterna, clearly exhibit the Puritans'
motives as I outline them: John Winthrop, "Christian Experience," in The
Winthrop Papers, 5 vols. (Boston: Massachusetts Historical Society, 1929),
I, 154-161, and John Winthrop, "Experiencia," in The Winthrop Papers, I,
161-9, 182-215, 235-8, 405, 412-3, II, 103; Thomas Shepard, "My Birth &
Life," Publications of the Colonial Society of Massachusetts, 27 (1932),
pp. 357-392, and Thomas Shepard, "The Autobiography of Thomas Shepard,"
Publications of the Colonial Society of Massachusetts, 27 (1932), pp.
352-6; Anne Bradstreet, "Religious Experiences," in The Works of Anne
Bradstreet, ed. John Harvard Ellis (1867; rpt. Gloucester: Peter Smith,
1962), p. 40; Roger Clap, The Memoirs of Roger Clap (Boston, 1731);
Increase Mather, The Autobiography of Increase Mather, ed. M. G. Hall
(Boston: American Antiquarian Society, 1974).

[20]_Puritanism in Old and New England_ (Chicago: Univ. of Chicago Press, 1953), p. 2.

[21]_A Farewel-Exhortation To The Church And People Of Dorchester In New-England_ (Cambridge, Massachusetts: Samuel Green, 1657), p. 9.

[22]"Preface to the Reader," in _A Farewel-Exhortation_.

[23]_Christian Cautions; or, The Necessity of Self-Examination_, in _The Works of President Edwards_, 10 vols. (1817; rpt. New York: Burt Franklin, 1968), IV, 381.

[24]_The Application of Redemption By the Effectual Work of the Word, and Spirit of Christ_, 2hd. ed. (London: Peter Cole, 1659), p. 216.

[25]_Design and Truth in Autobiography_ (London: Routledge & Kegan Paul, 1960), pp. 4-5.

[26]_The Autobiography of Increase Mather_, ed. M. G. Hall (Boston: American Antiquarian Society, 1974).

[27]For a detailed discussion of the structure and techniques of the Puritan sermon see Perry Miller, _The New England Mind_, pp. 280-330.

[28]"Biographical Technique in Cotton Mather's _Magnalia_," _William and Mary Quarterly_, 2 (1945), p. 155. Watters is the first to discuss the biographical parallel in Mather's work. For a more recent study see William R. Manierre II, "Cotton Mather and the Biographical Parallel," _American Quarterly_, 13 (1961), 153-160.

[29]Manierre, "A Description of 'Paterna,'" p. 186.

[30]Manuductio ad Ministerium (Boston: Printed for Thomas Hancock, 1726), pp. 104-5.

[31]Throughout his essay Manierre questions the value of Paterna for those who would approach it as a work offering detailed descriptions of the author's personal life. Readers of Puritan autobiographies (at least those written in the New England colonies) learn not to expect detail from these sources. Cotton Mather, whose Diary is a paradigm for abstraction and ambiguity, is no exception to this rule in his autobiography. Yet, I think Manierre's characterization of Paterna as a "dull," "curious," "remarkably uninformative document" is an overstatement of his case against Paterna. After all, abstract and ambiguous as it is, Paterna remains the only unified assessment of Cotton Mather's life by himself, and given the suggestions I offer for further studies of Paterna (see Introduction, section IV), I believe the work will become central to future studies of Puritan autobiography, literary art, and cultural history.

[32]The years for which Mather includes comment in Paterna but for which no diaries have survived are: 1682, 1684, 1687-90, 1694, and 1695. See Kenneth Silverman, Selected Letters of Cotton Mather (Baton Rouge: Louisiana State Univ. Press), pp. 6-7, for two Mather letters attributed to the late 1670's.

[33]Shortly before this edition went to its publisher, I was pleased to read Sacvan Bercovitch's The Puritan Origins of the American Self (New Haven: Yale Univ. Press, 1975). That recent study uses biography much in the same way that I suggest autobiography generally and Paterna specifically can be used to establish early American tendencies and literary influences which have survived into modern times.

Paterna

[1]"Therefore, I do not doubt the place of my authority, to excite you, if only because I have much authority."

[2]"What could be more useful to the son? What could be more pleasing to anyone?"

[3]"The life of man is nothing at all without prayer, groans, desires, sighs to the mercy of God."

[4]"On account of my deed I pulled you to imitation in a way not of discipline but example."

[5]"None could be more faithful to you in order to counsel you than one who teaches you what sort of true parents they are."

[6]Mather's "Reserved Memorials" or, as he occasionally refers to them, the "Revised Memorials" are his diaries which, along with Paterna, he intended to leave for the practical and spiritual benefit of his children. In both tone and content these "Memorials" are almost identical to Paterna, the major difference being their greater volume. Approximately seventy-five per cent of the information and events recorded in Paterna are taken directly from these "Memorials." See Appendix A for a comprehensive record of the diary entries incorporated into Paterna.

[7]These words are deleted in the manuscript. All deletions which I have been able to read in the manuscript are incorporated into the text in their proper places. Such deletions will be indicated, as is this one, by the following characters: ⟨⟨ . . . ⟩⟩ .

[8]See Proverbs 22: 6.

[9]"Their own books about themselves."

[10]The Private Christian's Witness For Christianity (London, 1697) has been attributed to Sir David Hamilton. The caution Mather observes here is argued for on pages 6-7.

[11]Although Daniel B. Shea has written that Mather's legacy to his son--Things, Talents, and monitors--suggests that "Puritan autobiography has . . . found a new way to be impersonal when a father can leave his son neither possessions nor expressions of feeling" (Spiritual Autobiography in Early America, p. 167), the significance Mather attaches to these terms in Bonifacius indicates that he personally places great value on such a legacy. "It is to be feared," Mather writes, "that we too seldome inquire after our OPPORTUNITIES TO DO GOOD. Our opportunities to do good are our TALENTS. An awful account must be rendered unto the great GOD, concerning our use of the TALENTS, wherewith He has entrusted us, in these precious opportunities. We do not use our opportunities, many times because we do not know what they are; and many times, the reason why we do not know, is because we do not think. Our opportunities to do good, lie by unregarded, and unimproved, and so 'tis but a mean account that can be given of them. We read of a thing, which we deride as often as we behold: there is, that maketh himself poor, and yet has great riches. It is a thing too frequently exemplified, in our opportunities to do good, which are some of our most valuable riches" (Bonifacius, pp. 31-32). It is important also to note that, as he states in a rather

subtle manner his legacy to his son, Mather also introduces one of the major themes which convey his advice in _Paterna_: the need to constantly seek out opportunities to do good.

THE FIRST PART

The First Three LUSTRES, of a Fathers Life.

[1]See Romans 15: 15-16.

[2]This sentence was originally entered in the margin of the manuscript. All marginal entries have been incorporated into the text and
will be indicated, as is this one, by the following characters:
{ . . . } .

[3]Ezekiel Cheever (1614-1708), a Londoner educated at Christ's Hos-
pital and Emmanuel College, was New England's most famous schoolmaster
and Mather's principal tutor during his early years. Cheever's Acci-
dence, a Short Introduction to the Latin Tongue endured as the standard
introductory Latin text for nearly two centuries. Mather's personal admiration for Cheever is reflected in this tribute, written in his
Corderius Americanus (Boston: John Allen, for Nicholar Boone, 1708),

     "'Tis Corlett's praise and Cheever's, we must own,

       That thou, New England, art not Scythia grown."

[4]"How praiseworthy is your diligence!"

[5]See Hebrews 7: 25.

[6]Except for what is recorded in Paterna there is no surviving record
by Mather of his personal affairs and public activities before 1681. As
Mather notes early in Paterna (p. 5), he was in the habit of keeping a
diary by his fourteenth year. A brief entry in the Diary for 1683 offers
some scant explanation for the "unhappy Casualty" referred to here: "My

Diaries, wherein I had written the Course of my Study and preaching, and the Resolves of Piety upon my Daily course of Meditation, I have thrown, as useless Papers into the Fire" (Diary, I, 73).

[7]Henry Scudder (d. 1659?), English divine of presbyterian persuasion. Scudder's The Christian's Daily Walke in Holy Securitie and Peace, a popular devotional manual, went through six editions by 1635. On the title-page it is described as "first intended for private use; now through importunitie published for the common good." (Dictionary of National Biography, XVII, pp. 1096-7.)

[8]While this particular society remains unidentified, Mather's interest in societies of "YOUNG MEN ASSOCIATED" was constant throughout his life. In Bonifacius, pp. 66-8, Mather argues the usefulness of such societies as a benefit to both the individuals involved and their neighborhoods and outlines nine points of conduct to order the government of such groups. The points of conduct recorded in Bonifacius are merely an expanded version of the activities Mather notes here.

[9]Presumably John Hall (d. 1707), English divine. Hall's Jacobs Ladder: or the Devout Souls Ascension to Heaven, in prayers, thanksgivings, and praises was published in a second, enlarged edition in London in 1676. An immensely popular work, it went through fourteen additional editions by 1728. Included among the methods for meditation which Hall suggests are: private devotions, family devotions for every day in the week, occasional devotions, and sacred poems upon select subjects. (Dictionary of National Biography, VIII, p. 956.)

[10] Page 10 is blank in the manuscript.

The Fourth Lustre

[1]This statement, as well as the following two (pp. 11-2), appears
to be a paraphrase of the main themes of Psalm 91.

[2]See Mark 4: 25.

[3]See I Timothy 1: 15-16 and Ephesians 3: 8.

[4]See Hebrews 2: 18.

[5]See Psalm 23: 6.

[6]See Matthew 28: 20.

[7]Nightmares

[8]Mather originally wrote "chosen" for "desired."

[9]Mather originally wrote "Study" for "Design."

[10]See Psalm 131: 1-2.

[11]Mather originally wrote "conscious" for "most Explicit."

[12]Mather published three works on the subject of "Early Religion" or
early piety: Early Piety, Exemplified in the Life and Death of Mr.
Nathaniel Mather (London: J. Astwood, for J. Dunton, 1689); Early Reli-
gion Urged (Boston: B[enjamin] H[arris], for Michael Perry, 1694); The
Duty of Children, Whose Parents have Pray'd for them. Or, Early and Real
Godliness Urged (Boston: [B. Green, and J. Allen], for the Booksellers, 1703).

[13]Mather identifies this gentleman in his diary for 1681 as "one
Mr. Middlecot" (Diary, I, 13). Worthington Chauncey Ford adds the following biographical information on Middlecot: "He was a merchant, son
of ---- Middlecot of Warminster, England, who served his apprenticeship
with a merchant of Bristol. Married Sarah Winslow, widow of Miles
Standish" (Diary, I, 13).

[14]See Job 42: 6.

[15]See Lamentations 3: 29.

[16]"Biting words."

[17]See Proverbs 23: 17.

[18]See I Peter 1: 6-9.

[19]See Mark 14: 24.

[20]See Mark 1: 4 and Luke 3: 3.

[21]See Psalm 19: 8.

[22]See Colossians 4: 5.

[23]Although this "Little Blank Book" has not, apparently, survived,
Mather may have eventually entered the Resolves and "Contrivances"
spoken of here in his diaries, during his numerous revisions of those
works.

[24]The extent of Mather's library and the titles of its holdings has never been completely determined. Thomas Goddard Wright, in his Literary Culture in Early New England (1920; rpt. New York: Russell & Russell, 1966), pp. 127, 177-9, estimates that by 1700 Mather had accumulated approximately three thousand books and by the end of his life "Mather's eagerness for books resulted in the gathering of probably four thousand volumes."

[25]Samuel Shaw (1635-1696), English nonconformist divine. Shaw's The Voice of One crying in the Wilderness was published in London in 1666. (Dictionary of National Biography, XVII, pp. 1382-3.)

[26]See Psalm 34: 1-3.

[27]See John 12: 32.

[28]See Psalm 103: 1, 22 and Psalm 104: 1, 35.

[29]The Honorable Robert Boyle (1627-1691), English natural philosopher, chemist, and writer on religious subjects. Boyle's Seraphic Love was published in 1660. (Dictionary of National Biography, II, pp. 1026-31.)

[30]El Shaddai literally translates "all-sufficient one." El Shaddai is the title of Mather's published funeral discourse on the death of Mrs. Katharin Willard in 1725 (Boston: B. Green, 1725).

[31]See I Peter 5: 6-7.

[32]See Proverbs 3: 27.

[33]Mather originally wrote "Before" for "'Ere."

[34]Although the diary for 1682 is missing, the following passage suggests that Mather had this particular "Memorial" at his disposal during the writing of this section of Paterna. Presumably then this diary was not among the early memorials which he threw, "as useless," "into the Fire" (Paterna, p. 7; Diary, I, 73). Perhaps this diary was among the papers destroyed in 1718 by Mather's third wife, Lydia Lee-George. See Diary, II, 583-4.

[35]"David's Counsil," according to Psalm 37, is "Rest in the Lord and Wait." The meditation or "Improvement" which begins here and extends through the following page is based on themes expressed throughout Psalm 37.

[36]The Honorable Robert Boyle (1627-1691). See earlier reference, Paterna, p. 51. Among Boyle's writings to which Mather may be referring here are: The Excellency of Theology compared with Natural Philosophy 1673, Some Considerations about the Reconcileableness of Reason and Religion (1675), and Of the High Veneration Man's Intellect owes to God (1685).

William Spurstowe, D. D. (1605?-1666), English Puritan divine. Spurstowe's The Wels of Salvation opened; or, a Treatise . . . of Gospel Promises was published in 1655 and his The Spiritual Chymist; or, Six Decads of Divine Meditations was published posthumously in two parts in 1666. (Dictionary of National Biography, XVIII, pp. 843-4.)

Sir William Waller (1597?-1668), English parliamentary general. Waller's Divine Meditations upon several Occasions, with a Daily Directory was published posthumously in 1680. (<u>Dictionary</u> <u>of</u> <u>National</u> <u>Biography</u>, XX, pp. 588-92).

[37]See Psalm 139: 2.

[38]See Psalm 119: 68.

[39]Page 60 is blank and unnumbered in the manuscript.

The Fifth Lustre.

[1]In Mather's Diary, I, 203, the "Knight" mentioned here is identified as Sir William Phips, Governor of Massachusetts (by royal appointment) from 1692 to 1694. There is little question that the Mathers, Increase and Cotton, had "Laid [him] under many Obligations." Phips's appointment as governor was arranged largely through the diplomacy of Increase. His baptism and full admission into the Church in 1690 was personally undertaken by Cotton.

[2]See Job 13: 23.

[3]John Corbet (1620-1680), English Puritan author. Corbet's An Account of Himself about Conformity was published with The Kingdom of God among Men in 1679. His Self-employment in Secret was published in 1681. (Dictionary of National Biography, IV, pp. 1126-27.

[4]See Genesis 24: 26-28.

[5]See I John 1: 7.

[6]See Proverbs 3: 9-10.

[7]See I Peter 1: 19.

[8]Mather originally wrote "to do" for "for the doing of."

[9]See Hebrews 4: 8-9.

[10]Thomas White (fl. 1702), English divine. The date of publication

for White's The Power of Godliness is uncertain. Mather takes note of
White and the usefulness of his works for the proper education of children
in his Addresses to Old Men, and Young Men, and Little Children (Boston:
R. Pierce, for Nicholas Buttolph, 1690), p. 109.

[11]Mather originally wrote "Glory" for "Service."

[12]"Read Exodus 34, 35, 36; Prayed; Examined the children; Read Des-
cartes; Read commentators on John 6: 37; Breakfasted; Prepared sermon;
Took part in family praper; Heard pupils recite; Read Salmon on medicine;
Dined; Visited many friends; Read various books; Prepared sermon; Heard
pupils recite; Meditated . . . Prayed; Dined; Prepared sermon; Took part
in family prayer."

[13]See Philippians 3: 13-14.

[14]See earlier reference, Paterna, p. 25.

[15]Mather originally wrote "Show" for "celebrate."

[16]The preceding three lines were originally written: "Friends
greatly dear unto me/Mee in thy Church thou dost Employ:/To Speak and
Write for thee."

[17]Five lines deleted by Mather.

[18]This entire paragraph appears nearly verbatim in Bonifacius, p.
85. In a manner reflective of the anonymity he attempts in Paterna,
Mather introduces the paragraph in Bonifacius, stating, "I have read this
experiment of one who had pupils under his charge."

[19]See Matthew 9: 2.

[20]See Psalm 21: 3.

[21]The "papers" mentioned here are, presumably, the diary for 1684, which is missing.

[22]See Isaiah 55: 6-7.

[23]See I Thessalonians 5: 9-11.

[24]See II Timothy 3: 16-17.

[25]" . . . through others . . . We ourselves are not worthy."

[26]"A few listeners were sufficient for me; one would be sufficient; none would be sufficient."

[27]The time is May, 1685, shortly after James II was proclaimed King. In April Mather entered the following in his Diary: "[April 20] K. James II, being this Day, proclaimed in Boston, and all people hereabouts generally attending the Solemnities of the Proclamation, I withdrew from the Noises of the World . . . particularly to deprecate the Confusions with which the Protestant Religion and Interest, were threatned by the Accession of that Prince unto the Throne; especially in our own unhappy Colony" (Diary, I, 93). Compounding the fears and difficulties of the "unhappy Colony" was the revocation of the Charter by Charles II in 1684 and the appointment of Colonel Percy Kirke, long despised in the colony, as his majesty's Lieutenant and Governor-General over the now royal

province of Massachusetts. The fate of the colony was generally thought
to rest in the hands of parliament, although ultimately it was decided
on the events of Increase Mather's later diplomacy abroad.

[28]See Hebrews 13: 20.

[29]Mather was elected "pastor" of the Second Church in Boston in
December, 1681. The "Elderly and Eminent Person" with whom he served as
a Collegue was his father, who was the official "teacher" of the church.

[30]Mather was ordained on May 13, 1685. Samuel Sewall, who was present, made the following record of the event in his diary: "Mr. Cotton
Mather is ordained Pastor by his Father, who said, My son Cotton Mather,
and in 's sermon spoke of Aaron's Garments being put on Eleazer, inti-
mating he knew not but that God might now call him out of the World. Mr.
Eliot gave the Right Hand of Fellowship, calling him a Lover of Jesus
Christ. Mr. Benjamin Eliot was there who hath not been at Town these
many years" (The Diary of Samuel Sewall, ed. M. Halsey Thomas, 2 vols.
(New York: Farrar, Straus and Giroux, 1973), I, 63. In his Life of his
father Samuel Mather refers to the event as "A truly primitive Ordination!" (p. 18).

[31]See I Peter 5: 2.

[32]Although he does not reproduce them verbatim, Mather argues for
the substance of these "Rules of Preaching" in both Bonifacius, pp. 71-2,
and Manuductio ad Ministerium, pp. 90-96.

[33]See Ephesians 5: 19.

[34]This "Young Gentleman" is identified in Mather's Diary, I, 104, as Mr. Daniel Royse. In a marginal note added in the Diary at a later date Mather writes, "This gentleman, afterwards joined unto our church and lived and died, a serious Christian." An entry in Sewall's diary completes the episode: " January 31, 1685/6 . . . Mr. Royse taken in and baptized in the North Church" (The Diary of Samuel Sewall, I, 95).

[35]See I Timothy 4: 7-9.

[36]George Swinnock (1627-1673), English nonconformist divine. Swinnock's exercises to which Mather here refers are probably those contained in his The Christian Man's Calling (London, 1661-5). (Dictionary of National Biography, XIX, p. 235.

[37]See II Timothy 2: 24-25.

[38]John Owen, D. D. (1616-1683), English theologian said to rank with Baxter and Howe as the most eminent of Puritan divines. Owen's Of the Mortification of Sin in Believers was published in 1668. (Dictionary of National Biography, XIV, pp. 1318-22.

[39]Ford, in his edition of Mather's Diary, notes that the "Evil Humours" may be a reference to the beginning of the witchcraft outbreak (Diary, I, 114 n). Although Mather never specifies what these "Evil Humours" are, we learn from Sewall's diary about "a Maid at Woburn who 'tis feared is Possessed by an evil Spirit" in an entry dated January 21, 1685/6. (The Diary of Samuel Sewall, I, 93). Two additional meanings for Mather's reference should not be overlooked. It may be that he is

thinking of the uncertain political state of the colony as an "evil hu-
mour." Interestingly, Sewall's diary contains a mention of this problem
within two weeks of his entry concerning the possible outbreak of witchcraft in the colony: "[February 7, 1685/6, Mr. Willard] . . . very sensible of the Countries Danger as to Changes" preached on Romans 8: 1 (The
Diary of Samuel Sewall, I, 96). One final suggestion as to the nature of
the "evil humours" is provided by the title of a publication "By the
Ministers of Christ at Boston in New England," An Arrow against Profane
and Promiscuous Dancing (Boston, 1684). This pamphlet was in fact written
by Increase Mather.

40See Psalm 23: 6.

41A seventh favor is not recorded in Paterna. The sixth favor listed
here is recorded as the seventh favor in Mather's diary. The sixth favor
as recorded in the Diary reads: "My Deliverance from the Chains upon my
Utterance" (Diary, I, 111). This is the reference which is missing in
Paterna and is an obvious allusion to Mather's speech impediment, a
stammer, which is addressed in some detail in the Diary, I, 55.

42See Colossians 1: 12.

43Mather notes in the margin of his Diary: "I did it, on Isa. 33.
17" (Diary, I, 112). Sewall's comments on Mather's sermon suggest that
Mather did not achieve the effect he intended. In an entry dated January
28, 1685/6, Sewall writes, "Isa. 33. 17. was preached from, by Mr. Cotton
Mather. Thine eyes shall see the King, &c. whoes Sermon was somewhat
disgusted for some expressions; as, sweet-sented hands of Christ, Lord

High Treasurer of AEthiopia, Ribband of Humility--which was sorry for, because of the excellency and seasonableness of the subject" (The Diary of Samuel Sewall, I, 94-5).

[44]The following passage on pastoral visits is reproduced nearly verbatim in Bonifacius, pp. 75-7. Mather introduces the subject in Bonifacius by acknowledging that the directions for pastoral visits are "from the memorials of one who long since did so, and then left his PATERNA to his son upon it." Mather includes a passage on pastoral visits in his Manuductio ad Ministerium, pp. 106-7, in which he reiterates the substance of his method as it is revealed in Paterna and Bonifacius. Interestingly, Mather wrote The Thoughts of a Dying Man (Boston: B. Green & J. Allen, for J. Wheeler, 1697) to leave with his church members at the close of his pastoral visits. He explains his motive for this publication in his Diary: "That I might render my pastoral Visits, the more significant, I published my Sermon . . . The Thoughts of a Dying Man, wherein I do, with all possible Pungency and Fervency, sett before my Neighbours, the Advice of what they will think, and choose, AT THE LAST, when they come to dy . . . It was my Purpose, every Week, to leave this Book, in several visited Families, at my Neighbours" (Diary, I, 224).

[45]See Luke 11: 1-2.

[46]Mather originally wrote "three of four" for "four or five."

[47]See Romans 8: 11 and Galatians 5: 16.

[48]Mather reproduces the remainder of this paragraph verbatim in his Manuductio ad Ministerium, pp. 74-5. He claims there that the passage is

"from the PATERNA, of One whom it may be, you are not wholly a Stranger to," although he does not reveal himself as the author of the passage.

[49]See Psalm 18: 22.

[50]See Psalm 32: 8.

[51]Mather originally wrote "whose company I might also at length have in" for "Who might accompany me to."

[52]See Psalm 55: 22.

[53]Mather originally wrote "whom God has made Your _Mother_" for "whom God made a Consort, & a Blessing to me." The "Worthy Young Gentlewoman" was Abigail Philips, "the Happy Daughter of JOHN, and KATHARIN PHILIPS" (_Diary_, I, 120), to whom Mather was married on May 4, 1686. She bore Mather nine children, among them Increase (1699-1724) for whom _Paterna_ was initially intended. Of the nine children Abigail bore only four were alive at her death in 1702.

[54]Mather originally wrote "your [?] Mother" for "my Consort."

[55]Three lines are deleted in the manuscript.

[56]See John 2: 1-11, concerning Jesus's first public miracle, performed at the wedding feast in Cana.

[57]See Luke 14: 14. Mather spoke to this effect on the second Sabbath following his marriage when, at Boston, he preached on "Psal. 119. 14 [24?], _Divine Delights_" (_Diary_, I, 127).

[58]In the following passage from his <u>Diary</u> Mather is using the term "promise" in a technical, biblical sense. Historically, the covenant between God and Adam, and the "New Covenant" later joined between God and Abraham, implied a promise on the part of God (see Leviticus 26). Hence, "promise" almost always refers in the <u>Bible</u> to the promises of God to His people; for instance, God's promise to give them a land of their own (Genesis 17: 8; Deuteronomy 1: 8; Joshua 21: 43; Hebrews 11: 9), an inheritance (Romans 4: 13), and a permanent kingdom under a son of David (II Samuel 7: 8-16). In terms of their spiritual content these promises receive their fulfillment through Christ and His salvific action (Acts 26: 6; II Corinthians 1: 20; Ephesians 3: 6). The fulfillment of these promises includes not only what Christ has done and what the Holy Spirit does (Acts 1: 4), but includes the completion of God's plan at the end of time (II Peter 3: 13) as well.

[59]Mather's statement that he had already established "Methods to <u>Serve</u> <u>God</u>, & to <u>Do</u> <u>Good</u>" and that he was now engaged in a "Variety of <u>Publick</u> <u>Employments</u>" is the only explanation we have for the absence of any diaries for his twenty-fifth through twenty-ninth years. Significantly, <u>Paterna</u> is the only work in which Mather comments upon his activities during these years.

[60]Abigail, his first child by Abigail Philips. Wendell is unsure of the child's year of birth (<u>Cotton</u> <u>Mather</u>, p. 81) which we can now state, on the basis of this <u>Paterna</u> entry, as 1687.

[61]See Colossians 3: 1-2.

[62]See Genesis 42: 36.

[63]See Luke 10: 18-19.

[64]See Mark 3: 28.

[65]"By the Holy Spirit of God."

[66]Page 110 is blank in the manuscript.

The Sixth Lustre

[1]Mather originally wrote "Lustres" for "years."

[2]Although Mather has left no substantial account of his activities
during this time (1688-1689), Samuel's Life together with Cotton's Parentator (Boston: B. Green, for Nathaniel Belknap, 1724) are sufficient to
fill in some informational gaps. By April, 1688, Increase Mather was already on his way to England, having slipped out of Boston at night, in
order personally to present James II an address of thanks, on behalf of
the New England ministers, for his 1687 Declaration of indulgence. Principal among Mather's motives for the journey, however, was the need to
argue for a new charter. Although James's Declaration was intended as a
relief for Catholics, Dissenters, in England and New England, grasped at
it as a legal means to procure their religious liberty. In New England,
the document meant much to those ministers closely associated with the
Mathers, for they had been forced to endure the rule of an unsympathetic
Sir Edmund Andros and his decidedly pro-Church of England policy for over
two years.

Upon Increase's departure Cotton was entrusted with the care of the
Mathers' Church, and he quickly assumed the position of political power
left vacant by his father. Samuel writes that shortly before the Revolution of 1689, which brought William and Mary to the throne of England,
"the principal Gentlemen of Boston met with Mr. Mather to consult what
was best to be done [concerning the mounting unrest of the populace over
Andros's rule]: and they all agreed, if possible that they would extinguish all Essays in our People to an Insurrection." These gentlemen also
agreed that if an outbreak of protest should occur, they would place

themselves at the head of it in order to prevent violence, "[and] a
Declaration was prepared accordingly."

Shortly before the insurrection began, Cotton Mather soothed the
raw nerves of the people with an "affectionate and moving Speech . . .
at which many fell into Tears and the whole Body . . . present immediately
united in the Methods of Peace Mr. Mather proposed unto them." Nevertheless, he was to be committed to prison for his "seditious" activities on
the very day that the revolution commenced. Samuel states that this
happy deliverance encouraged him to continue his efforts to keep "the
Peoples [from] proceeding any further than to reserve the Criminals for
the Justice of the English Parliament."

Samuel concludes his treatment of this period of Mather's life
with the following comment:

> Upon Discoursing with him of the Affairs, he has told me
> that he always pressed Peace and Love and Submission unto
> a legal Government, tho' he suffered from some tumultuous
> People, by doing so; and upon the whole, has asserted unto
> me his Innocency and Freedom from all known Iniquity in that
> time, but declared his Resolution, from the View he had of
> the fickle Humors of the Populace, that he would chuse to be
> concern'd with them as little as possible for the future.

It is in the light of these events that we must read the beginning of
"The Sixth Lustre" in Paterna.

[3]Mather originally wrote "One Night" for "Once."

[4]Mather's publications for the "French churches, in their own Lan-
guage," are: "Preface du Docte et Reverend Ministre Monsieur Cotton
Mather pour Servir d'approbation au present ecrit," in Ezechiel Carre,
Echantillon (Boston: Samuel Green, 1690); Le Vrai Patron des Saines
Paroles [Boston: T. Green (?), 1704]: Une Grande Voix du Ciel A La
France [Boston: B. Green (?), 1725].

[5]The other "Living Tongue" mastered by Mather was Spanish. The book he "composed and published" is La Fe del Christiano (Boston, 1699).

[6]See Matthew 16: 1-3.

[7]See Isaiah 48: 17.

[8]Mather reprinted the following section on "Particular Faiths" (pp. 119-125) in an abbreviated form in Parentator, pp. 189-191.

[9]See James 1: 6.

[10]" . . . Good man's prayer being effective."

[11]See Daniel 6: 22 and Acts 10: 1-3, respectively.

[12]The "Particular Faith" referred to here concerns the restoration of the Charter. Largely through the diplomacy of Increase Mather, a new charter was granted in 1691. Although the new charter was not equal to the one lost in 1684, Cotton felt a considerable relief and saw the charter as a victory for his father and for the colony.

[13]See Genesis 18: 27 and Job 30: 19.

[14]Mather originally wrote "Delusion" for "Deceit."

[15]See Matthew 11: 5 and Luke 7: 22.

[16]See John 11: 25-26.

[17]Mather originally wrote "caused me to fall into" for "Dissolved me into."

[18]Mather originally wrote "my" for "y[e]."

[19]See Ephesians 2: 8-9.

[20]See Ephesians 4: 30.

[21]"When my birthday in February advised me of the number of days until summer, and I came into the thirtieth year, depression suddenly struck me, and life took on new meaning; however, without a sense of motivation I discovered its summit, by which light became somewhat more obscure and our days began to decline. The face of things for the moment was changed, and then I realized for the first time that I was a person."

[22]Approximately one-half of the "caution" which follows is reproduced in Parentator, p. 195.

[23]This description of a particular faith as a "Jewel of God" is identical to Mather's description of "justifying faith" in Bonifacius, p. 29.

[24]Page 126 is blank in the manuscript.

The Seventh Lustre

[1]See Hebrews 1: 14.

[2]See I Peter 1: 12.

[3]See II Corinthians 12: 3-4.

[4]The "infallible Demonstration" follows, pp. 130-2.

[5]"A strange and memorable thing. After outpourings of prayer, with great fervor and fasting, there appeared an Angel, whose face shone like the noonday sun. His appearance was as that of a man, and beardless; his head was encircled by a splended tiara; on his shoulders were wings; his garments were white and glowing; his robe reached to his ankles; and about his loins was a belt like that of the people of the East.

"And this Angel said that he was sent by the Lord Jesus to bear an absolute answer to the prayers of a certain youth, and to carry his words back in reply.

"This Angel said many things which are not appropriate to say here. But among things not to be forgotten he declared that this youth's fate is to find complete expression for what in him was best; and this he said in the words of the prophet Ezekiel."

[6]"And in particular this Angel talked of the influence his reason would have, and of the books that this youth would publish. And he added certain special prophecies of the great work this youth would do for the Church of Christ in the coming revolutions.

"Lord Jesus! What is the meaning of this apparition? From the

cunning of Satan, I pray you, deliver and defend your most unworthy servant."

[7]Abigail (b. and d. 1687); Mary (b. before 1693, d. 1693); Increase
(b. malformed and d. 1693); Mehitabel (b. 1695, d. 1696); Samuel (b.
1700, d. 1700/01).

[8]See Romans 1: 16-17.

[9]Identified in Diary, I, 179, as his daughter Katherine (b. before
1693, d. 1716).

[10]See II Samuel 14: 7.

[11]See Luke 8: 40-42, 49-56, concerning Jesus's raising up from the
dead the daughter of Jairus.

[12]See II Chronicles 25: 9.

[13]See I Peter 5: 7.

[14]See Romans 8: 15.

[15]See Hebrews 13: 5.

[16]Mather originally wrote "Kingdome" for "Paradise."

[17]See Romans 15: 3.

[18]See II Samuel 23: 5.

[19]Several words deleted in the manuscript.

[20]See Romans 8: 26.

[21]See Psalm 6: 9.

[22]Mather originally wrote "HIM" for "the Lord."

[23]Mather originally wrote "to Engage to [be]" for "to become."

[24]Mather originally wrote "together with" for "in the Company of."

[25]Mather apparently acted on this plan in 1701 when he "[gave] to the publick two Discourses; one directing a Christian in his general Calling; another directing him in his personal Calling" (Diary, I, 403). These discourses were published as A Christian at His Calling (Boston: B. Green and J. Allen, for Samuel Sewall, Jr., 1701).

[26]Two lines are deleted in the manuscript. The remainder of the sentence as it now stands is written, in Mather's hand, between the lines which are deleted in the manuscript.

[27]See Mark 9: 24.

[28]See Canticles 8: 6.

[29]See Matthew 28" 18.

[30]Mather's page numbers skip from 161 to 164 in the manuscript.

[31]Although Mather's resolution to "become a _Remembrancer_ unto the Lord, for no less than whole _Peoples_, Nations, and Kingdomes," appears at the beginning of his _Diary_ for 1696, Mather was already at work on his great history, _Magnalia Christi Americana_. Conceived in 1693, the _Magnalia_ was completed in 1697 and published in London in 1702. The term "Lord's Remembrancer" is not original with Mather; it was used more than twenty years before by Urian Oakes in his _New England Pleaded with_ (Cambridge, 1673), p. 23. In his work Oakes urges that histories of New England and of the progress of the people of God there be written for the instruction of future generations.

[32]Mather's supplications "not here to be mentioned" deal with the sort of political and religious issues which he elsewhere deletes in _Paterna_, pp. 164, 177, 179, 180. The supplications are, however, entered in his _Diary_, I, 200.

[33]The town is identified as Salem in Mather's _Diary_, I, 201.

[34]See II Corinthians 4: 7.

[35]See Psalm 119: 34.

[36]See Titus 2: 14.

[37]See Psalm 22: 14.

[38]See Zechariah 9: 9.

[39]See Matthew 27: 28, 35; Mark 15: 24; John 19: 23.

[40]See Isaiah 61: 10.

[41]The child is identified in Mather's Diary, I, 185, as his daughter Mehitabel.

[42]Mather records that during the Spring of 1696 Massachusetts found itself with an "unusual Scarcity of provisions" (Diary, I, 191). In addition to the proposed remedy that follows, Mather organized a "Collection for the Releef of the Poor" and requested "the Ministers of Connecticut-Colony, that they would prevail with the Government in that Colony, to remitt the Embargo which they laid upon their Corn, unto our exceeding Detriment" (Diary, I, 190, 191). Finally, Mather notes that during the presentation of his Election Sermon in June, 1696, his "wrestling and melted Heart, expressed a strange Faith, on the Lord Jesus Christ that wonderful Releefs would bee sent in unto us, against the Famine that was now distressing us." To this is added the following: "Memorandum. The night following, there arrived, a little Fleet of Corn, and Floure, to us . . ." (Diary, I, 196).

[43]This document has not survived.

[44]See Exodus 3: 7-8.

[45]See Hebrews 12: 22.

[46]See Psalm 10: 14 and Hosea 14: 3.

[47]See Proverbs 3: 5.

[48]That is, the Second Coming of Christ, as foretold in the Book of Revelation.

[49]It is not clear which churches Mather has in mind. In February, 1696/7, he enters the following in his _Diary_: "The bereaved Condition of some Churches in this Wilderness, and the divided Condition of one, (that at _Watertown_,) I made a large Article of my Petitions" (_Diary_, I, 225). An entry in Sewall's _Diary_, dated April 8, 1697, suggests that among the churches out of order was Mather's own: "Mr. Cotton Mather gives notice that the Lecture hereafter is to begin at Eleven of the Clock, an hour sooner than formerly: Reprov'd the Towns people that attended no better; fear'd twould be an omen of our not enjoying the Lecture long, if did not amend" (_The Diary of Samuel Sewall_, I, 371).

[50]See Daniel 4: 17.

[51]See Habakkuk 2: 13.

[52]A considerable list of "Particular Articles" of the Lord's use of him is found in Mather's _Diary_, I, 227-8.

[53]See Matthew 26: 28.

[54]Mather's publications on the subject of _Free-Grace_ are: _A Seasonable Testimony To the Glorious DOCTRINES of GRACE_ (Boston, 1702); _Christianity Demonstrated_ (Boston, 1710); _Grace Defended_ (Boston: B. Green, for Samuel Gerrish, 1712); _The Old Pathes Restored_ (Boston: T. Green, 1711; rpt. London, 1712).

[55]See John 17: 24.

The SECOND Part.

No Longer Distinguished into

LUSTRES.

[1]Mather originally twice wrote and twice deleted "The Eighth Lustre" for "The SECOND Part."

[2]See Psalm 23: 3.

[3]Four and one-half lines are deleted in the manuscript.

[4]Mather originally wrote "should Come" for "Coming."

[5]Presumably Mather's "eighth lustre," 1697-1702. This would help explain Mather's meaning in what remains in this paragraph, for Increase, born in 1699, would be only two or three years old at the time Mather is writing.

[6]Several words are deleted in the manuscript.

[7]Mather originally wrote this sentence as follows: "For, My Son, it was not until this Lustre of my Life, that God bestow'd You upon me, a Son that Lived to Read what I write." Although Increase would only be two or three years old at this time, Mather's optimism is understandable. His first son, also named Increase, was born malformed and died shortly thereafter (1693). After the birth of the second Increase another son, Samuel, was born who did not survive his first year (1700-1700/1).

[8]Mather originally wrote the preceding two sentences as follows:
"The Day before You were born, I Spent in Praying and Fasting before the
Lord, and Crying to Heaven, for the Welfare of Your Excellent Mother, and
of her Expected off-spring. You had been foretold unto me, in an Extraordinary Way, some years before your birth; and in the Evening of the Day,
which I had now kept, I Entertained my Family, before o[e] Evening-Prayers,
with a Discourse on Joh. 16. 21."

[9]Six lines are deleted in the manuscript.

[10]Mather originally wrote "Lustre" for "part."

[11]One and one-half lines are deleted in the manuscript.

[12]Mather originally wrote "may" for "will."

[13]See Hebrews 1: 1-2.

[14]" . . . determination of future judgment . . .".

[15]Here ends the part of Paterna originally intended for Increase.
From this point on, including the revisions noted in the first eight pages
of "The SECOND Part," Mather is writing for his son Samuel.

[16]See Matthew 4: 1-11, concerning the victory of Jesus over the
temptations of Satan.

[17]See I Corinthians 10: 13.

[18]See I Peter 4: 14.

[19]See I Peter 4: 12, 13.

[20]See Matthew 26: 41 and Mark 13: 33; 14: 38.

[21]One and one-half lines are deleted in the manuscript. The remainder of the sentence as it now stands is written, in Mather's hand, between the lines which are deleted.

[22]The term "Sealing" is used here figuratively to indicate the outward identifying mark (sanctification) which suggests the inward state of the justified. (Romans 4: 11; I Corinthians 9: 2; II Corinthians 1: 22) As Mather notes, the "Sealing Work of ye Holy Spirit, is alwayes attended with ye Symptomes of a Sanctifying Work" (p. 200).

[23]The following paragraph is considerably enlarged in Mather's Signatus (Boston: Henchman, 1727), pp. 15-21.

[24]See Romans 8: 16-17.

[25]Mather originally wrote "Lord JESUS CHRIST!" for "GOD the SAVIOUR!"

[26]Mather apparently preached on the subject on August 30, 1702 (Diary, I, 440).

[27]See Revelation 1: 5.

[28]See Jeremiah 31: 3.

[29]See I Peter 1: 4-5.

[30]See I Corinthians 15: 58.

[31]See I John 3: 1.

[32]Maschil; Or, The Faithful Instructor (Boston: B. Green & J. Allen, for Samuel Phillips, 1702).

[33]The exact meaning of Maschil and Mictam has never been determined. The words occur in the titles to some of the Psalms and, according to Ford, they are derived from the transposition and corruption of letters (Diary, I, 426 n).

[34]Page 206 is blank in the manuscript.

[35]Although the following poem is mentioned in the Diary, I, 482, it is not printed there. It was printed, however, as the conclusion to Mather's Baptismal Piety (Boston, 1727), pp. 47-8.

[36]See Hebrews 3: 1.

[37]See Psalm 115: 4-8; 135: 15-18; Isaiah 44: 9-20.

[38]See Galatians 5: 19-21.

[39]The "Matter of great Consequence" is explained in Mather's Diary, I, 424: "I was in much Distress upon my Spirit, concerning my Church History [the Magnalia Christi Americana], and some other elaborate Composures, that I have sent unto London; about the Progress towards the Publication whereof, the Lord still keeps me in the Dark. To have those

Composures with all my Labours and Prayers about them, lost, would be a
terrible Trial to me."

[40]Mather's first wife, Abigail Phillips, "The Desire of my Eyes"
(Diary, I, 448), died on December 1, 1702. The record of "a Time, and a
Thing, wherein I was full of Distress," which begins here and continues
through page 214, concerns Mather's eight month period of "widowhood"
before his marriage, in August, 1703, to Mrs. Elizabeth Clark-Hubbard.
Abigail's death had a profound effect upon Mather, for it carried "that
most astonishing Sting in it; a Miscarriage of a Particular Faith" that
she would not die (Diary, I, 451). Within two months (February, 1702/3)
"a young Gentlewoman of incomparable Accomplishments . . . of rare Witt
and Sense . . . of comely Aspect . . . extremely Winning in her Conversation . . . [and who had] a Mother of an extraordinary Character for
her Piety," began to press Mather for a marriage. Mather's intention at
the time was to remain a "widow" indefinitely; his father and friends,
however, advised him to marry as soon as possible and proper. It was a
this point that Mather placed the matter at "the Door of Heaven."

Events developed quickly. By March 6 Mather learned that the
woman's reputation was not exactly spotless, although the exact nature
of her indiscretion is unclear. Rumors and gossip ensued within a week
and Mather immediately took to prayer with fasting and sacrificing. By
March 15 Mather renounced the woman. Having judged that a marriage with
the woman in question "will not be consistent with my public serviceableness," Mather writes, "I struck my Knife, into the Heart of my Sacrifice,
by a Letter to her Mother." Apparently, the people of Boston would not
let the matter die, as Mather describes himself for several weeks afterwards as "miserable Mather," "extremely Unhappy!" Fortunately, however,

during Mather's fasts in early July, the Lord directed his wandering mind
to thoughts of Mrs. Elizabeth Hubbard, a comely, discreet, and pious woman, with "a most unspotted Reputation," living nearby. They were
married on August 18, 1703.

The whole story is told by Wendell, Cotton Mather, pp. 202-9;
Mather's version is printed in his Diary, I, 450-495.

[41]See Corinthians 12: 8.

[42]Mather's exercises for the three day exercise which follows are
recorded and improved upon for young ministers in his Manuductio ad
Ministerium, pp. 16-8. There Mather states that the original outline of
the exercise is to be found in Cœlestinus, a Mather publication (Boston:
S. Kneeland, for Nath. Belknap, 1723), which he does not acknowledge in
Manuductio. In fact, Paterna is the real source of the passage.

[43]See Psalm 103: 21.

[44]See Psalm 34: 8.

[45]This episode and the ones following it probably occurred in 1704.
Unfortunately, Mather's diary for that year is not preserved. It may be
that Mather is exaggerating here, for neither Sewall nor Samuel Mather
records anything as spectacular as Mather does.

[46]"No one is equal to the Lord; whoever would deny that must have
his madness purged by a double dose of hellebore. But the grace of Christ
has restored some similar people, restored them shining in the likeness
of the heavenly Father, which is no small thing to me.

"MERCY, A guarantor is appointed; for we discern the clear image of the merciful Jesus while the flesh of Christ redeems the lost ones, so that the Grace of God is given to those called back from the snare of Satan."

[47]See Galatians 3: 13.

[48]See Psalm 86: 17.

[49]The publication of Mather's Mare Pacificum (Boston: T. Green, 1705) is probably the occasion for this remark. Mather writes in his Diary, I, 524, that "the Gentleman who was principally concerned in the publication, did of his own Accord, present one of the Books, to every Town in these Colonies, to be lent among the Inhabitants. Thus I have a strange Opportunity once again, to serve the Lord, in all His Congregations, from one End of the Countrey to the other."

[50]See Acts 9: 15-16.

[51]This paragraph and the one following appear in nearly the same form in Bonifacius, pp. 24-5.

[52]See Hebrews 12: 11.

[53]Samuel Mather was accepted into "the Evangelical Ministry." Samuel received the degree of A. B. from Harvard in 1723. During the summer of 1724 he began to preach at Castle William, remaining there as chaplain until 1732. In October 1724 he delivered a sermon at his father's church; in 1731 he became an assistant to the Reverend Joshua

Gee at the Second Church. On January 28, 1732, Samuel was chosen pastor of the Second Church, the last Mather to serve from its pulpit.

[54]It may be that in the lapse of time between the composition of the first and second parts of _Paterna_ Mather forgot that he had already addressed many of the following topics in the first part of the work, pp. 96-8.

[55]This passage, which extends to p. 232, is found, in a somewhat altered form, in _Bonifacius_, pp. 43-52.

[56]See I Peter 5: 10.

[57]See Psalm 128: 3.

[58]See Jeremiah 49: 15-16.

[59]Mather originally wrote "of devising" for "to _Devise._"

[60]The town to which this letter was sent is identified in Mather's _Diary_, I, 580-1, as Salem, a town which "has many _poor_ and _bad_ People in it; and such as are especially scandalous for staying at Home on the _Lords-dayes._" However, this letter is not reproduced in the _Diary_.

[61]Mather originally wrote "and not so very Good" for "both on Temporal and Spiritual Accounts."

[62]See Mark 16: 15.

[63]Mather elaborates upon "the Strains and Flights of Real CHRISTIAN-

ITY," which is <u>Manly</u> <u>Christianity</u>, in his <u>Manly</u> <u>Christianity</u> (London:
Printed for Ralph Smith, 1711). However, the following passage, which
extends to p. 249, is taken almost verbatim from Mather's <u>The</u> <u>Heavenly</u>
<u>Conversation</u> (Boston, 1710), pp. 7-30.

[64]See I Timothy 3: 16.

[65]See John 1: 18.

[66]See Hebrews 5: 7.

[67]See Deuteronomy 32: 13 and Psalm 81: 16.

[68]See John 14: 6.

[69]Mather originally wrote "precious" for "dear."

[70]See Matthew 19: 21 and Mark 10: 21.

[71]See Hebrews 5: 7.

[72]See Luke 23: 34 and John 19: 25-27.

[73]See Psalm 116: 7.

[74]See Acts 24: 16.

[75]See Isaiah 63: 9.

[76]See Luke 23: 34.

[77]Mather originally wrote "know Him & love Him" for "Obey Him, & have Him."

[78]See Hebrews 5: 9.

[79]See Isaiah 53: 3.

[80]See I Corinthians 4: 12-13.

[81]See II Corinthians 12: 21.

[82]See Galatians 2: 20.

[83]See Proverbs 15: 24.

[84]"No things are born except through penance."

[85]The following passage, which extends to p. 257, is taken almost verbatim from Mather's Dust and Ashes (Boston: B. Green, for T. Green, 1710), pp. 16-34. The substance of this same passage is repeated in Mather's Manuductio ad Ministerium, pp. 16-8.

[86]See Lamentations 3: 19.

[87]See Isaiah 6: 3 and Revelation 4: 8.

[88]See Exodus 12: 8 and Numbers 9: 11.

[89]See Acts 28: 3-6. "Treacle" refers to the various antidotes which are derived from venom. Mather published a discourse entitled, A Treacle Fetched out of a Viper (Boston: B. Green, for Benjamin Eliot, 1707); see

Diary, I, 580, for details of the publication of the work. The theme which Mather explores through this image—affliction should lead to repentance—is also addressed in the following Mather works: Bonifacius, pp. 37-9, and The Right Way to Shake off a Viper (London: Sarah Poppling, 1711; Boston: S. Kneeland, for S. Gerrish, 1720). Mather addresses the subject again in Paterna, p. 319.

[90]See Job 5: 21.

[91]See Job 42: 6.

[92]See Psalm 2: 11-12.

[93]One line is deleted in the manuscript.

[94]See John 6: 45.

[95]See Luke 10: 37.

[96]This document has not survived.

[97]In the following passage, which extends to p. 270, Mather elaborates on the method he finally adopted in 1709 to regulate entries or "Devices of Good" in his diaries. Although Mather's resolution to follow this method and an outline of his procedure are found in his Diary, II, 25-9, the Paterna version is considerably more detailed.

[98]Mather originally wrote "Subjects" for "Things."

[99]Mather originally wrote "were" for "have been."

[100] Mather originally wrote "Every other Week" for "When such an occasion . . . as for my Relatives."

[101] See Romans 12: 21.

[102] Mather devotes a chapter in Bonifacius, pp. 132-7, to the subject of "Reforming Societies." The following passage, which extends to p. 267, is taken verbatim from Bonifacius, pp. 136-7. Several years before the publication of Bonifacius Mather advertised his interest in reforming societies as "engines" that assist men to make good use of their talents when he anonymously published Methods and Motives for Societies [Boston, 1703].

[103] The following two paragraphs were entered into Paterna sometime after the original composition of this section. The first two lines were entered at the bottom of page 267; the remainder of the passage was entered in the inside margin of the same page.

[104] See Jude 23.

[105] Mather originally wrote "Take only this Thought" for "I will add only this one thing upon this Head."

[106] See Ecclesiastes 9: 10.

[107] The initial advice offered by Mather to young ministers in Manuductio ad Ministerium is that they should continually think upon their own "Approaching DEATH," pp. 1-4.

[108]The following paragraph is reproduced almost verbatim in Mather's Manductio ad Ministerium, pp. 23-4, where he introduces the paragraph as follows: "I will conclude this Matter with the Works of One who knew what he Wrote."

[109]The phrase, "Netts of Salvation," is Mather's own. Mather shared the conventional Puritan view that the sermon, when well prepared and preached, could be a sufficient occasion for an individual to recognize the motions of grace within himself. The sermon as, therefore, a net of salvation implies its sufficiency as a means to recognize grace. Mather addresses this theory at length in his The Nets of Salvation (Boston: Timothy Green, 1704). In the Manductio ad Ministerium, pp. 104-5, Mather urges young ministers to make the most of their sermons and to dexterously spread, through their sermons, the nets of salvation over their hearers.

[110]See I Timothy 1: 15-16.

[111]See Psalm 78: 25.

[112]See Romans 13: 14 and Galatians 3: 27.

[113]See Luke 24: 32.

[114]See Hosea 14: 3. The following passage, which extends to p. 275, is a concise statement of Mather's view on the role of Christ as the Father of the fatherless. In this autobiography for his sons Mather stresses this doctrine repeatedly, pp. 46, 176, 190, for reasons which this passage makes obvious. Mather published two works on this subject:

Orphanotrophium (Boston: B. Green, 1711) and Parentalia (Boston: J. Allen, for N. Boone, 1715).

[115]See II Corinthians 8: 12.

[116]See Psalm 27: 10.

[117]See I Chronicles 28: 9.

[118]See Proverbs 3: 6.

[119]See Psalm 90: 12.

[120]See Romans 1: 20-21.

[121]See Luke 17: 10.

[122]See Matthew 7: 7 and Luke 11: 9.

[123]See James 1: 17.

[124]See Isaiah 60: 19-20.

[125]See Psalm 119: 148.

[126]See Romans 13: 8.

[127]See Ecclesiastes 12: 6 and Jeremiah 2: 13. The "terrible Disease" referred to is the problem of incontinence.

[128]See Psalm 24: 4.

[129]Two lines are deleted in the manuscript.

[130]Mather originally wrote "Charity" for "Love."

[131]See I Corinthians 13: 4.

[132]See John 15: 16.

[133]The subject matter of the following passage, which extends to p. 289, is from Mather's 1712 Diary (see Appendix A). The subject of "Winter-Desires and Prayers" was, however, first addressed by Mather in his Winter Meditations (Boston: Benj. Harris, 1693), pp. 29-38. Mather addressed the subject again in Winter Piety (Boston: B. Green, for T. Green, 1712).

[134]See Psalm 51: 7.

[135]See Jude 24.

[136]See Job 29: 14 and Isaiah 59: 17.

[137]See Isaiah 23: 18.

[138]See Hebrews 10: 27.

[139]See Malachi 4: 2.

[140]See Philippians 1: 11.

[141]A possible allusion to one of Mather's own books, Songs of the Redeemed: A Book of Hymns (Boston: B. Green, for J. Allen, 1697).

Apparently no copy of this work has survived (see Thomas James Holmes,
Cotton Mather: A Bibliography of His Works, III, 1008).

[142] See Psalm 97: 11.

[143] See Isaiah 32: 2.

[144] See I Corinthians 10: 4.

[145] See Isaiah 49: 10 and Revelation 7: 16.

[146] See Psalm 126: 5.

[147] See Isaiah 64: 6.

[148] Mather has previously addressed a variety of methods for keeping
the Lord's day in Paterna, pp. 90, 178, 188 ff, 270.

[149] See Psalm 89: 15.

[150] See the Book of Revelation.

[151] See Isaiah 58: 10.

[152] This passage is taken from the 1712 Diary. Most likely, the
little son referred to here is Samuel or "Sammy" (1706-1785), the son for
whom Mather wrote the second part of Paterna. Samuel would have been
about six years old at the time Mather has him hear the prayers of the
servants.

[153] See Hebrews 5: 7-8.

[154] The following passage, which extends to p. 303, is taken nearly verbatim from Mather's The Sacrificer (Boston: Fleet, for Gerrish, 1714), pp. 28-45.

[155] See Ezekiel 24: 16.

[156] See Hebrews 9: 26.

[157] See Numbers 16: 30, 33.

[158] See Exodus 30: 12; Matthew 20: 28; Mark 10: 45; I Timothy 2: 6.

[159] See II Corinthians 5: 14-20.

[160] See Amos 4: 5.

[161] See Psalm 69: 31.

[162] See Psalm 39: 3.

[163] See Acts 21: 14.

[164] See Job 1: 21.

[165] See Psalm 113: 2.

[166] See Job 15: 11.

[167] Mather originally wrote "Suffering" for "Enduring."

[168] See Psalm 94: 19.

[169] See Matthew 26: 39.

[170] See James 1: 2.

[171] Here Mather is employing the term "Priesthood" in two senses, both derived from the New Testament. First, to the extent that he is assuming an identity with Christ, the "great SACRIFICER," Mather is looking to the role of Christ as the new high priest who offers himself as a sacrifice in order to continually intercede for his people before God. See Hebrews, chapters 5-9, for an explanation of the role of Christ as priest-sacrificer. The second meaning of priesthood which Mather is applying here is the general disposition in the New Testament to regard all believers in Christ as members of a universal priesthood. See I Peter 2: 9.

[172] The "Royal Priesthood" refers to the growth in Christian spirit of God's chosen people in the New Testament. According to Revelation, chapter 6, those who gave the most for the word of God, their lives, were given white robes to signify their glorious sacrifice.

[173] See Matthew 19: 28-30.

[174] Since Mather is still assuming an identity between himself and Christ, it is important to note that Christ is said to have descended into hell in order to "fill all things" (See Ephesians 4: 9-10 and I Peter 3: 18-22) and in order that "those that are dead . . . might be judged according to men in the flesh, but live according to God in the spirit" (See I Peter 4: 6).

[175]In the New Testament the "Peace of God" refers to the Christian believer's inner poise and tranquility which is derived from the knowledge of God's grace for him through Christ and the promise of God's continual interest in the welfare of His elect. See John 14: 27, II Peter 3: 14, and Mather's marginal note which follows in Paterna.

[176]Mather's principal essay at a "Philosophical Religion" is his Christian Philosopher (London, 1720).

[177]The following "Illustration," which extends to p. 305, is from Mather's Christian Philosopher, pp. 93-4.

[178]See Acts 17: 27.

[179]See Job 23: 8-9.

[180]See Job 23: 10.

[181]Mather originally wrote "Weight" for "Power."

[182]See Matthew 12: 35-37.

[183]See John 1: 29-34 and Revelation 21: 6.

[184]The following passage, which extends to p. 310, is taken almost verbatim from Mather's Valerius: or, Soul Prosperity (Boston: Fleet, for Gerrish, 1723), pp. 8-16. Mather repeats his theme in Manuductio ad Ministerium, p. 81. Mather's reference to "the Blood of my SAVIOUR . . . The Blood of my Physician: A Sovereign Balsam for all ye Distempers

of my Soul" (p. 309) contains allusions to two of his works: _Balsamum_
Vulnerarium ex Scriptura (Boston: Bartholomew Green and John Allen, for
Nicholas Buttolph, 1692) and _The Great Physician_ (Boston: Timothy Green,
1700).

[185]See Proverbs 12: 5.

[186]See Matthew 7: 12.

[187]See John 18: 11.

[188]See Revelation 21: 27.

[189]See Revelation, chapters 12 and 13, in which hell is represented
as inhabited by dragons.

[190]See John 3: 16.

[191]See II Corinthians 3: 18.

[192]See Isaiah 53: 3.

[193]See Isaiah 53: 7.

[194]See Matthew 9: 36; 14: 14; Mark 6: 34.

[195]One line is deleted in the manuscript.

[196]See Revelation 22: 1-2, in which the _Tree_ noted here is "the tree
of life," bearing fruit for those redeemed out of many nations, that is,
the elect.

[197]See II Timothy 3: 16-17 and II Peter 1: 21.

[198]The following paragraph appears in enlarged form in Mather's Manuductio ad Ministerium, pp. 81-2.

[199]"Having sent forth some pious requests, they observed with devoted attention, the affectation of sacred scripture, and they eagerly assumed the spirit of its message."

[200]See Luke 2: 14.

[201]The following passage, which extends to page 319, is paraphrased from Mather's "Of Equity," in Piety and Equity, United (Boston: Allen, for Starke, 1717), pp. 37, 34-5.

[202]"An Absolute Demonstration." Johann Arndt (1556-1621). The source of this quotation is uncertain, although Mather is known to have read and quoted from Arndt's De Vero Christianismo.

[203]See Job 1: 10.

[204]See Psalm 38: 4.

[205]See Ephesians 3: 19.

[206]See Leviticus 17: 11.

[207]One line is deleted in the manuscript.

[208]See Luke 23: 46.

[209]See I Thessalonians 5: 17.

[210]See Ephesians 3: 20.

[211]See II Corinthians 4: 18.

[212]Mather originally wrote "Consider" for "behold."

[213]See Timothy 6: 7.

[214]The occasion for this deleted remark is addressed by Mather in his Diary, II, 445-6. In March of 1717 a trader of Boston was commissioned by the residents of Cape Francois to transport a statue of St. Michael there from Boston. Mather and some of "our People" set up a mighty cry against "the brutish Papists," who, they assumed, intended to worship the idol. Mather, in consequence of the storm raised by his flock, engaged to interview the wife of the trader on "distinguishing between an ornamental Business, and an Idol." In a short while, the "wretched and bruitish Family" of the trader made a "vile Representation" of Mather's remarks which made him the subject of much ridicule throughout the colony. To answer the "Storm of Calumnies and Obloquies" raised against him, Mather published Iconoclastes: An Essay upon the IDOLATRY (Boston: John Allen, for Daniel Henchman, 1717).

[215]See Isaiah 26: 1.

[216]See Isaiah 54: 5.

[217]See Psalm 88: 10.

[218]See II Corinthians 7: 1.

[219]See Acts 18: 25 and Romans 12: 11.

[220]See Romans 12: 9.

[221]Mather originally wrote "Dedication" for "Consecration."

[222]See Revelation 4: 1.

[223]See Ephesians 1: 3.

[224]See Revelation 3: 19.

[225]See Hebrews 12: 6.

[226]See Psalm 56: 13; Isaiah 2: 5; I John 1: 7.

[227]See I Peter 1: 15.

[228]Mather originally wrote "Great" for "mighty."

[229]See Thessalonians 4: 14.

[230]A lengthy marginal note, to be inserted here, is deleted in the manuscript.

[231]See Exodus 40: 34-38 and I Kings 8: 10-11. The following paragraph is an altered version of a paragraph on the same subject in Mather's The Christian Temple (Boston: Bartholomew Green, 1706), pp. 35-6.

[232]"Sechinah" is a variant from of "Shekinah," the divine or glorious light representative of the divine presence.

[233]See Isaiah 63: 9.

[234]See I Corinthians 6: 19.

[235]See Ephesians 2: 19-22.

[236]See Matthew 16: 17.

[237]See Colossians 3: 3.

[238]See I John 3: 19-22.

[239]Two lines are deleted in the manuscript.

[240]See Colossians 2: 9.

[241]See I Thessalonians 4: 14.

[242]See Romans 5: 17.

[243]See Romans 5: 10 and Ephesians 2: 16.

[244]See Hebrews 13: 21.

[245]See Genesis 32: 12.

[246]See John 4: 24.

[247]See Philippians 3: 3.

[248]Mather originally wrote "Happy" for "Well of it."

[249]Mather originally wrote "on all occasions" for "and feeding upon Him."

[250]See Habakkuk 3: 17-18.

[251]See Psalm 22: 20.

[252]See Zechariah 9: 17.

[253]Incorrectly numbered page 244 in the manuscript.

[254]Incorrectly numbered page 245 in the manuscript.

[255]See Exodus 15: 23.

[256]See Psalm 40: 5.

[257]See Hebrews 4: 9-11.

[258]See Matthew 11: 28.

[259]See Psalm 130: 7.

[260]See Philippians 4: 4.

[261]See Isaiah 11: 10.

[262] See I John 5: 20.

[263] See John 5: 39.

[264] See Hebrews 9: 12.

[265] See Colossians 1: 13.

[266] See Romans 8: 28.

[267] One-half line is deleted in the manuscript.

[268] See Job 19: 13.

[269] See Philippians 4: 19.

[270] See Proverbe 30: 8.

[271] See John 6: 35, 48.

[272] See Ephesians 6: 14.

[273] See Isaiah 33: 16.

[274] See Psalm 88: 5.

[275] See Luke 23: 34.

[276] See Isaiah 14: 29.

[277] See Psalm 31: 5. and Luke 23: 46.

[278]See Hebrews 12: 2.

[279]See II Corinthians 4: 17.

[280]See II Corinthians 6: 9.

[281]The doctrine of the Trinity is amply addressed and illustrated by Mather in his A Christian Conversing with the Great Mystery of Christianity ([Boston:] T. Green, 1709).

[282]See Jude 21.

WORKS CITED

Bercovitch, Sacvan. "Cotton Mather." Major Writers of Early America. Ed. Everett H. Emerson. Madison: Univ. of Wisconsin Press, 1972.

Boas, Ralph and Louise. Cotton Mather: Keeper of the Puritan Conscience. 1928; rpt. Hamden, Connecticut: Archon Books, 1964.

Clap, Roger. The Memoirs of Roger Clap. Boston, 1731.

Edwards, Jonathan. Christian Cautions; or, The Necessity of Self-Examination. The Works of President Edwards. 10 vols. 1817; rpt. New York: Burk Franklin, 1968. IV, 379-420.

Hamilton, David. The Private Christian's Witness For Christianity. London, 1697.

Holmes, Thomas James. Cotton Mather: A Bibliography of His Works. 3 vols. Cambridge: Massachusetts Historical Society, 1940.

Hooker, Thomas. The Application of Redemption By the Effectual Work of the Word, and Spirit of Christ. 2nd ed. London: Peter Cole, 1659.

Levin, David. In Defense of Historical Literature: Essays on American History, Autobiography, Drama and Fiction. New York: Hill and Wang, 1967.

Manierre, William R. "Cotton Mather and the Biographical Parallel." American Quarterly, 13 (1961), 153-160.

————. "A Description of 'Paterna': The Unpublished Autobiography of Cotton Mather." Studies in Bibliography, 18 (1965), 185-205.

Mather, Cotton. Addresses to Old Men, and Young Men, and Little Children. Boston: R. Pierce, for Nicholas Buttolph, 1690.

————. Balsamum Vulnerarium ex Scriptura. Boston: Bartholomew Green and John Allen, for Nicholas Buttolph, 1692.

————. Baptismal Piety. Boston, 1727.

————. Bonifacius. Ed. David Levin. Cambridge: The Belknap Press of Harvard Univ. Press, 1966.

————. A Christian Conversing with the Great Mystery of Christianity. Boston: T. Green, 1709.

————. The Christian Philosopher. London, 1720.

————. The Christian Temple. Boston: Bartholomew Green, 1706.

——. Christianity Demonstrated. Boston, 1710.

——. Coelestinus. Boston: S. Kneeland, for Nath. Belknap, 1723.

——. Corderius Americanus. Boston: John Allen, for Nicholas Boone, 1708.

——. The Diary of Cotton Mather. Ed. Worthington Chauncey Ford. 2 vols. 1911-12; rpt. New York: Frederick Ungar Publishing Co., 1957.

——. The Diary of Cotton Mather for the Year 1712. Ed. William R. Manierre II. Charlottesville: The Univ. Press of Virginia, 1964.

——. Dust and Ashes. Boston: B. Green, for T. Green, 1710.

——. The Duty of Children, whose Parents have Pray'd for them. Or, Early and Real Godliness Urged. Boston: [B. Green, and J. Allen], for the Booksellers, 1703.

——. Early Piety, Exemplified in the Life and Death of Mr. Nathaniel Mather. London: J. Astwood, for J. Dunton, 1689.

——. Early Religion Urged. Boston: B [enjamin] H [arris], for Michael Perry, 1694.

——. Grace Defended. Boston: B. Green, for Samuel Gerrish, 1712.

——. The Great Physician. Boston: Timothy Green, 1700.

——. The Heavenly Conversation. Boston, 1710.

——. Iconoclastes: An Essay upon the IDOLATRY. Boston: J. Allen, for Daniel Henchman, 1717.

——. La Fe del Christiano. Boston, 1699.

——. Le Vrai Patron des Saines Paroles. [Boston: T. Green (?), 1704].

——. Manly Christianity. London: Printed for Ralph Smith, 1711.

——. Manuductio ad Ministerium. Boston: Printed for Thomas Hancock, 1726.

——. Mare Pacificum. Boston: T. Green, 1705.

——. Maschil; Or, The Faithful Instructor. Boston: B. Green & J. Allen, for Samuel Phillips, 1702.

——. Methods and Motives for Societies. Boston, 1703.

——. The Nets of Salvation. Boston: Timothy Green, 1704.

——. The Old Pathes Restored. Boston: T. Green, 1711; rpt. London, 1712.

——. Parentator. Boston: B. Green, for Nathaniel Belknap, 1724.

——. Piety and Equity, United. Boston: Allen, for Starke, 1717.

——. "Preface du Docte et Reverend Ministre Monsieur Cotton Mather pour Servir d'approbation au present ecrit." Ezechiel Carre. Enchantillon. Boston: Samuel Green, 1690.

——. The Right Way to Shake off a Viper. London: Sarah Poppling, 1711.

——. The Sacrificer. Boston: Fleet, for Gerrish, 1714.

——. A Seasonable Testimony To the Glorious DOCTRINES of GRACE. Boston, 1702.

——. Signatus. Boston: Henchman, 1727.

——. Songs of the Redeemed: A Book of Hymns. Boston: B. Green, for J. Allen, 1697.

——. A Treacle Fetched out of a Viper. Boston: B. Green, for Benjamin Eliot, 1707.

——. Une Grande Voix du Ciel A La France. [Boston: B. Green (?), 1725].

——. Winter Meditations. Boston: Benj. Harris, 1693.

——. Winter Piety. Boston: B. Green, for T. Green, 1712.

——. Valerius; or, Soul Prosperity. Boston: Fleet, for Gerrish, 1723.

Mather, Increase. An Arrow against Profane and Promiscuous Dancing. Boston, 1684.

——. The Autobiography of Increase Mather. Ed. M. G. Hall. Boston: American Antiquarian Society, 1974.

Mather, Richard. A Farewel-Exhortation To The Church And People Of Dorchester In New-England. Cambridge, Massachusetts: Samuel Green, 1657.

Mather, Samuel. The Life of the Very Reverend and Learned Cotton Mather, D. D. & F. R. S. Boston, 1729.

Middlekauff, Robert. The Mathers: Three Generations of Puritan Intellectuals. New York: Oxford Univ. Press, 1971.

Miller, Perry. The New England Mind: From Colony to Province. 1953;
    rpt. Boston: Beacon Press, 1961.

Murdock, Kenneth B. Literature and Theology in Colonial New England.
    Cambridge: Harvard Univ. Press, 1949.

Oakes, Urian. New England Pleaded with. Cambridge, 1673.

Pascal, Roy. Design and Truth in Autobiography. London: Routledge
    & Kegan Paul, 1960.

Piercy, Josephine K. Studies in Literary Types in Seventeenth Century
    America (1607-1710). New Haven: Yale Univ. Press, 1939.

Sewall, Samuel. The Diary of Samuel Sewall. Ed. M. Halsey Thomas.
    2 vols. New York: Farrar, Straus and Giroux, 1973.

Shea, Daniel B. Spiritual Autobiography in Early America. Princeton:
    Princeton Univ. Press, 1968.

Shepard, Thomas. "The Autobiography of Thomas Shepard." Publications
    of the Colonial Society of Massachusetts, 27 (1932), 352-356.

———. "My Birth & Life." Publications of the Colonial Society of
    Massachusetts, 27 (1932), 357-392.

Silverman, Kenneth. Selected Letters of Cotton Mather. Baton Rouge:
    Louisiana State Univ. Press, 1971.

Simpson, Alan. Puritanism in Old and New England. Chicago: Univ.
    of Chicago Press, 1953.

Watters, Reginald. "Biographical Technique in Cotton Mather's
    Magnalia." William and Mary Quarterly, 2 (1945), 154-163.

Wendell, Barrett. Cotton Mather: The Puritan Priest. New York:
    Dodd, Mead, and Co., 1891.

The Winthrop Papers. 5 vols. Boston: Massachusetts Historical
    Society, 1929.

Wright, Thomas Goddard. Literary Culture in Early New England. 1920;
    rpt. New York: Russell & Russell, 1966.